A rare book, like a friend, should be cherished.
                                    Anonymous

Outside of a dog, a book is a man's best friend.
Inside of a dog, it's too dark to read.
                                    Groucho Marx

The Used Book Lover's Guide To The South Atlantic States

Maryland, Washington, DC, Virginia, North Carolina, South Carolina, Georgia and Florida

By

David S. and Susan Siegel

Book Hunter Press
P.O. Box 193
Yorktown Heights, NY 10598

The Used Book Lover's Guide To The South Atlantic States (Revised Edition) by David S. and Susan Siegel.   © Copyright 1998   Book Hunter Press.

Printed and bound in the United States of America

Library of Congress Catalog Card Number 97-094389

ISBN 0-9634112-8-4

Dedication

This book is dedicated to the hundreds of anonymous service station attendants and strangers who we stopped on the streets and who helped two frustrated and weary travelers who got lost more often than they would like to admit.

It is also dedicated to the wonderful driver who, despite the neurosis of her traveling companion about wrong turns and bad neighborhoods, always reached her destination and greeted the bookstore proprietor with a smile.

Also Available From Book Hunter Press

The Used Book Lover's Guide to New England, a guide to over 750 used book dealers in Maine, New Hampshire, Vermont, Massachusetts, Connecticut and Rhode Island.

The Used Book Lover's Guide to the Mid-Atlantic States, a guide to over 1,000 used book dealers in New York, New Jersey, Pennsylvania and Delaware.

The Used Book Lover's Guide to the Midwest, a guide to over 1,000 used book dealers in Ohio, Indiana, Illinois, Michigan, Wisconsin, Minnesota, Iowa, Missouri, Kentucky and West Virginia.

The Used Book Lover's Guide to the Pacific Coast States, a guide to over 1,350 used book dealers in California, Oregon, Washington, Alaska and Hawaii.

The Used Book Lover's Guide to the Central States, a guide to over 1,200 used book dealers in the Rocky Mountain, Plains, Southwest and Southcentral States.

If you've found this book useful in your book hunting endeavors and would like to order copies of any of the other guides, you will find a convenient Order From at the back of this book. Or, you can call or write to us at:

Book Hunter Press
PO Box 193
Yorktown Heights, NY 10598
(914) 245-6608
Fax: (914) 245-2630
bookhuntpr@aol.com
http://members.aol.com/bookhuntpr/

Acknowledgments

We would like to thank the over 900 hundred book dealers listed in this Guide who patiently answered our questionnaire, responded to our phone calls, and chatted with us during our visits. Without their cooperation, this book would not have been possible.

We would also like to thank the Washington Antiquarian Booksellers' Association, Florida Antiquarian Booksellers Association, Antiquarian Book Dealers' Association of South Carolina and the Georgia Antiquarian Booksellers Association for their membership directories, and the dealers who compile *Booksellers in Virginia* and *North Carolina Antiquarian Booksellers* for their assistance.

Table of Contents

2

List of Maps

When Will It All End?

By now, those of our gentle readers who have read the Introductions in our other guides must have some sense of the frustrations and rewards inherent in the travels that have brought you the six volume *Used Book Lover's Guide Series*.

Even before we completed our coverage of the United States with the publication of our Central States Guide (a goal which we had only once dreamed about achieving), it became clear that given the number of changes that took place in the world of used books, keeping the guides up to date would be a never ending challenge.

As many of you know, we have approached this "problem" on two fronts. For the short run, we have initiated a series of Annual Supplements which describe new dealers as well as list closings, relocations and other changes. Readers who wish to keep their guides current can purchase the Annual Supplements for a modest sum.

Of course, after three years, the only practical way of insuring that the guides remain reliable and useful tools for the book hunter is to do complete revisions. Hence, our current cycle of Revised and Expanded editions, the latest example of which you are currently holding in your hand.

The question is: how long can two dedicated book hunters like us continue to travel thousands of miles a year? We aren't getting any younger and the quibbling we partake of involving which directions to follow, which shops to visit (alas, we can't visit them all), which motel to rest our weary bones in at the end of a long day, and other silly issues generated by the stress of being away from home for extended periods of time and spending 24 hours day with one's mate (as much as we profess love for one another) would put a strain on any relationship.

If we proceed as we have in the past, our next project should be a revised edition of our Midwest Guide. Just thinking about the number of weeks on the road such an effort would entail sends shivers down each of our spines.

Should we go on? Are these volumes worth the toll they take? How say ye gentle readers?

David S. and Susan Siegel
October, 1997

4

(Reprinted from first edition)

On The Road Again

"Turn left."

"No, go straight."

Anyone overhearing us as we travel in search of yet another used book shop would be amazed to learn that we actually do find most of the places we list without major mishap, and, still talking to each other by the end of the day.

To those dealers, loyal readers and fellow bookaholics who say to us, "Oh, what fun it must be to travel the country visiting used book shops," we smile graciously and try to explain that when we're on the road researching a guide, the "fun" is tempered by lots of hard work and a gruelling schedule: getting up at the crack of dawn so we can be at the first store as soon as it opens (or earlier, if the owner has agreed in advance to be there earlier), getting lost at least once or twice a day, eating on the run, checking into our motel sometimes well into the evening, trying to unwind while we write up the day's notes and double check the next day's schedule, and finally, arranging for a wake up call for the next morning.

There are compensations, however, the most notable being the opportunity we have during our travels to meet some of the most knowledgeable book people in the world. And of course, there's always the thrill that comes when we spot new titles in our own areas of interest.

Despite the relief we feel when a trip comes to an end and we're finally back home catching up on our mail and pouring through weeks of accumulated newspapers, we know that we wouldn't trade any of the frustrations for all the tea in . . . Sri Lanka.

David S. & Susan Siegel
December, 1993

How To Get The Most From This Guide

This guide is designed to help you find the books you're looking for, whether you visit used book shops in person or "browse" by mail or phone from the comfort of your home. It's also designed to help you access the collections of the three categories of used book dealers: open shop, by appointment and mail order.

Open shop dealers maintain regular store hours. Their collections can vary in size from less than a 1,000 to more than 100,000 books and can either be a general stock covering most subject categories or a specialized collection limited to one or more specialty areas.

By appointment or chance dealers generally, but not always, have smaller collections, frequently quite specialized. Many of these dealers maintain their collections in their home. By phoning these dealers in advance, avid book hunters can easily combine a trip to open shops as well as to by appointment dealers in the same region.

Mail order only dealers issue catalogs and/or sell to people on their mailing list or in response to written, phone or e-mail inquiries.

Antique malls. A growing number of dealers in all three of the above categories also rent space in multi dealer antique malls and some malls have more than one dealer. The size and quality of these collections vary widely from a few hundred fairly common titles to interesting and unusual collections, sometimes as large as what we have seen in individual book shops. While we include antique malls where we knew there were used book dealers, we have not, on a systematic basis, researched the multitude of antique malls in the South Atlantic States.

How this book is organized.

Because we believe that the majority of our readers will be people who enjoy taking book hunting trips, we have organized this guide geographically by state, and for open shop and by appointment dealers, within each state by location. Mail order dealers are listed alphabetically at the end of each state chapter.

To help the reader locate specific dealers or locations, at the beginning of each state chapter we have included both an alphabetical listing of all the dealers in that state as well as a geographical listing by location.

Within each listing, we have tried to include the kinds of information about book sellers that we have found useful in our own travels.

• *A description of the stock*: Are you likely to find the kinds of books you're searching for in this shop? Are the books reading copies or of collectible quality? Are they fairly common volumes or more difficult-to-find unusual ones? Are they recent publications or do they date back to earlier decades? What condition are the books in? How many volumes does the dealer have? What percentage of the store's stock is paperback? (When collections are a mix of new and used books, and/or hardcover and paperback, we have indicated the estimated percentage of the stock in each category, listing the largest category first.)

• *Detailed travel directions*: How you can get to the shop, usually from the closest major highway exit.

• *Special services*: Does the dealer issue a catalog? Accept want lists? Have a search service? Offer other services? Note that if the dealer issues a catalog, we generally have not listed "mail order" as a separate service.

• *Payment:* Will the dealer accept credit cards?

• *Comments:* Perhaps the most unique feature of this guide is the *Comments* section that includes our personal observations about a shop. Based on our actual visits to the shops, the comments are designed not to endorse or criticize any of the establishments we visited but rather to place ourselves in the position of our readers and provide useful insights.

• *Specialty Index:* If you're interested in locating books in specific categories, take a close look at the *Specialty Index* in the back of the book.

• *Owner's name:* Note that the owner's name is included in each listing only when it is different from the name of the business.

Maps

The guide includes a series of 20 state, regional and city maps designed to assist readers plan book hunting safaris to open shops and by appointment dealers.

With some exceptions, only locations with dealers who have general collections are included on the maps: locations with open shops are shown in regular type while locations that only have by appointment dealers are in italics. Locations of "mostly paperback" shops are not included on the maps. (See "Paperbacks" below.) Note that the maps are not drawn to scale and are designed to be used in conjunction with actual road maps.

Comments

We are often asked, "Do you actually visit every dealer who appears in your books?" The answer, we must confess, is "No." To do so, would require far more time than one could possibly imagine and would make this book far too expensive.

We try instead to visit the kinds of shops the majority of our readers are most interested in: open shops with a predominately hardcover general collection. We do not normally visit specialty open shops or by appointment and mail order dealers. There are, of course, exceptions, such as when a shop is either closed on the day that we're in the area or is too far off the route we have laid out for ourselves in order to make the most economical use of our travel time. For this reason, we always welcome input from readers who may have personal knowledge of such shops so that we can share the information with other book lovers in future editions.

A few caveats and suggestions before you begin your book hunting safari.

Call ahead. Even when an open shop lists hours and days open, we advise a phone call ahead to be certain that the hours have not changed and that the establishment will indeed be open when you arrive.

Is there a difference between an "antiquarian" and a "used" book store? Yes and no. Many stores we visited call themselves antiquarian but their shelves contain a large stock of books published within the past ten or fifteen years. Likewise, we also found many pre-20th century books in "used" book stores. For that reason, we have used the term "antiquarian" with great caution and only when it was clear to us that the book seller dealt primarily in truly antiquarian books.

Used and Out-of-Print. Some used book purists also make a distinction between "used" books and "out-of-print" books, a distinction which, for the most part, we have avoided.

Paperbacks. The reader should also note that while we do not list shops that are exclusively paperback, we do include "mostly paperback" shops, although these stores are generally not described in great detail. While philosophically we agree with the seasoned book dealer we met in our travels who said, "Books are books and there's a place for people who love to read all kinds of books," because we believe that a majority of our readers are interested in hardcover volumes, we have tried to identify "mostly paperback" shops as a caveat to those who might prefer to shop elsewhere. In those instances where we did visit a "mostly paperback" shop, it was because, based on the initial information we had, we thought the percentage of hardcover volumes was greater than it turned out to be.

Size of the collection. In almost all instances, the information regarding the size of the collection comes directly from the owner. While we did not stop to do an actual count of each collection during our visits, in the few instances where the owner's estimate seemed to be exaggerated, we made note of our observation in the *Comments* section. Readers should note, however, that the number of volumes listed may include books in storage that are not readily accessible.

Readers should also note that with a few exceptions, only dealers who responded to our questionnaire or who we were able to contact by phone are included in the guide. If the dealer did not respond to our multiple inquiries, and if we could not personally verify that the dealer was still in business, the dealer was not listed.

And now to begin your search. Good luck and happy hunting.

"And they said the Cold War was over."

District of Columbia

Alphabetical Listing By Dealer

Washington, DC
Map 2

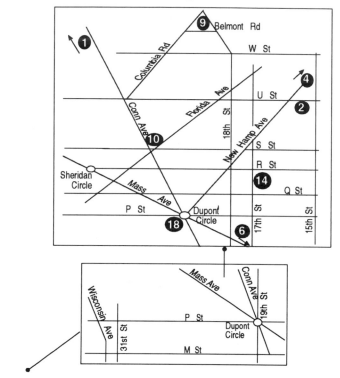

N

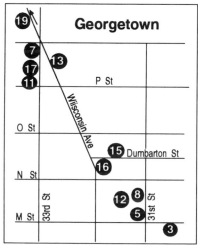

1.   Alphaville Bookshop
2.   Atticus Books
3.   Bartleby's Books
4.   Book Mark It
5.   Booked Up
6.   Capitol Hill Books
7.   Georgetown Book Exchange
8.   William F. Hale Books
9.   Idle Times Books
10. Kultura's Books & Records
11. The Lantern Bookshop
12. Logic and Literature Book Shop
13. Kinsey Marable & Company
14, Niel's Books
15. The Old Forest Bookshop
16. Olsson's Books & Records
17. J.F. Ptak Science Books
18. Second Story Books
19. Yesterday's Books

Alphaville Bookshop   **Open Shop**
5612-B Connecticut Avenue, NW 20015   (202) 363-2775

Collection:	General stock of hardcover and paperback.
# of Vols:	18,000
Specialties:	Scholarly
Hours:	Mon-Thu 11-8. Fri 11-9. Sat 10-9. Sun 11-5.
Services:	Accepts want lists.
Travel:	Rte 185 exit off I-495. Proceed south on Connecticut. Shop is two blocks south of Chevy Chase Circle on the right next to theater.
Credit Cards:	Yes
Owner:	Carlo Parcelli & Rosalie Gancie
Year Estab:	1993
Comments:	This small, neat shop specializes in more serious scholarly and/or academic titles with some lighter items interspersed. Most of the books are in quite good condition, and for the most part, seemed to be of more recent vintage. The shop also carries remainders.

Atticus Books   **Open Shop**
1508 U Street, NW 20009   (202) 667-8148
Web page: www.atticusbooks.com   E-mail: atticus@relix.net

Collection:	General stock of hardcover and paperback, CDs, zines and comics
# of Vols:	12,000
Specialties:	Literature; art; black studies; gay and lesbian.
Hours:	Mon-Sat 11-7. Sun 12-6.
Travel:	Between 15th & 16th Streets.
Credit Cards:	Yes
Owner:	Lucinda Ebersole & Richard Peabody
Year Estab:	1993
Comments:	A general shop with an almost even mix of hardcover and paperback volumes. Strong in the specialties noted above but plenty of interesting titles in other subject areas. Somewhat crowded but worth taking the time to browse. The shop sponsors weekly readings (except during summer).

Backstage   **Open Shop**
2101 P Street, NW 20037   (202) 775-1488
                                                         Fax: (202) 296-3430
                                          E-mail: BACKSTGBKS@aol.com

Collection:	Specialty books and related items.
Specialties:	Theatre; film.
Hours:	Mon-Sat 10-6, except Thu till 7.
Services:	Mail order
Travel:	Two blocks west of Dupont Circle.
Credit Cards:	Yes
Year Estab:	1982
Comments:	Used books are primarily scripts.

Bartleby's Books
3034 M Street, NW, 2nd Fl.
Mailing address: PO Box 15400 Chevy Chase 20825

Open Shop
(202) 298-0486
Fax: (202) 686-5697

Collection:	Specialty and some general stock.
# of Vols:	5,000
Specialties:	Americana; literature; art; economics.
Hours:	Tue-Sat 10-3.
Services:	Catalog, accepts want lists.
Travel:	In Georgetown, at corner of M and Thomas Jefferson St.
Credit Cards:	Yes
Owner:	John Thomson & Karen Griffin
Year Estab:	1984
Comments:	The stock in this shop (one flight up and a short block from another fine shop) offers a quality collection for the discerning reader.

Bay Street Books
1740 Bay Street, SE 20003

By Appointment
(202) 546-3893
E-mail: mercury@vais.net

Collection:	Specialty
# of Vols:	1,500
Specialties:	Civil War.
Services:	Appraisals, search service, accepts want lists, mail order.
Credit Cards:	No
Owner:	Ben Kirkconnell
Year Estab:	1990

Book Mark It
3507 12th Street NE 20017

Open Shop
(202) 529-2360

Collection:	General stock of hardcover and paperback.
# of Vols:	15,000-20,000
Hours:	Mon-Fri 10-5. Sat 10-4.
Travel:	New Hampshire Ave exit off I-495. Proceed south on New Hampshire which becomes North Capitol. Turn east on Michigan, then right on 12th St. Metro: Catholic University stop.
Credit Cards:	Yes
Owner:	John Lewis
Year Estab:	1994
Comments:	A modest collection of reading copies, both paperback and hardcover. Few surprises or rarities. A shop that no doubt meets the needs of its neighborhood.

Booked Up
1204 31st Street NW 20007

Open Shop
(202) 337-2749
Fax: (202) 298-6555

Collection:	General stock.
# of Vols:	4,000
Specialties:	Antiquarian

Hours:	Mon-Fri 11-3. Sat 10-12:30.
Travel:	In Georgetown, at M Street. Shop is on second floor.
Credit Cards:	Yes
Owner:	Marcia Carter
Year Estab:	1975
Comments:	A narrow outside metal staircase leads to a good sized room which displays volumes that may truly be classified as antiquarian. Their bindings, their age and their rarity all suggest that they have received tender loving care from all who have had the privilege of previous ownership. The owner, a charming southern belle, reminds the visitor that she also has a section of more traditional used books and indeed this is correct.

Capitol Hill Books
657 C Street SE 20003

Open Shop
(202) 544-1621

Collection:	General stock of mostly hardcover.
# of Vols:	10,000
Specialties:	Classics; history; modern first editions; biography.
Hours:	Mon-Fri 11:30-6. Sat & Sun 10-6.
Services:	Search service, accepts want lists, mail order.
Travel:	Off Pennsylvania Ave, between 6th and 7th Sts, across from Eastern Market. From Pennsylvania, turn on 7th St, then left on C St. Note: "C" St cannot be approached from Pennsylvania Ave.
Credit Cards:	Yes
Owner:	Martin "Jim" Toole
Year Estab:	1990
Comments:	Very much reminiscent of the bookshops of yore on New York City's Fourth Avenue. The shop is small, compact, overflowing with volumes displaying interesting titles and, if you're lucky enough to be able to locate the shop, worth a brief visit.

De Jure Antiquarian Books
2907 29th Street NW 20008

By Appointment
(202) 462-4959
Fax: (202) 328-7635
E-mail: dejure@erols.com

Collection:	Specialty
# of Vols:	1,500
Specialties:	Law; history (Scholarly books in English, French, German, Latin and Spanish).
Services:	Appraisals, accepts want lists, catalog.
Credit Cards:	Yes
Owner:	Edward Gordon
Year Estab:	1990

Georgetown Book Exchange
1660 33rd Street NW 20007

Open Shop
(202) 337-4348

Collection:	General stock of hardcover and paperback.

# of Vols:	25,000
Hours:	Mon-Sat 10-7. Sun 12-5.
Travel:	In Georgetown, at intersection of 33rd St and Wisconsin Ave.
Credit Cards:	Yes
Owner:	Hamid Afshar
Year Estab:	1997
Comments:	Stock is evenly divided between hardcover and paperback.

James M. Goode Fine Books   **By Appointment**
4301 Massachusetts Avenue NW, Ste. A303 20016   (202) 364-4301
Fax: (202) 364-2579

Collection:	Specialty
# of Vols:	6,000
Specialties:	Architecture; Americana.
Credit Cards:	Yes
Year Estab:	1997

William F. Hale Books   **Open Shop**
1222 31st Street, NW 20007   (202) 338-8272
Fax: (202) 338-8420
E-mail: wfhale@ix.netcom.com

Collection:	General stock.
# of Vols:	4,000
Specialties:	Art history; botany; early printed books.
Hours:	Mon-Sat 11:30-6.
Services:	Appraisals, occasional catalog, accepts want lists, mail order.
Travel:	In Georgetown, between M and N Streets.
Credit Cards:	Yes
Year Estab:	1978
Comments:	An eclectic mix consisting of some older volumes, some classics, some solid non fiction titles and a reasonable representation of antiquarian volumes (some with unusual bindings). Note that the dealer shares space with the Logic and Literature Book Shop and that the two collections are intershelved, giving, for all practical purposes, the appearance of one shop.

Joshua Heller Rare Books   **By Appointment**
PO Box 39114 20016   (202) 966-9411
Web page: www.abaa-booknet/usa/   Fax: (202) 363-5658
E-mail: HellerBkDC@aol.com

Collection:	Specialty
Specialties:	Private press; illustrated; printing history; books on books; modern fine bindings; contemporary artists' books.
Services:	Catalog
Credit Cards:	Yes
Owner:	Joshua & Phyllis Heller
Year Estab:	1985

Hooper's Books
1615 Eighth Street NW 20001-3102

By Appointment
(202) 387-3007
E-mail: rhooper451@aol.com

Collection:	Specialty
# of Vols:	2,000
Specialties:	Equestrian sports; tennis; dogs; T.E. Lawrence.
Services:	Appraisals, accepts want lists, catalog, search service.
Credit Cards:	No
Owner:	Richard Hooper
Year Estab:	1979

Idle Times Books
2410 18th Street, NW 20009

Open Shop
(202) 232-4774

Collection:	General stock of hardcover and paperback.
# of Vols:	50,000
Hours:	Mon-Thu 11-10. Fri & Sat 11-midnight.
Travel:	Between Columbia & Belmont.
Credit Cards:	Yes
Owner:	Jacques Morgan
Year Estab:	1981
Comments:	An interesting bi-level shop with a collection of mixed vintage books in mixed condition. We noted some interesting titles and recommend the shop as worth a visit. Moderately priced.

Kultura's Books & Records
1741 Connecticut Avenue, NW 20009

Open Shop
(202) 462-2541

Collection:	General stock of hardcover and paperback.
# of Vols:	55,000
Specialties:	Humanities
Hours:	Mon-Wed 11-9. Thu-Sat 11-10. Sun 11-7.
Services:	Accepts want lists, mail order.
Travel:	At S Street.
Credit Cards:	Yes
Owner:	Andrew MacDonald & Irene Coray
Year Estab:	1988
Comments:	A modest sized, comfortable to browse shop with a pleasant atmosphere. Most of the books we saw reflected scholarly topics such as politics, sociology and more serious literature and literary criticism. Most of the books were of more recent vintage and in generally good condition and with dust jackcts.

Lambda Rising
1625 Connecticut Avenue, NW 20009

Open Shop
(202) 462-6969
Fax: (202) 462-7257
E-mail: lrstaff@aol.com

Collection:	Specialty new and used.

# of Vols:	500-1,000 (used)
Specialties:	Gay and lesbian; bisexual and transgender.
Hours:	Daily 10-midnight.
Services:	Search service, accepts want lists, mail order.
Travel:	Between Q and R Streets.
Credit Cards:	Yes
Owner:	James Bennett & Deacon McCubbin
Year Estab:	1975

The Lantern Bookshop   **Open Shop**
3241 P Street, NW 20007   (202) 333-3222
Web page: www.heis.com/~lantern   E-mail: lantern@heis.com

Collection:	General stock.
# of Vols:	20,000
Hours:	Mon-Fri 11-4. Sat 11-5. Sun 12-4.
Services:	Search service, accepts want lists.
Travel:	In Georgetown, just off Wisconsin Avenue.
Credit Cards:	No
Year Estab:	1976
Comments:	Owned and operated by volunteers for the benefit of the Bryn Mawr College alumni scholarship fund. Bryn Mawr shops are always sources of potential bargains and this location is no exception. Although knowledgeable book people quickly gather up the more resalable items, fortunately the shop receives an ongoing stream of donations, usually from generous sources with good taste in books.

Latin American Books   **By Appointment**
PO Box 39090 20016   (202) 244-4173

Collection:	Specialty
# of Vols:	200,000
Specialties:	Latin America; Spain and Portugal and their former Asia and African colonies. All languages and all disciplines.
Services:	Search service, accepts want lists, mail order.
Credit Cards:	No
Owner:	David Clark
Year Estab:	1970's

Logic And Literature Book Shop   **Open Shop**
1222 31st Street, NW 20007   (202) 625-1668

Collection:	Specialty
# of Vols:	5,000-8,000
Specialties:	Philosophy; travel (Middle East); history (ancient to Renaissance); history of science and mathematics; classical studies.
Hours:	Mon-Sat 11:30-6.
Travel:	Shares space with William F. Hale Books. See above.
Owner:	Candee Harris
Comments:	See comments for William F. Hale Books above.

Kinsey Marable & Company   **Open Shop**
1531 Wisconsin Avenue, NW 20007   (202) 337-3460
                                                 Fax: (202) 337-5381

Collection: Specialty
Specialties: Architecture; interiors; gardening; cookbooks; social history; sports;
                  travel.
Hours: Mon-Sat 10-6.
Services: Catalog, accepts want lists.
Travel: In Georgetown, between P and Q Streets.
Credit Cards: Yes
Owner: Kinsey Marable
Year Estab: 1994
Comments: Shop also sells library furnishings.

Military Books   **By Appointment**
3226 Woodley Road, NW 20008   (202) 333-7308

Collection: Specialty
# of Vols: 5,000-10,000
Specialties: Military, including all American wars, Napoleonic wars; military avia-
                  tion, marine corps and naval, firearms, manuals, artillery and military
                  biography.
Services: Catalog, accepts want lists.
Credit Cards: No
Owner: R.P.W. Williams
Year Estab: 1983

Niel's Books   **Open Shop**
1615 17th Street NW, 2nd Fl. 20009   (202) 483-4737

Collection: General stock of hardcover and paperback.
# of Vols: 12,000
Specialties: Philosophy; 20th century theory; art; children's; labor history.
Hours: Mon-Thu 12-9. Fri-Sun 12-10.
Travel: Between Q and R Streets.
Credit Cards: Yes
Owner: Niel Rosen
Year Estab: 1995
Comments: A nice selection of mostly newer titles. Stronger in non fiction, par-
                  ticularly related to politics and history. The majority of the books we
                  saw sported dust jackets in shiny protective coverings. Some fiction
                  was on hand, again, mostly newer. Roomy and easy to browse.

The Old Forest Bookshop   **Open Shop**
3145 Dumbarton Street, NW 20007   (202) 965-3842

Collection: General stock of hardcover and paperback.
# of Vols: 10,000+
Specialties: Literature; history; art.

Hours:	Mon-Sat 11-6:30. Sun 12-6.
Travel:	In Georgetown, between Wisconsin and 31st Streets.
Credit Cards:	Yes
Owner:	Derrick Hsu
Year Estab:	1988
Comments:	Unlike some of the other used book shops in Georgetown that carry more scholarly titles, this bi-level shop stocks more recent vintage titles. The shop is well organized and easy to browse.

The Old Print Gallery   **Open Shop**
1220 31st Street, NW 20007   (202) 965-1818
                                                                          Fax: (202) 965-1869

Collection:	Specialty
Specialties:	Maps
Hours:	Mon-Sat 10-5:30.
Services:	Appraisals, search service, catalog, accepts want lists.
Travel:	In Georgetown, between M and N Streets.
Credit Cards:	Yes
Owner:	Judith Blakely & James von Ruster
Year Estab:	1971

Olsson's Books • Records   **Open Shop**
1239 Wisconsin Ave NW 20007   (202) 338-9544
Web page: www.olssons.com   Fax: 202-342-2342
                                                        E-mail: ordering@olssons.com

Collection:	General stock of mostly new and some used.
# of Vols:	1,500 (used)
Hours:	Mon-Thu 10am-11pm. Fri & Sat 10am-midnight. Sun 11-11
Travel:	In Georgetown between M and N Streets.
Owner:	Jim Tenney, Senior Buyer
Comments:	One of six stores in a chain of independent new booksellers that began selling used and out-of-print books in 1997. The used stock, primarily hardcover, is intershelved with the new books. The store anticipates building specialties in history; medieval studies; Byzantine, world regional studies, military, military intelligence and biography.

J.F. Ptak Science Books   **Open Shop**
1531 33rd Street NW 20007   (202) 337-0945
Web page: www.access.digex.net/~jfptak   E-mail: jfptak@access.digex.net

Collection:	Specialty books and related prints.
# of Vols:	50,000
Specialties:	Physics; mathematics; logic; electrical engineering; history of science; history of medicine.
Hours:	Tue-Sun 12-5.
Services:	Appraisals, accepts want lists, catalog, search service. Also publishes books on the history of science under the name Amphion Press.
Travel:	In Georgetown, between P and Volta Streets.

Credit Cards:	Yes
Owner:	John Ptak
Year Estab:	1984
Comments:	In all our travels, this is the first open shop we have seen devoted exclusively to used and out-of-print books dealing with science.

Second Story Books   Open Shop
2000 P Street, NW 20036   (202) 659-8884
Web page: www.paltech.com/secondstory   E-mail: ssbookguys@paltech.com

Collection:	General stock of hardcover and paperback books and records.
# of Vols:	50,000+
Hours:	Daily 10-10.
Services:	Search service, catalog.
Travel:	At Dupont Circle.
Credit Cards:	Yes
Owner:	Allan Stypeck
Year Estab:	1974
Comments:	A broad general collection with books in most subject areas in mixed condition and of mixed vintage. Prices tended to be average and slightly above average. When we stopped by, the shop was crowded with browsers, most always a sign of a shop with a good selection and satisfied customers.

Voyages Books & Art   By Appointment
4705 Butterworth Place, NW 20016   (202) 244-9636

Collection:	General stock.
# of Vols:	15,000
Specialties:	20th century literature; poetry.
Services:	Appraisals, search service, accepts want lists, subject catalogs upon request.
Credit Cards:	No
Owner:	William Claire
Year Estab:	1987
Comments:	Also displays at antique malls in Bethesda and Queenstown in Maryland (see Maryland chapter) and in antique malls in Delaware and Connecticut.

Yesterdays Books   Open Shop
4702 Wisconsin Avenue, NW 20016   (202) 363-0581

Collection:	General stock of hardcover and paperback.
# of Vols:	25,000
Hours:	Mon-Thu 11-9. Fri & Sat 11-10. Sun 1-7.
Services:	Appraisals, search service, accepts want lists, mail order.
Travel:	Rte 355 (Rockville Pike/Wisconsin Ave) exit off I-495. Proceed south on Wisconsin for 4-5 miles. Shop is on right at corner of Chesapeake.
Credit Cards:	Yes

Owner: Katina Stockbridge & Montez Swanner
Year Estab: 1973
Comments: This bi-level shop offers a cozy atmosphere with chairs, coffee and nut
                bread snacks to tempt the browser. While the first floor is somewhat
                crowded, the second floor is divided into several more roomy alcoves,
                each with a character of its own. The books are of mixed vintage and
                in mixed condition with few truly rare items but many interesting
                titles. There are, however, some more expensive items in a locked
                bookcase on the first floor.

Mail Order Dealers

East-West Features Service   Tel & Fax: (301) 236-5966
PO Box 15067 Washington, DC 20003   E-mail: eastwest@tidalwave.net

Collection: Specialty
# of Vols: 30,000+
Specialties: Russia; Belarus; Slavica; Siberia.
Services: Catalog, accepts want lists.
Credit Cards: No
Owner: Kozak/ Sasamoto
Year Estab: 1975

The Holy Land   (202) 965-4831
3041 Normanstone Terrace, NW Washington, DC 20008   Fax: (202) 965-1746
                                                     E-mail: shalperin@aypf.org

Collection: Specialty books and ephemera.
# of Vols: 4,000
Specialties: Holy Land; Judaica; Israel.
Services: Search service, accepts want lists.
Credit Cards: No
Owner: Dr. Samuel Halperin
Year Estab: 1975

The President's Box Bookshop   (703) 998-7390
PO Box 1255 Washington, DC 20013

Collection: Specialty books and ephemera
# of Vols: 2,000
Specialties: Assassination of American presidents.
Services: Appraisals, search service, catalog, accepts want lists.
Credit Cards: No
Owner: David A. Lovett
Year Estab: 1982

Florida

Alphabetical Listing By Dealer

Alphabetical Listing By Location

Atlantic Beach
(Map 3, page 32 & Map 4, page 54)

Tappin Book Mine   **Open Shop**
705 Atlantic Boulevard 32233   Tel & Fax: (904) 246-1388
Web page: users.southeast.net/~tappinbm   E-mail: tappinbm@southeast.net

Collection:	General stock of mostly hardcover.
# of Vols:	30,000
Specialties:	Nautical; military; modern first editions; Florida.
Hours:	Mon-Fri 10-8. Sat 10-6. Sun 12-5.
Services:	Appraisals, search service, catalog, accepts want lists.
Travel:	Rte 9A exit off I-95 south. Proceed south on Rte 9A to Atlantic Blvd then east on Atlantic Blvd for about seven miles.
Credit Cards:	Yes
Owner:	Douglas C. Tappin
Year Estab:	1975
Comments:	Quite a nice shop with quality books that are competitively priced. We saw a number of titles that were "out of the ordinary" and would certainly recommend a visit here to all but the most esoteric buyer. The books were in good to excellent condition. If you're looking for "better books," be certain to ask for admission to the catalog room.

Bartow

Family Book Exchange   **Open Shop**
140 South Wilson Street 33830   (941) 533-6338

Collection:	General stock of mostly paperback.
# of Vols:	15,000
Hours:	Mon-Fri 9:30-5:30. Sat 10-3.

Belleair Bluffs

Snoop Sisters Mystery Bookshop   **Open Shop**
566 North Indian Rocks Road 33770   Tel & Fax: (813) 584-4370

Collection:	Specialty new and used.
# of Vols:	Several hundred (used hardcover).
Specialties:	Mystery.
Hours:	Mon-Sat 10-4. Extended hours in season.
Services:	Search service, accepts want lists, newsletter.
Travel:	From Rte 19, turn west onto East Bay Dr which becomes West Bay Dr. Turn north onto Indian Rocks Rd and west into Antique Alley. Shop address is Indian Rocks Rd but entrance is from Antique Alley.
Credit Cards:	Yes
Owner:	Susan Rose
Year Estab:	1991

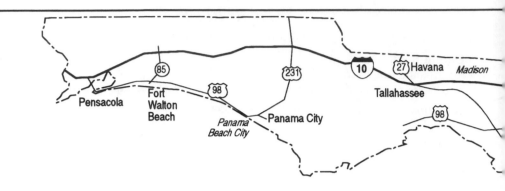

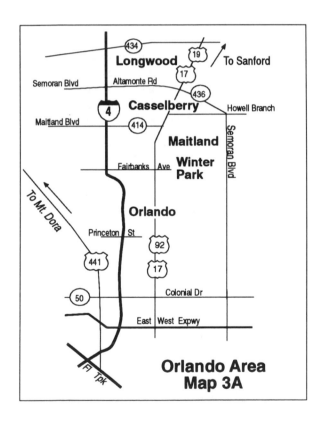

**Orlando Area
Map 3A**

Florida
Map 3

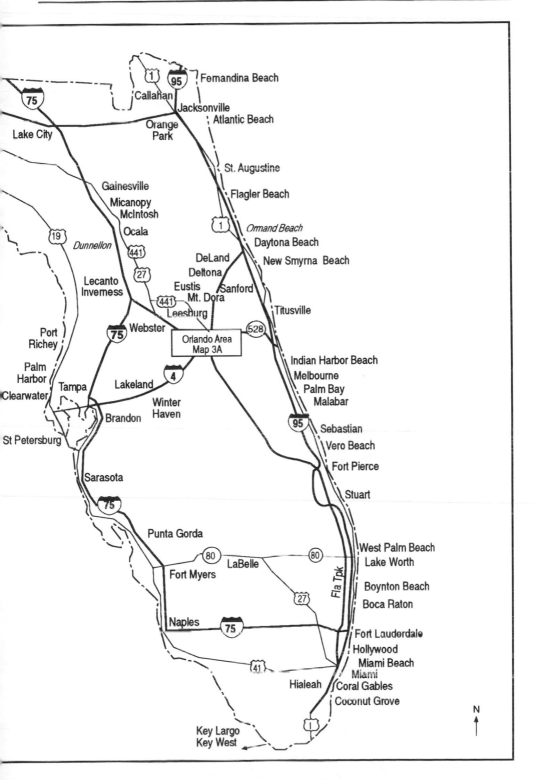

Boca Raton
(Map 3, page 32 & Map 5, page 68)

Booksmart   **Open Shop**
668 Glades Road 33431   (561) 394-6085
Web page: www.booksmartusa.com   Fax: (407) 394-6430
                                                     E-mail: booksmrt@gate.net

Collection: General stock of hardcover and paperback.
# of Vols: 20,000 (excluding textbooks)
Hours: Mon-Fri 9-7. Sat 11-5.
Services: Appraisals, search service, accepts want lists.
Travel: Glades Rd exit off I-95. Proceed east on Glades Rd for about 1½ miles.
                  Shop is on right in Oaks Plaza.
Credit Cards: Yes
Owner: David, Jim & Ann Wulf
Year Estab: 1992
Comments: A large selection of paperbacks and textbooks along with a modest
                  sized collection of mostly hardcover fiction and non fiction. Primarily
                  reading copies. Very reasonably priced.

Booksmart   **Open Shop**
146 NW 20th Street 33431   (561) 347-6455

Collection: General stock of paperback and hardcover.
# of Vols: 15,000
Hours: Mon-Sat 10-4.
Services: Accepts want lists.
Travel: Glades Rd exit off I-95. Proceed east on Glades Rd to 2nd Ave (Boca
                  Raton Blvd), then north on 2nd Ave and right on NW 20th St. Shop is
                  on right in 20th Street Shopping Plaza.
Credit Cards: Yes
Owner: David, Jim & Ann Wulf
Year Estab: 1992
Comments: Stock is approximately 70% paperback.

Brandeis Book Store   **Open Shop**
9060 Kimberly Boulevard, Ste. 47 33434   (561) 852-2650

Collection: General stock of hardcover and paperback.
Hours: Mon-Sat 9:30-5. Sun 10-4.
Travel: Glades Rd exit off I-95. Proceed west on Glades to Lyons Rd, then
                  north on Lyons to Kimberly.
Comments: A non profit shop. All books are donated.

Cohen Books And Collectibles   **By Appointment**
PO Box 810310 33481-0310   (561) 487-7888
Web page: www.bbai.onramp.net/bbai/cohen.htm   Fax: (561) 487-3117
                                                  E-mail: cohendisney@prodigy.com

Collection: Specialty books, ephemera and related items.

Specialties:	Disney
Services:	Appraisals, search service, accepts want lists, mail order.
Credit Cards:	No
Owner:	Joel Cohen
Year Estab:	1971

Debbie-Rand Memorial Thrift Shoppe   **Open Shop**
800 Meadows Road 33486   (561) 395-2208

Collection:	General stock of paperback and hardcover.
# of Vols:	500+
Hours:	Mon-Fri 10-3. Sat 9-1.
Travel:	Glades Rd exit off I-95. Proceed east on Glades Rd to 10th Ave then south on 10th Ave. Follow street till it becomes Meadows. Shop is on grounds of the Boca Raton Community Hospital.
Comments:	A non profit shop. All books are donated.

Paulette Greene: Rare & Unusual Books   **By Appointment**
7152 Via Palomar 33433   Tel & Fax: (561) 347-1948

Collection:	Specialty
# of Vols:	4,000
Specialties:	Art (modern); decorative arts; Latin American art; fine press books; illustrated.
Services:	Mail order.
Credit Cards:	No
Year Estab:	1967

Boynton Beach
(Map 3, page 32 & Map 5, page 68)

Stephen Koschal Autographs Inc.   **By Appointment**
PO Box 1581 33425   Tel & Fax: (561) 736-8409

Collection:	Specialty
Specialties:	Signed books; autographs.
Services:	Appraisals, search service, catalog, accepts want lists.
Credit Cards:	Yes
Year Estab:	1967

Victorian Parlor Book Store   **Open Shop**
513 East Ocean Avenue 33435   (561) 738-2018
                                    Fax: (561) 738-1914
                                    E-mail: janh@emi.net

Collection:	General stock and ephemera.
# of Vols:	15,000
Specialties:	Royalty; history.
Hours:	Tue-Sat 10-4:30.
Services:	Appraisals, search service, accepts want lists.
Travel:	Ocean Ave exit off I-95. Proceed west on Ocean. Shop is on north side of street, about 1/2 block west of Rte 1.

Credit Cards:	Yes
Owner:	Janet Hall
Year Estab:	1993
Comments:	A combination used book and collectibles shop. Most of the books we saw were older and in mixed condition. If you're on Rte 1 traveling up or down the Florida coast, this shop is only a half block off the main thoroughfare.

Bradenton

A Real Bookstore   **Open Shop**
5700 Manatee Avenue West 34209   (941) 795-2665

Collection:	General stock of mostly new and some used.
Hours:	Mon-Sat 10-6.
Travel:	Rte 64 exit off I-75. Proceed west on Rte 64 to 57th St.
Comments:	Stock is approximately 80% new.

Brandon
(Map 3, page 32 & Map 6, page 88)

Book Corner   **Open Shop**
728 West Lumsden Road 33511   (813) 684-1133
E-mail: bookcrnr@worldnet.att.net

Collection:	General stock.
# of Vols:	20,000
Specialties:	Florida; maritime; pirates and treasure; aviation; children's; modern first editions; Cuba; Panama Canal; travel (19th century).
Hours:	Mon-Sat 10-6. Sun by appointment.
Services:	Appraisals, search service.
Travel:	From I-75, proceed east on Rte 60 for about three miles, then right onto Kings. Shop is after the second light in the LaViva Plaza shopping center at corner of Kings and Lumsden.
Credit Cards:	Yes
Owner:	Michael & Victoria Tennaro
Year Estab:	1988
Comments:	An inviting shop that shares space with an antique store. The books are attractively displayed with most (including the older volumes) in reasonably good or better condition. We spotted a few really old treasures. The shop is comfortable to browse with chairs and a coffee pot close at hand.

Callahan
(Map 3, page 32)

Beaton's Book & Vitamin Shoppe   **Open Shop**
500 Kings Road South 32011   (904) 879-4042

Collection:	General stock of hardcover and paperback.
# of Vols:	10,000

Hours:	Mon-Sat 10-6.
Travel:	On Rte 1 just south of Rte A1A. Proceeding south, the shop is on the right in a small strip center.
Credit Cards:	Yes
Owner:	Ernest & Marilyn Beaton
Year Estab:	1984
Comments:	Once you realize that half of the shop is devoted to the sale of vitamins and the other half to paperbacks, religious books and just plain "old hardcover books," you may find your desire for a vitamin supplement greater than your desire to purchase a book.

Casselberry
(Map 3A, page 32)

A Novel Idea Bookshop   **Open Shop**
1466 Semoran Boulevard 32707   Tel & Fax: (407) 672-0095

Collection:	General stock of mostly paperback.
# of Vols:	20,000
Hours:	Mon 12-6:30. Tue-Fri 10-6:30. Sat & Sun 10-5:30.

Harbar Book Exchange   **Open Shop**
1033 Semoran Boulevard, Ste. 137 32707   (407) 834-0153

Collection:	General stock of mostly used paperbacks.
# of vols:	10,000
Hours:	Tue-Sat 10-5. Sun 12-4.
Travel:	On Rte 436 in Summitt Plaza Shopping Center.
Credit Cards:	No
Owner:	J. Shelby
Year Estab:	1980
Comments:	While we acknowledge that our visit to this shop was brief, had we a greater interest in paperbacks we might have stayed longer. As it was, the number of hardcover items in both the front and rear rooms was modest.

Leedy's Books   **Open Shop**
1455 Semoran Boulevard, #137 32707   (407) 677-4686

Collection:	General stock of mostly hardcover.
# of Vols:	27,000
Hours:	Mon-Sat 10-6, except Mon till 8.
Services:	Search service, accepts want lists.
Travel:	Exit 48 off I-4. Proceed east on Rte 436 (Semoran Blvd) to Howell Branch Rd. Shop is on right in Casselberry Commons Shopping Center just before Howell Branch.
Credit Cards:	No
Owner:	Robert Leedy
Year Estab:	1993
Comments:	An attractive shop with a nice collection of mostly hardcover volumes in good to very good condition. Quite reasonably priced. Easy to browse.

Clearwater
(Map 3, page 32)

Acquist Books & Antiques   **Open Shop**
1415 Cleveland Street 34615   (813) 443-7444

Collection:	General stock, maps and prints.
# of Vols:	40,000
Specialties:	Antiques; Americana; Napoleon; Florida; history; southern authors; children's.
Hours:	Mon-Sat 9-6. Sun (Nov-Apr) 9-6. Call for Sun hours during off season.
Services:	Appraisals, search service, accepts want lists, mail order.
Travel:	Rte 19 to Rte 60. Proceed west on Rte 60. At fork, make a hard right onto Highland, then left onto Cleveland. Shop is two blocks ahead on left.
Credit Cards:	Yes
Owner:	Lowell Kelly
Year Estab:	1978
Comments:	This shop is much larger than it appears from the outside and we suspect there may be more than the 40,000 books cited above. The shelves were jammed packed and each of the many small rooms we visited were filled to the brim. Most, but not all, of the books were of an older vintage and in mixed condition. A sharp buyer may well discover a treasure or two here.

Clearwater Books   **Open Shop**
425 Cleveland Street 33755   Tel & Fax: (813) 447-5722

Collection:	General stock of hardcover and paperback.
# of Vols:	20,000+
Hours:	Mon-Sat 11-7.
Services:	Search service, mail order.
Travel:	Rte 60 to Clearwater. Follow signs to Cleveland St/downtown. Cleveland St is Rte 60.
Credit Cards:	Yes
Owner:	Jim Rupp
Year Estab:	1982
Comments:	A small shop with a nice stock making good use of its space. Easy to browse. Very reasonably priced.

Paperback Palace   **Open Shop**
1293 South Missouri Avenue 33756   (813) 461-2160

Collection:	General stock of mostly used paperback.
Hours:	Mon-Fri 9-8. Sat 9-7. Sun 11-5.

E.J. Snyder, Bookseller   **Open Shop**
505 Howard Court, Ste. 200 34616   Tel & Fax: (813) 446-1521

Collection:	Specialty
# of Vols:	2,000
Specialties:	Naval history.
Hours:	Mon-Fri 10-5.

Services:	Appraisals
Year Estab:	1978

Coconut Grove
(Map 3, page 32 & Map 5, page 68)

Grove Antiquarian   **Open Shop**
3318 Virginia Street 33133   (305) 444-5362
E-mail: grovbook@interloc.com

Collection:	General stock.
# of Vols:	10,000
Specialties:	First editions; south Florida; Caribbean; Cuba.
Hours:	Daily 10-9.
Services:	Appraisals, search service, mail order.
Travel:	Bird Rd exit off Rte 826. Proceed east on Bird to Virginia St then south onto Virginia. Shop is several blocks ahead in a small cluster of stores set off from the street by a few steps.
Credit Cards:	Yes
Owner:	Ward & Viviana Arrington
Year Estab:	1989
Comments:	A roomy shop with books attractively displayed and in generally good condition. The shelves are well labeled and the books fairly priced. If you're interested in any of the specialties listed above, the shop is certainly worth a visit.

Coral Gables
(Map 3, page 32 & Map 5, page 68)

Books & Books   **Open Shop**
296 Aragon Avenue 33134   (305) 442-4408
Fax: (305) 444-9751

Collection:	General stock of new and used books.
# of Vols:	12,000 (used)
Specialties:	Limited editions; Cuba; art; Florida; fine bindings; first editions.
Hours:	Mon-Sat 9am-11pm. Sun 11-8.
Services:	Search service, accepts want lists, mail order.
Travel:	From Rte 1, proceed north on LeJeune Rd (42nd Ave), then east on Coral Way (Miracle Mile) and left on Salzedo. Shop is at next intersection.
Credit Cards:	Yes
Owner:	Nolly Ebert, Used Book Manager
Year Estab:	1981
Comments:	While the first floor of this combination new/used book shop is devoted entirely to new books, the second floor should prove a delight to any used book person who has an appreciation for books dealing with art and architecture. We saw some very rare items in both specialties that would make a particularly fine contribution to any university library. There were also several bookcases devoted to used books in the fiction/ literature category, most of which were in good to fine condition.

Crestview

Joy's Book Nook   **Open Shop**
625 Ferdon Boulevard North 32536   (850) 689-3739

Collection:	General stock of mostly paperback.
# of Vols:	25,000
Hours:	Tue-Fri 11-5. Sat 11-3 (except closed in summer).

Dania

Dania Books & News   **Open Shop**
310 East Dania Beach Boulevard 33004   (954) 923-0668

Collection:	General stock of new and mostly paperback used.
# of Vols:	4,000 (used)
Hours:	Mon-Sat 9-7. Sun 8-2.

Davie

Barrister Books   **By Appointment**
6901 SW 56th Court 33314   (954) 584-3775
                                                               (954) 436-0078

Collection:	Specialty
# of Vols:	2,500
Specialties:	First editions; Civil War; Florida; Cuba; children's; illustrated; Abraham Lincoln.
Services:	Appraisals, search service, subject lists, mail order.
Credit Cards:	No
Owner:	Sheldon C. & Rosalind Kurland
Year Estab:	1977

The Book Corner   **Open Shop**
8966 State Road 84 33324   (954) 423-1751

Collection:	General stock of mostly paperback.
# of Vols:	20,00
Hours:	Mon, Tue, Thu 10-5. Wed 10-2. Fri & Sat 10-6.

Daytona Beach
(Map 3, page 32)

Book Barn   **Open Shop**
2032 South Ridgewood Avenue, Ste 4   (904) 760-7027
Mailing address: 2032 S. Ridgewood Ave, Ste 4 South Daytona 32119

Collection:	General stock of mostly used and some new paperback and hardcover.
# of Vols:	100,000+
Specialties:	Modern first editions; cookbooks; crafts.
Hours:	Mon-Sat 10-7. Sun hours in season.
Services:	Search service, accepts want lists.

Travel:	Rte 400 exit off I-95. Proceed east on Rte 400 to Rte 1 (Ridgewood Ave). Turn south on Rte 1 and proceed for about one mile. Shop is on right in Big Tree Shopping Center at corner of Big Tree Rd and Rte 1.
Credit Cards:	Yes
Owner:	Mary Miller
Year Estab:	1984
Comments:	A mostly used paperback shop with a scattering of hardcover books intershelved with the paperbacks according to subject. Chances are you're not likely to spend a great deal of time here.

Mandala Books   **Open Shop**
204 International Speedway Boulevard 32114   (904) 255-6728

Collection:	General stock of hardcover and paperback.
# of Vols:	150,000
Specialties:	Modern literature; photography; art; fine arts; metaphysics; nautical; black studies; history; first editions.
Hours:	Mon-Sat 9:30-6:30. Sun 11-6.
Travel:	Daytona Beach exit off I-95. Proceed on Rte 92 (International Speedway Blvd).
Credit Cards:	Yes
Owner:	Victor Newman
Year Estab:	1980
Comments:	This is the type of shop that some of our "paperback mostly" friends consider a "real" book store. The shop has a large selection of mostly hardcover books in almost every field from scholarly to mystery, science fiction and cookbooks. The books we saw were in mixed condition and represented many generations. While the shop does carry paperbacks and records, its hardcover collection is respectable and well worth a visit. First editions and other rarities are located in a back room.

Deerfield Beach

Bargain Bestsellers   **Open Shop**
3240 West Hillsboro Boulevard 33442   (954) 480-9777

Collection:	General stock of mostly paperback.
# of Vols:	35,000
Hours:	Mon-Sat, except closed Tue, 10-6. Sun 12-5.

DeLand
(Map 3, page 32)

Cliff's Books   **Open Shop**
209 North Woodland Boulevard 32720   (904) 738-9464

Collection:	General stock of paperback and hardcover, comics and records.
# of Vols:	5,000-10,000
Specialties:	Science fiction; horror; mystery; vintage paperbacks.
Hours:	Mon-Fri 4-6. Sat 10-5.

(DeLand)

Travel:	See Muse Book Shop below.
Credit Cards:	No
Owner:	Cliff Weikal
Year Estab:	1983
Comments:	Specialty books are paperback only. Hardcover titles are general stock.

Family Book Shop (Second Hand Prose)   Open Shop
1301 North Woodland Boulevard 32720   Tel & Fax: (904) 736-6501
                                                        E-mail: Readit@totcon.com

Collection:	General stock of mostly used paperback and hardcover.
# of Vols:	150,000+
Hours:	Mon-Sat 10-6. Sun 1-5.
Services:	Accepts want lists, mail order.
Travel:	Exit 56 (Rte 44) off I-4. Proceed west on Rte 44 to Amelia Ave, then north on Amelia to Kentucky Ave and west on Kentucky to Woodland. Shop is at corner of Kentucky and Woodland.
Credit Cards:	No
Owner:	Judy Mathys
Year Estab:	1976
Comments:	Usually, when we visit a used book store that is close to a university campus (this shop is near Stetson University), we find the shops are heavy into scholarly titles. This shop was an exception to that rule. The majority of the books we saw were used paperbacks and comics with approximately 5,000 hardcover volumes that ran the gamut from recent bestsellers to older and more obscure items.

Muse Book Shop   Open Shop
112 South Woodland Boulevard 32720   (904) 734-0278

Collection:	General stock of mostly used.
# of Vols:	40,000 (used)
Specialties:	Florida
Hours:	Mon-Sat 9:30-5:30. Sun 1-5.
Services:	Appraisals, accepts want lists, occasional catalog.
Travel:	Exit 56 (New York Ave) off I-4. Proceed west on New York Ave, then left onto Hayden (just before Woodland Blvd) and first right onto Georgia. Shop is across the street from the parking.
Credit Cards:	Yes
Owner:	Janet Bollum
Year Estab:	1980
Comments:	An attractive combination new/used shop with a reasonable selection of used titles. Although the size of the collection we saw was smaller than the 40,000 cited above, there were enough books to pique one's interest. Most of the books were in good to better condition. It should not take the experienced browser a great deal of time to peruse the shop's wares. A majority of the books were serious and scholarly.

Rivertown Antique Mall   **Antique Mall**
114 South Woodland Boulevard 32720   (904) 738-5111

Hours:	Mon-Sat 10-5.
Travel:	On Rte 17/92.

Deltona
(Map 3, page 32)

Brenda's Book Haven   **Open Shop**
1200 Deltona Boulevard, #12 32725   Tel & Fax: (407) 574-1665

Collection:	General stock of paperback and hardcover.
# of Vols:	20,000
Specialties:	Children's; children's series; inspirational fiction; African American fiction; political science.
Hours:	Mon-Sat 10-6. Sun 12-6.
Services:	Accepts want lists, mail order.
Travel:	From I-4 westbound: Exit 53CA (Deltona). Proceed on Saxon Blvd, then right at second light onto Normandy and right at next light onto Deltona Blvd. Shop is on right in Deltona Plaza shopping center.
Credit Cards:	No
Owner:	Brenda Hardy
Year Estab:	1997
Comments:	At the time of our visit, the shop had only been open a short time. Most of the stock consisted of paperbacks, a rather modest supply of hardcover titles and some new trade paperbacks. We saw little that could be classified either as rare or collectible.

Dunedin

Book Swap   **Open Shop**
2109 Main Street 34698   (813) 736-5171

Collection:	General stock of paperback and some hardcover.
# of Vols:	60,000
Hours:	Mon-Sat 9-7.

Dunnellon
(Map 3, page 32)

Always Books   **By Appointment**
22008 SW Mango Lane 34431   (352) 489-0424

Collection:	General stock.
# of Vols:	5,000+
Specialties:	Modern first editions.
Services:	Search service, catalog, accepts want lists.
Credit Cards:	No
Owner:	Georgia C. Meyer
Year Estab:	1990

Book Depot Plus   **Open Shop**
11223-D North Williams Street 34432   (352) 465-1431
                                                                Fax: (352) 489-7033
                                                         E-mail: bookdepot@aol.com

Collection:	General stock of mostly used paperback and hardcover.
# of Vols:	20,000 (combined)
Hours:	Mon-Fri 8-6. Sat 9-3.
Services:	Search service, accepts want lists, mail order.
Travel:	Located on east side of Rte 41 in Food Lion Plaza.
Comments:	The stock is approximately 80% used, 80% of which is paperback.

Edgewater

Brown's Bookstore   **Open Shop**
106 Indian River Boulevard 32141   (904) 426-5477
                                                        E-mail: brownsbooks@aol.com

Collection:	General stock of mostly paperback and hardcover.
# of Vols:	20,000
Hours:	Mon-Sat 8-5. Sun (Oct-Apr) 8-5.
Travel:	Rte 442 exit off I-95. Proceed east on Rte 442 for about four miles.
Credit Cards:	No
Owner:	James & JoAnn Brown
Year Estab:	1991
Comments:	Overwhelmingly paperback with no more than a 1,000 (if that many) hardcover books (primarily reading copies) at the very rear of the shop and on the top shelves.

Eustis
(Map 3, page 32)

Raintree Books   **Open Shop**
432 North Eustis Street 32726   (800) 732-0078   (904) 357-7145
                                                                Fax: (904) 589-9093

Collection:	General stock of new and used hardcover and paperback.
# of Vols:	250,000
Hours:	Mon-Sat 9-5.
Services:	Appraisals
Travel:	Rte 441 to Rte 19 north. Once in Eustis, make left onto Hazard St (across from shopping center). Shop is in a stand alone yellow building at corner of Eustis and Hazard.
Credit Cards:	Yes
Owner:	Wendell "Jeff" & Jo Davis
Year Estab:	1963
Comments:	The shop is large, well organized and even though most of its stock is paperback, there are enough hardcover items scattered throughout the store to make a stop here worthwhile. The hardcover books are moderately priced and of mixed vintage and condition.

Fernandina Beach
(Map 3, page 32)

Book Ends   **Open Shop**
1004 South 14th Street 32034   (904) 277-0048

Collection:	General stock of mostly used paperback and some new.
# of Vols:	30,000
Hours:	Summer: Mon-Fri, except Wed, 10-6. Wed 2-6. Sat 10-3.
	Winter: Mon-Fri, except Wed, 11-5. Wed 2-5. Sat 11-3.
Travel:	From A1A, turn east on Sadler Rd, then left at next light onto 14th St. Shop is 1½ miles ahead on right in a shopping center.
Credit Cards:	No
Owner:	Sara Boatright & Brenda Ward
Year Estab:	1994
Comments:	Stock is 75% used, 75% of which is paperback.

Flagler Beach
(Map 3, page 32)

Pegasus By The Sea Books   **Open Shop**
300 South Central   (904) 439-1535
Mailing address: PO Box 219 Flagler Beach 32136   E-mail: pegasusbk@aol.com

Collection:	General stock of mostly hardcover and ephemera.
# of Vols:	40,000
Specialties:	Florida; maritime; science fiction; mystery; first editions; cookbooks; women's studies; black studies; military; Americana.
Hours:	Tue-Sun 9-6.
Services:	Appraisals, search service, accepts want lists, mail order.
Travel:	Exit 91 off I-95. Proceed east on Rte 100 to Flagler Beach, then right on Central.
Credit Cards:	Yes
Owner:	Bonnie Lee Scott
Year Estab:	1994
Comments:	Unfortunately, we didn't take our own advice to call ahead and missed this dealer who had changed her hours.

Fort Lauderdale
(Map 3, page 32 & Map 5, page 68)

All Books & Records   **Open Shop**
917 North Federal Highway 33304   (954) 761-8857
                                                        Fax: (954) 760-4797

Collection:	General stock of hardcover, paperback, comics and records.
# of Vols:	350,000
Hours:	Mon-Sat 9:30-9. Sun 12-7.
Travel:	Sunrise Blvd exit off I-95. Proceed east on Sunrise to Rte 1. Shop in on the corner in the Sears Town Shopping Center.

Credit Cards: Yes
Owner: Rod Cronk
Year Estab: 1981
Comments: A large shop that devotes almost as much space to records and CDs as it
                  does to books and has at least as many paperbacks as it does hardcover
                  titles. For the most part, the paperbacks and hardcovers in the same cat-
                  egory are shelved relatively near to one another. While most of the items
                  we saw were fairly common, there were exceptions and the very size of the
                  collection is such that there is always a good chance that if one arrives at
                  the right time and is patient enough, one may discover a rare gem hidden
                  among the more ordinary stock. The owner operates a second store in Fort
                  Lauderdale with a similar stock. See below.

All Books & Records   **Open Shop**
420 East Oakland Park Boulevard 33334   (954) 537-4899

Collection: General stock of paperback and hardcover, comics and records.
# of Vols: 200,000
Hours: Mon-Sat 10-9. Sun 11-7.
Travel: Oakland Park Blvd exit off I-95. Proceed east on Oakland Park to East
                  4th Ave. Shop is at the corner in a small strip mall.
Credit Cards: Yes
Owner: Rod Cronk
Year Estab: 1981
Comments: Stock is approximately 75% paperback. See above.

Robert A. Hittel, Bookseller   **Open Shop**
3020 North Federal Highway, Bldg. 6 33306   (800) 445-3358   (954) 563-1752
Web page: www.equa.com   Fax: (954) 563-9736
                                                                  E-mail: rh@equa.com

Collection: General stock.
# of Vols: 100,000
Hours: Mon-Sat 10-6. Other times by appointment.
Services: Appraisals, accepts want lists, mail order.
Travel: Oakland Park Blvd exit off I-95. Proceed east on Oakland to Rte 1,
                  then south on Rte 1 for one block. Shop is on left in Plaza 3000
                  Shopping Center, but you must proceed to next possible left turn.
Credit Cards: Yes
Year Estab: 1974
Comments: One of those shops that, based on the rave review that we gave it after
                  our first visit three years ago, we decided "should be seen by us
                  again." We were not disappointed and can only repeat what we said the
                  first time around:

                  We would have liked (and recommended) this well organized tri-level
                  shop even if we hadn't purchased several books during our visit. Not
                  only were there the expected number of books claimed by the owner,
                  but most subjects were represented in reasonable depth, making one's

browsing all that much more pleasurable. Be sure to ask for admission to the rare book room located on a mezzanine between the first and second floors (open Mon-Fri 10-6 and other times by appointment.) Needless to say, we would have loved to have spent more time here, in addition to more money.

Fort Myers
(Map 3, page 32)

Book Den South   **Open Shop**
2249 First Street 33901   Tel & Fax: (941) 332-2333

Collection:	General stock of mostly hardcover.
# of Vols:	25,000
Specialties:	Florida; mystery; military; nautical; Kipling; law
Hours:	Mon-Sat 10-5.
Services:	Appraisals, search service, accepts want lists, mail order.
Travel:	Exit 24 (Rte 80) off I-75 southbound. Proceed west four miles on Palm Beach to Hendry. Left onto Hendry and proceed for one block to First. Shop is at the corner.
Credit Cards:	Yes
Owner:	Greg Miller
Year Estab:	1983
Comments:	A very neat and clean shop with books attractively displayed. The shelves are well labeled and most of the books we saw were in good to very good to better condition. The shop is easy to browse as the aisles are wide, the visibility between bookcases open and clear and there are plenty of chairs. While the shop does stock paperbacks, the vast majority of the books were hardcover.

The Book Shop/Alex Shoe Bookseller   **By Appointment**
PO Box 1206 33902   (941) 334-0141

Collection:	General stock.
# of Vols:	10,000
Owner:	Alex Shoe

Fort Pierce
(Map 3, page 32)

All Around Books & Records   **Open Shop**
3347 South US Highway One 34982   (561) 464-5600

Collection:	General stock of hardcover and paperback.
# of Vols:	20,000
Specialties:	Cookbooks; music; fiction.
Hours:	Mon & Tue 10:30-4. Wed-Sat 2-8. Summer: Mon & Tue 12-6. Wed-Sat 2-8.
Services:	Appraisals, search service, accepts want lists, mail order.
Travel:	Midway Rd (Port St. Lucie) exit off I-95. Proceed east to Rte 1, then north on Rte 1 for two miles. Shop is on left.

Credit Cards: Yes
Owner: Florence Green
Year Estab: 1994
Comments: We didn't discover that this establishment had special summer hours until we arrived at the shop at 12:15 on a Monday. However, even though we arrived 15 minutes after the shop's scheduled opening, the store was still not open. Based on the numerous signs indicating that the shop sold music, CDs and tapes, we could only wonder how much of the stock actually consisted of books (Because the shop's blinds were drawn, it was impossible to view the inside of the shop.) Should you visit here, we would be pleased to have your impressions.

Fort Walton Beach
(Map 3, page 32)

Beal Street Books   **Open Shop**
700 NW Beal Parkway, Ste. D 32547   (850) 862-2001

Collection: General stock of paperback and hardcover.
# of Vols: 8,000
Hours: Mon-Sat 12-6.
Travel: Mary Esther Blvd exit off Rte 98. Proceed on Mary Esther to Beal, then left on Beal. Shop is after first light, on left in Fisherman's Square.
Credit Cards: Yes
Owner: John Fitzgerald
Year Estab: 1993
Comments: Stock is approximately 60% paperback.

Book & Game Emporium   **Open Shop**
311 Racetrack Road NW 32547   (850) 863-7964

Collection: General stock of paperback and hardcover.
# of Vols: 3,000-5,000
Hours: Mon 9-7. Tue-Sat 9-9. Sun 12-6.
Travel: Rte 85 exit off I-10. Proceed away from Crestview and towards Niceville. Turn right onto Racetrack Rd. Shop is about two to three miles ahead.
Comments: Stock is approximately 75% paperback.

Frostproof

Books-N-Stuff   **Open Shop**
10 North Scenic Highway 33843   (941) 635-3892

Collection: General stock of mostly paperback.
Hours: Summer: Mon, Thu, Fri 9:30-5. Sat 10-3. Call for winter hours.

Gainesville
(Map 3, page 32)

Book Gallery West
4121 NW 16th Boulevard 32605

Open Shop
(352) 371-1234
Fax: (352) 371 7154

Collection:	General stock of new and used paperback and hardcover.
# of Vols:	15,000 (used)
Hours:	Mon-Sat 9-9. Sun 11-7.
Travel:	Exit 76 (Newberry Rd) off I-75. Proceed east on Newberry for 1½ miles then left onto 43rd St. Shop is on right in Millhopper Shopping Center.
Credit Cards:	Yes
Owner:	Pat Landis & Sara Landis Stein
Year Estab:	1983
Comments:	A typical neighborhood book store that carries new as well as used paperbacks and hardcover books shelved together by subject. The store is spacious, the shelves well labeled and the used books (the majority of which are recent, although there were some exceptions) are most reasonably priced. The owners operate a second shop in Gainesville with a similar stock. See Omni Books below.

Books, Inc.
505 NW 13th Street 32601

Open Shop
(904) 374-4241

Collection:	General stock of paperback and hardcover.
# of Vols:	15,000 (hardcover)
Specialties:	Modern first editions; science fiction.
Hours:	Daily 10-10.
Services:	Search service, mail order.
Travel:	Exit 76 off I-75. Proceed east on Newberry Rd (Rte 26) which becomes University Ave. Left at 13th St. Shop is five blocks ahead on right.
Credit Cards:	Yes
Owner:	Anne Haisley
Year Estab:	1989
Comments:	What a pleasure to return to a shop after three years and to find that it has bloomed into one of the most attractive books stores in the state. One room contains several rows of bookshelves organized in a most exacting fashion. The books we saw, both fiction and non fiction, were in good to excellent condition and priced to sell. A second room doubles as a cafe for an adjoining vegetarian restaurant (open the same hours as the bookstore) and displays a full range of used paperbacks. You may begin by stopping here for a brief visit; we have a feeling you'll be staying longer.

Omni Books
99 SW 34th Street 32607

Open Shop
(352) 375-3755
Fax: (352) 371-7154

Collection:	General stock of used and new paperback and hardcover.

# of Vols:	10,000 (used)
Hours:	Mon-Sat 9-9. Sun 10-6.
Travel:	Newberry Rd exit off I-75. Proceed east on Newberry for about 2½-3 miles. Shop is on right in Westgate Publix Shopping Center.
Credit Cards:	Yes
Owner:	Sara Landis Stein & Bart Stein
Year Estab:	1983
Comments:	A slightly smaller version of the Book Gallery West (see above). Similar in ambience and stock.

The Philosophy Store   **By Appointment**
PO Box 13736 32604   (352) 378-6370

Collection:	General stock of mostly hardcover.
# of Vols:	5,000-10,000
Specialties:	Philosophy; science; history; economics.
Services:	Appraisals, search service, mail order.
Owner:	Jon Asfour
Comments:	Also displays at Webb's Antique Mall in Lake City. See below.

University Avenue Bookshop   **Open Shop**
804 West University Avenue 32601   (352) 371-0062

Collection:	General stock of hardcover and paperback.
# of Vols:	10,000+
Specialties:	Literature; philosophy.
Hours:	Mon-Sat 11-7. Sun 12-5. Other times by appointment.
Services:	Search service, accepts want lists.
Travel:	Exit 76 (Rte 26) off I-75. Proceed east on Rte 26 which becomes University Ave. Shop is near 8th St.
Credit Cards:	Yes
Owner:	Robert McNellis
Year Estab:	1991
Comments:	Unlike many used book stores whose shelves don't change much from month to month or year to year, it is apparent that this dealer replenishes his stock with new buys often enough to warrant frequent visits from regular customers. Chances are that his latest find (we hate to tease our readers so we won't mention the subject matter) will be long gone by the time this book is in print. The good news is that other materials are likely to show up in their place. Don't look for books in pristine condition here. What you'll find instead are nice titles of truly well read books in most areas of interest but particularly strong in the specialties listed above.

Goldenrod

Paper Americana   **By Appointment**
PO Box 2126 32733   (407) 657-7403

Collection:	Specialty books and ephemera.

# of Vols:	2,000
Specialties:	Financial histories; antique stocks and bonds; letters and manuscripts (business oriented); business biographies.
Services:	Mail order.
Credit Cards:	No
Owner:	David Beach

Gulf Breeze

The Book Corner   **Open Shop**
8 Harbourtown 32561   (850) 934-0688

Collection:	General stock of mostly paperback.
# of Vols:	11,000
Hours:	Mon-Fri 10-5.

Gulfport

Small Adventures Bookshop   **Open Shop**
3107 Beach Boulevard South 33707   (813) 347-8732

Collection:	General stock of mostly paperback.
# of Vols:	18,000
Hours:	Tue-Sat 10:30-5:30.

Haines City

Goodwill's Rereader Book Store   **Open Shop**
107 South 6th Street 33844   (941) 422-5397

Collection:	General stock of hardcover and paperback.
Hours:	Mon-Sat 9-5:30.

Havana
(Map 3, page 32)

Historical Bookshelf   **Open Shop**
104 East 7th Avenue   (850) 539-5040
Mailing address: PO Box 647 Havana 32333   E-mail: hisbks@interloc.com

Collection:	General stock and prints.
# of Vols:	10,000
Specialties:	Aviation; military; political biography; railroads; Civil War; guns; hunting; fishing.
Hours:	Mon-Sat 10-6 and other times by appointment. Best to call ahead.
Services:	Appraisals, search service, accepts want lists, mail order.
Travel:	Tallahassee exit off I-10. Proceed north on Rte 27 to Havana. Right onto East 7th.
Credit Cards:	No
Owner:	Jim & Pat Wilkinson
Year Estab:	1964

Comments: If your interests include the specialties listed above, this is definitely a shop worth visiting as the titles in most of these areas are broad enough to satisfy the tastes of most collectors in those fields. If, on the other hand, your book hunting interests lie elsewhere, the chances of your adding to your collection here are not very great.

Hernando

Book Nook   **Open Shop**
2780 North Florida Avenue, #18 34442   (352) 637-1182

Collection: General stock of mostly paperback.
# of Vols: 10,000
Hours: Mon-Fri 9-5. Sat 9-3.

Hialeah
(Map 3, page 32 & Map 5, page 68)

Trader Jack's Books   **Open Shop**
122 Hialeah Drive 33010   (305) 884-5524
    E-mail: ultrabyg@icanect.net

Collection: General stock of paperback and hardcover.
# of Vols: 7,000+ (hardcover)
Hours: Tue-Sun 11:30-7.
Travel: Rte 112 exit off I-95. Proceed north on LeJeune for one mile, then west one mile on Hialeah Dr.
Credit Cards: No
Owner: Ed Hartmann
Year Estab: 1992

Hollywood
(Map 3, page 32 & Map 5, page 68)

Book Fair   **Open Shop**
5650 Stirling Road 33021   (954) 987-6695

Collection: General stock of new and used paperback and hardcover.
# of Vols: 6,000 (used)
Hours: Tue-Fri 10-5:30. Sat 10-1:30.
Services: Accepts want lists, search service, mail order.
Travel: Stirling Rd exit off I-95. Proceed west on Stirling. Shop is on south side of street in Emerald Center.
Credit Cards: Yes
Owner: Marlo & Neece Schram
Year Estab: 1972
Comments: Used stock is approximately 60% paperback.

Trader John's Record & Book   **Open Shop**
1907 Hollywood Blvd 33020   (954) 922-2466
Collection: General stock of mostly paperback and records.
Hours: Mon-Sat 10-6. Sun 10-4:30.

Indian Harbor Beach
(Map 3, page 32)

Village Book Shoppe
1875 South Patrick Drive 32937

Open Shop
(407) 773-5223

Collection:	General of hardcover and paperback.
# of Vols:	6,000
Hours:	Mon-Fri 10-5. Sat 10-3.
Travel:	Cross Eau Gallie causeway, then first left onto South Patrick Dr. Shop is in Pines Plaza.
Credit Cards:	No
Owner:	Jeff Grinnell
Year Estab:	1989
Comments:	At press time, the shop was up for sale. Readers may therefore want to call ahead before visiting to confirm that the store is still in business.

Indian River Shores

Trafalgar Square
6210 N A1A 32963

Open Shop
(561) 231-6506

Collection:	General stock.
Hours:	Mon-Sat 10-5.
Comments:	A specialty gift shop with less than 100 older volumes.

Inverness
(Map 3, page 32)

Paperback Paradise
1221 Highway 41 North 34450

Open Shop
(352) 637-6777

Collection:	General stock of mostly paperback.
# of Vols:	25,000
Hours:	Mon-Fri 9:30-5. Sat 10-4.

Rainy Day Books
214 Tompkins Street 34450

Open Shop
(352) 637-3440

Collection:	General stock of mostly used paperback and hardcover.
# of Vols:	10,000
Hours:	Mon-Fri 9-5. Sat 9-3.
Year Estab:	1991
Comments:	Stock is approximately 65% paperback.

Jacksonville
(Map 3, page 32 & Map 4, page 54)

All Booked Up
10033 Atlantic Boulevard 32225

Open Shop
(904) 855-0243
(888) 812-5105

Collection:	General stock of paperback and hardcover.

# of Vols:	30,000
Hours:	Mon-Sat 9-5. Sun 12-5. Open most evenings till 8 or 9 but best to call ahead to confirm.
Services:	Accepts want lists, mail order.
Travel:	Atlantic Blvd exit off Rte 9A. Proceed west on Atlantic for .6 mile staying in right lane. (After third light on Atlantic, turn right into parking lot after the third building.)
Credit Cards:	Yes
Owner:	Chip Clemmons
Year Estab:	1995
Comments:	Most of the books we saw in this shop were in quite good condition, attractively shelved and priced reasonably. While antiquarians might not see an ancient tome here, other book hunters should enjoy their visit.

Books & Comics Unlimited   Open Shop
8608 Baymeadows Road 32256   (904) 448-5304

Collection:	General stock of mostly used paperbacks, comics and gifts.
# of Vols:	5,000+
Hours:	Mon-Thu 11-8. Fri 11-9. Sat 10-9. Sun 12-6.
Travel:	Baymeadows Rd (exit 100) off I-95. Proceed west on Baymeadows. Shop is about 1/2 mile ahead, on left, in Baymeadows Festival Shopping Center.
Comments:	If this shop had more than 1,000 hardcover items we had trouble locating them. If that isn't important to you and you're looking for paperbacks or comic books you may wish to visit.

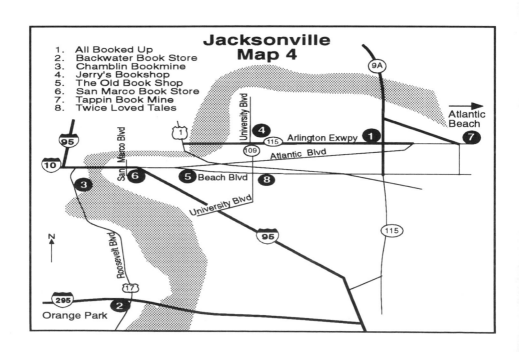

Jacksonville Map 4

1. All Booked Up
2. Backwater Book Store
3. Chamblin Bookmine
4. Jerry's Bookshop
5. The Old Book Shop
6. San Marco Book Store
7. Tappin Book Mine
8. Twice Loved Tales

Chamblin Bookmine   **Open Shop**
4551 Roosevelt Boulevard 32210   (904) 384-1685
                                                         Fax: (904) 384-6951
                                                   E-mail: bookmine@smart1.nct

Collection:	General stock of paperback and hardcover.
# of Vols:	500,000
Hours:	Mon-Fri 10-6, cxcept Wed till 8. Sat 10-5. Sun 1-5.
Services:	Appraisals, search service, accepts want lists, mail order.
Travel:	From intersection of I-295 and Rte 17, proceed north on Rte 17 for about three miles. The shop is on the right, just after the Ortega Bridge. Make an immediate right turn at end of bridge.
Credit Cards:	Ycs
Owner:	Ron Chamblin
Year Estab:	1976
Comments:	A very, very, very large shop with lots of space and more books than one can readily browse in a brief period. About one half the stock is paperback but the good news is that the other half consists of used hardcover books representing several time periods. While the shelves and sides of the bookcases are labeled, given the size of the shop, we wished there were some readily available directions such as a map indicating what subjects were shelved where. Also during our visit we found hardcover books in the fiction section mixed with mysteries without any rhyme or reason and without benefit of alphabetization. Despite these handicaps, the shop is still worth a visit, if only because of the magnitude of its collection and because a patient browser, with a little assistance from one of the employees, may be able to turn up several items of interest (as we did).

Jerry's Bookshop   **Open Shop**
917 University Boulevard North 32211   (904) 745-1600

Collection:	General stock of paperback and hardcover and comics.
# of Vols:	5,000-6,000 (hardcover)
Specialties:	Pulps; science fiction; collectible comics; first editions.
Hours:	Mon-Sat 10-7. Sun 1-6.
Travel:	Union St cxit off I-95. Proceed east on Union to Matthews Bridge, which cmpties into Arlington Expwy. Take University Blvd north exit off cxpressway. Shop is in Town and Country Shopping Center which is just off the exit.
Credit Cards:	Yes
Owner:	Jerry Corder
Year Estab:	1991
Comments:	If old pulp magazines of the 20's, 30's and 40's are your speed, and/or if you enjoy reprints of the same or any of the specialties listed above, your visit to this shop will be a lot of fun. On the other hand, if your interests relate to morc general fiction, history, biography, art, etc., your chances of striking it rich here are almost nil.

(Jacksonville)

The Old Book Shop   **Open Shop**
3142 Beach Boulevard 32207   (904) 398-6163

Collection:	General stock of paperback, hardcover and comics.
# of Vols:	25,000 (hardcover)
Hours:	Mon-Sat 10-6.
Travel:	From I-95 southbound: Beaches exit. Proceed on Beach for about one mile. Shop is on the right. From I-95 northbound: Emerson exit. Right onto Emerson and proceed to Beaches exit. Left on Beach and proceed as above.
Credit Cards:	Yes
Owner:	Robert L. Odom
Year Estab:	1970
Comments:	This shop offers an almost even mix of paperback and hardcover books. Most of the hardcover volumes we saw were in good condition, dust jacketed and were of recent vintage. Prices, we thought, were a bit lower than elsewhere.

Paperback Trade Mart   **Open Shop**
10578 St. Augustine Rd 32257   (904) 262-0297

Collection:	General stock of mostly paperback.
# of Vols:	65,000
Hours:	Tue-Fri 10-6. Sat 10-5.

Peb's Paperback Book Exchange   **Open Shop**
1537 Cesery Blvd 32211   (904) 743-2778

Collection:	General stock mostly used paperback.
# of Vols:	100,000
Hours:	Mon-Fri 10-6. Sat 10-5.
Travel:	From State St in downtown, cross Matthews Bridge. Continue on State St to Cesery exit. Take Cesery Ave north for about one mile. Shop is in Holland Mini Center.
Comments:	Stock is approximately 75% used, 80% of which is paperback.

San Marco Book Store   **Open Shop**
1971 San Marco Boulevard 32207   (904) 396-7597

Collection:	General stock of hardcover and paperback and records.
# of Vols:	15,000 (hardcover)
Specialties:	Florida; Marjorie K. Rawlings.
Hours:	Mon-Sat 10-5.
Services:	Appraisals, search service, accepts want lists, mail order.
Travel:	Southbound on I-95: San Marco Blvd exit, the first exit after crossing the St. John River. Make right turn onto San Marco and proceed for about one mile.
Credit Cards:	Yes
Owner:	Michael J. Blauer

Year Estab:	1978
Comments:	A nice shop with wide aisles and well labeled shelves. Most of the books we saw were in good to very good condition. With some exception, most of the books were of relatively recent vintage. Most categories were represented and the books were reasonably priced.

Twice Loved Tales   **Open Shop**
6630 Beach Boulevard 32216   (904) 725-9354
                                                Fax: (904) 727-9858

Collection:	General stock of hardcover and paperback.
# of Vols:	40,000
Specialties:	Literature; history; science fiction; romance.
Hours:	Mon-Fri 10-6. Sat 10-5.
Services:	Search service, accepts want lists, mail order.
Travel:	Beaches exit off I-95. Proceed east on Beach Blvd for about three miles.
Credit Cards:	Yes
Owner:	E.M. Volpe
Year Estab:	1990
Comments:	A good sized selection of both paperbacks and fairly recent hardcover books. While most of the hardcover items were dust jacketed and in good condition, we noted that among the more common items, particularly the omnibus editions but others as well, prices here were a tad higher than elsewhere.

Jensen

Jensen Book Exchange (aka Maggies Junque & Book Exchange)   **Open Shop**
843 NE Jensen Beach Blvd 34957   (561) 334-2538

Collection:	General stock of paperback and hardcover.
# of Vols:	70,000
Hours:	Mon-Sat 10-5.
Travel:	Two miles east of Rte 1, in Jensen Beach Plaza. Shop is on the left.
Comments:	After reading this shop's "aka," an astute or perhaps a discriminating reader should not require our guide to know whether the shop is worth visiting. We would guess that perhaps 2,000-3,000 of the shop's estimated 70,000 volumes were hardcover and most were located on the top shelves of each bookcase. Every once in a while one would see a book worth pulling off the shelf and examining; more often than not, the book would be returned to the shelf.

Jupiter

Annie's Book Stop   **Open Shop**
6671 West Indiantown Road 33458   (561) 575-5973

Collection:	General stock of mostly paperback used and new.
# of Vols:	20,000 (used)
Hours:	Mon, Tue, Thu, Fri 10-7. Wed 11-6. Sat 10-4.

Key Largo
(Map 3, page 32)

Flamingo Books   **Open Shop**
99513 Overseas Highway 33037   (305) 451-5303

Collection: General stock of paperback and hardcover.
# of Vols: 10,000
Hours: Mon-Fri 10-5:30. Sat 10-3.
Travel: On Rte 1, in Port Largo Plaza shopping center.
Credit Cards: Yes
Owner: James Burnside
Year Estab: 1989
Comments: Stock is approximately 70% paperback.

Key West
(Map 3, page 32)

Bargain Books & News Stand   **Open Shop**
1028 Truman Avenue 33040   (305) 294-7446

Collection: General stock of used and new paperback and hardcover.
# of Vols: 100,000
Specialties: Hemingway
Hours: Daily 7am-10pm.
Services: Appraisals, search service, accepts want lists, mail order.
Travel: On Rte 1. Shop is on left, about four blocks after road narrows from
                   four to two lanes.
Credit Cards: No
Owner: William Flagg
Comments: The largest used book store in Key West in terms of the number of
                   books, this shop carries both paperbacks and hardcover items with a
                   special section of Hemingway titles. Unfortunately, a large portion of
                   the hardcover books have seen not only better days but drier days as
                   well. We believe that too many of the used books we saw were in need
                   of care and were priced substantially higher than their market value.

Flaming Maggie's   **Open Shop**
830 Fleming Street 33040   (305) 294-3931

Collection: Specialty. Mostly new.
# of Vols: 1,000 (used)
Specialties: Gay and lesbian.
Hours: Daily 10-6.
Comments: Used stock is predominately hardcover.

Key West Island Books   **Open Shop**
513 Fleming Street 33040   (305) 294-2904
                                                                Fax: (305) 294-2920

Collection: General stock of mostly hardcover used and new books.

# of Vols:	10,000 (used)
Specialties:	Modern first editions; signed first editions; local authors.
Hours:	Daily 10-6.
Services:	Catalog
Travel:	From Truman, make right onto Duval, then right onto Fleming.
Credit Cards:	Yes
Owner:	John Boisonault
Year Estab:	1976
Comments:	A very neat and well organized shop that displays its books most attractively. The books were in good to very good condition and were reasonably priced. There's a rare book room in the back of the shop. Without question, the premier used book shop in Key West.

Salmonberry Book Rack   **Open Shop**
1114A Truman Avenue 33040   (305) 294-0810

Collection:	General stock of mostly paperback.
# of Vols:	25,000
Hours:	Mon & Tue 10-6. Wed & Thu 9-2. Fri-Sun 9-5.

LaBelle
(Map 3, page 32)

The Place   **Open Shop**
340 North Bridge Street   (941) 675-7904
Mailing address: PO Box 2458 LaBelle 33735

Collection:	General stock of mostly used paperback and hardcover.
# of Vols:	200,000+
Hours:	Mon-Sat 9-6.
Travel:	Rte 80 exit off I-75. Proceed east on Rte 80, then north on Rte 29, Shop is 1/2 block from drawbridge.
Credit Cards:	Yes
Owner:	Gene Johnson
Year Estab:	1989
Comments:	Plenty of paperbacks with a fair sized collection of hardcover volumes, most of which were older and not in particularly good condition.

Lake City
(Map 3, page 32)

Webb's Antique Mall   **Antique Mall**
Route 2, Box 6005 32024   (904) 758-5564

Hours:	Daily 9-6.
Travel:	Exit 80 off I-75. Turn west on Rte 441. Shop is on north side of Rte 441 along the I-75 frontage road.

Lake Worth
(Map 3, page 32 & Map 5, page 68)

The Bookworm   **Open Shop**
4111 Lake Worth Road 33461   (561) 965-1900

Collection:	General stock of paperback and hardcover.
# of Vols:	250,000
Hours:	Mon-Sat 9:30-5. Sun 1-5.
Travel:	10th Ave N exit off I-95. Proceed west on 10th Ave to Kirk Rd, then south on Kirk and right on Lake Worth. Shop is 1/2 block ahead.
Credit Cards:	No
Owner:	Judith H. & Robert L. Dewitt
Year Estab:	1968
Comments:	Two buildings, each with a far larger selection of paperbacks than hardcover volumes. The first building contained only a scattering of hardcover books along the top shelves and one had to strain to read the titles of these fairly common, frequently book club editions. We saw more hardcover books in the second building but not, at least as far as we could determine, many rare or collectible items. Oh yes, the shop also carries back issues of *Playboy, National Geographic* and other similar magazines.

Old Book Shop   **Open Shop**
1207 North Dixie Highway 33460   Tel & Fax: (561) 588-5129
                                                           E-mail: owenobs@gate.net

Collection:	General stock.
# of Vols:	12,000
Specialties:	Nautical; biography; show business; Florida; mystery; science fiction; British and Commonwealth authors and subjects.
Hours:	Tue-Sat 1-6. Other times by appointment.
Services:	Appraisals, search service, catalog, accepts want lists, bookbinding.
Travel:	10th Ave North exit off I-95. Proceed east to Dixie Hwy, then turn left (north). Shop is two blocks ahead.
Credit Cards:	Yes
Owner:	Jack Owen
Year Estab:	1985
Comments:	A modest sized shop with an interesting collection that has more than its share of collectibles at what we thought were quite reasonable prices.

Lakeland
(Map 3, page 32)

Book Bazaar   **Open Shop**
2120 South Combee Road 33801   (941) 665-3004

Collection:	General stock of mostly paperback.
# of Vols:	100,000
Hours:	Mon-Fri 9:30-5:30. Sat 9-5.
Travel:	Rte 33 exit off I-4. Proceed south on Rte 33 to Combee Rd, then left on Combee. Shop is about eight miles ahead.

Early Jackets
At Caseylynn Antiques
214 Traders Alley
Mailing address: 1418 Plantation Circle, #602 Plant City 33567

Antique Mall
Mall: (941) 682-2857
Home: (813) 759-2918
E-mail: ejackets@interloc.com

Collection: General stock.
# of Vols: 3,000
Specialties: All books are pre-1940, dust jacketed first editions. Many are signed.
Hours: Tue-Sat 10-5.
Travel: Exit 18 off I-4. Proceed south on Rte 98, then left on Pine St and left on Kentucky. Traders Alley is first left after turning onto Kentucky.
Owner: James Taylor
Comments: Additional books can be viewed by appointment.

Largo
(Map 6, page 88))

Book Bank USA
10500 Ulmerton Road, Ste 360 33771

Open Shop
(813) 588-0474

Collection: General stock of used and new paperback and hardcover.
# of Vols: 100,000
Hours: Mon-Thu 10-9. Fri & Sat 10-10. Sun 12-6.
Travel: From Rte 19 turn west onto Ulmerton Rd. Shop is in the Largo Mall.
Year Estab: 1995
Comments: Stock is approximately 75% used, 75% of which is paperback.

Lecanto
(Map 3, page 32)

Stokes Flea Market
5220 West Gulf to Lake Highway 34461

Flea Market
(352) 746-7200

Hours: Wed, Sat, Sun 7-3.
Travel: On Rte 44.

Leesburg
(Map 3, page 32)

J & B Books
600 West Main Street 34748

Open Shop
(352) 787-7574
Fax: (352) 787-6806
E-mail: j_bbooks@interloc.com

Collection: General stock and ephemera.
# of Vols: 20,000
Specialties: Film; military; poetry; first editions; review copies; Florida; Western Americana; science fiction.
Hours: Tue-Sat 10-5. Mon by appointment or chance. Evenings by appointment.
Services: Appraisals, search service, accepts want lists, mail order.
Travel: Exit 66 off I-75. Proceed east on Rte 44 which is Main St in downtown.

Credit Cards:	Yes
Owner:	Jim & Beverly Forsyth
Year Estab:	1989
Comments:	A most attractive shop with quality books in almost every category one can think of. We saw very few items that were not in very good to excellent condition and found prices were quite reasonable. A real pleasure to browse.

Longwood
(Map 3A, page 32)

Legible Leftovers   **Open Shop**
706-712 North Highway 17/92 32750   (407) 339-4043

Collection:	General stock of hardcover and paperback.
# of Vols:	100,000
Specialties:	Science fiction; military.
Hours:	Mon-Sat 10-6. Sun 12-5.
Services:	Accepts want lists.
Travel:	Rte 434 exit off I-4. Proceed east to Rte 17/92. Turn left onto Rte 17/92. Shop is about 3/4 of a mile ahead on left.
Credit Cards:	No
Owner:	V.E. Frederick
Year Estab:	1984
Comments:	Quite a large shop housing row after row after row of paperbacks and hardcover volumes intershelved and meticulously organized and labeled. We noted a large selection of mysteries as well as the other specialties listed above. Most of the hardcover books were of fairly recent vintage but we did see quite a few collectibles. The majority of the books were reading copies in mixed condition and quite reasonably priced.

Madeira Beach
(Map 6, page 88)

Books to the Ceiling   **Open Shop**
15126 Municipal Drive 33708   (813) 392-3070

Collection:	General stock of mostly used paperback and hardcover.
# of Vols:	65,000
Hours:	Mon-Sat 9-7. Sun 10:30-7.
Services:	Accepts want lists, mail order.
Travel:	Right turn after Tom Stuart Causeway bridge into Madeira Beach, then first right onto Municipal Drive. Shop is in shopping center.
Credit Cards:	Yes
Owner:	Judith Fish
Year Estab:	1988
Comments:	A mostly paperback shop with some new books as well as 3,000-4,0000 hardcover volumes, some intershelved with paperbacks and some shelved separately.

Madison
(Map 3, page 32)

Old Book Store
115 West Pinckney Street 32340

Collection:	General stock.
# of Vols:	10,000
Specialties:	Americana
Credit Cards:	No
Owner:	Mark Cherry
Year Estab:	1985

Maitland
(Map 3A, page 32)

Best Books
681 North Orlando Avenue 32751

Collection:	General stock of hardcover and paperback.
# of Vols:	15,000
Hours:	Mon-Sat 10-9. Sun 1-5.
Services:	Search service, accepts want lists.
Travel:	On Rte 17/92, one block south of Rte 414 and two miles east of I-4.
Credit Cards:	Yes
Owner:	John W. Wall
Year Estab:	1995
Comments:	Considering the size of this shop, we saw some nice books here. Some quite old. Some collectible. A good share of recent items and enough unusual titles to make for a pleasant if brief visit.

Malabar
(Map 3, page 32)

Warrior Books
1725 Krieger Drive
Mailing address: PO Box 7 Malabar 32950

Collection:	General stock of new and used hardcover and paperback.
# of Vols:	3,000
Specialties:	Engineering; electronics; physics; natural history; biology; physical sciences; history; herpetology; space science.
Hours:	Mon-Fri 9-4 (and most days till 5:30). 2nd & 4th Sat: 10-2. Other times by appointment.
Services:	Search service, catalog, accepts want lists.
Travel:	Exit 70 off I-95. Proceed east on Malabar Rd (Rte 514) for 2½ miles, then right on Glatter. Continue to Krieger Dr.
Credit Cards:	Yes
Owner:	Ann & Donald Krieger
Year Estab:	1989
Comments:	Stock is approximately 50% used, 80% of which is hardcover.

Marathon

Book Key and Gallery   **Open Shop**
11300 Overseas Highway 33050   (305) 743-5256

Collection:	General stock of new and mostly paperback used.
# of Vols:	10,000 (used)
Hours:	Mon-Fri 10-6. Sat 10:30-2:30.

Memories   **Open Shop**
9701 Overseas Highway 33050   (305) 743-2622

Collection:	Specialty ephemera.
Specialties:	Autographs
Hours:	Mon-Fri 10-5. Sat 10-2.
Owner:	Bob Smith
Year Estab:	1993

McIntosh
(Map 3, page 32)

O. Brisky's Book Barn   **Open Shop**
Route 441   (352) 591-2177
Mailing address: PO Box 585 Micanopy 32667

Collection:	General stock of mostly hardcover and ephemera.
# of Vols:	30,000+
Specialties:	Physics; natural history.
Hours:	Wed-Sun 10-5.
Travel:	On Route 441, about four miles south of Micanopy.
Owner:	O.J. Brisky
Year Estab:	1994
Comments:	Where else can a military or naval historian find a multi volume bound set of U.S. naval procedures from the 1870's to the early 20th century? That rare item, along with several other interesting volumes and a cornucopia of other titles (mostly older, in mixed condition but quite reasonably priced) are available in this book barn that is truly a barn.

Melbourne
(Map 3, page 32)

Chapter I Book Store   **Open Shop**
658 North Wickham Road 32935   (407) 242-7752

Collection:	General stock of mostly used paperback.
Hours:	Mon-Fri 10-6. Sat 10-5.

Eau Gallie Bookstore   **Open Shop**
559 West Eau Gallie Boulevard 32935   (800) 393-1275   (407) 255-5310
                                                                Fax: (407) 255-9092
                                                        E-mail: egbsbook@interloc.com

Collection:	General stock of mostly hardcover.
# of Vols:	30,000

Specialties:	Nautical; cookbooks; art; science; history; military; aviation; Civil War.
Hours:	Mon-Fri 10-6. Sat 10-5.
Services:	Appraisals, search service, accepts want lists, mail order.
Travel:	Exit 72 (Eau Gallie Blvd) off I-95. Proceed east on Eau Gallie to Rte 1. Cross over Rte 1 and continue on Eau Gallie which becomes Montreal. Left on Highland which is first light after crossing Rte 1. Shop is at corner of Highland and westbound lane of Eau Gallie Causeway.
Credit Cards:	Yes
Owner:	Jeffrey & Elizabeth Dennie
Year Estab:	1993
Comments:	A nice shop with quality books quite reasonably priced. If our trunk had not been almost filled to the brim at the time of our visit we probably would have left with several volumes. In any event, as usual, we regretted not having done so anyway.

The Health Hut Antiquarian Bookshop   **Open Shop**
1916 Waverly Place 32901   (407) 724-1212

Collection:	General stock.
# of Vols:	5,000
Hours:	Mon-Fri 10-5:30. Sat 10-4.
Services:	Accepts want lists, mail order.
Travel:	From I-95, proceed east on Rte 192 to Waverly Pl. Right on Waverly. Shop is first store on right.
Credit Cards:	Yes
Owner:	Tom & Grace Chadbourne
Year Estab:	1987
Comments:	Don't be confused by the name of the shop. Even though a portion of the store is taken up with displays of health food supplements, the majority of the shop is devoted to a very nice general collection of used books and we were able to spot several rare and unusual titles in many fields. Most of the books were reasonably priced. Although the selection is limited, the shop makes up in quality for what it lacks in numbers.

On The Shelf Bookstore   **Open Shop**
824 East New Haven Avenue 32901   (407) 724-2482

Collection:	General stock of mostly used paperback and hardcover and comics.
# of Vols:	75,000
Specialties:	Science fiction.
Hours:	Mon-Fri 10-5. Sat 10-4.
Travel:	Rte 1 to Rte 192. Proceed west on Rte 192. Shop is two blocks ahead.
Credit Cards:	Yes
Owner:	Joyce Pace
Year Estab:	1977
Comments:	Most of the hardcover books we saw were fairly common items with not a few book club editions and library discards. Persistent searching did, however, uncover a dozen or so rarer items in our field of interest that we have not usually seen in shops of this type. The shop is crowded with narrow aisles made even narrower by piles of books in the aisles.

Merritt Island

House of Books   **Open Shop**
141 South Courtenay Parkway 32952   (407) 454-4543
Collection: General stock of mostly used paperback.
# of Vols: 30,000 (used)
Hours: Mon-Fri 10-6:30. Sat 10-5:30.

Miami
(Map 3, page 32 & Map 5, page 68)

Book Barn Book Exchange   **Open Shop**
10597 Bird Road (SW 40th Street) 33165   (305) 223-0531
Collection: General stock of mostly paperback.
Hours: Mon 10-7. Tue & Wed 10-6. Thu-Sat 10-9. Sun 12-5.

Books & Cards   **Open Shop**
13130 Biscayne Boulevard 33181   (305) 893-8371
Collection: General stock of new and used paperback and hardcover.
Hours: Mon-Sat 10-9. Sun 12-6.
Travel: At 131st St.
Credit Cards: Yes
Year Estab: 1977
Comments: Stock is approximately 40% used, 70% of which is paperback.

Books & Prints Store   **Open Shop**
4329 South West 8th Street 33134   (305) 444-5001
Collection: General stock.
# of Vols: 100,000+
Hours: Mon-Sat 10-3.
Services: Accepts want lists, mail order.
Travel: Rte 836 exit off I-95. Proceed west on Rte 836 to LeJeune, then south
                   on LeJeune to SW 8th St (Tamiami Trail). Right onto Tamiami. Shop
                   is 1¼ blocks ahead.
Credit Cards: No
Owner: Marian B. Ledoux
Year Estab: 1958

Books For Less   **Open Shop**
12558 North Kendall Drive 33186   (305) 595-3749
Collection: General stock of paperback and hardcover.
# of Vols: 60,000
Hours: Mon-Thu 10-6. Fri & Sat 10-9. Sun 12-5.
Travel: At 125th St and North Kendall Dr in The Shops of Kendall.
Credit Cards: Yes
Year Estab: 1985
Comments: Stock is evenly divided between paperback and hardcover.

Books For Less
5753 SW 40th Street 33155

Collection:	General stock of paperback and hardcover.
# of Vols:	100,000+
Hours:	Mon-Sat 10-9. Sun 12-6.
Travel:	At 57th Ave and SW 40th St in Redbird Shopping Center.
Credit Cards:	Yes
Year Estab:	1967
Comments:	Stock is approximately 75% paperback.

Books of Paige's
420 NE 125th Street 33161

Open Shop
(305) 893-2931
E-mail: usedbooks2@aol.com

Collection:	General stock of paperback and hardcover
# of Vols:	25,000+
Hours:	Mon-Sat 10-8. Sun 10-5
Services:	Search service, accepts want lists, mail order.
Travel:	NE 125th St exit off I-95. Proceed east on NE 125th St for about five blocks. Shop is in Colonial Plaza Shopping Center.
Credit Cards:	Yes
Owner:	Michele & Robin Adams
Year Estab:	1988
Comments:	Stock is approximately 75% paperback.

Booksmart
1415 SW 107th Avenue 33174

Open Shop
(305) 226-4400
Fax: (305) 226-2156

Collection:	General stock of paperback and hardcover.
Hours:	Mon-Fri 9am-7pm. Sat 11-5. Shorter hours in summer.
Travel:	Tamiami Trail exit off Florida Tpk extension. Proceed east on Tamiami Trail for about one mile, then right on SW 107th Ave. Shop is on left in University Plaza Shopping Center.
Credit Cards:	Yes
Owner:	David, Jim & Ann Wulf
Year Estab:	1996
Comments:	A relatively new shop with an evolving mix of hardcover and paperback books in addition to textbooks. The owners operate two other shops in Boca Raton.

Pablo Butcher
737 NE 83rd Street 33138

By Appointment
(305) 758-7512
Fax: (305) 758-8318

Collection:	Specialty books and related maps, engravings and vintage photographs
# of Vols:	2,000
Specialties:	Latin America; Caribbean; Asia; Islamic World; Pacific region.
Services:	Catalog
Credit Cards:	No
Year Estab:	1995

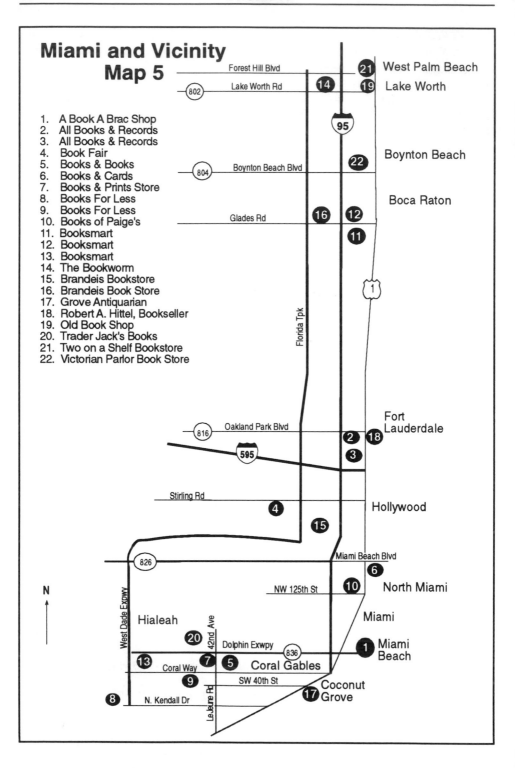

Miami and Vicinity
Map 5

1. A Book A Brac Shop
2. All Books & Records
3. All Books & Records
4. Book Fair
5. Books & Books
6. Books & Cards
7. Books & Prints Store
8. Books For Less
9. Books For Less
10. Books of Paige's
11. Booksmart
12. Booksmart
13. Booksmart
14. The Bookworm
15. Brandeis Bookstore
16. Brandeis Book Store
17. Grove Antiquarian
18. Robert A. Hittel, Bookseller
19. Old Book Shop
20. Trader Jack's Books
21. Two on a Shelf Bookstore
22. Victorian Parlor Book Store

Forest Hill Blvd
West Palm Beach
Lake Worth Rd
802
Lake Worth
95
Boynton Beach Blvd
Boynton Beach
804
Boca Raton
Glades Rd
Florida Tpk
Oakland Park Blvd
816
Fort Lauderdale
595
Stirling Rd
Hollywood
Miami Beach Blvd
826
North Miami
NW 125th St
N
West Dade Expwy
Hialeah
42nd Ave
Miami
Dolphin Exwpy
836
Miami Beach
Coral Way
Coral Gables
SW 40th St
Coconut Grove
N. Kendall Dr
Le Jeune Rd

Miami Memorabilia Co.   **By Appointment**
330 NE 96th Street 33138   (305) 757-1016

Collection:	Specialty books and ephemera.
# of Vols:	1,000
Specialties:	Florida; transportation.
Credit Cards:	No
Owner:	Seth & Myrna Bramson
Year Estab:	1955

Miami Beach
(Map 3, page 32 & Map 5, page 68))

A Book A Brac Shop   **Open Shop**
6760 Collins Avenue 33141   (305) 865-0092

Collection:	General stock and ephemera.
# of Vols:	6,000
Specialties:	Art; architecture; antiques and collectibles; hunting; fishing; firearms; military.
Hours:	Mon-Sat 3-9 but best to call ahead.
Services:	Appraisals, search service, accepts want lists, mail order.
Travel:	I-95 to any causeway that connects to Miami Beach to Collins Ave. Shop is at 67th St.
Credit Cards:	No
Owner:	Steven & Edie Eisenstein
Year Estab:	1987

Book Depot   **By Appointment**
350 Lincoln Road, Ste. 208 33139   (800) 438-2750   (305) 538-3111
                                             E-mail: Bk_Depot@aol.com

Collection:	General stock of mostly hardcover.
# of Vols:	1,000
Services:	Search service, accepts want lists.
Credit Cards:	Yes
Owner:	Andrew Delaplaine
Year Estab:	1992

W.B. Gebhard, Books   **By Appointment**
115 3rd Terrace   (305) 534-9244
San Marino Island 33139   E-mail: wgebgard@safari.net

Collection:	Specialty
# of Vols:	1,000
Specialties:	Modern first editions; children's.
Credit Cards:	No
Owner:	Wally Gebhard
Year Estab:	1989

Micanopy
(Map 3, page 32)

O. Brisky-Books   **Open Shop**
Cholokka Boulevard   (352) 466-3910
Mailing address: PO Box 585 Micanopy 32667

Collection:	General stock and ephemera.
# of Vols:	30,000+
Specialties:	Florida; nautical; music; Africa.
Hours:	Tue-Sun 10-5.
Services:	Appraisals, catalog, accepts want lists.
Travel:	Micanopy exit off I-75. Proceed east on Rte 441 for about one mile to village.
Credit Cards:	No
Owner:	O. J. Brisky
Year Estab:	1987
Comments:	We were quite fortunate, and pleased, on our latest southern sojourn to be able to visit this shop which was closed during our earlier visit three years ago. If we were rating shops with stars, this one would surely be "up there." Don't look for the latest best sellers here. Instead, expect to find (and you should not be disappointed) rare, unusual, antiquarian and significant titles in many areas of interest with a heavy emphasis on non fiction. The books are in generally good condition and quite reasonably priced.

Mount Dora
(Map 3, page 32)

Den of Antiquities   **Open Shop**
443 Donnelly Street 32757   (904) 383-1500

Collection:	General stock.
# of Vols:	2,000+
Hours:	Tue-Sat 10-4.
Travel:	Donnelly St exit off Rte 441. Proceed south on Donnelly.
Comments:	An interesting shop offering a variety of collectibles plus a back room filled with mostly reading copies. Worth a brief visit.

Dickens-Reed   **Open Shop**
140 West 5th Avenue 32757   (904) 735-5950

Collection:	General stock of mostly new and some hardcover used.
Hours:	Mon-Sat 9-9. Sun 12-5.
Services:	Search service, accepts want lists, mail order.
Travel:	Donnelly St exit off Rte 441. Proceed south on Donnelly, then right onto Fifth.
Credit Cards:	Yes
Owner:	Ruth Blake
Year Estab:	1992

Comments: Primarily a new book store with several hundred used volumes, most of which were in good condition. Not a shop where you're likely to find a rare or unusual used gem.

Highland Crossroads Book Shop
812 Shirley Avenue 32757

Open Shop
(352) 383-8127
(800) 472-0665
E-mail: hlcrrbks@interloc.com

Collection: General stock.
# of Vols: 6,000
Specialties: Military; Americana.
Hours: Mon-Wed 9-5. Fri 11-5. Sat 10-5. Sun 12-5. Normally closed July and August.
Services: Catalog, accepts want lists.
Travel: Rte 46 exit off Rte 441. Proceed west on Rte 46 into Mt. Dora, then left onto Highland (old Rte 441). Shop is at intersection of Highland and Shirley. Right on Shirley.
Credit Cards: No
Owner: Dick Costello
Year Estab: 1992
Comments: A small shop with limited space but some nice volumes, particularly in the specialties listed above. With exceptions, most of the titles we saw were a bit older and reasonably priced.

Old Towne Bookshop
411 North Donnelly Street, Ste. 204 32757

Open Shop
(352) 383-0878

Collection: General stock of hardcover and paperback.
# of Vols: 2,000
Hours: Mon-Sat 10-5.
Travel: See Den of Antiquities above.
Comments: A rather small shop located on the second floor of a building that caters primarily to tourists interested in crafts and gift items. The general selection of paperbacks and hardcover books is about what one might expect to find in such an establishment; basically reading copies of mixed vintage and in mixed condition.

Naples
(Map 3, page 32)

Bailey's Antiques & Country Pine
606 North Tamiami Trail 34102

Antique Mall
(941) 643-1953

Hours: Mon-Sat 10-5.
Travel: Located on Rte 41.

The Book Trader
170 10th Street North 33940

Open Shop
(941) 262-7562

Collection: General stock of new and used paperback and hardcover.
Hours: Mon-Sat 9-5:30.

Services:	Appraisals, search service.
Travel:	Central Ave exit off Rte 41. Proceed east on Central, the left onto 10th St North.
Credit Cards:	Yes
Owner:	Ray & Zena Nugent
Year Estab:	1976
Comments:	Stock is approximately 50% used, 50% of which is paperback.

New Smyrna Beach
(Map 3, page 32)

Irene's   **Open Shop**
1125 North Dixie Freeway 32168   (904) 423-0136

Collection:	General stock of hardcover and paperback.
# of Vols:	10,000
Hours:	Mon-Fri, except closed Wed, 10-5. Sat 10-2.
Travel:	On Rte 1, in Papa's Plaza.
Comments:	Stock is approximately 60% hardcover.

North Miami
(Map 5, page 68)

Brandeis Bookstore   **Open Shop**
R.K. California Club Mall   (305) 651-7566
850 Ives Dairy Road 33179

Collection:	General stock of hardcover and paperback.
# of Vols:	15,000
Hours:	Mon-Fri 10:30-7. Sat 10-4. Sun 12-4.
Travel:	Ives Dairy Rd exit off I-95. Proceed west on Ives Dairy for one mile. Shop is in an indoor shopping mall.
Credit Cards:	No
Year Estab:	1988
Comments:	Operated by volunteers for benefit of Brandeis University Library. All books are donated.

North Palm Beach

Book Exchange   **Open Shop**
807 Northlake Boulevard 33408   (561) 863-1555

Collection:	General stock of mostly paperback.
# of Vols:	150,000
Hours:	Mon-Sat 10-7:30. Sun 12-4.
Travel:	Northlake exit off I-95. Proceed east on Northlake for about two miles.
Credit Cards:	Yes
Owner:	Curt Bourque
Year Estab:	1987

Comments: A large selection of comic books, accompanied by a large selection of paperbacks, accompanied by a smaller collection of used hardcover items. As the owner pointed out to us, his customers aren't much into used hardcover books. This is confirmed by the selection of available books.

Ocala
(Map 3, page 32)

The Book Trader   **Open Shop**
8800 SW Highway 200 34481   (352) 873-0336

Collection: General stock of mostly paperback.
Hours: Mon-Fri 9-5. Sat 9-3.

Downtown Bookshop   **Open Shop**
16 South Magnolia 34474   (352) 620-9344
                                                          Fax: (352) 867-5696

Collection: General stock of hardcover and paperback.
# of Vols: 5,000-10,000
Specialties: Civil War; local interest.
Hours: Mon-Fri 10-5.
Services: Appraisals, search service, accepts want lists, mail order.
Travel: Rte 40 exit off I-75. Proceed east on Rte 40 to town square then right on South Magnolia.
Credit Cards: Yes
Owner: Robert & John Blauer
Year Estab: 1993
Comments: A modest shop with mostly recent hardcover items and a scattering of older volumes. Easy to browse. Reasonably priced.

Martin Nevers-Used & Rare Books   **Open Shop**
9180 South Highway 441 34480   (352) 245-0446

Collection: General stock of hardcover and paperback.
# of Vols: 20,000
Hours: Daily 10-5.
Services: Search service, accepts want lists, mail order.
Travel: Rte 484 exit off I-75. Proceed east on Rte 484 to Rte 441, then north on Rte 441 for three miles. Shop is on the left.
Credit Cards: No
Owner: Martin Nevers
Year Estab: 1985
Comments: Some paperbacks along with mostly older hardcover volumes in mixed condition and a few interesting titles. Quite reasonably priced. Not one of the neatest shops we have visited and some of the aisles are difficult to traverse because of books piled on the floor. If you're willing to devote the time here though, your chances of finding a collectible or two worth purchasing are, at least, even money.

Oldsmar

Sam's Shop   **Flea Market**
At Oldsmar Flea Market   (813) 527-3700
Antique Village, # 13 & 14
Mailing address: 711-47th Avenue North St. Petersburg 33703

Collection:	Specialty paperback and hardcover.
# of Vols:	3,500
Specialties:	Children's (modern and old).
Hours:	Sat & Sun 9-5.
Services:	Accepts want lists, mail order.
Travel:	At intersection of Tampa Rd/Hillsborough Ave/Race Track Rd.
Credit Cards:	No
Owner:	Sharon A. Micek
Year Estab:	1992
Comments:	Stock is evenly divided between hardcover and paperback.

Orange Park
(Map 3, page 32 & Map 4, page 54)

Backwater Book Store   **Open Shop**
418 Kingsley Avenue 32073   (904) 278-4992

Collection:	General stock of hardcover and paperback.
# of Vols:	20,000
Specialties:	Modern first editions.
Hours:	Mon-Fri 10-6. Sat 10-5.
Travel:	Rte 17 (Orange Park) exit off I-295. Proceed south on Rte 17 for about one mile, then right on Kingsley. Shop is one block ahead on left.
Credit Cards:	Yes
Owner:	Bob Disher
Year Estab:	1992
Comments:	An interesting mix of paperback and hardcover items. At the time of our visit, one room was devoted almost exclusively to romance paperbacks. Most of the hardcover items were of recent vintage, although the shop does have a reasonable number of collectibles.

Sunshine Books   **Open Shop**
997 Blanding Boulevard 32073   (904) 276-3992

Collection:	General stock of mostly paperback.
# of Vols:	50,000
Hours:	Mon-Fri 10-5:30. Sat 10-5.

Orlando
(Map 3, page 32 & Map 3A, page 32)

Charles Billings' Books   **Antique Mall**
At Annie's Antiques   Mall: (407) 896-0433
210 North Orange Avenue   Home: (407) 671-2762
Mailing address: 200 St. Andrews Boulevard, #3507 Winter Park 32792

Collection:	General stock.
# of Vols:	3,000
Hours:	Mon-Sat 10-4.
Services:	Appraisals, search service.
Travel:	Princeton exit off I-4. Proceed east on Princeton for one block then left on Orange. Shop is one block ahead.
Credit Cards:	Yes
Year Estab:	1989

The Bookery   **Open Shop**
1723 West Oakridge Road 32809   (407) 855-859

Collection:	General stock mostly paperback.
# of Vols:	30,000
Hours:	Mon-Fri 10:30-5:30. Sat 10-4.

Books and Ephemera   **Open Shop**
At College Park Antique Mall   (407) 839-1869
1317-19 North Edgewater   32804

Collection:	General stock and ephemera.
# of Vols:	5,000-10,000
Specialties:	Film; theater.
Hours:	Mon-Sat 10:30-4:30. Closed Mon Jun-Aug.
Travel:	Princeton exit (exit 43) off I-4. Proceed west on Princeton, then left onto Edgewater. Shop is 1/2 mile ahead on left.
Credit Cards:	Yes
Owner:	Joan McDaniel
Year Estab:	1988
Comments:	Located in the rear of an antique shop, the "book shop" stocks an interesting mix of mostly older titles, plus magazines and ephemera in mixed condition. This is the kind of shop that is always in the process of picking up new stock so regardless of what we may have seen when we visited, by the time you arrive, there will be more of some items and less of others.

Chapters Book Shop & Cafe   **Open Shop**
717 West Smith Street 32804   (407) 246-1546

Collection:	General stock.
# of Vols:	30,000
Specialties:	Florida; entertainment (all phases).
Hours:	Daily 9am-10pm.

Travel:	Exit 43 (Princeton St) off I-4. Proceed west on Princeton for one mile. After crossing Edgewater Dr, Princeton becomes Smith. Shop is third building on right.
Credit Cards:	Yes
Owner:	Jan & Marty Cummins
Year Estab:	1990
Comments:	Who can resist a tasty meal surrounded by thousands of books covering almost every subject under the sun? The books, an interesting mix that includes Reader's Digest condensed novels, book club editions, truly rare and collectible items and almost everything in-between, are attractively displayed and moderately priced. The shop is worth a visit, whether you're hunger is for intellectual gratification or for a good meal.

Keane's Books   **Open Shop**
1233 West Fairbanks Avenue 32804   (407) 644-0082

Collection:	General stock of mostly paperback.
# of Vols:	4,000
Hours:	Mon-Sat 10-8. Sun 11-5.
Travel:	Fairbanks Ave exit off I-4. Proceed west on Fairbanks.
Comments:	Anywhere from 500-1,000 hardcover books, along with several thousand paperbacks and a large supply of rental videos make up the stock of this small shop. The hardcover books we did see were a mix of general fiction and non fiction with few items that should cause you to rush here.

Words & Music   **Open Shop**
203 East Central Boulevard 32801   (407) 481-9122

Collection:	General stock of mostly paperback.
Hours:	Mon-Sat 11-6. Sat 10-6. Sun 12-6.

Ormond Beach
(Map 3, page 32)

Sandra & John Berryman - Fine Books   **By Appointment**
170 Laurelwood Lane 32174   (904) 677-2203
                                               Fax: (904) 677-7913
                              E-mail: bibliosandy@worldnet.att.net

Collection:	General stock.
# of Vols:	5,000
Specialties:	Cartographic reference; antique maps; horror; modern first editions.
Services:	Accepts want lists, mail order.
Credit Cards:	No
Year Estab:	1985

Book Shelf   **Open Shop**
611 South Yonge Street 32174   (904) 676-9850

Collection:	General stock of mostly paperback.
Hours:	Mon-Sat 9:30-5:30.

Lew Dabe Books
50 South Yonge Street, #2 32174

By Appointment
(904) 615-8755
Fax: (904) 677-4612

Collection:	General stock and ephemera
# of Vols:	8,000
Specialties:	Art; architecture; antiques; photography.
Services:	Appraisals, accepts want lists, mail order.
Credit Cards:	No
Year Estab:	1960

Palatka

The Bookworm
3112 St Johns Avenue 32177

Open Shop
(904) 325-2255

Collection:	General stock of mostly paperback.
Hours:	Mon-Sat 10-6.

Palm Bay
(Map 3, page 32)

Bookmark of Palm Bay
4700-20 Babcock Street NE 32905

Open Shop
(407) 725-1412

Collection:	General stock of new and used paperback and hardcover.
Hours:	Mon-Fri 10-6, except Fri till 7. Sat 9-6.
Travel:	Palm Bay Rd exit off I-95. Proceed east on Palm Bay, then right on Babcock. Shop is in Sabal Palm Shopping Center.
Comments:	We regret that all we can tell you for sure about this shop is that it is open for business and that it sells books. Despite a letter and several phone calls, we have been unable to update what we said about the store three years ago when we commented that the stock was approximately 65% used, 75% of which was paperback.

Palm Beach

Dominique's Antiquarian
96 Via Mizner Worth Avenue 33480

Open Shop
(561) 832-3885

Collection:	Specialty
Specialties:	Fine bindings; 18th & 19th century books.
Hours:	Mon-Sat 10:30-5:30. Summer: Tue-Sat 11-5.
Credit Cards:	Yes
Owner:	Dominique Skandalakis
Year Estab:	1991

Palm Beach Gardens

Book Rack
2532 PGA Boulevard 33410

Open Shop
(561) 622-0655

Collection:	General stock of mostly paperback.

# of Vols:	30,000
Specialties:	Mystery first editions.
Hours:	Mon-Sat 9:30-6.
Travel:	PGA Blvd exit off I-95. Proceed east on PGA Blvd for about two miles. Shop is in PGA Plaza.

Palm Harbor
(Map 3, page 32)

Book Swap   **Open Shop**
32840 US Highway 19 North 34684   (813) 785-2222

Collection:	General stock of paperback and hardcover.
# of Vols:	30,000
Hours:	Mon-Fri 10-6. Sat 10-5. Sun 12-4.
Travel:	On Rte 19 in Palm Lake Shopping Center.
Credit Cards:	Yes
Year Estab:	1983
Comments:	Stock is approximately 75% paperback.

Palm Harbor Bookstore   **Open Shop**
33633 US Highway 19N 34684   (813) 787-0551

Collection:	General stock of used and new paperback and hardcover.
# of Vols:	3,000-5,000 (used)
Hours:	Mon-Thu 9:30-7. Fri & Sat 9:30-6. Sun 12-4.
Comments:	Stock is approximately 70% used, 60% of which is paperback.

Panama City
(Map 3, page 32)

Ageless Book Shoppe   **Open Shop**
1090 Florida Avenue   (850) 763-5264
Mailing address: PO Box 2501 Panama City 32401

Collection:	General stock of hardcover and paperback.
# of Vols:	200,000 (See Comments)
Hours:	Mon-Fri 10-5. Sat 9-12.
Services:	Appraisals, search service, accepts want lists, mail order.
Travel:	Rte 231 into Panama City where Rte 231 becomes Harrison Ave. Right turn onto 11th St. Shop is at intersection of 11th and Florida.
Credit Cards:	Yes
Owner:	Ann Humphreys
Year Estab:	1983
Comments:	This bi-level shop has a good number of older books, most of which have seen better days. While there were certainly lots of books on display, our estimate of the number of books available for inspection would be somewhat less than 100,000 (perhaps even closer to 40,000-50,000). Of course, the owner may have additional books in storage. If you're looking for inexpensive reading copies, you'll certainly find lots on display here.

The Blue Room   **Open Shop**
2111 East Third Street 32401   (850) 914-0001

Collection:	General stock.
# of Vols:	3,000
Specialties:	Modern first editions; signed; Florida; biography.
Hours:	Generally Mon, Tue, Thu & Fri 11-6. Sat 10-3. Wed & Sun by appointment. Best to call ahead.
Services:	Search service, accepts want lists.
Travel:	From intersection of Rtes 77 and 231, proceed south on Rte 77 (Martin Luther King Blvd) to 5th St, then turn left. Cross Watson Bayou, then right onto Sherman Ave. Shop is at 3rd & Sherman.
Credit Cards:	Yes
Owner:	Marah Coleman
Year Estab:	1993

Book Bin   **Open Shop**
1415 Gulf Avenue 32401   (850) 785-4461

Collection:	General stock of mostly paperback.
# of Vols:	300,000
Hours:	Summer: Mon-Sat 10-5. Winter (From Oct 1): Mon-Sat 10-6.
Travel:	From Rte 98, turn south onto Lisenby Ave, then east on Gulf Ave.
Credit Cards:	No
Year Estab:	1977
Comments:	Stock ranges from 75%-90% paperback.

Book Bin   **Open Shop**
5428 East 15th Street 32404   (850) 763-6113

Collection:	General stock of mostly paperback.
# of Vols:	500,000+
Hours:	Mon-Sat 9:30-5.

JJ's Books   **Flea Market**
At 15th St Flea Market   (850) 763-8120
Mailing address: PO Box 4813 Panama City 32401-8813   Fax: (850) 769-5673
                                                    E-mail: jjscoll@interoz.com

Collection:	General stock.
Hours:	Sat & Sun 9-3.
Services:	Search service, accepts want lists, mail order.
Travel:	15th St exit off Rte 231 or Rte 98. Flea market is at Sherman Ave, across from fairgrounds.
Credit Cards:	No
Owner:	Joyce & John Soares
Year Estab:	1990

Panama City Beach
(Map 3, page 32)

Wheelerbooks   **By Appointment**
609 Granada Circle 32413   (850) 230-8693

Collection:	General stock.
# of Vols:	5,000
Specialties:	Americana; Florida; local history; first editions; military (regimental histories).
Services:	Appraisals, accepts want lists, mail order.
Credit Cards:	No
Owner:	Jack L. Wheeler
Year Estab:	1965

Pembroke Pines

Volume One Books   **Open Shop**
8910 Taft Street 33024   (954) 432-5188

Collection:	General stock of mostly paperback.
# of Vols:	30,000.
Hours:	Mon-Thu 9-6:30. Fri & Sat 9-7. Sun 12-5.

Pensacola
(Map 3, page 32)

Farley's Old & Rare Books   **Open Shop**
6200 Tippin Avenue 32504   (850) 477-8282
                                                              Fax: (904) 484-5564
                                              E-mail: mfarley@compuserve.com

Collection:	General stock.
# of Vols:	15,000
Specialties:	History; religion; fiction.
Hours:	Mon-Sat 10-5.
Services:	Appraisals, search service, accepts want lists, mail order, book repair and restoration
Travel:	Exit 5 (Rte 291/Davis Hwy exit) off I-10. Proceed south to Langley Ave, then left onto Langley and right at second light onto Tippin.
Credit Cards:	Yes
Owner:	Owen & Moonean Farley
Year Estab:	1975

Hawsey's Book Index   **Open Shop**
803 North Navy Boulevard 32507   (850) 453-1430

Collection:	General stock of used paperback and hardcover.
# of Vols:	60,000
Hours:	Tue-Sat 9-5.
Travel:	One block from intersection of Rte 98 and North Navy Blvd.
Credit Cards:	Yes

Owner:	Lana Creary & Dinah Tronu
Year Estab:	1968
Comments:	Stock is evenly divided between paperback and hardcover.

King & Queen Books
By Appointment
1305 Lansing Drive
(850) 477-2560
Mailing address: PO Box 15062 Pensacola 32514-0062

Collection:	General stock of mostly used.
# of Vols:	6,500
Specialties:	Florida; Southern Americana.
Services:	Catalog
Credit Cards:	No
Owner:	Lana Servies
Year Estab:	1975

Ruth's Books
Open Shop
314 South Alcaniz Street 32501
(850) 444-9999

Collection:	General stock.
# of Vols:	2,000-3,000
Hours:	Tue-Sat 10-5.
Travel:	Garden St exit of I-110. Continue on Garden, taking first opportunity to make U turn on Garden going in opposite direction. When Garden dead ends at Alcaniz, turn right on Alcaniz. Shop is 2½ blocks ahead on Seville Square.
Credit Cards:	No
Owner:	Ruth Colley
Year Estab:	1983
Comments:	At the time of our visit to Pensacola three years ago, this dealer was located in an antique mall. Since then, she has relocated into her own shop. Unfortunately, we did not have an opportunity to visit her at her new location for this revised edition. On our earlier visit we noted that she carried a mix of mostly older books, not always in the best condition, including an interesting selection of children's books, and a sampling of paperbacks and that most of the books were inexpensive.

Secondhand Prose Bookstore
Open Shop
8067 North Davis Highway 32514
(850) 477-8338

Collection:	General stock of paperback and hardcover.
# of Vols:	50,000
Hours:	Tue-Sat 9-5.
Travel:	Davis Hwy exit off I-10. Proceed north on Davis Hwy for about one mile. Shop is on left in a strip center.
Credit Cards:	No
Owner:	Marcia Crymes
Year Estab:	1989
Comments:	Stock is approximately 75% paperback.

Seville Bookstore　　　　　　　　　　　　　　　　**Open Shop**
660 East Government Street 32590　　　　　　(850) 434-0439

Collection:	General stock.
# of Vols:	7,000-10,000
Hours:	Mon-Sat 9-4.
Travel:	Located in Seville District at the end of Government St in downtown.
Credit Cards:	No
Owner:	Stephen G. & Mary B. Fluegge
Year Estab:	1979
Comments:	Since our visit to this shop three years ago, the original owner has died and his son has taken over the shop. At the time of our visit we noted that the shop carried books of varying ages, most in fairly good condition and priced quite reasonably. While the shelves were not labeled, the books were generally well organized and the shop was small enough (2+ rooms) to browse quickly and discover one's areas of interest. If you have an opportunity to visit this shop, we'd welcome your impressions on any changes that the new owner has introduced.

Pompano Beach

Robert Richshafer　　　　　　　　　　　　　**By Appointment**
700 North Ocean Blvd, #6 33062　　　　　　　(954) 784-8317
　　　　　　　　　　　　　　　　　　　　　　Fax: (954) 259-1983

Collection:	Specialty books and ephemera.
# of Vols:	5,000
Specialties:	Americana; voyages; travel; exploration; photography; historical documents; newspapers.
Services:	Appraisals, search service, accepts want lists.

Port Richey
(Map 3, page 32)

Book Store at Jasmine Center　　　　　　　　**Open Shop**
10622 Devco Drive 34668　　　　　　　　　　(813) 868-8731

Collection:	General stock of mostly used paperback and hardcover.
# of Vols:	125,000 (used)
Hours:	Mon-Sat 10-6.
Travel:	On Rte 19, just north of Jasmine Blvd. Note: Devco Dr is an access road that parallels Rte 19.
Credit Cards:	Yes
Owner:	Faye Wilson
Year Estab:	1978
Comments:	This shop serves its community by offering the usual selection of used paperbacks (at least one half the stock), a reasonable number of used hardcover items, not all in the best condition, and some new paperbacks and hardcover titles.

USA Flea Market   **Flea Market**
Route 19 34668   (813) 862-3583

Hours: Fri-Sun 8-4.
Travel: Just south of Rte 52.

Punta Gorda
(Map 3, page 32)

All Books   **Open Shop**
111 West Marion Avenue 33950   (941) 505-0345

Collection: General stock of hardcover and paperback.
# of Vols: 20,000
Specialties: Local authors.
Hours: Mon-Sat 9:30-5, except Fri till 7.
Services: Search service.
Travel: Rte 17 exit off I-75. Proceed west on Rte 17. Shop is just after crossing
                  Rte 41, on the left, across from Publix Plaza.
Credit Cards: No
Owner: Al Leonard
Year Estab: 1995
Comments: A good selection of unusual hardcover titles (including, at the time of
                  our visit, a two volume first edition of *In Darkest Africa* along with
                  some far more ordinary titles and paperbacks. All in all, we would say
                  that if the owner is able to continue to buy and shelve the same ratio of
                  unusual titles that were on hand at the time of our visit this shop should
                  be well worth visiting.

Saint Augustine
(Map 3, page 32)

Avenue Books & Gallery   **Open Shop**
142 King Street 32084   (904) 829-9744
                                                       E-mail: avebooks@interloc.com

Collection: General stock.
# of Vols: 50,000
Specialties: Art
Hours: Mon-Sat 10-7. Sun 12-5.
Services: Appraisals, accepts want lists.
Travel: Rte 1 to King St, then right onto King (towards historic district). Shop
                  is 1½ blocks ahead.
Credit Cards: Yes
Owner: Allan Gerth & Kathleen Mulholland
Year Estab: 1986
Comments: A particularly nice shop with quality titles in most categories, particu-
                  larly in the shop's specialty area. The books were in especially good
                  condition, the variety was intriguing and the shop has more than its
                  share of collectibles. We would definitely recommend a visit. The
                  shop also features an art gallery.

(Saint Augustine)

Bettye's Baubles & Books   **Open Shop**
60 Cuna Street 32084   (904) 823-9363

Collection:	General stock and ephemera.
# of Vols:	1,500
Hours:	Wed-Sun 10-5.
Services:	Accepts want lists, mail order.
Travel:	Rte 16 exit off I-95. Proceed east on Rte 16 to Rte 1 south, then left on Castillo Dr, right on Cordova and left on Cuna.
Credit Cards:	Yes
Owner:	Bettye Trites
Year Estab:	1990

Buy The Book   **Open Shop**
4255 US Highway 1 South, #3 32086   (904) 797-3388

Collection:	General stock of mostly paperback.
Hours:	Mon-Sat 9-5:30.

Karla's Thrift Store   **Open Shop**
179 San Marco Avenue 32095   (904) 824-9190

Collection:	General stock of paperback and hardcover.
# of Vols:	500
Hours:	Tue-Sat 11-5.

North Country Antiques   **Antique Mall**
At Lightner Antique Mall   (904) 829-2129
25 Granada Street 32084

Collection:	General stock and ephemera.
# of Vols:	500+
Hours:	Daily 11:30-4.
Travel:	From Rte 1, proceed east on King St, then right on Granada.

Second Read   **Open Shop**
51D Cordova Street 32084   (904) 829-0334

Collection:	General stock of paperback and hardcover.
# of Vols:	10,000
Hours:	Mon-Thu, except closed Tue, 10-6. Fri & Sat 10-7. Sun 10-6.
Travel:	From Rte 16, turn right on San Marco Ave, right on Orange, then left on Cordova.
Credit Cards:	No
Owner:	Susan Von Spreckelsen & Evelyn Young
Year Estab:	1995
Comments:	Stock is approximately 75% paperback.

Thinking Works   **Open Shop**
323 Anastasia Boulevard 32084   (800) 633-3742 (904) 824-0648
Mailing address: PO Box 468 Saint Augustine 32085-0468   Fax: (904) 824-8505
E-mail: thnkgwks@aug.com

Collection:	Specialty new and used.
# of Vols:	6,000 (used)
Specialties:	Self help; spirituality; women's studies; black studies; education.
Hours:	Mon-Sat 9-5.
Services:	Accepts want lists.
Travel:	From San Marco Ave, continue on Avenida Menendez, then turn left onto Rte A1A (Anastasia Blvd).
Credit Cards:	Yes
Owner:	Sandra Parks
Year Estab:	1987

Wolf's Head Books   **Open Shop**
48 San Marco Avenue   (904) 824-9357
Mailing address: PO Box 3705 St. Augustine 32085   E-mail: wolfhead@aug.com

Collection:	General stock and ephemera.
# of Vols:	22,000
Specialties:	Regional Americana; military; Civil War; children's series.
Hours:	Mon-Fri 11-7. Sat 11-5. Sun 12:30-5. Other times by appointment or chance.
Services:	Appraisals, search service, catalog, accepts want lists, collection development.
Travel:	From Rte 16 turn south (right) onto San Marco. Northbound on I-95: Rte 1 exit. Take Rte 1 to Rohde, then turn east on Rohde.
Credit Cards:	Yes
Owner:	Barbara E. Nailler & Harvey J. Wolf
Year Estab:	1980
Comments:	When we returned to this establishment three years after our earlier visit we felt well rewarded as the owners continue to maintain a broad selection of books in many many categories tempting the browser to leave the shop with an armful of goodies. The shop is a real class act with some vintage treasures. The books are nicely displayed and, for the most part, in good condition. During our visit, we noted a particularly nice mystery section, with most of the books having dust jackets and consisting of non book club editions.

Saint Augustine Beach

Booktown   **Open Shop**
4075 A1A South 32084   (904) 471-5556

Collection:	General stock of mostly paperback.
# of Vols:	40,000
Hours:	Mon-Sat 10:30-5.

Saint Petersburg
(Map 3, page 32 & Map 6, page 88)

Age of Reason   **Open Shop**
401 First Avenue North 33701   (813) 821-0892

Collection:	General stock hardcover and paperback.
# of Vols:	18,000
Specialties:	Metaphysics; philosophy; history.
Hours:	Mon-Sat 9-6.
Services:	Accepts want lists, mail order.
Travel:	At corner of 4th St.
Credit Cards:	No
Owner:	Bill Poulsen
Year Estab:	1990
Comments:	An airy corner shop that was easy to browse, perhaps because there seemed to be room for a few more bookcases or shelves than were on the premises when we visited. Most of the books were in good to better condition. Moderately priced.

Antique Exchange of St. Petersburg   **Antique Mall**
2535 Central Avenue 33713   (813) 321-6621

Hours:	Mon-Sat 10-5. Sun 12-5.
Travel:	Fifth Ave exit off I-275. Continue straight across to Central, then right on Central.

Attic Bookshop   **Open Shop**
6601 First Avenue South 33707   (813) 344-2398

Collection:	General stock of hardcover and paperback.
# of Vols:	35,000+
Specialties:	Sheet music.
Hours:	Mon-Fri 10:30-5:30. Sat 10:30-3.
Services:	Search service, accepts want lists.
Travel:	Fifth Ave exit off I-275. Proceed west to 66th St, then south five blocks to Central. The shop's parking lot is 1/2 block south of Central on 66th St.
Credit Cards:	No
Owner:	Osborne & Chris Gomez
Year Estab:	1985
Comments:	A relatively modest sized shop which uses every square inch of space to display a mix of hardcover books, paperbacks and sheet music. Our guess is that your visit here will be brief, but, because the shop does have a variety of items, including some older titles, you may well find something of interest. Prices were reasonable.

Books & Bagels on the Beach   **Open Shop**
119 108th Avenue 33706   (813) 367-8029

Collection:	General stock of mostly used paperback.
Hours:	Mon-Fri 9-5. Sat 9-12.

Brigit Books   **Open Shop**
3434 4th Street North 33704   (813) 522-5775
E-mail: brigit@mail.earthlink.net

Collection:	Specialty. Mostly new.
# of Vols:	1,000
Specialties:	Women's studies; lesbian fiction and non fiction.
Hours:	Mon-Thu 10-8. Fri & Sat 10-6. Sun 1-5. Summer only: Mon-Sat 10-6, except Mon & Thu till 8. Sun 1-5.
Services:	Accepts want lists, mail order, catalog (new books only).
Travel:	Exit 13 off I-275. Proceed east on 38th Ave N, then right on 4th St N.
Credit Cards:	Yes
Owner:	Patty Callaghan
Year Estab:	1989

Haslam's Book Store   **Open Shop**
2025 Central Avenue 33713   (813) 822-8616
Web page: www.haslams.com   Fax: (813) 822-7416

Collection:	General stock of new and used hardcover and paperback.
# of Vols:	300,000 (combined)
Hours:	Mon-Sat 9-5:30, except Fri till 9.
Services:	Search service, mail order.
Travel:	Between 20th & 21st Streets.
Credit Cards:	Yes
Owner:	Haslam-Hinst Families
Year Estab:	1933
Comments:	A most impressive shop and a treat to visit. We have no doubt that the shop's claim to being Florida's largest book store is accurate. While the owner readily admits that the shop is not a "rare" book store, the shop certainly has a very fine selection of used and out-of-print titles (about 30% of the shop's total stock) ranging from turn of the century titles to far more recent volumes. The huge shop (which could easily accommodate half a dozen typical used book shops) is extremely well organized with wide aisles and the new and used book shelves clearly identified by colored labels. We spotted several uncommon titles and suggest that unless you're an absolute purist in the world of antiquarian books, you should enjoy spending some time visiting here. We found the books to be very modestly priced.

Lighthouse Books   **Open Shop**
1735 First Avenue North 33713   (813) 822-3278
E-mail: lightbks@sprint.com

Collection:	General stock, maps, prints and ephemera.
# of Vols:	30,000
Specialties:	Florida; illustrated; Americana; Caribbean; southern writers.
Hours:	Tue-Sat 10-5. Other times by appointment.
Services:	Appraisals, search service, catalog, accepts want lists.

Travel: 5th Ave North exit off I-275. Left at first light, then right onto 16th St.
                  Proceed three blocks then right onto First Ave N. Shop is on right, just
                  beyond 17th St.
Credit Cards: Yes
Owner: Michael F. Slicker
Year Estab: 1977
Comments: A compact shop with older books taking up almost every available
                  square inch of space. We were impressed by the owner's taste in terms
                  of selecting his stock which is particularly strong in the areas cited
                  above but which also has a fine if limited selection of materials of a
                  more general nature. Quite reasonably priced.

Page After Page   **Open Shop**
2390 4th Street North 33704   (813) 894-4733

Collection: General stock of used and new paperback and hardcover.
# of Vols: 25,000 (used)
Hours: Mon-Sat 10-7. Sun 12-5.
Travel: Between 22nd & 30th Avenue.
Year Estab: 1996
Comments: Used stock is approximately 65% paperback.

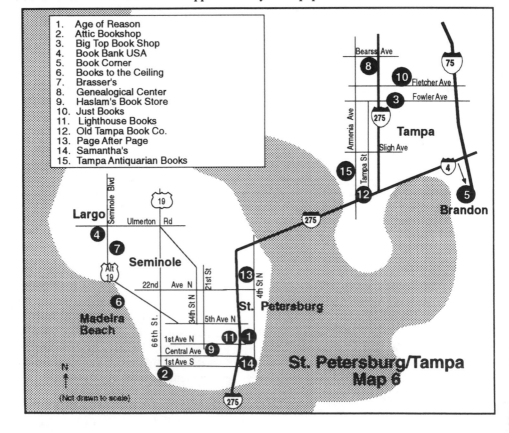

1. Age of Reason
2. Attic Bookshop
3. Big Top Book Shop
4. Book Bank USA
5. Book Corner
6. Books to the Ceiling
7. Brasser's
8. Genealogical Center
9. Haslam's Book Store
10. Just Books
11. Lighthouse Books
12. Old Tampa Book Co.
13. Page After Page
14. Samantha's
15. Tampa Antiquarian Books

St. Petersburg/Tampa
Map 6

Paperback Palace of St. Petersburg   **Open Shop**
A3725 49th Street North 33709   (813) 521-1171

Collection: General stock of mostly paperback.
Hours: Mon-Sat 9-8, Sun 12-5

Samantha's   **Open Shop**
670 Central Avenue 33701   (813) 894-1755
                                                                  Fax: (813) 823-9555
                                                        E-mail: samsbks@gte.net

Collection: General stock.
# of Vols: 15,000
Specialties: History; art; modern first editions; psychology.
Hours: Mon-Sat 10:30-5:30. Sun 10:30-5.
Services: Search service, accepts want lists, mail order
Travel: 9th St exit off I-375. Follow 9th St to Central Ave, then left on Central.
                  Shop is at corner of Central and 7th St.
Credit Cards: Yes
Owner: Paul Rebinskas
Year Estab: 1991
Comments: Unless we missed something, most of the books on display, with the
                  exception of the specialties listed above, appeared to be rather ordinary.

Wilson's Book World   **Open Shop**
2394 9th Street North 33704   (813) 896-3700

Collection: General stock of mostly used paperback.
# of Vols: 80,000
Hours: Mon-Fri 10-7. Sat 9-5.

Sanford
(Map 3, page 32)

Our House Books & Coffee   **Open Shop**
308 East Commercial Street 32771   (407) 324-0054
                                                        E-mail: ourhouse@ao.net

Collection: General stock of hardcover and paperback.
# of Vols: 10,000
Hours: Mon-Sat 10-10.
Travel: Rte 46 exit off I-4. Proceed east on Rte 46 to Sanford, then left on
                  Palmetto and right on Commercial. Shop is on left in Lakeview Plaza.
Credit Cards: No
Owner: Dan Mulvaney
Year Estab: 1997
Comments: Stock is approximately 65% hardcover.

Sanibel

MacIntosh Book Shop　　　　　　　　　　　　　　**Open Shop**
2365 Periwinkle Way 33957　　　　　　　　　　　(941) 472-1447

Collection:	General stock of mostly new.
# of Vols:	500 (used)
Specialties:	Florida; Hemingway and other Florida authors.
Hours:	Summer: Mon-Sat 10-5. Winter: Mon-Sat 9:30-5.
Travel:	After crossing Sanibel causeway ($3.00 charge to cross) turn right at four way stop sign onto Periwinkle. Shop is two miles ahead on left in a stand alone building with a clock tower.
Comments:	Used and out or print books are primarily first editions.

Sarasota
(Map 3, page 32)

A. Parker's Books　　　　　　　　　　　　　　**Open Shop**
1488 Main Street 34236　　　　　　　　　　　　(941) 366-2898
　　　　　　　　　　　　　　　　　　　　　Fax: (941) 957-3779
　　　　　　　　　　　　　　　　E-mail: aparkers@aol.com

Collection:	General stock.
# of Vols:	2,000-3,000
Specialties:	Fine bindings; art; first editions.
Hours:	Mon-Sat 10-6. Extended hours in season.
Services:	Occasional catalog.
Travel:	See Book Bazaar below.
Credit Cards:	Yes
Owner:	Robert Wildey, Manager
Comments:	Located in the back room of the Book Bazaar, this collection, eclectic in nature, offers a smaller, but in most cases, finer selection of books than in the main store, including some antiquarian items.

Book Bazaar　　　　　　　　　　　　　　　**Open Shop**
1488 Main Street 34236　　　　　　　　　　　　(941) 366-1373
　　　　　　　　　　　　　　　　　　　　　Fax: (941) 957-3779

Collection:	General stock of mostly hardcover.
# of Vols:	90,000
Specialties:	Travel; exploration; first editions; Florida; art.
Hours:	Mon-Sat 10-6. Extended hours in season.
Services:	Accepts want lists, mail order.
Travel:	Fruitville Rd exit off I-75. Proceed west on Fruitville Rd for six miles to Lemon. Left onto Lemon then right onto Main. Shop is on the left.
Credit Cards:	Yes
Owner:	Robert Wildey, Manager
Year Estab:	1990
Comments:	A very nice establishment that is well organized and has some wonderful titles in almost every section of the shop. Clearly we were im-

pressed with the quality of the books as well as with the selection and would definitely recommend a visit for any true book aficionado. The books are reasonably priced and there were lots of chairs for the browser's comfort.

Book Nook   **Open Shop**
3650 Weber Street 34232   (941) 922-8564

Collection:	General stock of mostly paperback.
# of Vols:	100,000
Hours:	Mon-Fri 10-5. Sat 10-4.
Travel:	Bee Ridge Rd exit off I-75. Proceed west on Bee Ridge, right on Beneva and right on Weber. Shop in Forest Lake Shopping Center.
Comments:	Stock is approximately 80% paperback.

The Book Nook   **Open Shop**
6549 Superior Avenue 34231   (941) 923-1989

Collection:	General stock of mostly paperback.
Hours:	Mon-Fri 10-5. Sat 10-4.

Brant's Used Books   **Open Shop**
3913 Brown Avenue 34231   Tel & Fax: (941) 365-3658
                                                       E-mail: brantbks@interloc.com

Collection:	General stock of hardcover and paperback.
# of Vols:	100,000
Hours:	Mon-Sat 9-5.
Services:	Search service, accepts want lists, mail order.
Travel:	From the corner of Rte 41 and Bee Ridge Rd, proceed west one block. Turn left onto Brown. Shop is in a former WW II vintage quonset hut.
Credit Cards:	Yes
Owner:	William & Mary Sciarretta
Year Estab:	1956
Comments:	This shop does indeed have a large collection with at least as many (if not possibly more) paperbacks as hardcover items. Unfortunately, the books, which are generally reading copies, were not all in terrific condition. We spotted some interesting titles and most of the books we saw were priced to sell. The shop is worth browsing. Arrive early since when the owner says she closes at 5pm, she means she closes at 5pm.

Christine's Books   **Open Shop**
1502 Main Street 34236   (941) 365-0586

Collection:	General stock.
# of Vols:	15,000+
Specialties:	Florida; circus; children's; Civil War; Americana; martial arts.
Hours:	Mon-Sat 10-5.
Services:	Search service.
Travel:	See the Book Bazaar above.
Credit Cards:	Yes

(Sarasota)

Owner:	Christine Pegram
Year Estab:	1984
Comments:	A spacious, easy to browse shop. While one is not overwhelmed by the volume of books on display, the books we saw were in good to very good condition, of mixed vintage and with lots of collectible titles.

Coral Cove Books   **Open Shop**
7282 South Tamiami Trail 34231   (941) 924-3848
Web page: www.bibliofind.com/coralcove.html   Fax: (941) 924-2884
                                                                     E-mail: jcz@gate.net

Collection:	General stock of hardcover and paperback.
# of Vols:	40,000+
Specialties:	Art; history; military; modern fiction.
Hours:	Mon-Sat 10-8. Sun 12-6. Call to confirm during off season.
Services:	Search service, accepts want lists, mail order.
Travel:	Exit 37 off I-75. Proceed west on Clark Rd which becomes Stickney Point Rd. Turn left (south) onto Rte 41 (Tamiami Trail). Shop is one mile ahead on right.
Credit Cards:	Yes
Owner:	John & David Zeiss
Year Estab:	1996
Comments:	Absolutely worth going out of your way to visit. The books are almost universally in excellent condition. The store is spacious, easy to browse, attractive, and perhaps best of all, the books are priced most competitively.

Helen's Book & Comic Shop   **Open Shop**
1531 Main Street 34236   (941) 955-2989

Collection:	General stock of mostly paperbacks and comics.
# of Vols:	50,000
Hours:	Mon-Sat 9:30-5:30. Sun 11:30-4:30.
Travel:	See Book Bazaar above. Shop is between Orange and Lemon.
Comments:	If comic books are your thing you might want to stop here. On the other hand, if you're looking for a hard-to-find hardcover volume, even though this shop does have a smattering of hardcover books, we suspect you would have far better luck elsewhere.

3rd Floor Books   **Open Shop**
1962 Main Street 34236   (941) 955-1978

Collection:	General stock of hardcover, paperback, used videos, books on tape and records.
# of Vols:	10,000 (hardcover)
Hours:	Mon-Sat 11am-10:30pm. Sun 11-6.
Travel:	See Book Bazaar above. Shop is located inside the Main Bookshop on the third floor.

Credit Cards:	Yes
Owner:	Randy Glenn
Year Estab:	1994
Comments:	A mix of paperbacks, cassettes, LPs and hardcover books. While most of the hardcover volumes were reading copies, there were enough titles in several different areas of interest (including some vintage items and some books in excellent condition) to make the three story climb worth the effort.

Used Book Heaven   **Open Shop**
5216 Ocean Boulevard 34242   (941) 349-0067

Collection:	General stock of mostly paperback.
# of Vols:	25,000
Hours:	Mon-Sat 10-8. Call for Sun hours in season.

Sebastian
(Map 3, page 32)

Michael J. Knox, Bookseller   **Open Shop**
1614 North US Highway 1 32958   (561) 388-5733
Web page: www.abebooks.com/home/KNOXBOOK   E-mail: knoxbook@cape.net

Collection:	General stock of hardcover and paperback.
# of Vols:	5,000
Specialties:	Modern first editions; fine bindings; military; Civil War; Florida; cookbooks.
Hours:	Oct-May: Mon-Sat 10-5. Jun-Sep: Tue-Sat 10-4.
Services:	Appraisals, search service, mail order.
Travel:	On Rte 1, midway between Melbourne and Vero Beach.
Credit Cards:	No
Year Estab:	1994
Comments:	Stock is approximately 60% paperback.

Seminole
(Map 6, page 88)

Brasser's   **Open Shop**
8701 Seminole Boulevard 33772   (813) 393-6707

Collection:	General stock.
# of Vols:	30,000
Specialties:	Florida; military; baseball; football; golf; tennis.
Hours:	Mon-Fri 9-4:30. Sat 9-4. Closed month of Sept.
Services:	Appraisals (specialty fields only), search service, accepts want lists, occasional catalog, mail order.
Travel:	Located on Alt. Rte 19, about two miles northwest of St. Petersburg.
Credit Cards:	No
Owner:	Thomas Brasser
Year Estab:	1972

Comments: At the time of our visit, this good sized establishment had a rather nice
selection of older hardcover used items, and, like many other Florida used
book shops, a healthy selection of paperbacks. Perhaps it was the heat, but
when we entered the shop, except for the entrance area, the entire store
was dark and we could only browse the shelves after requesting that the
lights be turned on, which the owner did. Most subject areas were represented and many areas had books specially wrapped for protection against
the dampness. We noted that in areas about which we consider ourselves
fairly knowledgeable, most books were priced higher (despite the fact that
they were certainly not in any better condition) than the same titles in
equal or better condition that we have seen elsewhere. Despite the previous comments, it is possible to find a book here you may have been
searching for for quite some time, that is, if you're willing to pay the
premium price for it. Note: At press time the shop was for sale.

Stuart
(Map 3, page 32)

The Book Rack   **Open Shop**
632 SW Monterey Road 34994   (561) 283-4644
Collection: General stock of mostly paperback.
# of Vols: 5,000
Hours: Mon-Fri 9:30-6. Sat 9:30-4.

Collections Inc. Books   **Antique Mall**
53 West Flagler Avenue 34994   (561) 288-0035
Collection: General stock.
# of Vols: 8,000
Hours: Mon-Sat 10-5.
Services: Appraisals, search service, mail order, book binding.
Travel: Rte 76 exit off I-95. Proceed east on Rte 76 which becomes Colorado.
After crossing railroad tracks, go 3/4 way around the circle, then turn
onto Flagler Ave. The shop is 1/4 mile ahead.
Credit Cards: No
Owner: Jane Cousins
Year Estab: 1993
Comments: There were plenty of antiques and collectibles in this shop and, in the
rear left hand corner, several bookcases containing older books. Some
were interesting, some certainly collectible (including a worn *Glenda
of Oz* at $40) and some rather undistinguished. If you like to gamble,
why not take a chance. At the time of our visit, there were fewer books
on display than noted above.

Sharon's Book Trader   **Open Shop**
2299 SE Federal Highway 34994   (561) 288-1977
Collection: General stock of mostly paperback.
# of Vols: 10,000
Hours: Mon-Fri 10-5. Sat 10-4.

Tallahassee
(Map 3, page 32)

Mahoney's Violins & Bows   **By Appointment**
806 Ivanhoe Road 32312-3025   (850) 385-9521
Web page: www.spindata.com/violin   Fax: (850) 386-2602
    E-mail: violinbk@polaris.net

Collection:	Specialty books and periodicals
Specialties:	Music (violin family of stringed instruments). Books in all languages.
Services:	Appraisals, search service, catalog (on line), accepts want lists.
Credit Cards:	No
Owner:	John P. Mahoney
Year Estab:	1990

Rubyfruit Books   **Open Shop**
739 North Monroe Street 32303   (850) 222-2627
    Fax: (850) 222-0411

Collection:	General stock of new and used.
Specialties:	Women's studies; metaphysics, new age.
Hours:	Mon-Sat 10:30-6:30, except Thu till 8.
Services:	Search service, accepts want lists (women's studies only).
Travel:	Exit 29 off I-10. Proceed south on Rte 27 for about four miles. Shop is just south of Thomaseville Rd.
Credit Cards:	Yes
Owner:	Susan M. Mayer
Year Estab:	1973
Comments:	Stock is about 20% used, 75% of which is paperback.

Tampa
(Map 3, page 32 & Map 6, page 88)

Almost New Books   **Open Shop**
3637 Henderson Boulevard 33609   (813) 873-8906

Collection:	General stock of mostly paperback.
Specialties:	Science fiction.
Hours:	Tue-Fri 9-5. Sat 9-3.

Ashley Douglas Booksellers   **Open Shop**
3649 South Manhattan Avenue 33629   (813) 837-5650

Collection:	General stock of mostly paperback.
# of Vols:	35,000
Hours:	Mon-Fri 10-6. Sat 10-3.

Big Top Book Shop   **Flea Market**
At Big Top Flea Market   (813) 821-9031
Fowler Avenue & I-75
Mailing address: 119 20th Avenue North St. Petersburg 33704

Collection:	General stock of hardcover and paperback.

(Tampa)

# of Vols:	9,400
Specialties:	Modern literature; military; children's; cookbooks; technical.
Hours:	Sat & Sun 9:30-5.
Services:	Search service.
Travel:	Fowler Ave exit off I-75. Proceed east on Fowler for 1/4 mile ahead.
Credit Cards:	No
Owner:	Catherine Slicker
Year Estab:	1990

Book Swap of Carrollwood   **Open Shop**
13020 North Dale Mabry Highway 33618   (813) 963-6979

Collection:	General stock of mostly used paperback.
Hours:	Mon-Fri 10-8. Sat 10-5. Sun 12-5.

Genealogical Center Inc.   **Open Shop**
14816 North Florida Avenue 33613   (813) 265-2191

Collection:	General stock.
# of Vols:	2,000
Specialties:	Genealogy
Hours:	Mon, Tue, Wed, & Fri 10-5. Thu 2-5. Weekends by chance.
Services:	Appraisals, accepts want lists, catalog.
Travel:	Southbound on I-275: Bearss Ave exit. Turn right on Bearss then left on Florida. Shop is 3/10 mile ahead in Windwood Plaza. Northbound on I-275: Fletcher Ave exit. Turn left on Fletcher, then right on Florida. Shop is one mile ahead.
Credit Cards:	No
Owner:	Mary Mahon & Myra Sims
Year Estab:	1995

Just Books   **Open Shop**
2002 East Fletcher Avenue 33612   (813) 977-4648

Collection:	General stock of paperback and hardcover.
# of Vols:	80,000
Specialties:	Literature; science fiction.
Hours:	Mon-Fri, except closed Wed, 11-7. Sat 11-6.
Services:	Accepts want lists.
Travel:	Fletcher Ave exit off I-275. Proceed east on Fletcher.
Credit Cards:	Yes
Owner:	Carl & Marilyn Jacoby
Year Estab:	1978
Comments:	A heavy concentration of paperbacks with a nice selection of hardcover books in the specialties listed above, particularly more recent titles. If you're looking for vintage items, we wouldn't take odds on you're finding them here. But, as the selection is broad enough and the owner has quite a large stock in storage, one never knows.

Merlin's Books   **Open Shop**
2368 Fowler Avenue East 33612   (813) 972-1766

Collection:	Specialty new and used books and comics.
# of Vols:	15,000 (used)
Specialties:	Metaphysics; science fiction; pulps.
Hours:	Mon-Sat 10-9. Sun 12-6.
Travel:	Fowler Avenue exit off I-275. Proceed east on Fowler.
Owner:	Richard Clear

Old Tampa Book Co.   **Open Shop**
507 Tampa Street 33602   (813) 209-2151
Web page: www.reddesign.com/otbc/home.html   E-mail: otbc@reddesign.com

Collection:	General stock.
# of Vols:	12,000-14,000
Specialties:	Automobiles; Florida; railroads; sailing and ships; modern first editions; literature; art; architecture.
Hours:	Mon-Fri 10-5. Sat 11-6.
Services:	Appraisals, search service, accepts want lists, mail order.
Travel:	Exit 25 (Downtown/West) off I-275. Proceed south on Tampa St for about eight blocks.
Credit Cards:	Yes
Owner:	Jim Shelton & David Brown
Year Estab:	1980
Comments:	With few exceptions (a nice fiction as well as humor section) the shop's stock is devoted mostly to serious subjects, i.e., the specialties listed above. The books we saw were primarily neat, clean dust jacketed copies, were fairly priced and offer an interesting variety to both the specialist and the general browser.

Out of Print Cookbooks   **Open Shop**
9915 US Highway 301 North 33637   (813) 988-3122

Collection:	Specialty
# of Vols:	17,000
Specialties:	Cookbooks
Hours:	Tue-Sat 10:30-6.
Services:	Accepts want lists.
Travel:	Four miles north of intersection of I-4. Shop is on right.
Credit Cards:	Yes
Owner:	Lynn Cooper

Vivian Shelton   **Open Shop**
At Inkwood Books   Store: (813) 253-2638
216 South Armenia   Home: (813) 876-0370
Mailing address: PO Box 20163 Tampa 33622

Collection:	General stock.
# of Vols:	200 (see Comments below)

Specialties:	Florida
Hours:	Mon-Sat 10-6 except Thu till 9. Sun 1-5
Travel:	Howard/Armenia exit off I-275. Proceed south on Armenia. Shop is in a former residence.
Year Estab:	1991
Comments:	Additional books can be viewed on a by appointment basis.

Sleuth Books   **By Appointment**
602 South Boulevard Annex 33606   (813) 251-4196
                                                                     Fax: (813) 251-0974
                                                             E-mail: bolter@atlantic.net

Collection:	Specialty
Specialties:	Children's series.
Owner:	Charles Bolter

Tampa Antiquarian Books & Collectibles   **Open Shop**
6306 North Armenia Avenue 33604   (813) 871-3919

Collection:	General stock and ephemera.
# of Vols:	25,000
Hours:	Tue-Fri 10-6. Sat 10-4.
Services:	Accepts want lists, mail order.
Travel:	Sligh Ave exit off I-275. Proceed west on Sligh to Armenia, then south on Armenia for about eight blocks.
Credit Cards:	No
Owner:	Jimmie Kaiser
Year Estab:	1988
Comments:	An interesting shop that tries, and succeeds, to carry most subject areas. The books we saw were of mixed vintage and in mixed condition. We saw few, if any, bargains.

Tequesta

My Book Place   **Open Shop**
124 Bridge Road 33469   (561) 747-9597

Collection:	General stock of mostly paperback.
# of Vols:	60,000
Hours:	Mon-Fri 10-5. Sat 10-12.

Titusville
(Map 3, page 32)

Brocket Books   **Flea Market**
At Frontenac Flea Market   Tel & Fax: (407) 568-2050
Route 1   E-mail: brocbook@interloc.com
Mailing address: Box 164 Christmas 32709

Collection:	General stock of hardcover and paperback.
# of Vols:	5,000 (hardcover)

Hours:	Fri-Sun 9-4 and other times by appointment.
Services:	Search service, accepts want lists.
Travel:	Located on Rte 1 between Titusville and Cocoa.
Owner:	Jan & C.A. Langston

Ken's Used Books   **Open Shop**
3659 South Hopkins Avenue 32780   (407) 267-7497

Collection:	General stock of paperback and hardcover.
# of Vols:	40,000
Hours:	Mon-Fri 10-8. Sat 9-6.
Travel:	From Rte 50, proceed north on Hopkins Ave for about two miles. Shop is in a strip mall on right.
Credit Cards:	No
Owner:	Kenneth Potter
Year Estab·	1992
Comments:	Stock is approximately 70% paperback.

Venice

Anderson's Paperback Book Exchange   **Open Shop**
2387 South Trail 34293   (941) 493-2766

Collection:	General stock of mostly paperback.
# of Vols:	60,000+
Hours:	Mon-Sat 10-5.
Travel:	On Rte 41, four blocks north of Jacaranda Blvd.
Comments:	The name says it all. I'm not sure why we stopped here except that I'm advised by my partner that "you can never tell." She was wrong. You can tell. We saw fewer than 500 hardcover volumes here at wonderful bargain prices of $2 and $3 each. (How does one spell facetious?)

Anderson's Paperback Book Exchange   **Open Shop**
900 Tamiami Trail South 34285   (941) 493-2766

Collection:	General stock of paperback and hardcover.
# of Vols:	60,000+
Hours:	Mon-Sat 9-5.

Books Et Cetera   **Open Shop**
4145 Tamiami Trail 34293   (941) 493-2589

Collection:	General stock of mostly new and some used.
# of Vols:	500 (used)
Hours:	Mon-Sat 10-6. Sun by appointment.
Travel:	On Rte 41 in Venice Village Shops shopping center.
Comments:	Primarily a new book store with a limited collection of used books most of which are intershelved with new books by subject. Better used books are shelved separately and can be viewed by appointment.

Vero Beach
(Map 3, page 32)

Elsey's Books   **Antique Mall**
At The Company Store Antique Mall   Mall: (561) 569-9884
6605 North US Hwy 1   Dealer: (888) 563-2244
Mailing address: 206 19th Avenue Vero Beach 32962   Fax: (561) 563-0718
                                                          E-mail: elseybks@gate.net

Collection:	General stock.
# of Vols:	500 (see Comments)
Specialties:	Mystery (available by appointment).
Hours:	Daily 10-5.
Services:	Catalog, search service, accepts want lists.
Travel:	From south: Exit 68 (Rte 60) off I-95. Proceed east on Rte 60 to Rte 1, then north on Rte 1. From north: Exit 69 (Rte 512) off I-95. Proceed east on Rte 512 to Rte 1, then south on Rte 1.
Credit Cards:	Yes
Owner:	Bill & Vi Elsey
Year Estab:	1994
Comments:	Only a portion of the stock is on display at the mall. If you don't see what you're looking for, call the owners directly.

Webster
(Map 3, page 32)

Jim & Mary's Out Of Print Books   **Flea Market**
Webster West Market   (352) 344-4627
Mailing address: 10436 East Irene Street Inverness 34450

Collection:	General stock.
Specialties:	Children's
Hours:	Monday only, 7am-4 pm.
Services:	Mail order.
Travel:	Webster exit off I-75. Proceed east on Rte 50, then north on Rte 478 to Webster Market. Shop is Booth # 33-35 in Maroon section.
Credit Cards:	No
Owner:	Jim & Mary Curls
Year Estab:	1965

West Palm Beach
(Map 3, page 32 & Map 5, page 68)

Joseph Rubinfine   **By Appointment**
505 South Flagler Drive, Ste. 1301 33401   (561) 659-7077

Collection:	Specialty
Specialties:	American historical documents.
Services:	Catalog, accepts want lists.
Credit Cards:	No
Year Estab:	1967

Two on a Shelf Bookstore
7637 South Dixie Highway 33405
Web page: www.emi.net/~twoonshelf/

Open Shop
(561) 582-0067
E-mail: twoonshelf@emi.net

Collection:	General stock of mostly hardcover.
# of Vols:	20,000
Specialties:	Metaphysics; occult; literature; fine arts; natural history; architecture; John D. McDonald.
Hours:	Tue-Fri 10-5:30. Sat 10-5.
Services:	Appraisals, search service, accepts want lists, occasional catalog.
Travel:	From I-95 north, Forest Hill Blvd exit. Proceed east on Forest Hill to Rte 1, then south on Rte 1. Shop is five blocks ahead in Palm Coast Plaza.
Credit Cards:	Yes
Owner:	Cynthia & Ray Plockelman
Year Estab:	1983
Comments:	We were pleased to return to this shop at its new, larger location. The shop offers a collection of very good books, the vast majority of which are in good to excellent condition. The shop is organized for easy browsing and is definitely worth a visit.

Winter Haven
(Map 3, page 32)

Book Inn
2824 Recker Highway 33880-1941
Web page: home1.get.net/fgilliam/bookinn.htm

Open Shop
Tel & Fax: (941) 294-8982
E-mail: fgilliam@gte.net

Collection:	General stock of hardcover and paperback.
# of Vols:	60,000
Hours:	Mon-Sat 10-6.
Services:	Appraisals, search service, accepts want lists.
Travel:	Recker Hwy exit off Rte 92. Proceed south on Recker Hwy (Rte 655) to Village Square Plaza. From Rte 17, turn west on Lake Ship Dr which becomes Recker Hwy. Continue on Recker to shopping center.
Credit Cards:	Yes
Owner:	May Gilliam & Shirley Wimberly
Year Estab:	1996
Comments:	Stock is approximately 70% hardcover.

The Booktraders
301 West Central Avenue 33880

Open Shop
(941) 299-4904

Collection:	General stock of paperback and hardcover.
# of Vols:	200,000+
Hours:	Mon-Sat 9-9. Sun 1-6.
Travel:	From I-4 westbound: Rte 27 exit. Proceed south on Rte 27 to Rte 542, then right onto Rte 542. Shop is seven miles ahead.
Credit Cards:	Yes
Owner:	Sue & Frank Ujlaki

Year Estab: 1983
Comments: We entered this shop with a bit of trepidation having spotted scores of paper bags filled with paperbacks through the side window; we wondered if this would be one of those "romance and sci fi paperback dominated shops." Clearly, the shop does have an extensive paperback selection but, it also carries a relatively large selection of hardcover volumes representing both vintage and more current titles. While it will require a good deal of patience to peruse all of the shelves, unless your tastes are esoteric, that patience should be rewarded.

Winter Park
(Map 3A, page 32)

Brandywine Books   **Open Shop**
114 South Park Avenue, Suite 32789   (407) 644-1711
                                          E-mail: branwine@interloc.com

Collection: General stock.
# of Vols: 5,000
Specialties: Florida; history; literature; first editions; art; architecture; antiques; children's; movies; theater; music; religion.
Hours: Mon-Sat 10-5:30.
Services: Search service, mail order.
Travel: Exit 45 (Fairbanks Ave) off I-4. Proceed east on Fairbanks (Rte 426) for about two miles to Park Ave, then north on Park. Shop is five blocks ahead on right in Greeneda Court (set off from the street), across from the Amtrak station.
Credit Cards: Yes
Owner: Evelyn W. Pettit
Year Estab: 1984
Comments: A small shop in which the owner makes the best use of the limited space available. We saw some very nice books on display in mostly good condition and recommend the shop as worth a visit.

Zephyrhills

Piles of Paperbacks   **Open Shop**
37325 State Road 54 West 33541   (813) 783-8105

Collection: General stock of mostly paperback.
# of Vols: 13,000
Hours: Mon-Fri 10-5. Sat 10-3.

A Novel Idea   (800) 277-9990   (941) 378-0990
5590 Bee Ridge Road, Ste. 3 Sarasota 34233-1505   Fax: (941) 378-1040

Collection:	Specialty
# of Vols:	3,000
Specialties:	First editions; signed; mystery; suspense; uncorrected proofs and review copies. Primarily fiction, with a few memoirs and a cat humor section.
Services:	Catalog
Credit Cards:	Yes
Owner:	Sandra E. Herron
Year Estab:	1995
Comments:	Collection may be viewed by appointment.

Aceto Bookmen   (941) 924-9170
5721 Antietam Drive Sarasota 34231-4903

Collection:	Specialty
# of Vols:	300
Specialties:	Genealogy
Services:	Accepts want lists.
Credit Cards:	No
Owner:	Charles D. Townsend
Year Estab:	1968

Alec R. Allenson   (850) 956-2817
Route 1, Box 464 Westville 32464

Collection:	Specialty
# of Vols:	50,000
Specialties:	Religion; philosophy; bibliography; titles in series; periodicals.
Services:	Accepts want lists.
Credit Cards:	No
Owner:	Robert D. Allenson
Year Estab:	1924

Bomar n' Things   (941) 494-6499
12193 SE County Road 763 Arcadia 34266

Collection:	General stock.
# of Vols:	100,000
Services:	Search service, accepts want lists.
Credit Cards:	No
Owner:	Ralph Bojanowski
Year Estab:	1985

Brightlight Books   (407) 894-2450
805 North Hyer Avenue Orlando 32803   E-mail: brightlight@mindspring.com

Collection:	Specialty
# of Vols:	3,500
Specialties:	Religion (Christian theology with a scholarly emphasis).
Services:	Occasional catalog, search service, accepts want lists.

Credit Cards: No
Owner: Scott Huber
Year Estab: 1994
Comments: Collection can be viewed by appointment.

Don Brown, Bookseller   Tel & Fax: (954) 946-5306
2521 NE 47th Street Lighthouse Point 33064   E-mail: dbrown@laker.net
Web page: www.laker.net/dbrown

Collection: Specialty
# of Vols: 3,000
Specialties: Children's series.
Credit Cards: No

Cover To Cover Booksellers   (941) 482-5885
1490 Memoli Lane Fort Myers 33919   E-mail: covrcovr@interloc.com

Collection: General stock.
# of Vols: 3,000
Credit Cards: No
Owner: Rosemary Maurice
Year Estab: 1987

Ralph Curtis Publishing   (941) 454-0010
PO Box 459 Sanibel 33957   Fax: (941) 395-2727

Collection: Specialty
# of Vols: 200
Specialties: Wildlife; reptiles; military.
Services: Occasional catalog, accepts want lists.
Credit Cards: Yes
Year Estab: 1962

Ensign Books   (561) 995-0751
PO Box 1442 Boca Raton 33429

Collection: Specialty
Specialties: US Navy cruise books; Office of Naval Intelligence Reports.
Services: Catalog, search service, accepts want lists.
Credit Cards: No
Owner: Tony Miele
Year Estab: 1992

Philip Grossman   (941) 921-1564
PO Box 721 Osprey 34229

Collection: Specialty
# of Vols: 2,000
Specialties: Modern first editions.
Services: Occasional catalog, accepts want lists.
Credit Cards: No
Year Estab: 1988

Herpetological Booksellers (561) 220-7988
PO Box 1906 Palm City 34991-1906 Fax: (561) 220-1509
Web page: www.herp books.com E-mail: lit@herp books.com

Collection:	Specialty new and used books and related prints and posters.
Specialties:	Reptiles and amphibians.
Services:	Appraisals, search service, catalog, accepts want lists.
Credit Cards:	No
Owner:	Barbara Marzec
Year Estab:	1982

Key Books (813) 867-2931
PO Box 58097 Saint Petersburg 33715

Collection:	Specialty
# of Vols:	4,000
Specialties:	Science; technology; exploration; books on books.
Services:	Catalog, accepts want lists.
Credit Cards:	No
Owner:	Raymond D. Cooper
Year Estab:	1975

Long's Books (850) 438-1956
711 West Lakeview Avenue Pensacola 32501-1964

Collection:	General stock.
# of Vols:	3,000
Specialties:	First editions; biography.
Services:	Accepts want lists.
Credit Cards:	No
Owner:	Catherine D. Long
Year Estab:	1958

Dave Mattson Nautical Books (813) 772-5723
PO Box 803 Cape Coral 33910

Collection:	Specialty new and used.
# of Vols:	5,000 (used)
Specialties:	Nautical
Services:	Catalog, accepts want lists.
Credit Cards:	No
Year Estab:	1987

O.S. McFarland
112 North Gilchrist Avenue Tampa 33606

Collection:	Specialty
# of Vols:	5,000
Specialties:	Horror; science fiction; mystery; fantasy.
Services:	Catalog

McQuerry Orchid Books   Tel & Fax: (904) 387-5044
5700 West Salerno Road Jacksonville 32244-2354
Collection: Specialty
Specialties: Orchids
Services: Catalog, accepts want lists.
Credit Cards: Yes
Owner: Mary McQuerry
Year Estab: 1972
Comments: Collection can also be viewed by appointment.

Mickler's Antiquarian Books   (407) 365-3636
PO Box 660038 Chuluota 32766-0038
Collection: Specialty books, maps and memorabilia.
# of Vols: 3,500
Specialties: Florida
Services: Search service, subject lists.
Credit Cards: No
Owner: Florida Breezes, Inc.
Year Estab: 1960
Comments: Collection can be viewed by appointment.

The Midnight Bookman   (813) 536-4029
1908 Seagull Drive Largo 34624
Collection: General stock.
# of Vols: 1,000
Services: Appraisals
Credit Cards: No
Owner: Lee J. Harrer
Year Estab: 1981

Arthur H. Minters, Booksellers   Tel & Fax: (813) 579-1132
500 110th Avenue North, #507 Saint Petersburg 33716
Collection: Specialty books and ephemera.
Specialties: Art; architecture; modern literature; photography; modern illustrated
                   books.
Services: Appraisals, search service, catalog, accepts want lists, collection de-
                   velopment, auction representative.
Credit Cards: Yes
Year Estab: 1957

Gary Nippes Books   (352) 373-4541
PO Box 78 Micanopy 32667
Collection: Specialty
# of Vols: 2,000
Specialties: Art; art reference; photography.
Services: Search service, catalog, accepts want lists.
Credit Cards: No
Year Estab: 1994

Oriental Book Shelf (813) 867-7978
6940 9th Street South St. Petersburg 33705 E-mail: OrientialBookShelf@msn.com

Collection:	Specialty
# of Vols:	15,000
Specialties:	Orient
Services:	Catalog
Credit Cards:	No
Owner:	James Roberts
Year Estab:	1982

Martin B. Raskin, Medical Books (561) 439-0339
4349 Trevi Court Lake Worth 33467

Collection:	Specialty
# of Vols:	8,000
Specialties:	Medicine
Services:	Catalog
Credit Cards:	No
Year Estab:	1979

Serpent's Books (904) 760-7675
2090 South Nova Road South Daytona 32129

Collection:	Specialty new and used.
# of Vols:	2,000 (used)
Specialties:	Metaphysics
Services:	Catalog, search service, accepts want lists.
Credit Cards:	Yes
Owner:	Steve Savedow
Year Estab:	1989

Neil Shillington (561) 545-3269
PO Box 610 Hobe Sound 33475   E-mail: neilsbks@ecqual.net

Collection:	General stock.
# of Vols:	12,000
Specialties:	History; religion; fine bindings.
Services:	Occasional catalog, search service, accepts want lists.
Credit Cards:	No
Year Estab:	1985

Mike Smith, Bookseller (813) 784-8840
5437 Oakridge Drive Palm Harbor 34685   E-mail: mikebook@interloc.com

Collection:	Specialty
# of Vols:	5,000
Specialties:	Genealogy; Americana; modern first editions; Southern Americana.
Services:	Appraisals, search service, accepts want lists.
Credit Cards:	No
Year Estab:	1989

Gene Snyder - Books
991 McLean Street Dunedin 34698

Collection:	Specialty
Specialties:	Hawaii; Polynesia; ukuleles; horse drawn vehicles.
Credit Cards:	No
Year Estab:	1968

Southeastern Library Service   Tel & Fax: (352) 372-3823
PO Box 44 Gainesville 32602-0044

Collection:	Specialty new and used hardcover and paperback.
# of Vols:	22,000
Specialties:	Antique reference; Americana; Florida; nature; Native Americans.
Services:	Catalog, accepts want lists.
Credit Cards:	No
Owner:	Gerry & Harold Haskins
Year Estab:	1968

Suncoast Bookworm   (941) 342-3495
PO Box 864 Sarasota 34230-0864   E-mail: bookworm@home.com

Collection:	Specialty used and new.
# of Vols:	1,000+
Specialties:	Mystery; detective; contemporary literature and fiction.
Services:	Search service, accepts want lists.
Credit Cards:	No
Owner:	Maureen Waddell
Year Estab:	1996
Comments:	Stock is approximately 50% used.

Virgil Wilhite   Tel & Fax: (813) 461-4541
PO Box 10001, Clearwater 33757-8001   (813) 446-9362
                                                    E-mail: wilcobks@gte.net

Collection:	Specialty
# of Vols:	2,000
Specialties:	L. Ron Hubbard
Services:	Search service, accepts want lists.
Credit Cards:	Yes
Year Estab:	1981
Comments:	Former owner of Wilhite Collectibles Bookstore in Clearwater, FL.

Undercover Books   (941) 352-1745
4300 15th Avenue SW Naples 34116

Collection:	General stock and ephemera.
# of Vols:	10,000
Specialties:	First editions.
Services:	Search service, book binding and repair.
Credit Cards:	No
Owner:	Richard & Carol Wright
Comments:	Also displays at Baileys Antique Mall in Naples. See above.

Georgia

Alphabetical Listing By Dealer

Alphabetical Listing By Location

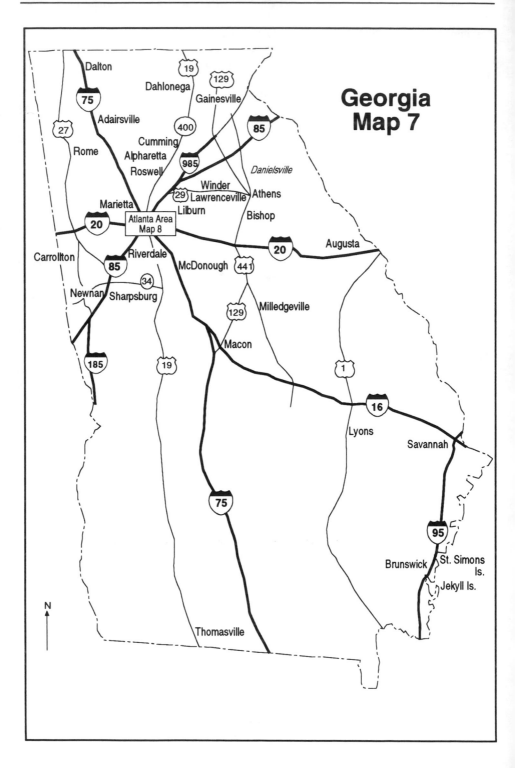

Georgia
Map 7

Adairsville
(Map 7, page 114)

Book Cottage
At 1902 Stock Exchange Antique Mall 30103
124 Public Square

Antique Mall
(770) 773-1902

Collection: General stock.
# of Vols: 3,000+
Hours: Tue-Sat 10-5. Sun 1-5.
Travel: Exit 128 off I-75. Proceed west on Rte 140 for one mile to downtown.

Albany

Booke Shoppe
2401-L Dawson Road 31707

Open Shop
(912) 436-5883

Collection: General stock of mostly used paperback.
# of Vols: 50,000 (used)
Hours: Tue-Sat 11-5:45.

Livingston Books
1129 West Broad Avenue 31707

Open Shop
(912) 883-7526

Collection: General stock of mostly paperback.
# of Vols: 100,000
Hours: Tue-Sat 10-6.

Alpharetta
(Map 7, page 114)

Charing Cross Booksellers
3000 Old Alabama Road, #120 30022

Open Shop
(770) 667-8319
Fax: (770) 448-7084

Collection: General stock of hardcover and paperback.
# of Vols: 8,000
Hours: Mon 1-7. Tue-Fri 11-7. Sat 9:30-6:30.
Services: Search service, accepts want lists, mail order.
Travel: Exit 8 off Rte 400. Proceed east on Haynes Bridge to Old Alabama. Shop is at the corner in Haynes Market Shopping Center.
Credit Cards: Yes
Owner: H. Lee Dunagan
Year Estab: 1992
Comments: Stock is approximately 65% hardcover.

Hollingsworth, Fine Books
2940 Francis Road 30004

By Appointment
(770) 410-9047

Collection: General stock.
# of Vols: 2,500
Specialties: Children's; illustrated; southern writers; Civil War; Southern Americana.
Services: Appraisals, search service, catalog, accepts want lists.

Credit Cards:	No
Owner:	Giles & Helen Hollingsworth
Year Estab:	1988
Comments:	Former owner of Atlanta Vintage Books in Chamblee.

Athens
(Map 7, page 114)

Blue Moon Books   **Open Shop**
282 East Clayton Street 30601   (706) 549-0993
                                                    E-mail: bluemoon@negia.net

Collection:	General stock of mostly new and some used hardcover and paperback and postcards.
# of Vols:	3,000+ (used)
Hours:	Mon-Sat 11:30-5:30.
Services:	Accepts want lists.
Travel:	Downtown, between Clayton and Broad.
Comments:	Stock is approximately 80% new. Used stock is evenly divided between hardcover and paperback.

Emeritus Books   **By Appointment**
145 Woodhaven Ridge 30606   (706) 546-0378

Collection:	Specialty
# of Vols:	6,000
Specialties:	Medicine; science.
Services:	Appraisals, catalog
Credit Cards:	No
Owner:	G.S.T. (Terry) Cavanagh
Year Estab:	1970

Jackson Street Books   **Open Shop**
260 North Jackson Street 30601   (706) 546-0245

Collection:	General stock of hardcover and paperback.
# of Vols:	42,000
Specialties:	Georgia; southern writers; first editions; general academic.
Hours:	Mon-Sat 11-6.
Services:	Appraisals, search service, accepts want lists.
Travel:	Downtown Athens, 1½ miles north of the University of Georgia.
Credit Cards:	Yes
Owner:	Susan & Edward Wilde
Year Estab:	1984
Comments:	A spacious shop with well labeled shelves and lots of fine books in most areas (with a heavy emphasis on the scholarly). Some of the shop's better books are kept in glass cases. Moderately priced. While the shop also has several shelves of paperbacks, this in no way diminishes the quality of the hardcover selections.

Atlanta
(Map 7, page 114 & Map 8, page 119)

A Book Nook   **Open Shop**
3342 Clairmont Road, NE 30329   (404) 633-1328

Collection:	General stock of used and new, hardcover and paperback, CDs and records, comics and videos.
# of Vols:	100,000+
Hours:	Mon-Sat 9-10:30 pm. Sun 10-10:30 pm.
Travel:	Off I-85, one mile east on Clairmont Rd. At corner of Buford Hwy.
Credit Cards:	Yes
Owner:	Alex Nunan
Year Estab:	1974
Comments:	Judging from the sound of the cash register which kept ringing during our visit, we suspect that this establishment must be a popular one with local book lovers. The owner is quick to concede that it's not likely you'll find a truly rare or antiquarian item in this large shop. What you will find, though, is a large selection of paperbacks and hardcovers, mostly of recent vintage and priced to sell. Approximately two thirds of the stock was paperback.

A Cappella Books   **Open Shop**
1133 Euclid Avenue 30307   (404) 681-5128

Collection:	General stock of hardcover and paperback.
# of Vols:	15,000
Specialties:	Modern literature; literary criticism; beat generation; music (non classical); baseball.
Hours:	Apr-Sep: Mon-Thu 11-10. Fri & Sat 11-midnight. Sun 12-7. Oct-Mar: Mon-Sat 11-7. Sun 12-6.
Services:	Search service, accepts want lists, mail order.
Travel:	Moreland Ave exit off I-20. Proceed north for one mile, then left onto Euclid. Shop is one block ahead on left. Located in city's bohemian district.
Credit Cards:	Yes
Owner:	Frank Reiss
Year Estab:	1989
Comments:	This neat and well organized shop was a pleasure to visit. The books on display were in generally good condition, were of mixed vintage and represented most subject areas though few in any great depth. A good portion of the stock reflected the type of community in which the shop is located (see above). A back room was devoted to paperbacks.

Antiquarian Books & Bindery   **Open Shop**
2855 Piedmont Road NE 30305-2767   (404) 814-0220
Web page: www.abcbooks.com/home/kaolink/   Fax: (404) 814-1324
                                                         E-mail: kaolink@msn.com

Collection:	Specialty with some general stock and ephemera.

# of Vols:	5,000
Specialties:	Early printed books.
Hours:	Mon-Fri 10-6. Sat 10-4.
Services:	Appraisals, search service, catalog, accepts want lists, hand binding.
Travel:	Buford Hwy exit off I-85 north. Left on Sydney Marcus Blvd, then right on Piedmont Rd. Shop is two block ahead on right.

Atlanta Book Exchange   **Open Shop**
1000 North Highland Avenue 30306   (404) 872-2665
Web page: www.creativeloafing.com/mall/beaver   Fax: (404) 876-1068

Collection:	General stock of hardcover and paperback.
# of Vols:	75,000
Specialties:	Literature; literary criticism; theology; history; biography, art; architecture.
Hours:	Mon-Sat 10-10. Sun 1-6.
Services:	Mail order.
Travel:	Corner of Virginia & North Highland.
Credit Cards:	Yes
Owner:	Charles & Beverly Henson
Year Estab:	1976
Comments:	A crowded shop with lots of nooks and crannies. The collection is a mixture of remainders, and reading copies of some slightly older volumes and very few truly old volumes. Moderately priced, but little out of the ordinary.

Back Pages   **Open Shop**
800 Miami Circle, NE, Ste 100   30324   (404) 231-9107

Collection:	General stock.
# of Vols:	4,000
Specialties:	History (scholarly); fine bindings; sets.
Hours:	Mon-Sat 10-5:30
Services:	Search service.
Travel:	Piedmont Rd exit off I-85. Proceed north on Piedmont to Miami Circle. Shop shares space with Books, Cases & Prints (see below).
Credit Cards:	Yes
Owner:	Howard McAbee
Year Estab:	1991

Banbury Cross   **By Appointment**
992 Oakdale Road, NE 30307   (404) 373-3511

Collection:	Specialty
# of Vols:	2,500
Specialties:	Children's (first editions).
Services:	Accepts want lists, mail order.
Credit Cards:	No
Owner:	Judy Gutterman
Year Estab:	1992

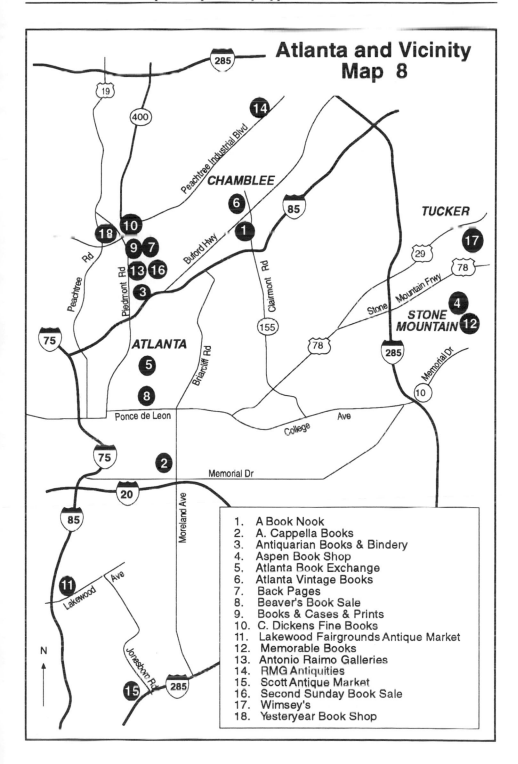

Atlanta and Vicinity
Map 8

CHAMBLEE

TUCKER

STONE MOUNTAIN

ATLANTA

Ponce de Leon

College Ave

Memorial Dr

Memorial Dr

Lakewood Ave

Jonesboro Rd

N

1. A Book Nook
2. A. Cappella Books
3. Antiquarian Books & Bindery
4. Aspen Book Shop
5. Atlanta Book Exchange
6. Atlanta Vintage Books
7. Back Pages
8. Beaver's Book Sale
9. Books & Cases & Prints
10. C. Dickens Fine Books
11. Lakewood Fairgrounds Antique Market
12. Memorable Books
13. Antonio Raimo Galleries
14. RMG Antiquities
15. Scott Antique Market
16. Second Sunday Book Sale
17. Wimsey's
18. Yesteryear Book Shop

(Atlanta)

Beaver's Book Sale   **Open Shop**
696-A Cleburne Terrace 30306   (404) 876-1068

Collection:	General stock of used paperbacks and hardcover and remainders.
# of Vols:	60,000
Hours:	Tue-Wed 11-8. Thu-Sat 11-10. Sun 12-8.
Travel:	Located in Plaza Shopping Center at intersection of Ponce de Leon and N. Highland.
Owner:	Charles & Beverly Henson

Books & Cases & Prints   **Open Shop**
800 Miami Circle, NE Ste. 100 30324   (404) 231-9107 (800) 788-9107
                                                          Fax: (404) 237-1062
                                                 E-mail: booksetc@compuserve.com

Collection:	Specialty books and some ephemera.
# of Vols:	12,000
Specialties:	Fine bindings; early printing; antiques; decorative arts; art; fore-edge paintings; some general stock.
Hours:	Mon-Sat 10-5:30.
Services:	Appraisals, search service, accepts want lists, mail order.
Travel:	See Back Pages above.
Credit Cards:	Yes
Owner:	Virginia Velleca
Year Estab:	1989
Comments:	The dealer also organizes and displays at the Second Sunday group sale. See below.

C. Dickens Fine, Rare and Collectible Books   **Open Shop**
3393 Peachtree Road, NE 30326   (404) 231-3825
Web page: www.cdickens.com   Fax: (404) 364-0713
                                                     E-mail: books@cdickens.com

Collection:	General stock.
# of Vols:	10,000
Specialties:	*Gone With The Wind*; Civil War; Charles Dickens; fiction; children's; science fiction; mystery; medicine.
Hours:	Mon-Sat 10-9. Sun 12-6.
Services:	Appraisals, search service, catalog.
Travel:	Lenox Rd exit off I-85 (north of Atlanta). Shop is located in lower level of Lenox Square Shopping Mall at corner of Lenox and Peachtree.
Credit Cards:	Yes
Owner:	Tom Hamm
Year Estab:	1977
Comments:	While most of the books we saw were in quite good condition and the store is attractively laid out with lots of sales help to assist the browser, in our travels we have seen many of the same books available else-

where at a much more competitive price. Our assumption (which we recognize could be flawed) is that the prices of the books reflect the rent paid for a location in an upscale mall.

G. Davis Rare Books
PO Box 8332 31106
Web page: www.antiqnet.com/gdavis

By Appointment
(404) 872-6084
Fax: (404) 874-0859

Collection:	Specialty
# of Vols:	2,000
Specialties:	Early printed books; fine bindings; sets; English and American literature and history (to 1901); fore-edge paintings; Ian Fleming.
Services:	Appraisals, accepts want lists, mail order.
Credit Cards:	Yes
Owner:	Greg Davis
Year Estab:	1992

Gallery 515
515 East Paces Ferry Road 30305

Open Shop
(404) 233-2911

Collection:	Specialty
Specialties:	Maps; ephemera; prints.
Hours:	Tue-Fri 10-6. Sat 11-5.
Services:	Accepts want lists.
Travel:	West Paces Ferry Rd exit off I-75. Proceed east on West Paces Ferry for about five miles. After crossing Peachtree Rd shop is about 1/4 mile ahead at intersection of Maple Dr and East Paces Ferry.
Credit Cards:	Yes
Owner:	Michael Sisk & Deborah McAfee
Year Estab:	1975

Hardy & Halpern
2575 Peachtree Road, NE
Plaza Towers, CU7 30305

By Appointment
(404) 261-4447
Fax: (404) 261-4673

Collection:	General stock and manuscripts.
# of Vols:	500-1,000
Services:	Appraisals, search service.
Credit Cards:	No
Owner:	Roderick Hardy & Jack Salling
Year Estab:	1970
Comments:	Primarily an appraisal firm that handles the sale of large private libraries. Inventory varies widely in both number and kind.

Lakewood Fairgrounds Antique Market
Off Lakewood Freeway

Antique Mall

Hours:	Second weekend of each month: Fri & Sat 9-6. Sun 10-5.
Travel:	Lakewood Freeway exit off I-85/I-75. Proceed east on Lakewood and follow signs for fairgrounds.

(Atlanta)

Laval Antiques   **By Appointment**
4092 East Brookhaven Dr, NE 30319   (404) 237-7389

Collection:	Specialty
# of Vols:	500+
Specialties:	French language books, primarily in fine bindings.
Owner:	June K. & Philippe Laval

McDonough Fine Art   **By Appointment**
2887 North Fulton Drive 30305   (404) 814-0533
                                                            Fax: (404) 814-1022

Collection:	Specialty books, maps and prints.
# of Vols:	1,000-2,000
Specialties:	Charles Dickens; fine bindings; natural history; color plate books; children's illustrated.
Services:	Appraisals, mail order, picture framing.
Credit Cards:	Yes
Owner:	Joseph D. McDonough
Year Estab:	1984

Old New York Book Shop   **By Appointment**
660 Spindlewick Drive 30350   (404) 881-1285   (770) 393-2997
                                                            Fax: (770) 393-1288

Collection:	General stock.
# of Vols:	5,000
Services:	Accepts want lists, catalog.
Credit Cards:	Yes
Owner:	Cliff Graubart
Year Estab:	1971

Antonio Raimo Galleries   **Open Shop**
700 Miami Circle, NE Ste 350 30324   (404) 841-9880
                                                            Fax: (404) 841-9230
                                                            E-mail: araimo@aol.com

Collection:	General stock and prints.
# of Vols:	10,000
Specialties:	Children's; pop-ups; women's studies; sets; fine bindings.
Hours:	Mon-Sat 9-6. Sun 12-6.
Services:	Appraisals, search service, accepts want lists, catalog.
Travel:	Off Piedmont Road and Sydney Marcus Blvd.
Credit Cards:	Yes
Year Estab:	1980

Scott Antique Market   **Antique Mall**
Jonesboro Road

Hours:	Second weekend of each month: Thu-Sun 9-6.
Travel:	Exit 40 off I-285. Proceed on Jonesboro Rd inside the loop. Market is in the old Atlanta Expo building.

Second Sunday Book Sale
764 Miami Circle, NE, Ste 206 30324

Open Shop
(404) 231-9107
(800) 788-9107

Collection:	General stock.
# of Vols:	10,000
Hours:	Second Sunday of each month 12-5:30.
Travel:	See Back Pages above.
Owner:	Virginia Velleca (Organizer)
Comments:	Sponsored by a group of area dealers.

Yesteryear Book Shop
3201 Maple Drive NE 30305

Open Shop
(404) 237-0163
Fax: (404) 365-0441

Collection:	Specialty books, maps, prints and ephemera.
# of Vols:	12,000
Specialties:	Modern first editions; Americana; Georgia; Southern Americana; Civil War; books about books; art; decorative arts; architecture; illustrated; autographs and documents; maps.
Hours:	Mon-Fri 10-5:30. Sat 11-4:30.
Services:	Appraisals, catalog, accepts want lists.
Travel:	In Buckhead neighborhood, about six miles north of downtown. Maple Dr is a few yards from intersection of Peachtree and Piedmont.
Credit Cards:	Yes
Owner:	Frank O. Walsh, III & Polly G. Fraser
Year Estab:	1971
Comments:	A modest sized shop with books attractively displayed. Most of the books appear to have been selected by the owners for their very good to fine condition. Prices reflect the condition of the books. As one never knows where the inveterate book hunter will find just the title he or she is looking for, this shop certainly deserves a visit. The owners also display at an antique mall in Marietta (see below).

Augusta
(Map 7, page 114)

Augusta Book Exchange
1631 Gordon Highway 30906

Open Shop
(706) 793-7796

Collection:	General stock of mostly paperback.
# of Vols:	3,000 (hardcover)
Hours:	Mon & Tue 10-6. Wed-Sat 10-8. Sun 1-6.

Augusta Book Exchange
592 Bobby Jones Expressway 30907

Open Shop
(706) 860-6553

Collection:	General stock of mostly paperback.
# of Vols:	1,000 (hardcover)
Hours:	Mon & Tue 10-6. Wed-Sat 10-8. Sun 1-6.

Estate Books   **Antique Mall**
At The Antique Market   Mall: (706) 860-7909
3179 Washington Road   Home: (706) 868-8564
Mailing address: 717 Stillwater Drive Augusta 30907

Collection:	General stock.
# of Vols:	5,000
Specialties:	History; biography; cookbooks.
Hours:	Mon-Sat 10-7. Sun 12-7.
Travel:	Washington Rd exit off I-20. Proceed west one mile. Shop is in Village West Shopping Center.
Owner:	Barry Speth

Research Ltd.   **By Appointment**
3214 York Drive 30909   (706) 738-1037

Collection:	General stock.
# of Vols:	10,000-12,000
Specialties:	Georgia; Southern Americana.
Services:	Search service, accepts want lists, mail order.
Owner:	Esther Young Mewihsen
Year Estab:	1940's

Bishop
(Map 7, page 114)

Book Worm   **Open Shop**
5531 Macon Highway 30621   (706) 769-5986

Collection:	General stock.
# of Vols:	10,000
Hours:	Daily 10-5.
Travel:	On Rte 441, south of Watkinsville bypass. Shop is on the right, inside Reed's Odd's and Ends.
Credit Cards:	No
Owner:	Janice Reed
Comments:	The sign outside this establishments reads: "old books." That is not an exaggeration. At least two rooms in this "odds & ends" shop have used book on display, many of them of a more common variety and a few sporting interesting titles. The general condition of the books could be classified as fair to almost good. Considering the condition of the books, don't expect to find bargains.

Brunswick
(Map 7, page 114)

The Book Shop, Inc.   **Open Shop**
1519 Newcastle Street 31520   (912) 262-6708   (888) 262-6708
                                                                    Fax: (912) 262-6938
                                                        E-mail: b_hobson@interloc.com

Collection:	General stock of new and used hardcover and paperback.

# of Vols:	5,000+
Specialties:	Children's; southern writers; Civil War; cookbooks; religion.
Hours:	Mon-Sat 9-6. Sun by appointment.
Services:	Search service.
Travel:	Exit 7 off I-95. Proceed south on Rte 341 which becomes Newcastle St in downtown.
Credit Cards:	Yes
Owner:	Virginia & Harold Hobson Hicks
Year Estab:	1968
Comments:	If your tastes include southern literature or anything else hailing from south of the Mason Dixon line, your chances of finding a copy here are fairly good. Whether or not the owner has the particular item you're searching for, she'll certainly do her best to find it for you as she is one persistent book person. In addition to the specialties listed above, the open shop also carries new books, stationary and gift items. If you have a few extra minutes, enjoy a cup of coffee with the charming owner. And, if you're lucky, you may have an opportunity to visit the owner's warehouse where the real treasures are stored. In all of our travels this is the only shop we have visited whose owner takes pride in having almost gone to jail for the right to sell books.

Carrollton
(Map 7, page 114)

Horton's Books & Gifts   **Open Shop**
410 Adamson Square 30117   (770) 832-8021
                                              Fax: (770) 838-1152
                               E-mail: ddittmanhortons@juno.com

Collection:	General stock of new and used hardcover and paperback.
# of Vols:	15,000
Hours:	Mon-Fri 9-6. Sat 9-5:30.
Services:	Appraisals, accepts want lists.
Travel:	Exit 5 off I-20. Proceed west on Rte 61 which becomes Rte 166 and goes through town to Adamson Square.
Credit Cards:	Yes
Year Estab:	1892
Comments:	If you're looking for a book store that displays attractive new books (including some charming children's books), as well as greeting cards, framed pictures, religious items and even some attractive canes, you'll find them all here. On the other hand, if you're looking for rare or unusual used books, we were not able to spot any during our brief visit to this shop's lower level. What we did see were lots of recent vintage used paperback and hardcover items selling for the usual fraction of their original cost.

Cartersville

Candlewick Book Shop   **Open Shop**
21 North Wall Street 30120   (770) 382-7276

Collection:	General stock of mostly paperback.
# of Vols:	15,000+
Hours:	Tue-Sat 10-5:30.

Chamblee
(Map 8, page 119)

Atlanta Vintage Books   **Open Shop**
3660 Clairmont Road 30341   (770) 457-2919
Web page: www.abebooks.com/home/AVB/   Fax: (770) 458-5637
                                              E-mail: aotten@worldnet.att.net

Collection:	General stock and ephemera.
# of Vols:	40,000+
Specialties:	Children's; military; travel; exploration; black studies; modern first editions.
Hours:	Mon-Sat 10-6.
Services:	Appraisals, search service, catalog, accepts want lists.
Travel:	Two miles north of Clairmont exit off I-85. Clairmont Rd is Rte 155. Shop is on left, just after crossing Dresden.
Credit Cards:	Yes
Owner:	Alice & Clarke Otten
Year Estab:	1987
Comments:	One of the most attractive shops we had the pleasure of visiting during our South Atlantic trip. The shop offers quality books in every category, attractively displayed with a real touch of class. One part of the store carried primitive and oriental artifacts in addition to books. Whether or not you make a purchase here, you'll surely enjoy your visit and see items of every description that would tantalize the most discriminating book person.

RMG Antiquities   **Antique Mall**
At Antique City   (770) 458-7131
5180A Peachtree Industrial Boulevard 30341   Fax: (770) 451-7173

Collection:	General stock.
# of Vols:	3,000+
Specialties:	Literature; illustrated; fine bindings.
Hours:	Mon-Sat 10-6. Sun 12-6.
Travel:	I-85 to I-285 westbound. Peachtree Ind Blvd South exit off I-285. Shop is 1½ miles ahead on right.
Owner:	Robert M. Giannetti

Cleveland

The Keystone
897 South Main Street, #8 30528

Open Shop
(706) 865-9826

Collection:	General stock of mostly used paperback.
# of Vols:	18,000 (used)
Hours:	Mon-Sat 10-8.
Travel:	On Rte 129, about one mile south of town square.
Comments:	Stock is approximately 80% used, 80% of which is paperback.

Conyers

Book Shelf
875 Flat Shoals Road SE 30094

Open Shop
(770) 922-2566

Collection.	General stock of mostly paperback.
# of Vols:	15,000+
Hours:	Mon-Wed 10-5:30. Thu & Fri 10-7. Sat 10-3.

Cumming
(Map 7, page 114)

D. Brooke & Son Booksellers
PO Box 611 30028

By Appointment
(770) 781-5047

E-mail: dbrookeandson@compuserve.com

Web page: www.abebooks.com/home/DBROOKE/

Collection:	General stock.
# of Vols:	12,000
Specialties:	Modern first editions; signed; Civil War; Americana.
Services:	Mail order.
Credit Cards:	Yes
Owner:	Dennis Richards
Year Estab:	1996

Humpus Bumpus Books!
703 Atlanta Road 30130

Open Shop
(770) 781-9705
Fax: (770) 781-4676

Collection:	General stock of new and used paperback and hardcover.
# of Vols:	15,000 (used)
Hours:	Mon-Sat 10-8. Sun 1-5.
Services:	Accepts want lists.
Travel:	Exit 14 off Rte 400. At end of ramp, make right onto Rte 20 north. After 3/4 of a mile, turn left onto Atlanta Rd. Shop is 3/4 of a mile ahead in a free standing building in the Merchant Square Shopping Center.
Credit Cards:	Yes
Owner:	Paul Cossman
Year Estab:	1990
Comments:	Stock is approximately 35% used, 75% of which is paperback.

Dahlonega
(Map 7, page 114)

Quigley's Antiques and Rare Books   **Open Shop**
170 North Public Square 30533   (706) 864-0161

Collection: General stock and ephemera.
# of Vols: 5,000
Specialties: Children's; Civil War; poetry.
Hours: Mon-Sat 11-5. Sun 12-5.
Services: Accepts want lists.
Travel: Rte 60 into Dahlonega. Shop is on northwest corner of public square.
Credit Cards: Yes
Owner: Tim Quigley
Year Estab: 1994
Comments: Located in the center of a charming square surrounded by antique and
                   specialty shops, restaurants and a gold mining museum. The shop offers
                   lots of oldies in mixed condition and more than a few collectibles. Not the
                   place for your typical last year's best seller. Priced accordingly.

Dalton
(Map 7, page 114)

Book Nook of Dalton   **Open Shop**
1207 Cleveland Highway 30721   (706) 226-8886

Collection: General stock of paperback and hardcover.
Hours: Mon-Sat 10-6.

Clements & Christie Books   **Open Shop**
815-A North Tibbs Road 30720   (706) 278-1205

Collection: General stock of mostly hardcover.
# of Vols: 10,000-20,000
Specialties: Georgia; Southern Americana.
Hours: Mon-Thu 9-4. Fri 9-1.
Services: Appraisals, accepts want lists, mail order, book binding and restoration.
Travel: Exit 136 off I-75. Proceed west on Walnut Ave for one block, then
                   right on College Dr, and left on Tibbs. Shop is about 3/4 mile ahead on
                   left.
Credit Cards: Yes
Owner: David Clements
Year Estab: 1989
Comments: Mindful of the dangers of traveling miles out of one's way only to find
                   a shop closed, we phoned this establishment at least three times the day
                   before and the day of our planned visit. On each occasion, a recording
                   advised of the shop's hours (see above). However, as our calls were
                   made during those very hours, we were reluctant to drive the extra 2½
                   hours without a live confirmation that the store would indeed be open
                   when we arrived. If you visit here, please let us know what we missed.

Danielsville
(Map 7, page 114)

McMeans Books
Route 3, Box 3181 30633

By Appointment
(706) 789-3206
E-mail: jmcmeans@negia.net

Collection:	General stock and ephemera.
# of Vols:	5,000
Specialties:	Southern literature and history; modern first editions; maps.
Services:	Search service, accepts want lists.
Credit Cards:	No
Owner:	Judi & Jim McMeans
Year Estab:	1986
Comments:	Also displays at the Lakewood Fairgrounds Antique Market in Atlanta (see above).

Decatur

Thomas Dorn - Bookseller
PO Box 2585 30031

By Appointment
(404) 320-6010

Collection:	Specialty
# of Vols:	8,000
Specialties:	Literary first editions; fiction in translation; signed; private press.
Services:	Catalog, accepts want lists.
Credit Cards:	No
Year Estab:	1990

Duluth

Books For Less
2180 Pleasant Hill Road, A2 30136

Open Shop
(770) 623-6884

Collection:	General stock of mostly paperback.
# of Vols:	60,000
Hours:	Mon-Sat 10-7. Sun 12-6.

Fort Oglethorpe

Books & Bytes
1503 Lafayette Road 30742

Open Shop
(706) 861-0774

Collection:	General stock of new and mostly paperback used.
# of Vols:	50,000+
Hours:	Mon-Fri 9-8:30. Sat 9-6.
Comments:	Stock is approximately 50% used, 85% of which is paperback.

Gainesville
(Map 7, page 114)

Appletree Books   **Open Shop**
5013 Cleveland Highway   30506   (770) 983-9198
                                                          E-mail: appletree@applied.net

Collection:	General stock of hardcover and paperback.
# of Vols:	15,000+
Specialties:	Modern first editions; children's; older fiction.
Hours:	Wed-Sat 10-6.
Services:	Search service, accepts want lists, mail order.
Travel:	Exit 7 off I-85. Turn west on Rte 23 (Old Cornelia Hwy) for a very short distance, then right onto Limestone Pkwy. At end of parkway, turn right and continue north on Rte 129. Shop is about 10 miles ahead on left in a stand alone building that looks like a private residence.
Credit Cards:	Yes
Owner:	Ann Dayton
Year Estab:	1997
Comments:	This shop carries a modest selection of fairly recent vintage items along with a few old timers and a fair share of paperbacks. While we were unable to spot any truly rare items here, the shop is out of the way enough to suggest that possibility.

Discount Books   **Open Shop**
235 Pearl Nix Pkwy, #7   30501   (770) 532-2305

Collection:	General stock of new, remainders and mostly used paperback.
# of Vols:	600+ (used hardcover)
Hours:	Mon-Sat 10-7. Sun 1-5.

Jekyll Island
(Map 7, page 114)

Jekyll Books and Antiques   **Open Shop**
101 Old Plantation Road   31527   Tel & Fax: (912) 635-3077
                                                          E-mail: thehamer@thebest.net

Collection:	General stock and ephemera.
# of Vols:	30,000
Specialties:	History; literature (modern and world); travel; mystery; Georgia; South America; Caribbean.
Hours:	Daily 9:30-5:30.
Services:	Appraisals, search service, catalog, accepts want lists.
Travel:	Exit 6 off I-95. Proceed to Jekyll Island. Turn right at first "historic district" sign, then right into complex at second "historic district" sign. Shop is immediately to your right in the Goodyear Infirmary Building.
Credit Cards:	Yes
Owner:	Robert Hamer & John Eckhoff
Year Estab:	1995

Comments: When in Georgia we strongly recommend that you spend at least one half to a full day on the island that is the home of this book store; it certainly is a national treasure and will allow you to take a pleasant rest from your book hunting endeavors. The shop offers an opportunity for book hunters with both a comfortable wallet as well as those buying on a budget; in one of the shop's specialty areas, we saw first editions, not always in the best condition, selling at a rather healthy price while in another section, books in the same genre were available at most reasonable prices.

Lawrenceville
(Map 7, page 114)

More Than Books   **Open Shop**
155B Gwinnett Drive 30245   Tel & Fax. (770) 513-1532
                                                                        E-mail: morethanbooks@worldnet.att.net

Collection: General stock of paperback and hardcover.
# of Vols: 12,000 (hardcover)
Specialties: Computer software and books; religion (Christian).
Hours: Mon-Fri 11-7. Sat 11-6.
Services: Accepts want lists, mail order.
Travel: Northbound on I-85: Exit 41. Proceed east on Rte 316 to Sugar Loaf Pkwy, then right on Sugar Loaf, left on Lawrenceville Hwy (Rte 29) and right on Gwinnett Dr. Shop is on right after the school buildings.
Credit Cards: Yes
Owner: Jack Mason
Year Estab: 1996
Comments: A nice community shop. Most of the hardcover books we saw were reading copies of fairly recent vintage in good condition and sporting dust jackets.

Lilburn
(Map 7, page 114)

Paul Blicksilver, Antiquarian Bookseller   **By Appointment**
3235 Alcazar Drive 30047   (404) 296-5933

Collection: General stock.
# of Vols: 10,000+
Hours: Evenings and weekends.
Services: Search service.
Credit Cards: Yes
Year Estab: 1981
Comments: The dealer also operates an open shop in Stone Mountain that stocks paperbacks and reading copies.

Book Nook   **Open Shop**
4664 Highway 29 30047   (770) 564-9462

Collection: General stock of paperback and hardcover, CD's, cassettes, movies and comics.

# of Vols:	200,000
Hours:	Mon-Sat 10-8. Sun 1-8.
Travel:	Indian Trail exit off I-85. Proceed east on Indian Trail to Rte 29, then north on Lawrenceville Hwy. Shop is just ahead on right.
Credit Cards:	Yes
Owner:	Alex Nunan
Year Estab:	1991
Comments:	See comments on Atlanta store.

Lyons
(Map 7, page 114)

Bellmore's Books   **Open Shop**
132 SE Broad Street 30436   (912) 526-4456

Collection:	General stock of hardcover and paperback.
# of Vols:	75,000
Hours:	Wed-Sat 10-6.
Travel:	Broad St is Rte 280/292.
Credit Cards:	No
Year Estab:	1988
Comments:	Stock is evenly divided between hardcover and paperback.

Macon
(Map 7, page 114)

Aequanimitas Medical Books   **By Appointment**
PO Box 13527 31208   (912) 471-6994
                                                                                          Fax: (912) 471-9410
                                                                                 E-mail: aeqbks@hom.net

Collection:	Specialty
# of Vols:	4,000
Specialties:	Medicine
Services:	Appraisals, search service, catalog.
Credit Cards:	Yes
Owner:	Alice & Martin Dalton
Year Estab:	1995

Golden Bough Vintage Books   **Open Shop**
371 Cotton Avenue 31201   (912) 744-2446
Web page: www.goldenbough.com   E-mail: lilly@goldenbough.com

Collection:	General stock.
# of Vols:	10,000
Specialties:	Southern Americana; Middle Georgia writers; Civil War; modern first editions; literature; art.
Hours:	Tue-Sat 10-6.
Services:	Search service, mail order.
Travel:	From I-75, take I-16 cutoff to Spring St exit. Make right onto Spring,

then left onto Mulberry, right onto Second and right onto Cotton. Shop is about one block ahead on right in downtown.

Credit Cards:	Yes
Owner:	Lilly Brannon
Year Estab:	1989
Comments:	A quality shop with a modest stock of books in generally good to very condition. Reasonably priced and easy to browse.

Madison

Cover to Cover Books   **Open Shop**
1402 Eatonton Road 30650   (706) 343-0089

Collection:	General stock of mostly used paperback.
# of Vols:	14,000
Hours:	Mon-Fri 10-6. Sat 10-4.

Marietta
(Map 7, page 114)

Book Exchange High Roads   **Open Shop**
1951 Canton Road 30066   (770) 427-4848

Collection:	General stock of mostly paperback.
# of Vols:	500,000
Hours:	Mon-Sat 10-6. Sun 1-5.
Travel:	Exit 114A off I-75. At first light off ramp turn right on Sandy Plains and proceed for one block, then left on Canton Rd. Shop is on left in Canton Road Plaza.
Comments:	We would not be surprised if there were more than half a million paperback books among the numerous alcoves dotting the floor of this establishment. On the other hand, we would be surprised if there were more than 1,000 hardcover volumes scattered throughout the shop, few of which would not be more readily available and easier to locate elsewhere.

Book Nook   **Open Shop**
595 Roswell Street 30060   (770) 499-9914

Collection:	General stock of mostly paperback and CDs, cassettes and movies.
# of Vols:	30,000
Hours:	Daily 11:30-7:30
Travel:	Marietta Loop exit off I-75. Proceed west on Rte 120 (Marietta Pkwy). Roswell St is Rte 120.
Owner:	Alex Nunan
Comments:	See comments for Atlanta store.

Downs Books   **Open Shop**
351 Washington Avenue   (770) 971-1103
Mailing address: 774 Mary Ann Drive, NE Marietta 30068

Collection:	General stock.

(Marietta)

# of Vols:	15,000
Specialties:	Children's; Georgia; Civil War.
Hours:	Wed & Sat 10-4 and other times by appointment.
Travel:	Rte 120 (Marietta Loop exit) off I-75. Take loop west to Cobb Pkwy (Rte 41). Proceed north on Rte 41 to Roswell Rd. Left onto Roswell, then right onto Fairground and left onto Washington. Shop is across from cemetery, in the rear of building.
Credit Cards:	No
Owner:	Katherine Downs
Year Estab:	1981
Comments:	A small but compact two room shop with a nice selection of mixed vintage books in mixed condition.

Georgia Bookman   **Antique Mall**
At Dupre's Antique Market   (770) 428-2667
17 Whitlock Avenue SW   30064

Collection:	General stock, prints and ephemera.
# of Vols:	2,000+
Specialties:	Southern history; military; Civil War; literature; art; antique reference; cookbooks.
Hours:	Mon-Sat 10-5:30. Sun 1-5.
Services:	Appraisals, accepts want lists.
Travel:	Located in historic town square.
Credit Cards:	Yes
Owner:	Frank O. Walsh, III & Polly G. Fraser
Year Estab:	1996
Comments:	Owners also operate an open shop in Atlanta. See Yesteryear Book Shop above.

Robert Murphy, Bookseller   **By Appointment**
3113 Bunker Hill Road 30062   (770) 973-1523
                                                         Fax: (770) 973-3291

Collection:	Specialty books and related material.
# of Vols:	2,000
Specialties:	Movies; autographs.
Services:	Catalog, accepts want lists.
Year Estab:	1970

Page One, Antiques   **Antique Mall**
At Mountain Mercantile   Mall: (770) 429-1889
315 Church Street   Home: (770) 971-2171
Mailing address: 1765 Holly Springs Road Marietta 30062

Collection:	General stock.
# of Vols:	1,000
Specialties:	Regional; political; cookbooks; children's; first editions.

Hours:	Mon-Sat 10:30-5. Sun 1-5.
Services:	Accepts want lists.
Travel:	N. Marietta Pkwy (Rte 120 Loop) off I-75. Proceed to Church St, then turn left on Church. Shop is just north of town square on right.
Credit Cards:	Yes
Owner:	Neal & Jo Ellen Page
Year Estab:	1991

Pot Luck Books   **Open Shop**
3721 Austell Road SW 30060   (770) 319-5994

Collection:	General stock of mostly paperback.
# of Vols:	15,000
Hours:	Mon-Fri 10-6. Sat 10-5.
Travel:	Exit 111 (Delk Rd) off I-75. Proceed south on Rte 280 for about four miles to Austell, then right onto Austell. Shop is about five miles ahead, on left, in a small shopping center.
Comments:	It would be embarrassing to reveal the not so gentle disputes the authors sometimes have about which shops to visit while researching this book. David lost this battle. After several corrections in the above travel directions, we finally reached this shop only to discover lots of CDs, videos, paperbacks and, oh yes, a few hardcover books. We hope we have saved our readers valuable time and effort by making this report.

McDonough
(Map 7, page 114)

Pleasant Hill Books   **Open Shop**
512 Nail Road 30253   (770) 957-9835

Collection:	General stock.
# of Vols:	8,000-10,000
Specialties:	Old fiction; Southern Americana.
Hours:	Wed & Sat 10-5. Other times by appointment.
Travel:	Exit 70 off I-75. Proceed west on Rte 20 for one mile to Nail Drive, then right on Nail. At fork, bear left onto Nail Road. Shop is 1/4 mile head in a residence.
Credit Cards:	No
Owner:	Ramona Beshcar
Year Estab:	1993

Milledgeville
(Map 7, page 114)

The Book Corner   **Open Shop**
101 West Hancock Street 31061   (912) 452-0937
                                          E-mail: book@accucom.net

Collection:	General stock of hardcover and paperback and ephemera.
# of Vols:	25,000
Specialties:	Southern Americana; children's.

Hours:	Mon-Sat 10-6.
Services:	Appraisals, search service, accepts want lists, mail order.
Travel:	Rte 441 (Wayne St) into downtown Milledgeville. If proceeding south, turn left on Hancock St. If northbound, stay on Rte 441 to corner of Hancock and Wayne.
Credit Cards:	Yes
Owner:	Larry & Elaine Raulerson
Year Estab:	1993
Comments:	This shop offers an almost equal balance between paperbacks and hardcover volumes, including an interesting selection of older books in mixed condition, along with a scattering of ephemera and some non book collectibles. Prices are reasonable. The kind of place where you may well find that certain book you've been seeking.

Newnan
(Map 7, page 114)

Clemens & Co. Used Books   **Open Shop**
284A Bullsboro Drive 30263   (770) 304-0017

Collection:	General stock of paperback and hardcover.
# of Vols:	45,000
Specialties:	Military; science fiction; fantasy; mystery; modern first editions.
Hours:	Mon-Sat 10-7. Sun 1-6 (but best to conform).
Services:	Accepts want lists, mail order.
Travel:	Exit 9 off I-85. Proceed west on Rte 34 (Bullsboro Dr) for 1.1 miles. Shop is on right in Newborn Shopping Center.
Credit Cards:	Yes
Owner:	John Leidner
Year Estab:	1994
Comments:	An easy and spacious shop to browse with two large rooms each shelving paperbacks down their respective center aisles and hardcover books along the outer walls. Most of the hardcover volumes we saw wore dust jackets and were of fairly recent vintage. While not necessarily rich in collectibles or older volumes, it was clear to us from our brief visit that the local community finds this shop inviting.

Guy's Book Nook   **Open Shop**
32 Perry Street 30263   (770) 253-1769

Collection:	General stock of paperback and hardcover.
# of Vols:	5,000+
Hours:	Tue-Sat 10-5.
Services:	Search service.
Travel:	Rte 34 to Jackson St in downtown. Left on Jackson, left on East Broad and right on Perry. Shop is just ahead on the right.
Credit Cards:	No
Owner:	Bunny Guy
Year Estab:	1996

Comments: A modest sized shop with a mix of paperbacks and hardcover books, most of the latter being in mixed condition and of mixed vintage. Some items were overpriced, some on target, making one wonder how such matters are determined.

Norcross

Corners Book Exchange   **Open Shop**
5450 Peachtree Parkway 30092   (770) 729-8660

Collection: General stock of mostly paperback.
# of Vols: 70,000
Hours: Mon-Fri 10-6. Sat 10-5.

Riverdale
(Map 7, page 114)

Book Nook   **Open Shop**
6569 Riverdale Road 30274   (770) 994-3444

Collection: General stock of mostly paperback and hardcover, CDs, cassettes, movies and comics.
# of Vols: 100,000
Hours: Mon-Sat 11:30-7:30. Sun 1-7:30.
Travel::   I-85 to I-285 East, then I-75 south to Rte 85. Proceed south on Rte 85 into Riverdale. Right on Howard St and continue straight ahead. Shop is in Chateau Plaza shopping center.
Credit Cards: Yes
Owner: Alex Nunan
Year Estab: 1997
Comments: See comments for Atlanta store.

Rome
(Map 7, page 114)

Booklover's Den   **Open Shop**
524 Broad Street 30161   Tel & Fax: (706) 295-5988

Collection: General stock of mostly used paperback and hardcover.
# of Vols: 85,000 (used)
Specialties: Southern Americana; Civil War; religion; new age.
Hours: Mon-Thu 10-6. Fri 10-7. Sat 10-5:30. Sun 1-5.
Travel: In downtown.
Credit Cards: Yes
Owner: George Anderson
Year Estab: 1993
Comments: This shop has books galore, the vast majority of which are in fair to near good condition. The great pity is that the shop is so overcrowded that one can hardly find space to stand in in order to peruse the titles. What the owner needs is a larger shop (we were advised that this search is already underway) with more display space and/or a slightly

better way to organize titles or the removal of some of the excess books
that can't be displayed properly. A patient scout might well find some
items of interest here.

Reader's Paradise   **Open Shop**
411 Broad Street 30161   (706) 232-4838

Collection: General stock of mostly paperbacks and comics.
# of Vols: 35,000
Hours: Mon-Sat 10-6.

Roswell
(Map 7, page 114)

A Book Deal   **Open Shop**
10479 Alpharetta Highway 30075   (770) 587-5377

Collection: General stock of paperback, hardcover and comics.
# of Vols: 25,000+
Hours: Mon-Fri 10-6. Sat 10-5.
Travel: Rte 400 to Holcomb Bridge Rd, then left on Alpharetta Hwy. Shop is .2
                 mile ahead on left.
Comments: Stock is approximately 75% paperback.

Roswell Book Store   **Open Shop**
11055 Alpharetta Highway 30076   (770) 992-8485

Collection: General stock of paperback and hardcover.
# of Vols: 100,000
Hours: Mon-Wed & Fri 10-6. Thu 1-8. Sat 10-5.
Travel: Rte 400 to Holcomb Bridge (Rte 140), then west on Holcomb Bridge to
                 Alpharetta and north on Alpharetta (Rte 120) for one mile. Turn right
                 on Sun Valley Dr and make an immediate left into parking lot. (The
                 shop is located on the building's lower level and the entrance is off
                 Sun Valley Dr, not Alpharetta Hwy.)
Comments: While the stock in this shop is overwhelmingly paperback, one can
                 find some hardcover items of mixed vintage. Recent titles are easily
                 recognizable and older items (1930's-1960's) are referred to as "col-
                 lectibles." Despite these observations, a sharp eye at the right time
                 could well reveal a gem that we may have missed.

Saint Simons Island
(Map 7, page 114)

Beachview Books   **Open Shop**
215 Mallory Street 31522   (912) 638-7282
                                           E-mail: beachview@thebestnet.com

Collection: General stock of hardcover and paperback.
# of Vols: 10,000-15,000
Hours: Daily 10-5:30.
Services: Accepts want lists, mail order.

Travel:	From I-95, take causeway to St. Simons Is. At end of causeway, turn right on Kings Way, then right on Mallory. Shop is a block ahead on right.
Credit Cards:	Yes
Owner:	Nancy Thomason
Year Estab:	1976
Comments:	Considering its location in the heart of a tourist area, we anticipated a neater, more attractive shop than the one we found. The shop carries hardcover books in mixed condition that appeared to be shelved haphazardly. We note that as our visit occurred late in the day, it might well have been that the store had been inundated by buyers earlier and that by the following morning the shelves would be neatly arranged again. If you have a chance to visit here, we would be interested in hearing from you.

Forgotten Lore   **By Appointment**
130 Brockinton Drive 31522   (912) 638-7897

Collection:	General stock.
# of Vols:	3,000
Specialties:	Illustrated
Services:	Accepts want lists.
Credit Cards:	No
Owner:	Ed Ginn
Year Estab:	1977

Savannah
(Map 7, page 114)

Book Lady   **Open Shop**
17 West York Street 31401   (912) 233-3628

Collection:	General stock.
# of Vols:	10,000
Specialties:	Georgia; black studies; Southeastern Americana.
Hours:	Mon-Fri 10-5. Sat 10-2.
Services:	Search service, accepts want lists, mail order.
Travel:	Exit 17 off I-95. Proceed east on I-16 to end into Savannah. Continue to York. Right on York. Shop about three blocks ahead (just before Bull St) on right, across from post office.
Credit Cards:	No
Owner:	Anita Raskin
Year Estab:	1984
Comments:	A quaint shop with attractive books, many with art or regional themes such as Georgia's Low Country, attractively displayed. In addition to the main display area in the front of the shop, there are two smaller rooms in the rear. Several shelves had "bargain books." While most subject areas are represented in the collection, both the size of the shop and the size of the collection make it impossible for any one subject to be covered in great depth.

(Savannah)

Books On Bay   **Open Shop**
11 West Bay Street 31401   (912) 231-8485

Collection:	General stock of hardcover and paperback.
# of Vols:	15,000+
Hours:	Mon-Sat 11-5. Sun 12-6.
Services:	Search service.
Travel:	I-16 to the end. Continue on Montgomery St (going around the square) to Bay St. Right on Bay. Shop is three blocks ahead on right.
Credit Cards:	Yes
Owner:	Beth L. Walker
Year Estab:	1996
Comments:	A combination used book shop and coffee shop. The collection (both paperback and hardcover items) was varied enough with representation in most areas. The majority of the items we saw were of fairly recent vintage and most appeared to be reading copies.

Dolphin Book Exchange   **Open Shop**
11615 Abercorn Street 31419   (912) 920-0354

Collection:	General stock of mostly paperback.
# of Vols:	25,000
Hours:	Mon-Sat 10-9. Sun 12-6.
Travel:	Exit 16 off I-95. Proceed east on Rte 204 which becomes Abercorn. Shop is on the right in Media Play Plaza, across from St. Joseph's Hospital.
Comments:	With apologies to those dealers who refer to their shops as "exchanges" but who nonetheless carry an ample supply of hardcover books, this shop fits the more traditional mold. The shop is 95% to 98% paperback with only a small selection of hardcover books. While clearly such a shop meets the needs and desire of its customers, it does not, in our view, require a lengthy visit.

Jacqueline Levine   **By Appointment**
107 East Oglethorpe Avenue 31401   (912) 233-8519

Collection:	General stock.
# of Vols:	4,000-5,000
Specialties:	Exploration; nautical; Georgia; fore-edge paintings.
Services:	Catalog
Credit Cards:	No
Year Estab:	1963

The Printed Page   **By Appointment**
211 West Jones Street 31401   (912) 234-5612

Collection:	General stock.
# of Vols:	4,000-5,000
Specialties:	Southern Americana; Civil War.
Services:	Appraisals, accepts want lists, mail order.

Credit Cards:	No
Owner:	Rita Trotz
Year Estab:	1966

V & J Duncan Antique Maps, Prints & Books   **Open Shop**
12 East Taylor Street 31401   (912) 232-0338
Fax: (912) 232-3489

Collection:	Specialty books, maps and prints.
# of Vols:	1,500
Specialties:	Regional Americana (books only). Maps and prints cover all geographic areas and subjects.
Hours:	Mon-Sat 10-5.
Services:	Appraisals, accepts want lists, mail order.
Travel:	On Monterey Square.
Credit Cards:	Yes
Owner:	Virginia & John Duncan
Year Estab:	1983

Senoia

Book Stop & Swap   **Open Shop**
2594 Highway 85 South 30276   (770) 599-8200

Collection:	General stock of mostly paperback.
# of Vols:	15,000
Hours:	Daily, except closed Wed & Sun, 12-6.
Comments:	Stock is approximately 80% paperback.

Flintside Gallery   **By Appointment**
1200 Sid Hunter Road 30276   Tel & Fax: (770) 254-0334
E-mail: flintside@worldnet.att.net

Collection:	Specialty books, prints and ephemera and sporting collectibles and art.
# of Vols:	2,500
Specialties:	Hunting; fishing; natural history; southern history; southern literature.
Credit Cards:	No
Owner:	Frank Jarrell
Year Estab:	1974

Sharpsburg
(Map 7, page 114)

Banks Books   **Antique Mall**
At Collector's Corner Mini Mall   Mall: (770) 251-6835
8861 Highway 54   Home: (770) 463-3370
Mailing address: PO Box 590 Palmetto 30268

Collection:	General stock.
# of Vols:	10,000
Specialties:	Civil War; religion; Georgia; Southern Americana.
Hours:	Mon-Sat 10-6. Sun 1-6.

Services:	Search service, accepts want lists.
Travel:	Intersection of Rtes 54 & 34, 12 miles east of exit 9 off I-85. Shop is on the second floor.
Credit Cards:	Yes
Owner:	H. Douglas Banks
Year Estab:	1991
Comments:	Most of the books here fit into the "older" category. If the shop's specialties are of interest to you, you may find some unique titles to whet your appetite. And, if you have extra time, you may find some of the other booths in this antique/collectible/crafts mall worth perusing. At the time of our visit, the number of books on display was less than the number indicated above.

Smyrna

Epona Books   **By Appointment**
1800 Mackinaw Place 30080   (770) 436-1332
                                                      E-mail: eponabks@interloc.com

Collection:	Specialty with some general stock.
# of Vols:	4,000-5,000
Specialties:	Mystery; horses; dogs; modern first editions.
Services:	Search service, catalog, accepts want lists.
Credit Cards:	Yes
Owner:	Linda Voss
Year Estab:	1982

Stockbridge

Book End   **Open Shop**
6041 North Henry Boulevard 30281   (770) 474-1032

Collection:	General stock of mostly paperback.
# of Vols:	20,000
Hours:	Mon-Wed 11-7. Thu-Sat 11-8. Sun 12-6.

The Book Place   **Open Shop**
5222-H North Henry Boulevard 30281   (770) 389-3700
                                                             Fax: (770) 507-6703
                                                 E-mail: kkimsey@mindspring.com

Collection:	General stock of mostly paperback.
# of Vols:	30,000
Hours:	Mon-Sat 11-6.

Stone Mountain
(Map 8, page 119)

Americana Books   **By Appointment**
5717 Wells Circle 30087   (770) 879-5816

Collection:	Specialty books and ephemera.

# of Vols:	2,000
Specialties:	Civil War; southern and regional Americana (emphasis on history and literature); Native Americans.
Owner:	David Hamilton
Comments:	Also displays at Lakewood Fairgrounds Antique Market in Atlanta. See above.

Aspen Book Shop   **Open Shop**
5986 Memorial Drive 30083   (404) 296-5933

Collection:	General stock of paperback and hardcover and remainders.
# of Vols:	100,000
Specialties:	Civil War; black studies; cookbooks; fiction.
Hours:	Mon-Fri 10-7. Sat 10-6. Sun 12-6.
Services:	Appraisals, search service, accepts want lists.
Travel:	Memorial Dr exit off I-285. Proceed east on Memorial for about four miles. Shop is on the left, at the corner of North Hairston & Memorial, in Stonewood Village Shopping Center.
Credit Cards:	Yes
Owner:	Paul Blicksilver
Year Estab:	1976
Comments:	The majority of the books in this shop were paperback and most of the hardcover items we saw were rather common. The owner also sells better used books on a by appointment basis from his home in Lilburn. See above.

The Bent Book   **Open Shop**
5055 Memorial Drive 30083   (404) 292-4069

Collection:	General stock of mostly paperback.
# of Vols:	90,000
Hours:	Mon-Thu 10-7. Fri & Sat 10-6. Sun 1-5:30.

Memorable Books   **Open Shop**
5380 Manor Drive 30083   (770) 469-5911

Collection:	General stock.
# of Vols:	30,000
Specialties:	Literature; history; philosophy; science; biography; religion; arts and crafts; military; cookbooks; foreign languages; music.
Hours:	Tue-Sat 11-5.
Travel:	Stone Mountain exit off Rte 78 east (Stone Mountain Fwy). Proceed south to next exit, then left onto Ponce de Leon.
Credit Cards:	Yes
Owner:	George M. Hoak
Year Estab:	1980
Comments:	We returned to this shop three years after our first visit thinking that perhaps the description we wrote at that time (see below) might have changed somewhat. Upon our arrival at 4:20 on a Tuesday afternoon we found the shop closed despite a sign on the door indicating that the

store was open till 5pm. A cursory glance through the window suggests that not much has changed since our initial visit when we noted:

The shop was overloaded with books not only filling every available inch of space on the shelves, but also taking up much of the narrow aisle space. The owner did indicate that he had plans to raise the height of the shelves to accommodate his growing stock. While there was some organization, in most instances, it will take persistent and patient browsing (or advice from the owner) in order to find the subject categories you're looking for. Most of the books we saw were quite reasonably priced with bargains to be had, and indeed, we did purchase our share. Many of the books were older, and again, we suspect that there are treasures to be had.

Mountain Mysteries   **By Appointment**
1786 Tilling Way   (770) 491-8283
Mailing address: PO Box 870966 Stone Mountain 30087

Collection:	Specialty
# of Vols:	8,000
Specialties:	Detective; suspense; espionage.
Services:	Catalog, accepts want lists.
Credit Cards:	No
Owner:	Jim & Kathleen Wood
Year Estab:	1994
Comments:	Stock is almost exclusively hardcover.

Olde Books and Collectibles   **By Appointment**
PO Box 289 30086   (770) 938-7023

Collection:	General stock.
# of Vols:	8,000-10,000
Specialties:	Fine bindings; Americana.
Services:	Appraisals, mail order.
Credit Cards:	No
Owner:	Harold & Jean Ballew
Year Estab:	1973
Comments:	Also displays at the Lakewood Fairgrounds Antique Market in Atlanta. See above.

Thomasville
(Map 7, page 114)

The Bookshelf   **Open Shop**
108 East Jackson Street 31792   (912) 228-7767
                                                              Fax: (912) 228-4478

Collection:	General stock of mostly new and some used paperback and hardcover.
Hours:	Mon-Fri 9:30-6. Sat 9:30-5:30.
Travel:	Located on Hwy 319.
Comments:	Stock is approximately 80% new. Used stock is approximately 70% paperback.

Tucker
(Map 8, page 119)

Wimsey's   **Open Shop**
2346 Main Street 30084   Tel & Fax: (770) 938-6465
E-mail: wimsey@mindspring.com

Collection:	General stock of paperback and hardcover books.
# of Vols:	20,000
Hours:	Mon-St 9:30-6.
Travel:	Exit 28 (La Vista) off I-285. Proceed east on La Vista for 2.1 miles, then right on Main. Shop is about two blocks ahead on right.
Credit Cards:	Yes
Owner:	Patty Tucker
Year Estab:	1996
Comments:	A nice selection of paperback and hardcover books showing promise for a shop that, at the time of our visit, had only been open for one year. Although somewhat disconcerting (at least for some book hunters) seeing hardcover and paperbacks intershelved, for the person looking for a particular title in one or the other format, we suppose it doesn't make much difference. We saw several "neat" titles on hand along with the usual run-of-the-mill selections. If you're scouting, give the shop a try.

Warm Springs

Trudy's Corner   **Open Shop**
7 Roosevelt Walk   (706) 655-9050
Mailing address: PO Box 558 Warm Springs 31830

Collection:	General stock of mostly used paperback and new books.
Hours:	Daily 10-6.

Waycross

Bargain Books & Things   **Open Shop**
816 Memorial Drive 31501   (912) 283-4166

Collection:	General stock of mostly paperback.
# of Vols:	25,000
Hours:	Mon-Sat 10-6.

The Tebeauville Store-Book Exchange   **Open Shop**
801 Tebea Street 31501   (912) 285-1377

Collection:	General stock of mostly paperback.
# of Vols:	70,000+
Hours:	Mon-Sat 9-5.

Winder
(Map 7, page 114)

Corner Bookstore   **Open Shop**
32 East Athens Street 30680   (770) 867-5800
                                                         E-mail: tvail@dscga.com

Collection: General stock of hardcover and paperback.
# of Vols: 100,000
Specialties: Cookbooks; military; southern history; local authors.
Hours: Mon-Fri 9:30-6. Sat 9:30-4.
Services: Appraisals, accepts want lists.
Travel: Exit 48 off I-85. Proceed south on Rte 211 for about 10 miles to
                   downtown Winder.
Credit Cards: Yes
Owner: Tom Vail
Year Estab: 1978

Woodstock

AGD Books   **By Appointment**
PO Box 93 30188   (770) 591-1394

Collection: General stock.
# of Vols: 20,000

Kenneth E. Schneringer   **By Appointment**
271 Sabrina Court 30188   (770) 926-9383

Collection: Specialty books and ephemera.
Specialties: Trade catalogs.
Services: Catalog
Credit Cards: No
Owner: Kenneth E. Schneringer
Year Estab: 1989

The Wild Honeysuckle   **Open Shop**
2295 Towne Lake Parkway, Ste 140 30189   (770) 516-1427
                                                                  Fax: (770) 516-8182

Collection: Specialty
# of Vols: 2,000
Specialties: Antiquarian (16th-19th century).
Hours: Mon-Sat 10-6.
Travel: I-75 to I-575, then exit 5 (Towne Lake Pkwy) off I-575. Proceed west
                   on Towne Lake Pkwy. Shop is on right, in Kroger Shopping Center.
Credit Cards: Yes
Owner: Lester "Sonny" Ideker, Jr.
Year Estab: 1994
Comments: Also displays at Scott Antique Market in Atlanta (under B11 sign). See
                   above.

Arabesque Books   Tel & Fax: (404) 264-9649
PO Box 12312 Atlanta 30355

Collection:	Specialty
# of Vols:	3,500
Specialties:	Southern Americana; Georgia; Civil War; Native Americans; travel and exploration; architecture; antiques; Edgar Allan Poe.
Services:	Accepts want lists, mail order.
Credit Cards:	No
Owner:	John Schulz
Year Estab:	1978

Auldfarran Books   (404) 373-3044
PO Box 1691 Decatur 30031   E-mail: jprozier@mindspring.com

Collection:	Specialty
# of Vols:	4,000
Specialties:	First books; British history; travel; Georgia.
Services:	Search service, accepts want lists.
Credit Cards:	No
Owner:	J.P. Rozier
Year Estab:	1993

Brewer's Books   (706) 862-2650
PO Box 202 Menlo 30731   E-mail: rbrewer@wavegate.com
Web page: www.abebooks.com/home/brewers

Collection:	Specialty books and ephemera.
# of Vols:	12,000
Specialties:	Black studies; labor history; economics; socialism; "sixties"; women's studies.
Credit Cards:	Yes
Year Estab:	1986

Coleman's Books   (770) 498-2094
491 Hickory Hill Trail Stone Mountain 30083 E-mail: pcoleman@mindspring.com

Collection:	General stock of mostly hardcover.
# of Vols:	1,000+
Specialties:	Fine bindings of: mathematics; science; technical; medicine. Also some modern first editions.
Services:	Search service, accepts want lists.
Owner:	Patrick J. Coleman
Year Estab:	1996

Midnight Book Company   (404) 926-1102
3929 Ebenezer Road Marietta 30066

Collection:	Specialty
# of Vols:	4,000
Specialties:	Science fiction; fantasy; science fiction and fantasy art.
Services:	Appraisals; search service, accepts want lists, mail order.
Owner:	Harold Dricks
Year Estab:	1970

The Overlook Connection   (770) 926-1762
PO Box 526 Woodstock 30188   Fax: (770) 516-1469
Web page: www.horrornet.com/overlook.htm   E-mail: overlookcn@aol.com

Collection:	Specialty new and used.
# of Vols:	5,000
Specialties:	Horror; science fiction; fantasy; mystery; Stephen King.
Services:	Catalog, accepts want lists.
Credit Cards:	Yes
Owner:	David Hinchberger
Year Estab:	1987
Comments:	Stock is approximately 50% used.

Prize Editions   (404) 373-4527
868 Springdale Road, NE Atlanta 30306   E-mail: prizeeds@aol.com

Collection:	Specialty
# of Vols:	200
Specialties:	Modern first editions.
Services:	Accepts want lists.
Owner:	Roger Stroud
Year Estab:	1996

Henry Ramsey   (706) 543-8867
573 Hill Street Athens 30606

Collection:	General stock.
# of Vols:	6,000
Specialties:	19th century Americana; slavery.
Services:	Appraisals, search service, accepts want lists, catalog.
Year Estab:	1985

Bernard Rogers, Jr. - Bookseller   Tel & Fax: (706) 632-8974
22 Swiss Lane Blue Ridge 30513   E-mail: aarts@athens.net
Web page: www.athens.net/~aarts

Collection:	Specialty
Specialties:	Nautical charts, maps, prints.
Credit Cards:	Yes
Year Estab:	1980

Whistle in the Woods Museum Services   (706) 375-4326
PO Box 309 Chickamauga 30707   E-mail: oldgoat@voy.net

Collection:	Specialty. Mostly used and some new.
# of Vols:	600-700
Specialties:	Railroads; steam engines, wind and water power; mining; manufacturing, history of technology; industrial archaeology, trade catalogs; related magazines.
Services:	Appraisals; search service, catalog, accepts want lists.
Credit Cards:	No
Owner:	Robert L. Johnson
Year Estab:	1958
Comments:	Collection may be viewed by appointment.

Maryland

Alphabetical Listing By Dealer

Alphabetical Listing By Location

New Market	C.W. Wood Bookshop	184
Oakland	Appalachian Background Books	184
Ocean City	Bookworld	185
	Bookshelf Etc.	184
	The Mason Collection	185
Olney	T.A. Borden	185
Parkton	Stephen A. Goldman Historical Newspapers	200
Pasadena	Books From X To Z	199
Poolesville	The Thankful Chase	185
Potomac	Quixote Books	201
Prince Frederick	Second Looks Books	186
Queenstown	Chesapeake Antique Center	186
Riverdale	Riverdale Bookshop & Coffee Depot	186
Rock Hall	America's Cup Cafe	187
	The Cup Runneth Over	187
Rockville	Book Alcove	187
	The Book Emporium	199
	Leaf Through	188
	Robert A. Madle SF/Fantasy Books	188
	Peter Pun Books	188
	Quill & Brush	189
	Q.M. Dabney & Company	202
	Second Story Books	189
	Washington Used Book Center	189
	Yak & Yeti Books	190
Saint Michaels	The Book Nook	190
Salisbury	Henrietta's Attic	190
	Market Street Books	191
Savage	The Book Guy	191
Silver Spring	Ground Zero Books	201
	Hirschtritt's '1712' Books	191
	Imagination Books	192
	Silver Spring Books	192
Smithsburg	Boyer's Book Bank & Emporium	193
Solomons	Lazy Moon Bookshop	193
Sykesville	Jerome Shochet	202
Takoma Park	Takoma Emporium	193
Taneytown	Taneytown Antique Shoppes	194
Tilghman Island	Book Bank	194
Towson	Jean-Maurice Poitras & Sons	201
Trappe	Unicorn Bookshop	194
Waldorf	Ellie's Paperback Shack	195
Walkersville	First Place Books	195
Westminster	Record and Book Heaven	195
Wheaton	The Barbarian Book Shop	196
	Bonifant Books	196
	Books of Colonial America	196
	Friends' Store	197

Washington Beltway Map 2

Area Code Changes

Two new area codes will go into effect in Maryland in 1998. At press time, the tentative plan is for NEW listings in the 410 code to be assigned 443. NEW listings in the 301 code area will be assigned 240.

Annapolis
(Map 9, page 170)

The Book Shelf   **Open Shop**
1918 Forest Drive 21401   (410) 267-6727

Collection:	General stock of paperback and hardcover.
# of Vols:	30,000
Hours:	Mon-Fri, except closed Tue, 10-6. Sat 10-4. Sun 12-4.
Travel:	Rte 665 exit off Rte 50. Left at first light onto Chiquapin Round Rd, then an immediate left onto Forest Dr. Shop is in Gardner Shopping Center.
Credit Cards:	No
Owner:	Cathy Toth
Year Estab:	1989
Comments:	Stock is approximately 65% paperback.

Briarwood Bookshop   **Open Shop**
88 Maryland Avenue 21401   (410) 268-1440

Collection:	General stock of mostly hardcover.
# of Vols:	15,000
Specialties:	Philosophy; religion; military history; United Kingdom; literature.
Hours:	Daily 10-6.
Services:	Appraisals
Travel:	Exit 24 off Rte 50. Proceed on Rowe Blvd toward downtown Annapolis. Left onto College, then first right onto North. Take North to State Circle and State Circle to Maryland, then right onto Maryland. Shop is just ahead on the left in the heart of the historic district and a few steps away from the State Capitol building.
Credit Cards:	Yes
Owner:	David Grobanie
Year Estab:	1989
Comments:	An immaculate and well organized shop with books in universally good condition. The collection has a strong emphasis on the scholarly and serious fiction. We saw several bargains in terms of pricing.

See-Worthy Books   **Antique Mall**
At Recapture the Past Antiques   Mall: (410) 216-9067
69 Maryland Avenue   Bus: (410) 268-8398
Mailing address: 921 Boucher Avenue Annapolis 21403

Collection:	General stock, prints and ephemera.

# of Vols:	1,000+
Specialties:	Nautical; naval; children's; American history; American literature; regional.
Hours:	Mon-Sat 10-5. Sun 1-5.
Travel:	See Briarwood Bookshop above.
Credit Cards:	Yes
Owner:	Paul M. Foer
Year Estab:	1996

Baltimore
(Map 10, page 160)

Allen's Bookshop   **Open Shop**
416 East 31 Street, 2nd Floor 21218   (410) 243-4356

Collection:	General stock of mostly hardcover.
# of Vols:	30,000
Specialties:	Music; Maryland; railroads, cookbooks; philosophy; mathematics.
Hours:	Mon-Fri 1-6. Sat 12-5.
Services:	Search service, accepts want lists, mail order.
Travel:	28th St exit off I-83 (Jones Falls Expwy). Cross 28th St and make left onto Charles St. Continue on Charles to 31st St, then right onto 31st St.
Credit Cards:	No
Owner:	David & Marcia Ray
Year Estab:	1974
Comments:	One flight up a steep metal outside staircase, this shop offers a modest sized collection of both hardcover and paperback books in generally good condition and reasonably priced. What the shop lacks in volume, it makes up for in quality. At the time of our visit, there were fewer books on display than noted above.

Alternate Realities   **Open Shop**
3360 Greenmount Avenue 21218   (410) 889-0099
                                                    E-mail: mhorn@welch.jhu.edu

Collection:	Specialty new and used.
# of Vols:	4,000 (used)
Specialties:	Science fiction; horror; fantasy.
Hours:	Mon-Sat 12-7.
Travel:	At 34th Street.
Credit Cards:	Yes
Owner:	Melissa Horn & Charlie Kimbrough
Year Estab:	1980
Comments:	Stock is approximately 50% used.

Shirley Balser, 16th-20th Century Paintings, Prints & Books   **By Appointment**
PO Box 5803 21282-5803   (410) 484-0880

Collection:	General stock, paintings and prints.
# of Vols:	10,000

Specialties:	Art; illustrated; Americana; literature, first editions; documents.
Services.	Appraisals, accepts want lists, mail order.
Credit Cards:	No
Year Estab:	1961

Baltimore Book Company   **Open Shop**
2114 North Charles Street 21218   (410) 659-0550

Collection:	General stock.
# of Vols:	1,000
Hours:	Mon-Fri 12-5.
Travel:	At 22nd Street.
Credit Cards:	No
Owner:	Chris Bready
Year Estab:	1989
Comments:	Owner also operates a catalog auction business.

BNN Books   **Open Shop**
12 West 25th Street 21218   (410) 243-8559

Collection:	General stock of paperback and hardcover.
Hours:	Tue-Sat 11:30-6.
Travel:	Just west of Charles St.
Credit Cards:	No
Year Estab:	1992
Comments:	A non profit shop operated by the Baltimore News Network.

Book Miser   **Open Shop**
2133 Gwynn Oak Avenue, 2nd Fl 21207   ** (410) 276-9880
Web page: www.bookmiser.com   Fax: (410) 276-1405
                                  E-mail: info@bookmiser.com

Collection:	General stock.
# of Vols:	20,000
Specialties:	Performing arts; American history and politics; religion.
Hours:	Tue-Fri 12-6. Sat 9-3. Other times by chance or appointment.
Services:	Search service, accepts want lists, mail order.
Travel:	Exit 17 east (Security Blvd) off I-695. Proceed on Security Blvd to third light, then left on Gwynn Oak Ave. Shop is just after second light where Gwynn Oak intersects with another road at a fork. Shop is on second floor of a two story red brick building.
Credit Cards:	Yes
Owner:	Stan Modjesky
Year Estab:	1992
Comments:	We visited this dealer at his Fell's Point location prior to his pending move to a larger shop. Having visited the store on two previous occasions, it seems reasonable to assume that at his new location, the dealer will continue to exhibit the same care in the selection and display of his books.

** *The phone number may change after 1998.*

(Baltimore)

The Book Rendezvous   **Open Shop**
805 Light Street 21230   (410) 332-1664
                                                          E-mail: cliffsbks@erols.com

Collection:	General stock of hardcover and paperback.
# of Vols:	25,000-30,000
Hours:	Daily 12-7.
Travel:	I-395/Camden Yards exit off I-95. Continue on I-395, passing Camden Yards, to Conway St. Right on Conway and continue for three blocks to Light. Right at Light St. Shop is four blocks ahead, after passing the Inner Harbor, at the intersection of Light and Montgomery.
Credit Cards:	No
Owner:	Cliff Panken
Year Estab:	1995
Comments:	Stock is evenly divided between paperback and hardcover.

Marilyn Braiterman   **By Appointment**
20 Whitfield Road 21210   (410) 235-4848

Collection:	Specialty
# of Vols:	2,500
Specialties:	Art; architecture; landscape design; illustrated; private press; Judaica.
Services:	Appraisals, catalog.
Credit Cards:	No
Year Estab:	1979

Continental Divide Trail Society   **By Appointment**
3704 North Charles Street, #601 21218   (410) 235-9610
Web page: www.gorp.com/cdts/   Fax: (410) 366-4310
                                                          E-mail: cdtsociety@aol.com

Collection:	Specialty
# of Vols:	1,000
Specialties:	Rocky Mountains; Southwest Americana; exploration history.
Services:	Accepts want lists, mail order. Also publishes Continental Divide Trail guidebooks.
Credit Cards:	No
Owner:	James R. Wolf
Year Estab:	1978

Drusilla's Books   **Open Shop**
817 North Howard Street   (410) 225-0277
Mailing address: PO Box 16 Lutherville 21094-0016   Fax: (410) 321-4955
                                                          E-mail: drusilla@interloc.com

Collection:	Specialty and small general stock.
# of Vols:	20,000
Specialties:	Children's; illustrated; antique reference.
Hours:	Tue-Sat 12-5. Sun also in Nov & Dec. Other times by appointment.

Services:	Appraisals, search service, catalog, accepts want lists.
Travel:	Exit 53 (I-395 exit) off I-95. Proceed on Martin Luther King, Jr. Blvd, then right on Pratt and left on Howard.
Credit Cards:	Yes
Owner:	Drusilla P. Jones
Year Estab:	1977

Goodwill Book Nook
3101 Greenmont Avenue

Open Shop
(410) 467-7505

Collection:	General stock of paperback and hardcover and records.
Hours:	Mon-Wed 10-6. Thu-Sat 10-7.
Travel:	Between 31st and 32nd Streets.

Kelmscott Bookshop
32 West 25th Street 21218

Open Shop
(410) 235-6810
Fax: (410) 366-4286

Collection:	General stock.
# of Vols:	100,000
Specialties:	Literature; first editions; travel; history; illustrated; H.L. Mencken.
Hours:	Mon-Sat 10-6.
Services:	Appraisals, search service, accepts want lists, mail order, book binding.
Travel:	One block west of Charles St.
Credit Cards:	Yes
Owner:	Donald & Teresa Johanson
Year Estab:	1977
Comments:	We made our third visit to this shop for the current edition of this book and are pleased to report that everything we said about the shop in our earlier edition (see below) remains valid.

If you ever have a fantasy of being locked in a bookshop overnight or over a weekend, this is the place you want it to be. The shop is, without question, Baltimore's premier used book shop and one of the finest shops along the east coast. The books are in excellent condition and are meticulously shelved by category and subcategory. The bi-level shop is divided into several small rooms, each with one, and in many cases, several comfortable chairs. Make sure you visit both upper levels which are reached by separate staircases and are not connected to one another.

Lambda Rising
241 West Chase Street 21201

Open Shop
(410) 234-0069

Collection:	Specialty new and used.
Specialties:	Gay and lesbian.
Hours:	Daily 10-10.
Travel:	Between Martin Luther King Blvd and Read St.

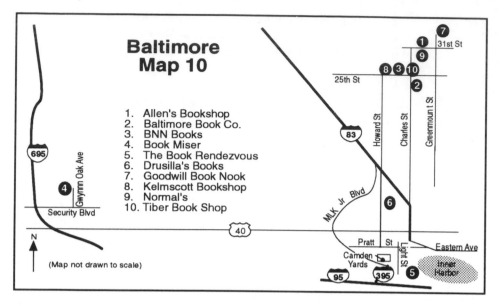

Baltimore Map 10

1. Allen's Bookshop
2. Baltimore Book Co.
3. BNN Books
4. Book Miser
5. The Book Rendezvous
6. Drusilla's Books
7. Goodwill Book Nook
8. Kelmscott Bookshop
9. Normal's
10. Tiber Book Shop

(Map not drawn to scale)

E. Christian Mattson
4 Turtlerock Court 21234

By Appointment
(410) 668-4730
Fax: (410) 882-9137
E-mail: emattson@qis.com

Collection:	Specialty
# of Vols:	5,000
Specialties:	Arthur Conan Doyle; Charles Dickens; H. Rider Haggard; fore-edge paintings.
Services:	Search service, accepts want lists, catalog.
Credit Cards:	No
Year Estab:	1962

Mystery Loves Company
1730 Fleet Street 21231

Open Shop
Tel & Fax: (410) 276-6708

Collection:	Specialty new and used.
# of Vols:	2,000 (used)
Specialties:	Mystery; signed first editions.
Hours:	Tue-Sat 11-5. Sun 12-5.
Services:	Search service, catalog, accepts want lists.
Travel:	Eastern Ave exit off I-95. Turn east on Eastern Ave and proceed seven blocks to Ann St, then south on Ann to Fleet and right onto Fleet.
Credit Cards:	Yes
Owner:	Paige Rose & Kathy Harig
Year Estab:	1991
Comments:	If you're into mysteries and are looking for out-of-print or reprinted titles of older classics, there's a good chance you may find your favorite here. While the shop specializes primarily in new books, it does have a healthy selection of used hardcover and paperback titles at

reasonable prices. The owner, who is knowledgeable in her field, is ready to help you locate the missing titles you may have long sought.

19th Century Shop   **By Appointment**
1047 Hollins Street 21223   (410) 539-2586
Web page: www.19thcentury.com   Fax: (410) 727-2681
                            E-mail: the19thcenturyshop@mindspring.com

Collection:	Specialty
Specialties:	First editions and manuscripts in literature; history; science; technology.
Services:	Appraisals, catalog, accepts want lists.
Credit Cards:	Yes
Owner:	Stephen Loewentheil
Year Estab:	1982

Normal's   **Open Shop**
425 East 31st Street 21218   (410) 243-6888

Collection:	General stock of hardcover and paperback and records.
# of Vols:	50,000
Specialties:	Women's studies; philosophy; new age.
Hours:	Sun-Fri 11-6. Sat 10-6.
Services:	Accepts want lists.
Travel:	Just off Greenmount Ave.
Credit Cards:	Yes
Owner:	John Berndt, Alfred Merchlinksy, Walt Novash & Rupert Wondslowski
Year Estab:	1990
Comments:	In addition to carrying LPs, cassettes and CD's, the shop also displays a reasonable selection of hardcover and paperback volumes consisting mostly of reading copies in mixed condition. Nicely organized.

The Perfect Ending   **By Appointment**
3008 Howard Park Avenue 21207   (410) 448-5340

Collection:	Specialty
Specialties:	Children's; collectible cartoons; French cartoon characters.
Credit Cards:	No
Owner:	Moyna Denise Anderson
Year Estab:	1987

The Rug Book Shop   **By Appointment**
2603 Talbot Road 21216   (410) 367-8194

Collection:	Specialty. Mostly new and some used.
# of Vols:	5,000
Specialties:	Oriental rugs; Navajo blankets; ethnographic textiles; Balkan costumes and textiles; European carpets and tapestries; Asiatic textiles.
Services:	Search service, catalog, accepts want lists.
Credit Cards:	No
Owner:	Paul Kreiss
Year Estab:	1969

Cecil Archer Rush, Fine Books   **By Appointment**
1410 Northgate Road 21218-1549   (410) 323-7767

Collection:	Specialty
# of Vols:	4,000
Specialties:	Art of Tibet, Nepal and India; illustrated.
Services:	Appraisals, search service, accepts want lists, mail order.
Credit Cards:	No
Year Estab:	1942

Tiber Book Shop   **Open Shop**
8 West 25th Street 21218   (410) 243-2789
Web page: www.bibliofind.com   E-mail: tiber@erols.com

Collection:	General stock.
# of Vols:	100,000
Hours:	Mon-Sat 12-6.
Services:	Appraisals, search service, accept want lists, mail order.
Travel:	Just west of Charles St.
Credit Cards:	Yes
Owner:	Whit Drain & Bob Kotansky
Year Estab:	1983
Comments:	This bi-level shop, located just a few doors away from another fine used book shop, offers a good collection of scholarly books, as well as its share of "general stock" titles. The shop is subdivided into several small rooms, is well organized, and well worth a visit. The books are moderately priced.

Beltsville
(Map 9A, page 170)

Antiquariat Botanicum   **By Appointment**
4606 Brandon Lane 20705   Tel & Fax: (301) 937-2561

Collection:	Specialty
# of Vols:	5,000+
Specialties:	Botany; color plate books; gardening; horticulture; landscape architecture; ornithology; science. (Books from 16th-20th centuries).
Services:	Appraisals, search service, catalog, accepts want lists.
Credit Cards:	No
Owner:	Eugene L. Vigil
Year Estab:	1988

JoAnn's Books   **Open Shop**
10438 Baltimore Avenue 20705   (301) 937-0259
                                              E-mail: joannsbk@erols.com

Collection:	General stock of hardcover and paperback.
# of Vols:	23,000
Hours:	Wed-Fri 11-7. Sat 10-6. Sun 12-5.
Services:	Mail order.
Travel:	Exit 25A off I-495. Proceed north on Rte 1 for about 8/10 of a mile. Shop is on left behind gas station.

Credit Cards:	Yes
Owner:	JoAnn Innocente
Year Estab:	1992
Comments:	A modest sized but comfortable shop with a small children's reading area, coffee and cookies and chairs for the weary browser. The hardcover volumes are of more recent vintage. This is a good place to find reading copies of popular titles but not a likely source for scarce or rare items. Moderately priced.

Bethesda
(Map 2, page 154)

Antiquarian Bookworm   **Open Shop**
7315 Wisconsin Ave 20814   (301) 656-3779
                                              E-mail: weetall@erols.com

Collection:	Specialty
# of Vols:	2,500
Specialties:	Travel; exploration; Americana; Civil War; art; architecture.
Hours:	Mon-Fri 10-6. Sat by appointment.
Services:	Appraisals, search service, subject lists, accepts want lists, mail order.
Travel:	Rte 355 exit off I-495. Proceed south on Wisconsin Ave. Shop is two blocks past Old Georgetown Rd, on the left, in the east lobby of the Air Rights Center (an office building).
Credit Cards:	Yes
Owner:	Howard Weetall
Year Estab:	1968

The Book Cellar   **Open Shop**
8227 Woodmont Avenue 20814   (301) 654-1898

Collection:	General stock.
# of Vols:	40,000
Specialties:	Foreign languages.
Hours:	Wed-Mon 11-6.
Services:	Search service, accepts want lists, mail order.
Travel:	Rte 355/Wisconsin Ave exit off I-495. Proceed south on Wisconsin for about one mile past the National Institutes of Health, then bear right onto Woodmont Ave. Shop is just after the first intersection (Battery Lane) and across the street from a parking garage. Look for the words "Books downstairs" stenciled on the door.
Credit Cards:	Yes
Owner:	Don & Linda Bloomfield
Year Estab:	1976
Comments:	Once you've found this tightly packed basement level shop, you won't regret having looked for it. The shop carries a little bit of almost every subject and while the emphasis in the collection is on the scholarly, browsers will also find a good selection of titles in less esoteric categories like humor, entertainment and mystery. We spotted several titles that we thought were underpriced and would be real bargains.

(Bethesda)

Georgetown Book Shop
7770 Woodmont Avenue 20814

Open Shop
(301) 907-6923

Collection:	General stock.
# of Vols:	15,000-20,000
Specialties:	History; military; presidents; art; photography; baseball; cookbooks; children's illustrated; vintage magazines; literature.
Hours:	Daily 10-6. Closed only Thanksgiving, Christmas and New Year's Day.
Services:	Appraisals, accepts want lists, mail order.
Travel:	See The Book Cellar above. The shop is on right after the fifth light. A parking garage is available on right just after shop.
Credit Cards:	Yes
Owner:	Andy Moursund
Year Estab:	1984
Comments:	A very attractive shop with books tastefully selected for display. Almost all the volumes we saw were in good to excellent condition and reasonably priced. While most subject areas are represented, the specialties listed above are clearly areas not to be ignored. While it is not unusual to find shops with signs advising customers with bags to leave them at the front counter, this shop enforces that rule strictly. We found the discount policy for dealers to be rather unique.

Iranbooks
6831 Wisconsin Avenue
Mailing address: 8014 Old Georgetown Rd. Bethesda 20814
Web page: www.iranbooks.com

Open Shop
(301) 718-8188
Fax: (301) 907-8707
E-mail: info@iranbooks.com

Collection:	Specialty new and used.
Specialties:	Iran; Persian language books.
Hours:	Mon-Sat 10-6. Sun 12-5.
Services:	Search service, accepts want lists.
Travel:	Exit 34 off I-495. Proceed south. Shop is in Shops of Chevy Chase shopping center.
Credit Cards:	Yes
Owner:	Farhad Shirzad
Year Estab:	1979
Comments:	Stock is approximately 85% new.

Jahan Book Co.
5516 Westbard Avenue 20816
Web page: www.erols.com/jahan/index.html

By Appointment
(301) 657-1412
Fax: (301) 654-1330
E-mail: jahan@erols.com

Collection:	Specialty new and used.
Specialties:	Middle East.
Services:	Appraisals, catalog.
Credit Cards:	No
Owner:	Hasan Javadi

Year Estab: 1980
Comments: Stock is approximately 75% new.

Mystery Bookshop   **Open Shop**
7700 Old Georgetown Road 20814   (301) 657-2665
                                                                            (800) 572-8533

Collection: Specialty. Mostly new.
# of Vols: Limited used.
Specialties: Mystery
Hours: Mon-Fri 10-7. Sat 10-6. Sun 12-5.
Travel: One block from Georgetown Book Shop (see above). Shop is located
                  in a multi story red brick office building at the corner of Moorland and
                  Georgetown Rd. The shop's entrance is through the lobby. An on site
                  parking garage is available.
Credit Cards: Yes
Owner: Jean & Ron McMillen
Year Estab: 1989
Comments: If you're looking for a good read in the mystery genre, you won't have
                  any trouble picking out a title or two in this attractively decorated shop
                  that carries mostly new books, puzzles and games. The used books are
                  in a small room in the rear of the shop and consist mostly of rather run
                  of the mill older titles. If you're looking for an older or rare mystery
                  classic, this is not the shop for you.

Olsson's Books • Records   **Open Shop**
7647 Old Georgetown Road 20814   (301) 652-3336
                                                                       Fax: (301) 907-4987

Collection: General stock of mostly new and some used.
# of Vols: 300+ used
Hours: Mon-Thu 10-10. Fri & Sat 10-10:30. Sun 11-8
Travel: Between Woodmont and Fairmont.
Owner: Bill Lloyd, Manager
Comments.   The second shop in this six-store chain of independent new bookstores
                  to open a used and out-of-print section in 1997. Unlike the Georgetown
                  location that intershelves new and used titles, this store displays its
                  used books in a separate section.

R. Quick, Bookseller   **Co-op Market**
At Montgomery Farm Women's Co-op Market   Home: (301) 654-5030
7155 Wisconsin Avenue 20815   Market: (301) 652-2291

Collection: General stock.
# of Vols: 3,000 (see comments)
Specialties: Children's
Hours: Wed & Sat 7-3.
Travel: A few blocks south of Rte 410 (East-West Hwy).
Comments: Approximately 500 books are on display at the market. Additional
                  books can viewed by appointment.

Schweitzer Japanese Prints   **By Appointment**
6313 Lenox Road 20817   (301) 229-6574
                                                                   Fax: (301) 229-0345

Collection: General stock of mostly hardcover.
# of Vols: 1,500+
Specialties: Japan; Japanese print references; modern Japanese fiction and mysteries.
Services: Appraisals, search service, accepts want lists.
Credit Cards: No
Owner: Paul & Agnes Schweitzer
Year Estab: 1967

Second Story Books   **Open Shop**
4836 Bethesda Avenue   (301) 656-0170
Mailing address: 12160 Parklawn Drive Rockville 20852   Fax: (301) 770-9544
Web page: www.paltech.com/secondstory   E-mail: ssbookguys@paltech.com

Collection: General stock of mostly hardcover.
# of Vols: 40,000
Hours: Daily 10-10.
Services: Appraisals, search service, catalog, accepts want lists.
Travel: Between Arlington and Woodmont. Metro Red Line: Bethesda Station.
Credit Cards: Yes
Owner: Allan Stypeck
Year Estab: 1974
Comments: Somewhat smaller and less crowded than the chain's Dupont Circle
                   shop in Washington, we found the ambience of this store far more
                   relaxing. The book selection was ample, if not quite as large as the
                   other shop, and there was more room for sitting and browsing as well
                   as a delightful children's corner. The variety of the stock, from older
                   leatherbound volumes and first editions to newer titles (remainders?),
                   paperbacks and ephemera offers enough variety to suit a wide range of
                   tastes. In short, a shop worth visiting.

Washington Antiques Center   **Antique Mall**
6708 Wisconsin Avenue 20815   (301) 654-3798
Hours: Daily 11-6.
Travel: Wisconsin Ave exit off Beltway (I-495).

Bowie
(Map 9A, page 170)

Deja Vu Books   **Open Shop**
13600 Annapolis Road 20720   (301) 464-2999

Collection: General stock of paperback and hardcover and records.
# of Vols: 12,000
Hours: Tue-Fri 10:30-8. Sat 10-5. Sun 12-5.
Travel: Rte 450 (Annapolis Rd) exit off I-495. Proceed east on Rte 450 for
                   about six miles. Shop is on left.

Credit Cards:	Yes
Owner:	Shelley Tidd
Year Estab:	1995
Comments:	Stock is approximately 70% paperback.

Brinklow

Old Hickory Bookshop   **By Appointment**
20225 New Hampshire Avenue 20862   (301) 924-2225

Collection:	Specialty
# of Vols:	5,000
Specialties:	Medicine
Services:	Appraisals, search service, accepts want lists, mail order
Credit Cards:	No
Owner:	Johanna Grimes
Year Estab:	1973

Cambridge
(Map 9, page 170)

Mill's Antiques   **Open Shop**
2951 Ocean Gateway 21613   (410) 228-9866

Collection:	General stock of hardcover and paperback.
# of Vols:	30,000
Hours:	Mon-Sat 11-3 but best to call ahead.
Travel:	Located on Rte 50.
Credit Cards:	No
Owner:	Raymond Mills
Year Estab:	1960's
Comments:	Our itinerary brought us to Maryland's eastern shore on a Sunday when this shop is normally closed. We have it on good authority though that the shop, which sells antiques and collectibles in addition to books, can best be described as "an experience" for the book person who likes well organized shops. As for the books, alas, we cannot comment on them. If perchance you get to visit here, we'd welcome your comments.

Chestertown
(Map 9, page 170)

Chestertown Used Book Store   **Open Shop**
6612 Churchill Road 21620   (410) 778-5777

Collection:	General stock of hardcover and paperback.
# of Vols:	60,000
Hours:	Mon-Sat 10-5:30, except Fri till 7.
Travel:	Centreville exit off Rte 50. Proceed north on Rte 213 (Churchill Rd). Shop is on right about one mile before bridge. Shop is located inside the Chestertown Antique & Furniture Center.
Credit Cards:	No

Owner:	John Woodfield
Year Estab:	1970's
Comments:	If you enjoy adventure, we suspect you'll find your visit here a worthwhile experience. Don't look for pristine copies of recent best sellers (although you might find a few.) What the owner of this high turnover shop offers are low priced books of every kind that he has purchased from estate sales and house liquidations. The vast majority of what we saw were fairly common reading copies but interspersed were a healthy number of collectible items offered at bargain prices.

Clear Spring

Cornerstone Books   **By Appointment**
12324 Big Pool Road 21722   (301) 842-3784
Fax: (301) 733-5669

Collection:	Specialty
# of Vols:	18,000
Specialties:	Religion; bibles.
Services:	Occasional catalog.
Owner:	Gene Albert

College Park
(Map 2, page 154)

Book Nook   **Open Shop**
9933 Rhode Island Avenue 20740   (301) 474-4060

Collection:	General stock of paperback and hardcover.
Hours:	Mon-Sat 10-5, except Wed till 7:30.
Owner:	Mary Monteith
Comments:	Approximately 70% paperback.

Columbia
(Map 9A, page 170)

John Gach Books   **By Appointment**
5620 Waterloo Road 21045   (410) 465-9023
Web page: www.clark.net/pub/sws/gachbook   Fax: (410) 465-0649
E-mail: john.gach@clark.net

Collection:	Specialty
# of Vols:	40,000
Specialties:	Psychology; psychiatry; philosophy.
Services:	Catalog, search service, accepts want lists.
Credit Cards:	Yes
Year Estab:	1968

Second Edition Used & New Books   **Open Shop**
6490M Dobbin Road 21045   (410) 730-0050

Collection:	General stock of used and new hardcover and paperback.
# of Vols:	53,000

Hours:	Mon-Sat 11-8. Sun 12-6.
Services:	Accepts want lists, search service.
Travel:	Rte 175 East exit off Rte 29. Proceed east on Rte 175 and make right at third light onto Dobbin, then right at second light into Columbia Business Center, a combination office park/shopping center.
Credit Cards:	Yes
Owner:	Marty Lookingbill & Vonnie Frazier
Year Estab:	1983
Comments:	The collection is quite a bit larger than the one we saw during our earlier visit. In addition to new books and used paperbacks, the hardcover used items are mostly reading copies of fairly new titles. Plenty to see but not necessarily strong in any one category.

Damascus
(Map 9, page 170)

L & L Books   **Open Shop**
26133 Ridge Road 20872   (301) 253-2510
                                                    E-mail: luedeke@erols.com

Collection:	General stock of hardcover and paperback.
# of Vols:	40,000
Hours:	Sun & Mon 12-5. Tue-Thu 10-6. Fri & Sat 10-8.
Services:	Accepts want lists.
Travel:	From Washington, DC: Exit 16 off I-270. Proceed north on Rte 27 (Ridge Rd) to Damascus. Shop in on right in High Point Shopping Center. From Baltimore: Exit 68 off I-70. Proceed south on Rte 27.
Credit Cards:	Yes
Owner:	Linda Burdette, Donna Fuller & Linda Luedeke
Year Estab:	1994
Comments:	If you don't make some of the wrong turns we did trying to locate this shop and you do get to visit, you may well wonder what brought you here. The shop offers a selection of both new and used hardcover and paperback books, most of fairly recent vintage, and little that is not normally available in a typical neighborhood used book store or at a library sale.

Darnestown

Steven C. Bernard-First Editions   **By Appointment**
15011 Plainfield Lane 20874   (301) 948-8423
                                                       Fax: (301) 947-8223

Collection:	Specialty
# of Vols:	5,000
Specialties:	Modern first editions; signed first editions; mystery; science fiction; fantasy; horror; black literature.
Services:	Catalog, accepts want lists.
Credit Cards:	Yes
Year Estab:	1974
Comments:	Deals exclusively in first editions.

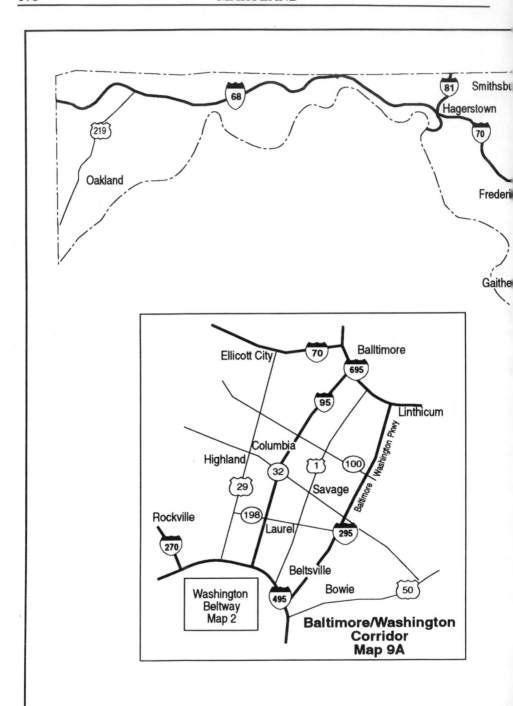

Smithsbu

81

Hagerstown

70

68

219

Oakland

Frederi

Gaithe

Ellicott City

70

Balltimore

695

95

Linthicum

Columbia

Highland

32

1

100

29

Savage

Baltimore / Washington Pkwy

Rockville

198

Laurel

295

270

Beltsville

Washington
Beltway
Map 2

495

Bowie

50

**Baltimore/Washington
Corridor
Map 9A**

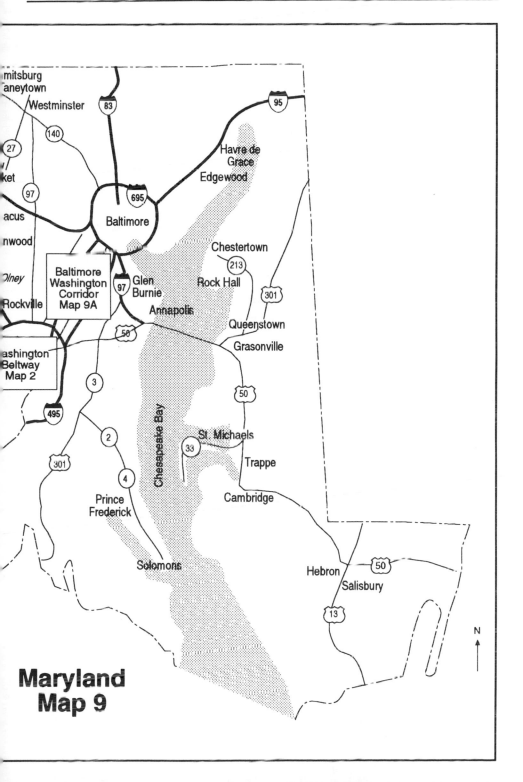

Maryland
Map 9

Edgewood
(Map 9, page 170)

Carol's Used Book Shop   **Open Shop**
2002 Pulaski Highway 21040   (410) 676-3560

Collection:	General stock of paperback and hardcover.
# of Vols:	25,000
Hours:	Mon-Sat 10-6, except Fri till 8. Sun 11-4.
Travel:	Exit 75 (Edgewood) off I-95. Proceed east on Old Emmerton Rd to second light and make a right onto Rte 40. Shop is 1/2 block ahead on right.
Credit Cards:	Yes
Owner:	Carol Aguilar
Year Estab:	1976
Comments:	Located in a trailer-like prefab building, this mostly paperback shop is divided into several rooms, each with its own specialty and an abundance of chairs for the browser's comfort. While there are some hardcover books on hand, most are of the book club variety and not at all unusual.

Ellicott City
(Map 9A, page 170)

Deeds Book Shop   **Open Shop**
8020 Main Street   (410) 465-9419
Mailing address: PO Box 85 Ellicott City 21041   E-mail: deedjohn@interloc.com

Collection:	General stock of mostly hardcover.
# of Vols:	6,000
Specialties:	Maryland; children's; classic literature; classic poetry.
Hours:	Wed-Sun 12-5. Best to call ahead.
Services:	Appraisals, search service, accepts want lists, mail order.
Travel:	From Baltimore, proceed west on Rte 40. Turn right at Rogers Ave and follow signs to historic district. Shop is located at bottom of hill.
Credit Cards:	Yes
Owner:	Jean Mattern
Year Estab:	1972
Comments:	A small, crowded shop with mostly older one-of-a-kind fiction and non fiction titles. The shop is definitely worth a visit if you're into vintage books or classics.

Gramp's Attic Books   **Open Shop**
8304 Main Street 21043   (410) 750-9235

Collection:	General stock.
# of Vols:	10,000
Specialties:	Medicine; maritime.
Hours:	Tue-Sat 11-5:30. Sun & Mon 12-5.
Travel:	See above.
Credit Cards:	Yes
Owner:	Walter & Bernice Jackson
Year Estab:	1991

Comments: A compact shop that makes the most of its limited space by packing books into narrow aisles. Most of the volumes we saw were in very good condition. The emphasis here is on non fiction although other subjects are certainly represented. If you're a medical maven, you'll certainly want to browse here.

Emmitsburg
(Map 9, page 170)

It's About Time   **Antique Mall**
At Emmitsbury Mall   (301) 447-6471
1 Chesapeake Street
Mailing address: 15308 Delphinium Lane Rockville 20853

Collection: General stock
# of Vols: 4,000
Hours: Daily 10-5.
Services: Accepts want lists.
Travel: From Rte 15 north turn left at second flashing light and proceed one mile. Right onto Potomac Ave and an immediate left onto Chesapeake.
Credit Cards: Yes
Owner: Robert G. Luther
Year Estab: 1987
Comments: Oft times there seems to be little rhyme or reason in the pricing of books found in used book booths in multi dealer antique malls. This booth was no exception and in our judgment, considering the condition of the books we saw on this visit, the books were a tad overpriced.

Finksburg

Trish Hughes, Bookseller   **By Appointment**
3140 Wheatfield Road 21048   (410) 840-9626
                                            E-mail: uhbooks@ix.netcom.com

Collection: Specialty
# of Vols: 1,500+
Specialties: Native American literature; natural history literature; some modern first editions; art; photography; biography; history; travel.
Services: Subject catalogs (also available on-line), accepts want lists.
Credit Cards: Yes
Year Estab: 1993

Frederick
(Map 9, page 170)

The Antique Station   **Antique Mall**
194 Thomas Johnson Drive 21701   (301) 695-0888

Hours: Daily, except closed Wed, 10-6.
Travel: Motter St exit off Rte 15 north. Make right at exit, then right at second light. Shop is third building on right.

(Frederick)

Off The Deep End   **Open Shop**
712 East Street 21701   (301) 698-9006
Web page: www.offthedeepend.com   Fax: (301) 698-0375
                                           E-mail: chilimon@offthedeepend.com

Collection:	General stock of hardcover and paperback and ephemera.
# of Vols:	14,000+
Hours:	Mon-Sat 10-7. Sun 10-6.
Travel:	Exit 56 (Patrick St) off I-270. Continue on Patrick St. Right on East.
Credit Cards:	Yes
Owner:	Sally & Steve Colby
Year Estab:	1990
Comments:	Looking for old memorabilia or novelty items? The first level of this shop has plenty to offer. Down one flight of stairs, you'll find paperback and hardcover books, not all in the best condition, with several shelves labeled "Pre 1960 Children's" and "Pre-1960 Fiction" containing books that are not necessarily hard-to-find old gems but rather books that have seen their day. We did spot a couple of shoppers browsing through a section of religious and inspirational titles and so we assume that the shop meets the needs of certain customers.

Wonder Book   **Open Shop**
1306 West Patrick Street 21703   (301) 694-5955

Collection:	General stock of used and new hardcover and paperback, prints, CDs, videos and comics.
# of Vols:	300,000
Hours:	Mon-Sat 10-10. Sun 12-10.
Services:	Search service.
Travel:	From I-270 westbound: Rte 15, then exit 6 off Rte 15 and proceed north on Rte 40 (West Patrick St) for 1¾ miles. Turn left onto McCain Drive and an immediate right into shopping center. From I-70 northbound: exit at exit 53 onto Rte 15 north and proceed as above.
Credit Cards:	Yes
Owner:	Charles E. Roberts
Year Estab:	1980
Comments:	Before you start browsing this large collection, or if your interests are very specific, you may want to pick up a copy of the handy store map that will guide you through the long rows of tightly packed and often overflowing shelves in this well stocked shop. Most of the hardcover books we saw during our visit were of fairly recent vintage but there were a few older items interspersed on the shelves. The shop also sells new books. Although the shop does not list any specialty areas (with 300,000 titles to choose from, you're likely to find something in most any category of interest), we noted particularly strong sections in entertainment, mystery and humor. Rare and collectible books are located in a series of locked glass bookcases in the front of the store.

Wonder Book   **Open Shop**
425 South Jefferson 21702   (301) 662-2774

Collection:	General stock of used and new hardcover and paperback, prints, CDs, videos and comics.
# of Vols:	100,000
Hours:	Mon-Sat 10-10. Sun 12-10.
Services:	Search service, accepts want lists, mail order.
Travel:	Located in Prospect Plaza Shopping Center, about five minutes from the other Wonder Book shop.
Credit Cards:	Yes
Owner:	Charles E. Roberts
Year Estab:	1980
Comments:	Smaller than its sister store, for the most part, this shop carries a similar stock, although we did see more older volumes on the shelves. If you visit the first shop, we believe there is less need to visit this location, especially if you're pressed for time.

Gaithersburg
(Map 9, page 170)

A-Z Used Books   **Open Shop**
373 Muddy Branch Road 20878   (301) 590-0022

Collection:	General stock of hardcover and some paperback.
# of Vols:	40,000
Hours:	Mon-Fri 10:30-8. Sat 10:30-7. Sun 11-5.
Services:	Search service, accepts want lists, mail order.
Travel:	Exit 9B off I-270. Proceed west on Rte 370 to Diamondback Dr, then right on Diamondback. Right at second light onto Muddy Branch Rd. Proceed for 3/4 of a mile. Shop is in Festival Shopping Center.
Credit Cards:	Yes
Owner:	Rennie Fagan
Year Estab:	1992
Comments:	It is initially difficult to determine whether this shop carries brand new books in addition to its used selections. That's because a fair number of the shop's books consist of review copies, many of which appear never to have been opened (probably not even by the reviewer to whom the book was initially sent). Customers looking for new literature, particularly in the field of science fiction, must have a field day here. The shop is neat, clean, well organized and easy to browse with plenty of paperbacks on hand as well as hardcover volumes in most popular subject areas. Not likely to be a place for antiquarian or vintage buffs. At the time of our visit, we saw fewer books on hand than noted above. There may, however, be additional books in storage.

(Gaithersburg)

Battle Books   **Open Shop**
18779-B North Frederick Road 20879   (301) 963-2929
Web page: www.oldesoldierbooks.com   Fax: (301) 963-9556
                                                E-mail: mail@oldesoldierbooks.com

Collection:	Specialty used and new.
# of Vols:	8,000-10,000
Specialties:	Military
Hours:	Mon-Sat 9-3.
Services:	Appraisals, search service, accepts want lists, catalog.
Travel:	See Olde Soldier Books below.
Credit Cards:	Yes
Owner:	Dave Zullo
Year Estab:	1975
Comments:	For Civil War books only, see Olde Soldier Books below.

Book Alcove   **Open Shop**
15976 Shady Grove Road 20877   (301) 977-9166

Collection:	General stock of hardcover and paperback
# of Vols:	200,000+
Hours:	Mon-Fri 10-8. Sat 10-7. Sun 12-6.
Services:	Accepts want lists, mail order.
Travel:	Shady Grove Rd exit off I-270. Proceed east on Shady Grove. Make left at second light (Gaither Rd) into shopping center. Shop is in the rear of the center.
Credit Cards:	Yes
Owner:	Ray Sickles
Year Estab:	1974
Comments:	If we were planning a return trip to Maryland and only had time to visit one of the two Book Alcove shops, we would choose this one over the Rockville location. What particularly attracts us to this shop is its larger number of older volumes and the meticulous way the shelves are organized into so many sub categories. The books are quite moderately priced and we think there is a good chance you may find more than one gem to your liking. The shop is aptly named as the store is subdivided into what appears to be a never ending series of alcoves for the book lover to explore.

Olde Soldier Books   **Open Shop**
18779-B North Frederick Road 20897   (301) 963-2929
Web page: www.oldesoldierbooks.com   Fax: (301) 963-9556
                                           E-mail: mail@oldesoldierbooks@aol.com

Collection:	Specialty books and related items.
# of Vols:	14,000
Specialties:	Civil War, including autographs, documents and photographs.
Hours:	Mon-Sat 9-3.
Services:	Appraisals, search service, accepts want lists, catalog.

Travel:	Exit 11 (Rte 124 East) off I-270. Make left onto Rte 355 and proceed north for about 1.2 miles. Right onto Game Preserve Rd. Shop is the first building on the right.
Credit Cards:	Yes
Owner:	Dave Zullo
Year Estab:	1975
Comments:	Stock is approximately 80% used. Owner operates a second business with general military books. See Battle Books above.

Glen Burnie
(Map 9, page 170)

Book Nook II   **Open Shop**
143 Delaware Avenue, NE 21061   (410) 766-5758

Collection:	General stock of paperback and hardcover.
# of Vols:	60,000
Hours:	Mon-Sat 10-5, except Wed till 7.
Travel:	Proceeding south from Baltimore on Rte 2 (Gov Ritchie Hwy), the shop is in a small cluster of shops just off the highway and just before the Hurandale Mall.
Comments:	If you happen to be looking for a particular paperback title, there's a good chance of finding it in this shop which is about 85% paperback. If you're searching for a hard to find hardcover title, though, we doubt if you'd be successful here.

Glenwood
(Map 9, page 170)

Books With A Past   **Open Shop**
2465 Washington Road, Ste 4 21738   (410) 442-3740
                                                             Fax: (410) 442-3741
                                                     E-mail: bwapast@erols.com

Collection:	General stock of hardcover and paperback.
# of Vols:	40,000
Specialties:	Cryptology; science fiction.
Hours:	Mon-Fri 11-7. Sat & Sun 11-5ish. Holidays 11-4ish.
Services:	Accepts want lists, mail order.
Travel:	Exit 76 (Rte 97) off I-70. Proceed south on Rte 97 for 1¼ miles. Shop is in Inwood Village Shopping Center.
Credit Cards:	Yes
Owner:	Mary Alice & Marvin Schaefer
Year Estab:	1990
Comments:	This shop has a little bit of everything; old books, new books, paperbacks, hardcover volumes, best sellers, ex library and book club editions, a multi volume collection on the life of Theodore Roosevelt and you name it. It's the kind of shop in which you may see so many common titles that it will require a bit of patience to spot the winners.

Grasonville
(Map 9, page 170)

Delmarva Book Shop   **Open Shop**
300 Drummer Drive 21638   (410) 827-9400

Collection:	General stock.
# of Vols:	60,000
Specialties:	Nautical; naval history; military; biography; history.
Hours:	Thu-Sun 10-6. Mon-Wed by appointment.
Services:	Limited appraisals, search service, accepts want lists, collection development.
Travel:	Proceeding eastward, exit 44B (Evans Ave) off I-50/301. Right onto Drummer Dr. Proceeding westbound, exit at Nesbitt Rd overpass off I-50/301. Right onto Rte 18, then right onto Evans and left on Drummer. Shop is located in the rear of a larger building housing a flea market.
Credit Cards:	Yes
Owner:	Christopher Dobbyn
Year Estab:	1991
Comments:	After our visit to this shop we made the following observations:

While many of the shelves carried the typical identification labels such as biography, history, business and such, we also noted many shelves simply designated "old books." Condition varied as did prices. The owner indicates a high turnover rate so one cannot really guess what might be on the shelves on any given visit. At the time of our visit, a sizeable portion of the stock was not displayed.

It is, of course, possible that changes have been made since that visit.

Hagerstown
(Map 9, page 170)

Barnwood Books   **Open Shop**
103 South Potomac Street 21740   (301) 790-0606

Collection:	General stock of hardcover and paperback.
# of Vols:	75,000
Hours:	Mon-Sat 10-5.
Services:	Appraisals
Travel:	Located off Rte 40 in downtown Hagerstown, across from the public library.
Credit Cards:	No
Owner:	Eva Delle & Jack Staley
Year Estab:	1983
Comments:	Probably the largest used book dealer in western Maryland. The shop consists of one large room devoted exclusively to paperbacks with a second, equally large room devoted to hardcover non fiction titles. A third room at the rear of the store offers hardcover mysteries, science fiction and general fiction. The stock is well labeled and well orga-

nized and the majority of the hardcover titles are of fairly recent vintage with multiple copies of the same title. We did, however, spot some older volumes interspersed. Prices vary. Given the size of the collection and the fact that most general categories are represented, it's certainly possible for the book hunter to find an unusual title or two. The owner takes pride in having helped several younger dealers get their start in the business.

Wonder Book   **Open Shop**
1701 Massey Boulevard 21740   (301) 733-1888

Collection:	General stock of mostly used hardcover and paperback, remainders, prints, CDs and comics.
# of Vols:	200,000
Hours:	Mon-Sat 10-10. Sun 12-10.
Services:	Search service, accepts want lists, mail order.
Travel:	Halfway Blvd exit off I-81. Proceed east on Halfway for about 1/2 mile. Left on Massey and right into Valley Plaza shopping center.
Credit Cards:	Yes
Owner:	Charles E. Roberts
Year Estab:	1995
Comments:	See comments for Wonder Book in Frederick.

Havre de Grace
(Map 9, page 170)

Courtyard Bookshop   **Open Shop**
313 St. John Street 21078   (410) 939-5150

Collection:	General stock of hardcover and paperback.
# of Vols:	16,000
Specialties:	Military; nautical.
Hours:	Mon-Fri 10-6. Sat 10-6. Sun 12-5.
Services:	Search service, accepts want lists, mail order.
Travel:	Havre De Grace exit off I-95. Proceed on Rte 155 to end. After passing under railroad overpass, make a right onto Juniata St, then left at first light onto Ostego, then right onto Union. After crossing railroad, swing left at statue of Lafayette and make quick right onto St. John. Shop is about two blocks ahead on left.
Credit Cards:	Yes
Owner:	Jack Kelly
Year Estab:	1989
Comments:	More books on hand than we saw during our first visit three years ago. Most of the books were reading copies, nicely organized in several small rooms. Hardcover books outnumber paperbacks and the shop offers a nice general collection. If there were rare titles on hand we failed to spot them.

(Havre de Grace)

Golden Vane Antiques   **Antique Mall**
408 North Union Avenue 21078   (410) 939-9595

Hours: Sun 11-5. Mon, Fri & Sat 11-6. Thu 11-9.
Travel: See Courtyard Bookshop above.

Splendor in Brass   **Open Shop**
123 Market Street 21078   (410) 939-1312

Collection: General stock of hardcover and paperback.
# of Vols: 20,000+
Hours: Daily 9:30-6.
Travel: See Courtyard Bookshop above. From Union St, continue to Congress
                  Ave. Left on Congress then right on Market.
Comments: If you're looking for older books, not necessarily in the best condition
                  but priced "to sell," you might want to check out the basement of this
                  furniture/collectible shop. Note that the basement is usually only open
                  to browsers on Saturday and Sunday from 9:30-4 in conjunction with a
                  weekend flea market. You'll probably have better luck at the two other
                  shops in town.

Washington Street Books   **Open Shop**
131 North Washington Street 21078   (410) 939-6215
                                                                 Fax: (410) 939-5176

Collection: General stock of hardcover and paperback and ephemera.
# of Vols: 15,000
Specialties: Civil War; science fiction; Mark Twain; modern first editions; vintage
                  paperbacks.
Hours: Wed-Sun 12-6.
Services: Accepts want lists.
Travel: From Union St (see Courtyard Bookshop above), proceed to first light
                  and make left onto Congress, then first left onto Washington. Shop is
                  just ahead on right.
Credit Cards: Yes
Owner: John & Kathy Klisavage
Year Estab: 1992
Comments: This shop carries both collectibles and books with an almost even
                  amount of space devoted to each. Many of the books we saw were in
                  line with the antique motif of the shop in that they dated back to the
                  late 19th and early 20th century. Some newer volumes were also on
                  hand. Subjects ranged from military history to children's to general
                  fiction. The owner notes that he has an additional 18,000 volumes in
                  storage.

Hebron
(Map 9, page 170)

Gateway Books **Open Shop**
26550 Ocean Gateway 21830 (410) 860-9750
Fax: (410) 860-2964

Collection: General stock and ephemera.
# of Vols: 8,000
Specialties: Newspapers (historic and birthdate).
Hours: Mon-Fri 8-5. Sat 10-2. Other times by chance or appointment.
Services: Mail auctions for historic newspapers and ephemera.
Travel: On Rte 50 at mile marker #104.
Credit Cards: No
Owner: Robert L. Mooers
Year Estab: 1973

Highland
(Map 9A, page 170)

Second Hand Prose **Open Shop**
13376 Clarksville Pike 20777 (301) 854-2440

Collection: General stock of hardcover and paperback.
# of Vols: 15,000-20,000
Hours: Mon-Sat 10-6. Sun 12-4.
Travel: From Rte 29, turn west onto Rte 216. Shop is at intersection of Rte 216 and Rte 108 (Clarksville Pike).
Credit Cards: No
Owner: Jean Lorenzen
Year Estab: 1996
Comments: When one sees a single volume containing three complete novels by John Ludlum on a shelf marked "First Editions" one has to wonder how this dealer defines the term "first edition." The shop carries an ample supply of paperbacks and hardcover books (many in shiny dust jackets), plenty of recent best sellers, as well as a healthy selection of older books. Pricing is, in our judgment, erratic. The shop is roomy and easy to browse. A long visit should not be necessary for you to determine if the elusive book you've been searching for is here.

Kensington
(Map 2, page 154)

All Books Considered **Open Shop**
10408 Montgomery Avenue 20895 (301) 929-0036
E-mail: all_boox@interloc.com

Collection: General stock.
# of Vols: 20,000
Specialties: Metaphysics; theology; history; Americana; military; Modern Library; antiques reference; university histories; business histories.
Hours: Tue-Sat 11-5. Sun 12-5

(Kensington)

Travel:	Rte 185 (Connecticut Ave) exit off I-495. Proceed north on Rte 185 to Howard. Right on Howard. Shop is three blocks ahead on right across from railroad station. (Note: Howard goes around a bend and becomes Montgomery.)
Credit Cards:	Yes
Owner:	Donald Ramsey
Year Estab:	1992
Comments:	A strong collection of esoterica with the balance of the collection notable for its atypical titles in the more popular subjects areas. In our judgment, well worth a visit for anyone looking for an out of the ordinary title.

Brandeis University Book Store
3716 Howard Avenue 20895

Open Shop
(301) 942-4707

Collection:	General stock of hardcover and paperback.
Hours:	Tue-Sun 10:30-5.
Travel:	See above. Shop is located across from the train station in a small white building that also houses the Prevention of Blindness Society.
Comments:	Operated by volunteers. All books are donated.

Children's BookAdoption Agency
PO Box 643 20895-0643

By Appointment
(301) 565-2834
Fax: (301) 585-3091

Collection:	Specialty
# of Vols:	12,000+
Specialties:	Black studies (children's and adult).
Services:	Search service, catalog, accepts want lists, gives talks on children's books and authors.
Credit Cards:	No
Owner:	Barbara & Bill Yoffee
Year Estab:	1987

Patrick W. Edwards Books
3218 Edgewood Road 20895-2904

By Appointment
(301) 933-2025
Fax: (301) 933-7351
E-mail: pedwards@interloc.com

Collection:	Specialty new and used.
Specialties:	Mystery; science fiction; literature; children's.
Services:	Appraisals, search service, catalog, accepts want lists.
Credit Cards:	Yes
Year Estab:	1990

Feng's Antiques and Appraisals
3786 Howard Avenue 20895

Open Shop
(301) 942-0137

Collection:	General stock.
# of Vols:	500+
Hours:	Mon-Sat 11-5:30. Sun 12-5:30.
Comments:	Several hundred older books in an antique/collectible shop.

Laurel
(Map 9A, page 170)

Attic Books   **Open Shop**
100 Washington Boulevard 20707   (301) 725-3725

Collection:	General stock of hardcover and paperback.
# of Vols:	25,000
Specialties:	Science fiction; mystery; military.
Hours:	Mon-Sat 11-7.
Travel:	Corner of Rte 1 (south) and Main St.
Credit Cards:	Yes
Owner:	Richard Cook
Year Estab:	1973
Comments:	A modest sized, well organized shop with books in generally good condition and reasonably priced.

John W. Knott, Jr.   **By Appointment**
8453 Early Bud Way 20723-1085   Tel & Fax: (301) 317-8427
                                                                 E-mail: jwkbooks@millkern.com

Collection:	Specialty new and used.
# of Vols:	4,500
Specialties:	Science fiction; horror; fantasy; mystery; adventure; first editions (in listed genres).
Services:	Catalog, accepts want lists.
Credit Cards:	Yes
Year Estab:	1988

Linthicum
(Map 9A, page 170)

Toomey's Bookshop   **Open Shop**
203 Transmission Court   Tel & Fax: (410) 850-0831
Mailing address: PO Box 122 Linthicum 21090

Collection:	General stock of hardcover and paperback.
# of Vols:	20,000
Specialties:	Maryland; Civil War.
Hours:	Mon-Fri 11-6. Sat 11-5. Closed Sat during summer.
Travel:	Exit 6B (Camp Meade) off I-695. Proceed south on Camp Meade through first light. Shop is just head, on left, in Shipley Linthicum Shopping Center.
Credit Cards:	Yes
Owner:	Daniel Toomey
Year Estab:	1993
Comments:	A neat store with a rather modest collection of clean hardcover and paperback volumes, mostly newer titles with a bent toward the specialties listed above. At the time of our visit, the number of books on display were fewer than noted above.

New Market
(Map 9, page 170)

C.W. Wood Bookshop   **Open Shop**
42 Main Street 21774   (301) 831-6118
                                                          Fax: (301) 865-5976

Collection:	General stock.
# of Vols:	15,000
Specialties:	Poetry; Maryland.
Hours:	Sat & Sun 1-5. Other times by appointment.
Services:	Appraisals, search service, accepts want lists, subject catalogs by request, mail order.
Travel:	Exit 62 off I-70. Proceed west on Rte 144 (Main St) for about 1/2 mile. Shop is on left across from Town Hall.
Credit Cards:	No
Owner:	Howard & Susan Wood Wilson
Year Estab:	1960
Comments:	This relatively small shop, located in a quaint community and on a street lined with antique shops, carries mostly older books. If you're interested in 19th century or early 20th century volumes, you might find books here to meet your taste. And even if you don't find a long lost title you've been searching for, you're likely to enjoy the visit to New Market. The shop also sells antiques.

Oakland
(Map 9, page 170)

Appalachian Background Books   **Open Shop**
4167 Maryland Highway 21550   (301) 334-4334

Collection:	General stock and ephemera.
# of Vols:	10,000
Specialties:	Children's; first editions; science fiction; mystery; vintage paperbacks; early magazines.
Hours:	Sat 10-4. Other times by appointment.
Services:	Accepts want lists, mail order.
Travel:	In western Maryland. Take Rte 219 to Oakland, then east on Oak St which becomes Maryland Hwy. Shop is about four miles ahead.
Credit Cards:	No
Owner:	S. Ivan Rowe
Year Estab:	1971

Ocean City

Bookshelf Etc.   **Open Shop**
8006 Coastal Highway 21842   (410) 524-2949

Collection:	General stock of mostly paperback.
# of Vols:	15,000
Hours:	May-Sep: Daily 10-8. Oct-Nov & Feb-Apr: Weekends 10-4. Closed Jan & Dec.

Bookworld   **Open Shop**
1st & Boardwalk 21842   (410) 289-7466

Collection: General stock mostly paperback.
# of Vols: 20,000
Hours: Mem Day-Oct 31: Daily 9am-11pm. Remainder of year: call for hours.

The Mason Collection   **Open Shop**
Shantytown   (410) 213-0041
Mailing address: PO Box G Fruitland 21826

Collection: General stock of mostly paperback.
Hours: May-Sep: Daily 10-10.

Olney
(Map 9, page 170)

T.A. Borden   **By Appointment**
17119 Old Baltimore Road 20832   Tel & Fax: (301) 774-4669
                                                                    E-mail: taborden@interloc.com

Collection: General stock.
# of Vols: 11,000-12,000
Specialties: Americana; performing arts; fine art; architecture; photography; deco-
                rative arts; literature; travel; science; nature; humanities; social sci-
                ences; history.
Services: Appraisals, accepts want lists, subject lists, mail order.
Credit Cards: No
Owner: Guy Gran & Therese Borden
Year Estab: 1987

Poolesville

The Thankful Chase   **By Appointment**
The John Poole House   (202) 955-5758   (301) 972-7298
Mailing address: PO Box 277 Poolesville 20837   Fax: (301) 428-8313
                                                                    E-mail: willisvd@aol.com

Collection: Specialty
# of Vols: 2,000
Specialties: Cookbooks; wine.
Services: Appraisals, search service, catalog, accepts want lists.
Credit Cards: No
Owner: Willis Van Devanter
Year Estab: 1973

Prince Frederick
(Map 9, page 170)

Second Looks Books   **Open Shop**
759 Solomons Island Road North   Tel & Fax: (410) 535-6897
Mailing address: PO Box 600 Prince Frederick 20678 E-mail: slbooks@prodigy.net

Collection:	General stock of paperback and hardcover.
# of Vols:	30,000
Hours:	Mon-Wed 10-7. Thu & Fri 10-8. Sat 10-5. Sun 12-4.
Services:	Accepts want lists.
Travel:	Located in Fox Run Shopping Center which is visible from Rte 2/4.
Credit Cards:	Yes
Owner:	Elizabeth A. Prouty & Richard C. Due
Year Estab:	1991
Comments:	The majority of the stock in this neat and well organized shop is paperback and most of the hardcover titles are of relatively recent vintage. Prices are quite reasonable. We saw little in the way of antiquarian or rare titles when we visited.

Queenstown
(Map 9, page 170)

Chesapeake Antique Center   **Antique Mall**
Route 301 21658   (410) 827-6640

Hours:	Daily 10-5.
Travel:	Ten miles east of Bay Bridge and 1/2 mile after Rtes 301 and 50 split.

Riverdale
(Map 2, page 154)

Riverdale Bookshop & Coffee Depot   **Open Shop**
4701 Queensbury Road 20737   (301) 277-8141

Collection:	General stock of mostly hardcover.
# of Vols:	15,000
Hours:	Mon-Fri 7am-8pm. Sat & Sun 9-6.
Travel:	Rte 1 exit off I-95. Proceed south on Rte 1 for about five miles, then left on Queensbury Rd. Shop is about two blocks ahead, on right, at the train station.
Credit Cards:	No
Owner:	Simon Plog & Audrey Bragg
Year Estab:	1950's
Comments:	How nice to find a shop that serves coffee and snacks whose book collection is actually worth a visit. Most of the books we saw here were older volumes in mixed condition. Several unusual titles. The shop is organized for easy browsing and the books are most reasonably priced.

Rock Hall
(Map 9, page 170)

America's Cup Cafe   **Open Shop**
5745 Main Street 21661   (410) 639-7361

Collection:	General stock of paperback and hardcover.
# of Vols:	2,000+
Hours:	Mon-Fri 7am-9pm. Sat & Sun 7am-10pm.
Travel:	See The Cup Runneth Over below.
Credit Cards:	No
Owner:	Arlene Douglas
Year Estab:	1996

The Cup Runneth Over   **Open Shop**
5761 Main Street   (410) 639-7486
Mailing address: PO Box 510 Rock Hall 21661

Collection:	General stock of paperback and hardcover.
# of Vols:	5,000
Hours:	Sun-Thu 10-8. Fri & Sat 10-10.
Travel:	From Chestertown, continue on Rte 213 to Rte 20, then Rte 20 to Rock Hall. At intersection with blinking light turn left on Main Street. Shop is just ahead on left.
Credit Cards:	No
Owner:	Peter Hiler
Year Estab:	1997
Comments:	Stock is approximately 65% paperback. The owner's main store is The Book Trader, in Philadelphia.

Rockville
(Map 2, page 154 & Map 9, page 170)

Book Alcove   **Open Shop**
706H Rockville Pike 20852   (301) 309-1231

Collection:	General stock of hardcover and paperback.
# of Vols:	150,000+
Hours:	Mon-Sat 10-9. Sun 12-6.
Services:	Accepts want lists, mail order.
Travel:	Rte 355 (Rockville Pike) exit off I-495. Proceed north on Rte 355 for about five miles. Shop is on the right, just north of Wintergreen Plaza. From I-270: Exit 6. Proceed east on Rte 28, then south on Rte 355.
Credit Cards:	Yes
Owner:	Ray Sickles
Year Estab:	1980
Comments:	If you're willing to overlook unshelved books on the floor in several of the aisles, some books not alphabetized by author, a healthy supply of paperbacks and Reader's Digest volumes and you're willing to exercise a little bit of patience, you might (as we did) find a couple of titles worth purchasing here. Perhaps its all just a matter of aesthetics.

(Rockville)

modern
good
(across
from
SAS)

Leaf Through   **Open Shop**
1701-L Rockville Pike 20852   (301) 230-8998

Collection:	General stock of paperback and hardcover.
# of Vols:	30,000
Hours:	Tue-Fri 10-7, except Thu till 8. Sat 10-5. Sun 12-5.
Travel:	Rockville Pike exit off I-495. Proceed north on Rockville Pike for about 3.5 miles. Shop is on left in Congressional South Shopping Center. Turn left at Halpine Rd traffic light into shopping center. At end of traffic divider, turn left into parking lot. Shop is to the left.
Credit Cards:	Yes
Owner:	Carol Perone
Year Estab:	1995
Comments:	A little tricky to find but once you do you'll discover a very neat shop with a fairly typical selection of newer volumes, i.e., recent best sellers, paperbacks, book club editions, etc. Not likely that a long lost treasure will turn up here, but there are enough goodies to satisfy local readers.

Robert A. Madle SF/Fantasy Books   **By Appointment**
4406 Bestor Drive 20853   (301) 460-4712

Collection:	Specialty new and used.
# of Vols:	20,000
Specialties:	Science fiction; fantasy; pulps.
Services:	Catalog, accepts want lists, mail order.
Credit Cards:	Yes
Year Estab:	1970
Comments:	We do not often visit "by appointment" dealers but the specialty of this particular dealer intrigued us and we were privileged to see his collection located in the basement of his home. If your interests lie in out of print and rare fantasy, science fiction and/or pulps and you're anywhere in the region, try to visit as the owner's catalog cannot possibly list all of the wondrous items on hand.

Peter Pun Books   **By Appointment**
835 Bowie Road 20852   (301) 762-4062

Collection:	Specialty
# of Vols:	5,000
Specialties:	Americana; literary first editions; military; American history; Civil War; literary manuscripts and correspondence.
Services:	Accepts want lists.
Credit Cards:	No
Owner:	Joseph E. Jeffs
Year Estab:	1991

Quill & Brush   **By Appointment**
14717 Janico Drive   20853   (301) 460-3700
Web page: qb.com/pub/q-and-b   Fax: (301) 871-5425
                                                        E-mail: firsts@qb.com

Collection:	Specialty
# of Vols:	8,000
Specialties:	First editions (19th & 20th century); literature; poetry; mystery; science fiction.
Services:	Appraisals, search service, catalog, accepts want lists, price guides.
Credit Cards:	Yes
Owner:	Patricia & Allen Ahearn

Second Story Books   **Open Shop**
12160 Parklawn Drive 20852   (301) 770-0477
Web page: www.paltech.com/secondstory   E-mail: ssbookguys@paltech.com

Collection:	General stock.
# of Vols:	150,000
Hours:	Sun-Thu 10-7. Fri & Sat 10-9.
Services:	Appraisals, search service, catalog, accepts want lists.
Travel:	Rte 355 (Rockville Pike) exit off I-495. Proceed north on Rte 355 to Randolph Rd. Right onto Randolph, then left onto Parklawn. Shop is on the right, set back about 75 feet from the street in a warehouse like building. Metro Red Line: Twinbrook Station.
Credit Cards:	Yes
Owner:	Allan Stypeck
Year Estab:	1974
Comments:	Unlike the chain's two storefront retail shops in Washington and Bethesda, this headquarters location is a warehouse setting. While we would certainly recommend your visiting all three shops, if your time in the Washington area is limited and you can only visit one location, we suggest this one because of its larger collection and better prices and also because the books here are of generally older vintage than the titles found in the retail stores. Given the size of the collection and the wide array of categories represented, we suggest you plan to stay awhile so that you can adequately browse all that is available. A separate rare book room is open by appointment.

Washington Used Book Center   **Open Shop**
11910 Parklawn Drive 20852   (301) 984-7358

Collection:	General stock.
# of Vols:	50,000
Hours:	Mon-Fri 10-5:30. Sat 10-4. Sun 12-4.
Travel:	See Second Story Books above. Turn right onto Parklawn Dr. Shop is fourth building on right.
Credit Cards:	Yes
Owner:	Michael E. Schnitter, Manager
Year Estab:	1997

Comments: We were not disappointed by our visit to this group shop, finding, once
                   more, that dealers who display at such locations tend to put their best
                   foot forward. The volumes we saw were in good to excellent condition,
                   non fiction is well represented, and the titles were not your typical used
                   book store selections. If you have scholarly tastes and want to be
                   tempted, you'll enjoy a visit here. Indeed, even if you're a vintage
                   mystery buff, you can find titles here generally not seen elsewhere.

Yak & Yeti Books   **By Appointment**
PO Box 5736 20855   (301) 869-5860

Collection: Specialty
# of Vols: 4,000
Specialties: Himalayan region; Tibet; Central Asia; Mongolia.
Services: Catalog
Owner: Daniel W. Edwards
Year Estab: 1982

Saint Michaels
(Map 9, page 170)

The Book Nook   **Open Shop**
411 Talbot Street 21663-0453   (410) 745-5742

Collection: General stock of hardcover and paperback.
# of Vols: 15,000
Hours: Daily 2-5. Best to confirm.
Travel: From Rte 50, proceed west on Rte 33.
Comments: Stock is approximately 60% hardcover.

Salisbury
(Map 9, page 170)

Henrietta's Attic   **Open Shop**
205 Maryland Avenue 21801   (410) 546-3700
                                                                      (800) 546-3744

Collection: General stock and ephemera.
# of Vols: 8,000
Specialties: Cookbooks; children's; American history; Maryland; Delaware.
Hours: Mon-Sat 10-5.
Services: Search service, accepts want lists, mail order.
Travel: Five blocks south of the hospital on Bus Rte 13 (South Salisbury Blvd).
                   Right onto Maryland Ave. Shop is just ahead on right.
Credit Cards: Yes
Owner: Henrietta J. Moore
Year Estab: 1980
Comments: A crowded shop with one room devoted to books and ephemera and a
                   second to collectibles. The books are reasonably priced, in mixed condi-
                   tion and of mixed vintage. The shop is not as well organized as it could be
                   and you may need a few extra minutes to browse most of the titles.

Market Street Books	**Open Shop**
146 West Market Street 21801	(410) 219-3210

Collection: General stock of hardcover and paperback.
# of Vols: 25,000+
Specialties: Children's
Hours: Tue-Sat 10:30-4.
Services: Accepts want lists, search service, mail order.
Travel: Rte 50 to Salisbury. Traveling eastbound, after crossing the Wicomico Bridge, turn right onto Mill St, then immediate left and immediate right onto Market. Shop is at end of street on right.
Credit Cards: No
Owner: Betsy Henry
Year Estab: 1993
Comments: We're always happy to pay a return visit to a shop that was just getting started at the time the first edition of this book was published. This dealer has obviously been quite busy in the intervening years. Hardly an inch of space on the shop's first level is wasted with books displayed in every nook and cranny. Just prior to our visit, the shop had expanded to a second floor and we saw several additional rooms available for further expansion.

Savage

(Map 9A, page 170)

The Book Guy	**Antique Mall**
At Antique Center II	(301) 604-2665
8600 Foundry Street 20763	E-mail: abookguy@interloc.com

Collection: General stock.
Specialties: Genealogy; children's; modern first editions; history.
Hours: Sun-Wed 10-6. Thu-Sat 10-9.
Services: Search service, accepts want lists.
Travel: Rte 32 exit off I-95. Proceed east on Rte 32 to Rte 1, then south on Rte 1 to Howard St. Right on Howard then left on Foundry.
Credit Cards: Yes
Owner: Jim Johnson & Pamela Lever
Year Estab: 1996

Silver Spring

(Map 2, page 154)

Hirschtritt's "1712" Books	**By Appointment**
1712 Republic Road 20902	(301) 649-5393

Collection: General stock.
# of Vols: 3,000
Specialties: Golf; Americana; Japan.
Services: Appraisals, search service, accepts want lists, mail order.
Owner: Ralph & Anita Hirschritt
Year Estab: 1970

(Silver Spring)

Imagination Books   **Open Shop**
946 Sligo Avenue 20910   (301) 589-2223
                                                                 Fax: (301) 229-2749

Collection:	General stock of hardcover and paperback and records.
# of Vols:	40,000+
Hours:	Mon-Sat 10-6. Sun 10-4.
Services:	Accepts want lists, catalog.
Travel:	Georgia Ave exit off I-495. Proceed south on Georgia to Sligo, then left on Sligo. Shop is just ahead on right.
Credit Cards:	Yes
Owner:	Elisenda D. Hopper
Year Estab:	1972
Comments:	A second visit to this establishment three years after the first visit hasn't changed our view. Once you enter this deceptively small looking shop you proceed from small room to small room to still another small room, each filled from floor to ceiling and representing every area of interest most book people would be attracted to. The books are of mixed vintage and mixed condition and are priced to sell. We believe there are bargains to be had here and would certainly recommend a visit for the serious book collector.

Silver Spring Books   **Open Shop**
938 Bonifant Street 20910   (301) 587-7484

Collection:	General stock of hardcover and paperback.
# of Vols:	40,000
Specialties:	Science fiction; black studies; literature.
Hours:	Mon, Thu, Fri, Sat 10:30-6:30. Sun 10:30-5.
Services:	Search service, accepts want lists.
Travel:	Rte 29 (Georgia Ave) exit off I-495. Proceed south on Georgia, then left onto Bonifant. Shop is just ahead on the right.
Credit Cards:	No
Owner:	D. Goodwin, C. Parker, W. Morgan & P. Def
Year Estab:	1972
Comments:	A well organized group shop owned and operated by four dealers, each with a distinctively different collection. If you happen to be interested in any of the shop's specialty areas, particularly mystery, there's a good chance you may find a title you've been looking for. The co-owner you happen to meet on the day of your visit will depend on which owner is manning the store at the time. The books are reasonably priced.

Smithsburg
(Map 9, page 170)

Boyer's Book Bank & Emporium   **Open Shop**
1 South Main Street   (301) 824-3733
Mailing address: PO Box 252 Smithsburg 21783

Collection:	General stock of mostly used paperback and hardcover.
Hours:	Tue-Fri 10:30-5:30. Sat 9-2.
Travel:	Exit 35 off I-70, then north on Rte 66 to downtown. Shop is on the square.
Credit Cards:	No
Owner:	Harold Boyer
Year Estab:	1994

Solomons
(Map 9, page 170)

Lazy Moon Bookshop   **Open Shop**
14510 Main Street   (410) 326-3720
Mailing address: PO Box 1141 Solomons 20688

Collection:	General stock of hardcover and paperback.
# of Vols:	20,000
Specialties:	Nautical; military; mystery; literature; history; philosophy; Maryland; Chesapeake Bay; music; science fiction; cookbooks; children's.
Hours:	Summer: Daily 10-6. Winter: Thu-Mon 11-5.
Services:	Accepts want lists.
Travel:	From Washington Beltway, take Rte 4 south to Solomons. (If you go over the Thomas Johnson Bridge, you've gone too far.)
Credit Cards:	Yes
Owner:	Jim Gscheidle
Year Estab:	1988
Comments:	A charming bi-level shop. The majority of the hardcover books we saw were in very good condition (most with dust jackets). The stock was a combination of hard to find titles mixed in with more common items. Although somewhat out of the way, the shop is certainly worth driving a few extra miles for.

Takoma Park
(Map 2, page 154)

Takoma Emporium   **Open Shop**
1107 Sligo Creek Parkway 20912   (301) 270-0640
                                                    Fax: (301) 891-3695

Collection:	General stock.
# of Vols:	1,000
Hours:	Sun-Fri 11-7.
Travel:	New Hampshire/Takoma Park exit off I-495. Proceed south on New Hampshire to Sligo Creek Pkwy, then right on Sligo Creek.

Credit Cards: Yes
Owner: Toni Bruce
Comments: Shop also sells antiques, original art and vintage clothing.

Taneytown
(Map 9, page 170)

Taneytown Antique Shoppes   **Open Shop**
7 Frederick Street 21787   (410) 756-4262
                                                           (410) 775-7083

Collection: General stock.
# of Vols: 5,000
Hours: Tue & Fri 11-5. Sat & Sun 10-6. Other times by appointment.
Services: Search service, accepts want lists, mail order.
Travel: In the heart of Taneytown at intersection of Rtes 194 & 140.
Credit Cards: Yes
Owner: Linda Bilo
Year Estab: 1982
Comments: While this bi-level shop offers more collectibles than books, it does
                  have enough older books (in mixed condition) to justify a brief stop,
                  but only if you're passing through the community.

Tilghman

Book Bank   **Open Shop**
5782 Tilghman Island Road   (410) 886-2230
Mailing address: 5520 N. 16th St. Arlington, VA 22205   Fax: (703) 534-8562
                                                       E-mail: bookbank@msn.com

Collection: Specialty. Mostly used and some new.
# of Vols: 12,000
Specialties: Nautical, naval; Chesapeake; maritime art; whaling; exploration; rivers;
                  everything "watery".
Hours: Sat & Sun 10-6.
Services: Search service, accepts want lists, mail order.
Travel: Rte 50 to Easton, then west on Rte 322 to Rte 33 through St. Michaels
                  to Tilghman Island where Rte 33 becomes Main St.
Credit Cards: Yes
Owner: Gary & Susan Crawford
Year Estab: 1992

Trappe
(Map 9, page 170)

Unicorn Bookshop   **Open Shop**
3935 Ocean Gateway   (410) 476-3838
Mailing address: PO Box 154 Trappe 21673

Collection: General stock.
# of Vols: 25,000

Specialties:	Maryland; Civil War; decorative arts; maps; first editions.
Hours:	Daily 9-5.
Services:	Mail order.
Travel:	Located on Rte 50 between Easton and Cambridge. Proceeding south on Rte 50, the shop is on the left, in a stand alone red brick building. Look for the sign of the unicorn.
Credit Cards:	Yes
Owner:	James Dawson
Year Estab:	1975
Comments:	This shop is a winner. The shelves are filled with books in almost every conceivable category. The books are quite reasonably priced and for the most part are in very good condition. A "better book room" displays rare volumes, first editions and fine bindings and maps are attractively displayed in a small second floor loft like space. Even if you don't see a book you have been searching for (and by the way, we did), you're sure to enjoy your search.

Waldorf

Ellie's Paperback Shack   **Open Shop**
2700 Crain Highway 20601   (301) 934-3140

Collection:	General stock of mostly paperback.
Hours:	Mon-Fri 10-6. (Longer in summer) Sat 10-5. Sun 12-5.

Walkersville

First Place Books   **By Appointment**
PO Box 561 21793   (301) 845-1248
Web page: www.radix.net/~fpbooks   E-mail: fpbooks@radix.net

Collection:	Specialty
# of Vols:	5,000
Specialties:	Nautical fiction; mystery; modern first editions; hypermodern first editions.
Services:	Search service, catalog, accepts want lists.
Credit Cards:	No
Owner:	Kevin Kinley
Year Estab:	1994

Westminster
(Map 9, page 170)

Record and Book Heaven   **Open Shop**
25 East Main Street 21157   (410) 876-8920
                                                 E-mail: bookstor@cct.infi.net

Collection:	General stock of hardcover and paperback and records.
# of Vols:	6,500
Hours:	Mon-Fri 10-5. Sat 10-6. Sun 12-5.

Services:	Accepts want lists, search service.
Travel:	I-795 north to Rte 140. Proceed west on Rte 140 to Main St. Shop is in downtown Westminster, across from library.
Credit Cards:	Yes
Owner:	Raymond Reed
Year Estab:	1993
Comments:	Stock is approximately 65% hardcover.

Wheaton
(Map 2, page 154)

The Barbarian Book Shop   **Open Shop**
11234 Grandview Avenue 20902   (301) 946-4184

Collection:	General stock of paperback and hardcover.
# of Vols:	10,000
Hours:	Tue-Sun 12-6:30.
Travel:	Near intersection of Georgia Ave, University Blvd and Viers Mill Rd.
Credit Cards:	Yes
Owner:	Carl & Janice Bridgers
Year Estab:	1969
Comments:	Primarily a paperback and comics shop with a relatively small hardcover collection. The shop seems to cater to a younger crowd. Judge for yourself.

Bonifant Books   **Open Shop**
11240 Georgia Avenue 20902   (301) 946-1526

Collection:	General stock and records.
# of Vols:	50,000
Specialties:	History; literature; science fiction; mystery.
Hours:	Mon-Fri 10-8. Sat 10-6. Sun 11-6.
Travel:	Georgia Ave exit (Rte 97) off I-495. Proceed north on Rte 97 for about one mile. Shop is just south of University Blvd, on the left. There's a limited amount of parking in the front of the store and a large parking lot in the rear.
Credit Cards:	Yes
Owner:	Julie Marquette
Year Estab:	1988
Comments:	This shop offers a very good selection of books in most categories. The shop is clean, neat and the collection is well organized. The owner's listing of mystery as one of her specialties is no understatement. The books, which are moderately priced, are in mixed condition and of mixed vintage.

Books of Colonial America   **By Appointment**
3611 Janet Road 20906   (301) 946-6490

Collection:	Specialty
# of Vols:	5,000

Specialties:	History; military.
Services:	Search service, accepts want lists, mail order.
Credit Cards:	No
Owner:	George Young
Year Estab:	1983
Comments:	Also displays at the Gettysburg Civil War & Antique Center in Gettysburg, PA.

Friends' Store   **Open Shop**
11160 Viers Mill Road 20902   (301) 217-3880

Hours:	Mon-Sat 10-9:30pm. Sun 12-6.
Travel:	Georgia Ave exit off I-495. Proceed north on Georgia Ave to where Viers Mill Rd forks off at left. Shop is in Wheaton Plaza, just where road forks.
Comments:	A non profit shop operated by volunteers for the benefit of the public library.

An invitation

Alder Books   (301) 854-9542
13743 Lakeside Drive Clarksville 21029   Fax: (301) 854-9543
                                                    E-mail: carl@idsonline.com

Collection: Specialty
Specialties: Horticulture; gardening; natural history; botany.
Services: Search service, accepts want lists.
Credit Cards: No
Owner: Carl R. Hahn
Year Estab: 1993

Angela Instruments   (301) 725-0451
10830 Guilford Rd, Ste 309 Annapolis Junction 20701   Fax: (301) 725-8823
Web page: www.angela.com   E-mail: steve@angela.com

Collection: Specialty
# of Vols: 2,000
Specialties: Vacuum tube electronics; hi fi; audio electronics.
Services: Catalog (on-line)
Credit Cards: Yes
Owner: Stephen Melkisethian
Year Estab: 1977

Antique Books   (410) 268-0845
PO Box 6395 Annapolis 21401

Collection: General stock.
# of Vols: 25,000
Specialties: Antiques and collectibles.
Services: Search service, accepts want lists.
Credit Cards: No
Owner: David & Kathleen Way
Year Estab: 1974

Art Reference Books   (301) 933-0197
PO Box 552 Garrett Park 20896   E-mail: arteref@aol.com
Web page: www.abebooks.com

Collection: Specialty. Mostly used.
# of Vols: 1,000
Specialties: Art (Native American, pre-Columbian, Latin American, new world);
                   anthropology; archaeological art; American history; mystery; children's
                   illustrated.
Services: Appraisals, search service, accepts want lists.
Owner: Sarah M. Quilter
Year Estab: 1996

Ashe & Deane Fine Books   (301) 588-9590
PO Box 15601 Chevy Chase 20825

Collection: General stock.
# of Vols: 10,000
Specialties: Art; travel; literature; mystery; history; private press.

Services:	Appraisals, search service, catalog, accepts want lists.
Credit Cards:	Yes
Owner:	Anita Macy
Year Estab:	1986

Book Arbor (410) 367-0338
PO Box 20885 Baltimore 21209 Fax: (410) 367-5202
E-mail: bkarbor@erols.com

Collection:	Specialty
# of Vols:	3,000-5,000
Specialties:	Landscape architecture; gardening history; horticulture.
Services:	Informal search service, accepts want lists, catalog.
Credit Cards:	No
Owner:	Judith Bloomgarden
Year Estab:	1990

The Book Emporium (301) 926-6035
17045 Briardale Road Rockville 20855 E-mail: bkemporium@aol.com

Collection:	Specialty
# of Vols:	4,000
Specialties:	First editions (fiction); mystery.
Owner:	Thomas Lee
Year Estab:	1995

Books From X To Z Tel & Fax: (410) 360-9602
PO Box 487 Pasadena 21123-0487 E-mail: booksxtoz@aol.com
Web page: http://members.aol.com/booksxtoz

Collection:	Specialty
# of Vols:	5,000
Specialties:	Business management; economics; psychology; public administration.
Services:	Catalog, accepts want lists.
Credit Cards:	Yes
Owner:	Daniel Martin
Year Estab:	1988

Books Unlimited (410) 788-5115
PO Box 3193 Baltimore 21228 Fax: (410) 747-7659

Collection:	General stock of hardcover and paperback.
# of Vols:	12,000
Specialties:	Vintage paperbacks.
Services:	Catalog, accepts want lists.
Credit Cards:	No
Owner:	Albert Cunniff
Year Estab:	1992
Comments:	Stock is approximately 50% hardcover.

Butternut and Blue (410) 256-9220
3411 Northwind Road Baltimore 21234 Fax: (410) 256-8423

Collection:	Specialty new and used.

# of Vols:	4,000
Specialties:	Civil War; baseball.
Services:	Catalog
Credit Cards:	Yes
Owner:	James & Judy McLean
Year Estab:	1983
Comments:	Collection can also be viewed by appointment. Stock is approximately 40% used, all of which is hardcover.

C. Wm. Beebe Books
113 Windsor Avenue Centreville 21617

Collection:	Specialty
# of Vols:	100+
Specialties:	C. Wm. Beebe
Credit Cards:	No
Owner:	Oliver A. Stromberg
Year Estab:	1991

Chervyl's Cookbooks   (301) 977-8033
18705 Capella Lane Gaithersburg 20877

Collection:	Specialty
Specialties:	Cookbooks
Services:	Search service, catalog, accepts want lists.
Credit Cards:	No
Owner:	Chervyl Hammerley
Year Estab:	1991

Culpepper, Hughes, & Head   (410) 730-1484
9770 Basket Ring Road Columbia 21045

Collection:	Specialty
Specialties:	Black studies, including Afro American and Caribbean African; cookbooks; photography; women's studies.
Services:	Search service, catalog, accepts want lists.
Credit Cards:	No
Owner:	Betty M. Culpepper
Year Estab:	1983

Lionel Epstein - Bookseller   (301) 949-8622
9909 Old Spring Road Kensington 20895-3247   Fax: (301) 949-0413

Collection:	Specialty
Specialties:	Law; economics; American history.
Services:	Search service, catalog, accepts want lists.
Credit Cards:	No
Year Estab:	1990

Stephen A. Goldman Historical Newspapers   (410) 357-8204
PO Box 359 Parkton 21120   E-mail: saghnoldnews@msn.com

Collection:	Specialty
Specialties:	Historic newspapers.

Services: Appraisals, catalog.
Credit Cards: No
Year Estab: 1977

Ground Zero Books (301) 585-1471
PO Box 1046, Blair Station Silver Spring 20910

Collection: Specialty books and ephemera.
# of Vols: 40,000
Specialties: Military history; Holocaust, military medicine; unit histories.
Services: Appraisals, catalog, accepts want lists.
Credit Cards: No
Year Estab: 1978

Miles Apart Tel & Fax: (301) 571-8942
5929 Avon Drive Bethesda 20814

Collection: Specialty new and used.
# of Vols: 1,000
Specialties: South Atlantic Islands.
Services: Catalog, accepts want lists.
Credit Cards: No
Owner: Laurence Carter
Year Estab: 1994

The Owl and the Buffalo Books (301) 949-0469
PO Box 527 Kensington 20895 Fax: (301) 933-8623

Collection: Specialty
# of Vols: 7,000
Specialties: Western Americana; history of medicine; frontier medicine.
Services: Catalog, accepts want lists.
Credit Cards: No
Owner: Mary Olch
Year Estab: 1990

Jean-Maurice Poitras & Sons (410) 821-6284
107 Edgerton Road Towson 21286 Fax: (410) 828-8025

Collection: Specialty
# of Vols: 50,000
Specialties: Medicine
Services: Catalog
Credit Cards: No
Year Estab: 1980

Quixote Books (301) 469-6215
PO Box 59101 Potomac 20854 Fax: (301) 365-4606
E-mail: dgogarty@erols.com

Collection: Specialty
# of Vols: 2,000
Specialties: Ireland; Irish interests.

Services: Catalog, accepts want lists.
Credit Cards: No
Owner: Denise B. Gogarty
Year Estab: 1990

Q.M. Dabney & Company   (301) 881-1470
11910 Parklawn Drive Rockville 20852   E-mail: qmdabney@interloc.com

Collection: Specialty
# of Vols: 25,000
Specialties: Military; European history; American history; law.
Services: Catalog, accepts want lists.
Credit Cards: Yes
Owner: Michael Schnitter
Year Estab: 1963

John C. Rather, Old & Rare Books   (301) 942-0515
PO Box 273 Kensington 20895-0273   E-mail: ratherjc@pipeline.com

Collection: Specialty
# of Vols: 10,000
Specialties: Chess; backgammon; magic; mountaineering; photography; art history.
Services: Appraisals, catalog, accepts want lists.
Credit Cards: No
Year Estab: 1976

Jerome Shochet   (410) 795-5879
6144 Oakland Mills Road Sykesville 21784

Collection: Specialty
# of Vols: 1,500
Specialties: Boxing
Services: Catalog, accepts want lists.
Credit Cards: No
Year Estab: 1978

Samuel Smith - First Editions   (410) 754-8935
109 Buena Vista Avenue Federalsburg 21632   Fax: (410) 754-3058

Collection: General stock and some ephemera.
# of Vols: 5,000
Specialties: Charles Bukowski; Loujon Press; beat generation. (Almost all books
                   are first editions).
Services: Search service, catalog, accepts want lists.
Credit Cards: No
Year Estab: 1987

North Carolina

Alphabetical Listing By Dealer

Alphabetical Listing By Location

Asheboro
(Map 11, page 212)

Collectors Antique Mall   **Antique Mall**
211 Sunset Avenue 27203   (910) 629-8105
Hours: Mon 10-8. Tue-Sat 10-6. Sun 1-5.
Travel: From Rte 220 southbound: Take second Asheboro exit (Sunset Ave.)
                Turn east on Sunset.

Asheville
(Map 11, page 212)

Blue Ridge Antique Mall   **Antique Mall**
126 Swannanoa River Road   (704) 258-3444
Hours: Daily 10-5.
Travel: Near Biltmore Estate.

The Captain's Bookshelf   **Open Shop**
31 Page Avenue 28801   (704) 253-6631
                                                                       Fax: (704) 253-4917
                                                          E-mail: capbbooks@aol.com
Collection: General stock.
# of Vols: 15,000
Specialties: Literature; photography; art; horticulture; natural history.
Hours: Mon-Fri 10-6. Sat 10-5.
Services: Appraisals, accepts want lists, catalog.
Travel: Eastbound on I-240: Exit 4C. At top of ramp proceed straight for one
                 block. Turn left. Shop is one block ahead. Westbound on I-240. Exit
                 4C. At top of ramp turn left and proceed to first light. Left onto
                 Haywood and proceed to first light, then right onto O'Henry, then first
                 left. Shop is one block ahead.
Credit Cards: Yes
Owner: Chandler & Miegan Gordon
Year Estab: 1976
Comments: A class act shop located in the heart of downtown. The books are in
                 pristine condition. The non fiction books are of a scholarly nature and
                 the fiction items include some of the best known writers and their
                 difficult to find titles. Considering the quality and condition of the
                 books we saw, prices were most reasonable.

The Christian Bookshop   **Open Shop**
842 Haywood Road 28806   (704) 253-8358
Collection: Specialty new and some used.
# of Vols: Limited (used)
Specialties: Religion
Hours: Mon-Sat 9-6.
Travel: I-40 to I-240 eastbound, then Brevard exit off I-240. Left at second
                 light onto Haywood Rd.

(Asheville)

Credit Cards: Yes
Owner: Robert R. Doom
Year Estab: 1976

Downtown Books And News   **Open Shop**
67 North Lexington Avenue 28801   (704) 253-8654
                                              E-mail: dbnbooks@mindspring.com
Collection: General stock of hardcover and paperback.
# of Vols: 25,000
Hours: Mon-Sat 8-6. (Jun-Aug: Fri & Sat till 8). Sun 6-6.
Services: Appraisals, search service, accepts want lists.
Travel: Westbound on I-240: Merrimon Ave exit. Proceed south one block, then
                  west one block and south again. Eastbound on I-240: Merrimon exit.
                  Proceed straight to Woodfin, Right on Woodfin. Left on Lexington.
Credit Cards: Yes
Owner: Lindig Hall Harris, Manager
Year Estab: 1988
Comments: One does not usually expect to find a strong book collection (both
                  hardcover and paperback) in the type of shop that opens as early as
                  6am on a Sunday morning and also features the latest newspapers and
                  a wide variety of new magazines. This shop offers a most respectable
                  selection of hardcover titles, both recent and vintage, in most subject
                  areas. While the majority of the books are clearly reading copies, we
                  saw a number of collectibles as well as some older multi volume sets.
                  Moderately priced.

Lexington Park Antique Mall   **Antique Mall**
65 West Walnut Street   (704) 253-3070
Hours: Mon-Sat 10-6. Sun 1-6.
Travel: Westbound on I-40: Merrimon Ave exit. Proceed south on Merrimon,
                  then right on Walnut. Eastbound on I-40. Merrimon Ave exit. Turn left
                  onto Merrimon, then right on Walnut.

Pattie's Book Swap   **Open Shop**
1569 Patton Avenue 28806   (704) 258-0652
Collection: General stock of mostly paperback.
Hours: Tue-Fri 10-5:30. Sat 10-5.

The Reader's Corner   **Open Shop**
31 Montford Avenue 28801   (704) 285-8805
                                                          Fax: (704) 285-0801
                                              E-mail: readerscorner@mindspring.com
Collection: General stock of mostly hardcover, records and ephemera.
# of Vols: 20,000
Specialties: Poetry; cookbooks; metaphysics; western North Carolina; southern lit-
                  erature.

Hours:	Mon-Fri 11-7. Sat 10-6. Sun 1-6.
Travel:	Exit 4C off I-240. Eastbound: Right at end of exit, then first right onto Montford. Westbound: turn right at exit. Shop is just ahead on right.
Credit Cards:	Yes
Owner:	Gillian Coats, Manager
Year Estab:	1996
Comments:	A recently opened second location for a long established Raleigh dealer. The shop offers a nice collection of mostly dust jacketed hardcover items of recent vintage, some trade paperbacks as well as CDs and LPs. In addition to the specialties listed above, the store has a modest selection of more general titles. Quite reasonably priced.

E. N. Treverton   **Antique Mall**
At Asheville Antiques Mall   Mall: (704) 253-3634
43 Rankin Avenue   Home: (704) 298-1882
Mailing address: 115 Cisco Rd Asheville 28805   Fax: (704) 298-2222
E-mail: e.treverton@worldnet.att.net

Collection:	General stock.
# of Vols:	5,000
Specialties:	Art; antique reference; literary first editions; mystery first editions.
Hours:	Mon-Sat 10-5. Sun 1-5.
Travel:	Merrimon exit off I-240. Proceed south into downtown. Right onto Walnut. Shop is at corner of Walnut and Rankin.
Services:	Appraisals, search service, accepts want lists, mail order.
Credit Cards:	Yes
Year Estab:	1983
Owner:	Edward Treverton
Comments:	Also displays at Black Mountain Antiques Mall in Black Mountain.

Banner Elk
(Map 11, page 212)

Reader's Den   **Open Shop**
4820 Highway 105, Ste 1A   (704) 898-8356
Mailing address: 150 Watauga River Road, Unit B Banner Elk 28604

Collection:	General stock of paperback and hardcover.
# of Vols:	7,000
Hours:	Summer: Mon-Sat 10-6. Sun 1-6. Call for winter hours.
Travel:	On Highway 105, one mile north of Rte 184 junction.
Credit Cards:	No
Owner:	Scott Evans
Year Estab:	1996
Comments:	If you enjoy a good cigar, you might want to stop here as the shop sells these smokes along with a selection of paperbacks (filling one room) and a relatively small number of hardcover books, mostly reading copies of fairly recent vintage, filling another. The sign outside reads: Used & Rare Books. All we can vouch for is that the stock consists of used books.

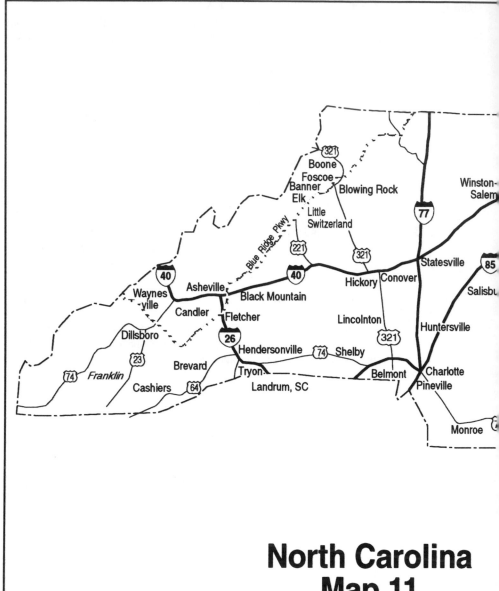

**North Carolina
Map 11**

N

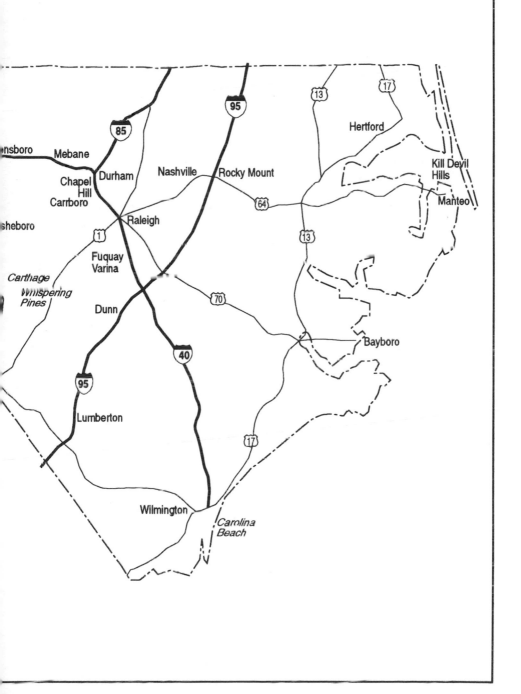

Bayboro
(Map 11, page 212)

Buckhorn Books   **Open Shop**
109 Main Street   (919) 745-3569
Mailing address: PO Box 443 Bayboro 28515   E-mail: cn3038@coastalnet.com

Collection: General stock (primarily non fiction) of hardcover and paperback.
# of Vols: 15,000
Specialties: Natural history; cooking.
Hours: Mon-Sat 9:30-5.
Services: Accepts want lists, mail order.
Travel: Rte 70 east to New Bern, then Rte 55 east to Bayboro. Main St is Rte
                    55. Shop is at intersection of Rtes 55 and 304.
Credit Cards: No
Owner: David W. & Dorothy R. Lupton
Year Estab: 1992
Comments: The owners describe their establishment as being "in the middle of
                    nowhere." True book hunters are rarely put off by such challenges and
                    adventurous book hunters may even enjoy some of the scenery on the
                    way to the shop. The shop itself, modest in size, is divided into several
                    rooms, each with its own theme. At least one half the stock is paper-
                    back and most of the hardcover items are of fairly recent vintage. We
                    did, however, spot a few older items and indeed some collectibles at
                    very reasonable prices.

Belmont
(Map 11, page 212)

Books Etc.   **Open Shop**
15B South Main Street 28012   (704) 825-2668
                                                             E-mail: mflock@bellsouth.net

Collection: General stock of hardcover and paperback.
# of Vols: 24,000+
Hours: Tue-Sat 11-6. Other times by chance.
Travel: In downtown, about 1¼ miles from I-85. Westbound on I-85. Exit 27.
                    Proceed south on Rte 272, then west (right) on 7th St and continue to
                    "T" intersection. Left on Main. Shop is two blocks ahead on left.
Credit Cards: No
Owner: Mary B. Flock
Year Estab: 1992
Comments: The nice owner of this shop arrived early on the day of our visit to
                    accommodate our travel plans. The shop is modest in size with paper-
                    backs and hardcover books shelved together. Most of the hardcover
                    items we saw were reading copies of rather recent vintage although we
                    did spot a fair number of older volumes.

Black Mountain
(Map 11, page 212)

Mysteries in the Mountains   **Open Shop**
221½ State Street 28711   (704) 669-4433

Collection:	Specialty
Specialties:	Mystery; science fiction; historical fiction; southern writers; signed.
Hours:	Mon-Sat 11-6. Occasional Sun. Call for winter hours.
Services:	Accepts want lists, mail order.
Travel:	Exit 64 off I-40. Proceed to downtown. Book store entrance is in back, off parking lot.
Credit Cards:	No
Owner:	Mary Southworth
Year Estab:	1996

Second Look Books   **Open Shop**
103 Cherry Street 28711   (704) 669-8149

Collection:	General stock of hardcover and paperback.
# of Vols:	35,000
Hours:	Apr-Dec (and most times Jan-Mar): Mon-Sat 10-5.
Services:	Accepts want lists, mail order.
Travel:	Exit 64 off I-40. Shop is just off Rte 70, one block west of Rte 9, in center of town.
Credit Cards:	No
Owner:	Gene & Charlie Chilton
Year Estab:	1990
Comments:	A small shop with an interesting collection of mixed vintage, but mostly newer books, in generally good condition.

E.N. Treverton   **Antique Mall**
At Black Mountain Antiques Mall   Mall: (704) 669-6218
100 Sutton Street   Home: (704) 298-1882
Mailing address: 115 Cisco Road Asheville 28805   Fax: (704) 298-222
                                                      E-mail: e.treverton@worldnet.att.net

Collection:	General stock.
# of Vols:	7,000
Specialties:	Art; antiques reference; military; fiction.
Hours:	Mon-Sat 10-5. Sun 1-5. (Closed Wed during winter.)
Services:	Appraisals, search service, accepts want lists.
Travel:	Rte 9 exit off I-40. Proceed north on Rte 9 into town. Shop is on left after crossing railroad tracks.
Credit Cards:	Yes
Owner:	Edward Treverton
Year Estab:	1983
Comments:	Also displays at Asheville Antiques Mall in Asheville. See above.

Blowing Rock
(Map 11, page 212)

Antique Bookshop at Happy Apple Farm   **Open Shop**
Blackberry Road   (704) 295-7367
Mailing address: PO Box 1723 Blowing Rock 28605

Collection:	General stock of hardcover and paperback and ephemera.
# of Vols:	12,000
Specialties:	Religion
Hours:	Mar 1-Dec 31: Daily 10-5. Jan & Feb: by appointment.
Services:	Accepts want lists, mail order.
Travel:	From Rte 321, two miles south of Blowing Rock city limits, turn left at church onto Blackberry Rd. Continue on Blackberry for about 1/2 mile. Shop is on right in a barn-like building.
Credit Cards:	Yes
Owner:	Donna & George E. Moore
Year Estab:	1990
Comments:	Once you've left the main highway and traveled a short distance on a gravel road to discover this shop, you'll find a collection of older hardcover books along with some paperbacks and ephemera. The books we saw were in mixed condition, some turn of the century, some early 19th century, and a fewer more recent items. Reasonably priced. If you enjoy rustic settings, you should enjoy your visit here.

Boone
(Map 11, page 212)

The Curiosity Shop   **Open Shop**
123 East King Street 28607   (704) 264-9600

Collection:	General stock of mostly used paperback and hardcover and new books.
Hours:	Mon-Sat 9:30-5:30. Sun 12:30-5.
Travel:	On Rtes 421/321.
Comments:	Stock is approximately 65% paperback. Hardcover stock comes from trades only.

Dragon's Den Comics   **Open Shop**
681 West King Street 28607   (704) 265-4263

Collection:	Specialty paperback and hardcover and new comics.
# of Vols:	1,000+ (books)
Specialties:	Science fiction; fantasy.
Hours:	Mon-Sat 11-8. Sun 12-6.

The Old Book Corner   **Open Shop**
At Wilcox Warehouse Emporium   (704) 262-0234
161 Howard Street   E-mail: oldbkcor@interloc.com
Mailing address: PO Box 1793 Blowing Rock 28605

Collection:	General stock of mostly hardcover.

# of Vols:	6,000
Specialties:	First editions; modern fiction; history; biography.
Hours:	Mem Day-Jan: Mon-Sat 10-9. Sun 1-6. Remainder of year: Mon-Sat 10-6. Sun 1-6.
Services:	Search service.
Travel:	One block off King St (Bus Rte 421).
Credit Cards:	Yes
Owner:	Amy Hobbs
Year Estab:	1996
Comments:	Located in a corner room on the first level of an attractive antique/collectible/crafts mall, the shop carries a modest number of recent titles (all with dust jackets), older volumes, including several collectibles, and a number of multi volume sets. Whether or not you make a purchase, you should find a visit to this emporium a pleasant way to spend an afternoon.

Brevard
(Map 11, page 212)

Book Nook — **Open Shop**
15 South Broad Street 28712 — (704) 883-9745

Collection:	General stock of paperback and hardcover.
# of Vols:	50,000+
Hours:	Mon-Sat 9-5:30.
Travel:	Located on Rte 64 in center of town, one block from courthouse.
Credit Cards:	Yes
Owner:	Allen Baltezore
Year Estab:	1978
Comments:	At the time of our visit, about 50% or more of the books were paperback and a large proportion of the hardcover books appeared to be library discards. While it's certainly possible you might find an unusual collectible here, we saw few items that would fit that category.

Bryson City

R & R 1/2 Price Books — **Open Shop**
145 North Everett Street 28713 — (704) 488-2665

Collection:	General stock of mostly paperback.
# of Vols:	30,000
Hours:	Mon-Sat 9:30-4:30.

Burlington

Viator Used & Rare Books — **By Appointment**
PO Box 2924 27216-2924 — (910) 226-3620
E-mail: romerj@netpath.net

Collection:	Specialty
# of Vols:	2,000

Specialties: Travel; exploration; foreign travellers in North America; some foreign
                    language titles; early scholarly titles.
Services: Catalog, accepts want lists.
Credit Cards: No
Owner: James Romer
Year Estab: 1988

Burnsville

Mimma's Books & Music   **Open Shop**
Highway 19 East   (704) 675-5095
Mailing address: Route 8, Box 818 Burnsville 28714

Collection: General stock of mostly used paperback.
# of Vols: 30,000+
Hours: Mon-Fri, except closed Wed, 10-5. Sat 10-2.

Candler
(Map 11, page 212)

Hominy Creek Bookstore   **Open Shop**
835 Pisgah Highway 28715   (704) 665-0035

Collection: General stock.
# of Vols: 5,000+
Specialties: Metaphysics; military (especially World Wars, Korean and Vietnam);
                    American history; biography (20th century); literature (20th century).
Hours: Call for hours.
Services: Accepts want lists.
Travel: From Asheville, proceed west on I-40 to Rte 19/23 exit. Continue
                    south (left) on Rte 151 for about five miles. Shop is on left in a four
                    story building.
Credit Cards: No
Owner: Bon Summers
Year Estab: 1997 (See Comments)
Comments: Anticipated opening in 1998. In addition to books, the store will fea-
                    ture an art gallery and an antique shop.

Carolina Beach
(Map 11, page 212)

Christine Gilboe, Bookseller   **By Appointment**
PO Box 2066 28428   Tel & Fax: (910) 458-4048
                                                     E-mail: chgilboe@wilmington.net

Collection: General stock.
# of Vols: 2,500
Specialties: Modern first editions; Civil War, Southern Americana.
Services: Accepts want lists, mail order, search service.
Credit Cards: Yes
Year Estab: 1988

Carrboro
(Map 11, page 212 & Map 13, page 244)

The Book Market   **Open Shop**
200 North Greensboro Street 27510   (919) 929-7264

Collection:	General stock of mostly paperback.
Hours:	Mon-Sat 10-6.

Nice Price Books   **Open Shop**
100 Boyd Street 27510   (919) 929-6222

Collection:	General stock of hardcover and paperback and records.
# of Vols:	100,000
Hours:	Mon-Sat 10-10. Sun 12-10.
Services:	Appraisals, accepts want lists.
Travel:	From Chapel Hill, continue north on Franklin where the road becomes Main St as you enter Carrboro. Shop is on the left as soon as you enter Carrboro.
Credit Cards:	Yes
Owner:	Cynthia Kamoroff
Year Estab:	1985
Comments:	Unlike its sister shop in Raleigh, this location offers a larger selection of hardcover volumes (mostly newer editions) in good condition. The shop is well organized, spacious and has a generous supply of chairs. The owner also operates a third shop in Durham.

H.E. Turlington Books   **By Appointment**
PO Box 848 27510   (919) 644-0831
                                              E-mail: het@mindspring.com

Collection:	Specialty
# of Vols:	2,500
Specialties:	Literature; southern writers and culture; British and American first editions; manuscripts.
Services:	Appraisals, catalog, accepts want lists.
Year Estab:	1979

Carthage
(Map 11, page 212)

Perry's Books   **By Appointment**
687 Brinkley Road 28327   (940) 947-2209

Collection:	General stock.
# of Vols:	25,000
Specialties:	Golf; Pinehurst and Moore Counties; North Carolina history.
Hours:	Most days, 2-6.
Services:	Appraisals, search service, accepts want lists, mail order.
Credit Cards:	No
Owner:	Perrell F. Payne Jr.
Year Estab:	1981

Cashiers
(Map 11, page 212)

Book & Specialty Shop   **Open Shop**
Highway 107 South   (704) 743-9930
Mailing address: PO Box 646 Cashiers 28717

Collection: General stock of used and new. Mostly hardcover.
# of Vols: 5,000+
Hours: May 1-Nov 1: Mon-Sat 10-5.
Services: Search service, accepts want lists.
Travel: One half mile south of intersection of Rtes 64 & 107. Shop is on right
                    in a stand alone building.
Credit Cards: No
Owner: Else S. Young
Year Estab: 1954
Comments: Stock is approximately 65% used.

Chapel Hill
(Map 11, page 212 & Map 13, page 244)

The Avid Reader Used and Rare Books   **Open Shop**
462 West Franklin Street 27516   (919) 933-9585
Web page: www.avidreader.com   Fax: (919) 933-1599
                                                    E-mail: avid@avidreader.com

Collection: General stock.
# of Vols: 125,000
Specialties: Americana; scholarly; genealogy.
Hours: Daily 10-10.
Services: Appraisals, search service, accepts want lists, on line catalog.
Travel: Rte 15/501 exit off I-40. Proceed west on Rte 15/501 toward Chapel
                    Hill. Bear right onto East Franklin St. (West Franklin begins at inter-
                    section with Columbia St.) Shop is four blocks ahead on right.
Credit Cards: Yes
Owner: Barry F. Jones
Year Estab: 1989
Comments: This wonderful, well organized, tri-level spacious shop just a block or
                    so away from an equally fine shop, offers the browser an opportunity to
                    spend a leisurely period of time enjoying a quality collection of books
                    representing most subjects. With few exceptions, the books are in good
                    to better condition. Prices are moderate.

The Bookshop   **Open Shop**
400 West Franklin Street 27516   (919) 942-5178
                                               E-mail: bookshop@mindspring.com
Collection: General stock of hardcover and paperback.
# of Vols: 150,000
Specialties: North Carolina; southern history; southern literature; military; detec-
                    tive; humanities (scholarly).

Hours:	Mon-Fri 11-9. Sat 11-6. Sun 1-5.
Services:	Catalog, accepts want lists, mail order.
Travel:	See Avid Reader above.
Credit Cards:	Yes
Owner:	Bill Loeser & Linda Saaremaa
Year Estab:	1979
Comments:	An absolutely splendid shop that is really two shops in one. The first bookshop, to the right of the entrance, stocks books dealing with every state in the union and every country in the world as well as a rich history section. The second shop contains books on every other subject imaginable. Whenever we manage to purchase several titles, we always feel that the store is a winner and this shop proved no exception. Add to this the fact that about a block away is another quality used book shop, and the book hunter should be able to enjoy several hours browsing Chapel Hill's riches.

Andrew Cahan Bookseller   **By Appointment**
3000 Blueberry Lane 27516   (919) 968-0538
Web page: www.cahanbooks.com   Fax: (919) 968-3517
                                                        E-mail: acahan@cahanbooks.com

Collection:	Specialty
# of Vols:	8,000
Specialties:	Photography; Americana; literature; art.
Services:	Catalog, accepts want lists.
Credit Cards:	Yes
Year Estab:	1975

Chapel Hill Rare Books   **By Appointment**
143 West Franklin Street, Ste 310W 27516   (919) 929-8351
                                                        Fax: (919) 967-2532

Collection:	General stock.
# of Vols:	10,000
Specialties:	Southern Americana; Civil War; literary first editions.
Services:	Appraisals, accepts want lists, catalog.
Credit Cards:	Yes
Owner:	Douglas & Maureen O'Dell
Year Estab:	1982

Second Foundation Bookstore   **Open Shop**
136 East Rosemary Street 27514   (919) 967-4439

Collection:	Specialty new and used books and comics
# of Vols:	4,000 (used)
Specialties:	Science fiction; horror; fantasy.
Hours:	Mon-Sat 10-6. Sun 12-5.
Travel:	Between Columbia and Henderson Streets.
Credit Cards:	Yes
Owner:	Daniel J. Breen

Year Estab: 1979
Comments: Approximately 65% of the used collection is paperback.

Skylight Exchange Bookstore & Cafe   **Open Shop**
405½ West Rosemary Street 27516   (919) 933-5550

Collection: General stock of mostly paperback, records and CDs.
# of Vols: 22,000.
Hours: Daily 11-11.

Charlotte
(Map 11, page 212)

Appleton's Books & Genealogy   **Open Shop**
8700 Pineville-Matthews Road, #610 28226   (704) 341-2244
Web page: www.appletons.com   Fax: (704) 341-0072
                                        E-mail: catalog.request@appletons.com

Collection: General stock of hardcover and paperback.
# of Vols: 12,000
Specialties: Genealogy; mystery; science fiction; fantasy.
Hours: Sun-Thu 10-8. Fri & Sat 10-10.
Services: Search service, accepts want lists.
Travel: I-485 exit off I-77. Proceed east on I-485 to Hwy 51 north exit. Shop is
                    on the left, in the Tower Place Shopping Center, two blocks after the
                    second light on Hwy 51.
Credit Cards: Yes
Owner: Blaine & Jennifer Schmidt
Year Estab: 1997
Comments: Stock is approximately 75% hardcover.

Book Rack   **Open Shop**
8326-401 Pineville Matthews Road 28226   (704) 544-8006

Collection: General stock of mostly paperback.
# of Vols: 40,000
Hours: Mon-Fri 11-7. Sat 10-6.

Carolina Bookshop   **Open Shop**
2440 Park Road 28203   (704) 375-7305

Collection: General stock.
# of Vols: 65,000
Specialties: Civil War; southern history; North Carolina; South Carolina; military;
                    hunting; fishing; southern writers, Americana; genealogy.
Hours: Tue-Sat 10:30-6. Mon by chance or appointment.
Services: Appraisals, accepts want list lists, catalog.
Travel: Woodlawn Road exit off I-77. Proceed east to Park Rd then left onto
                    Park. Follow Park for about one mile to intersection with Kenilworth
                    Ave. At light, bear left, staying on Park. Shop is just ahead on left in
                    the Park Square Shopping Center.

Credit Cards: Yes
Owner: Gordon Briscoe, Jr.
Year Estab: 1975
Comments: One of the nicest shops we've seen in the state. The vast majority of the
                  books are in good to excellent condition. The shop is extremely well
                  organized and except for some very high shelves, the shop is easy to
                  browse and the selection of books is outstanding. This is one of those
                  places we would have liked to have stayed longer in and believe that once
                  you've seen the shop for yourself you'll agree with our assessment.

Dilworth Books   **Open Shop**
2035 South Boulevard 28203   (704) 372-8154

Collection: General stock of hardcover and paperback and prints.
# of Vols: 50,000
Specialties: Modern first editions; maps.
Hours: Tue-Fri 10:30-6. Sat 10:30-5. Mon by chance.
Services: Appraisals, search service, accepts want lists, mail order.
Travel: From I-77 northbound: Exit 8 (Remount). Turn right on Remount and
                  proceed east for one mile to South Blvd, then left on South. From I-77
                  southbound: Exit 9 (West blvd). Turn left on West and proceed for
                  about one mile to South. Right on south. From I-85 northbound: Billy
                  Graham Pkwy exit which becomes Woodlawn. Proceed east on Billy
                  Graham/Woodlawn for two miles to South Blvd, then left on South.
Credit Cards: Yes
Owner: Haze Honeycutt
Year Estab: 1988
Comments: A good sized shop with lots of paperbacks and hardcover books in
                  mixed condition. While there were some collectibles on hand, the
                  majority of the books we saw appeared to be reading copies. The
                  friendly owner seems anxious to please his customers. The owner also
                  displays at the Salisbury Emporium in Salisbury and the Town &
                  Country Antique Mall in Pineville. See below.

Interiors Marketplace   **Antique Mall**
At Atherton Mill   (704) 377-6226
2000 South Boulevard 28203

Hours: Mon-Sat 10-6. Sun 1-5.
Travel: See Dilworth Books above.

MacNeil's   **Open Shop**
2 Nationsbank Plaza 28280   (704) 377-5331

Collection: Specialty
# of Vols: Limited
Specialties: Fine bindings.
Hours: Mon-Fri 10-5:30. Sat 10-3.
Travel: In center of downtown, at corner of Trade and Tryon, underneath the
                  Radison Hotel lobby.

Credit Cards:	Yes
Owner:	Brown MacNeil & William E. Hodgson
Year Estab:	1977

Poplar Street Books   **Open Shop**
226 West 10th Street 28202   (704) 372-9146

Collection:	General stock of hardcover and paperback.
# of Vols:	50,000
Specialties:	Poetry; art; classics; first editions; children's cookbooks.
Hours:	Tue-Sat 10-6.
Services:	Accepts want lists, mail order.
Travel:	Graham St exit off I-277. Left at bottom of ramp, and proceed one block to Poplar St. Shop is in a two story house at corner of 10th & Poplar.
Credit Cards:	Yes
Owner:	Rosemary Latimore
Year Estab:	1983
Comments:	Located on the first floor of a two story private home, this shop is jam packed with books in every category. The shop would have been a bit easier to browse had there been labels on the shelves and fewer books on the floor in front of many of the shelves. Prices were moderate. The books were of mixed but mostly newer vintage.

Conover
(Map 11, page 212)

Conover Antique Mall   **Antique Mall**
446 Conover Boulevard West 28613   (704) 465-0300

Hours:	Mon-Sat 10-6. Sun 1-6.
Travel:	Exit 128 off I-40. Proceed south on Rte 321, then left at light onto Rte 70. Shop is two miles ahead on left in Villa Park Shopping Center.

Dillsboro
(Map 11, page 212)

Another World   **Antique Mall**
At Old School Antique Mall   (704) 293-5197
Highway 441 South
Mailing address: PO Box 1119 Dillsboro 28725

Collection:	General stock.
# of Vols:	200-300
Hours:	Tue-Sat 10-5. Sun 12-5.

Time Capsule   **Open Shop**
10 Craft Circle   Tel & Fax: (704) 586-1026
Mailing address: PO Box 429 Dillsboro 28725   E-mail: timecaps@interloc.com

Collection:	General stock of mostly hardcover and ephemera.
# of Vols:	10,000

Specialties:	Appalachia; Cherokee Indians; Civil War; southern fiction and history; railroads.
Hours:	Mon-Sat 10-5:30. Sun (Jun-Oct) 11-4. Nov-Mar: Mostly open but call first.
Services:	Search service; catalog, accepts want lists.
Travel:	On Rte 441, one mile south of intersection with Rte 74 (Sylva-Dillsboro by-pass). Shop located on the left, at Riverwood Shops, just after passing the turn-off to the business district.
Credit Cards:	Yes
Owner:	Bill Lee
Year Estab:	1992
Comments:	A very well organized two story shop with a modest selection of books, priced to sell, in most subject areas. Paperbacks, children's books and ephemera (including magazines, post cards and sheet music) are located on the second floor. What the shop lacks in quantity, it makes up for in charm.

Dunn
(Map 11, page 212)

Ellen Murphy, Books   **Antique Mall**
At The Antique Showplace   (910) 892-1511
201 East Cumberland Avenue   E-mail: ellenm12@aol.com
Mailing address: 216 North Main Street Franklinton 27525

Collection:	General stock.
Specialties:	Southern Americana; children's.
Hours:	Mon-Sun 9:30-5.
Travel:	Exit 73 off I-95. Follow signs to downtown Dunn.
Credit Cards:	Yes
Year Estab:	1988

Durham
(Map 11, page 212 & Map 13, page 244)

The Book Exchange   **Open Shop**
107 West Chapel Hill Street 27701   (919) 682-4662

Collection:	General stock of hardcover and paperback.
# of Vols:	250,000+
Hours:	Mon-Sat 8:45-6.
Services:	Accepts want lists.
Travel:	Gregson St exit off I-85. Proceed south on Gregson for about 1.5 miles to Chapel Hill St, then left onto Chapel Hill. Shop is six blocks ahead, on right, just after the railroad overpass.
Credit Cards:	Yes
Owner:	Lena Marley
Year Estab:	1930's

(Durham)

Comments: This very large shop caters primarily to the local university trade and
                   has room after room and shelf after shelf filled with textbooks, both
                   new and used. However, in addition to its humongous textbook stock,
                   if you're willing to walk up a flight of stairs, you'll also find a rather
                   nice selection of used books, mostly but not all, of a scholarly nature.
                   While we may not go as far as the owner who, on a sign outside the
                   shop, proclaims the store as "The South's great bookstore," we cer-
                   tainly think the shop is worth a visit.

Books Do Furnish A Room   **Open Shop**
1809 West Markham Avenue 27705-4806   (919) 286-1076

Collection: General stock of paperback and hardcover, comics and records.
# of Vols: 5,000+
Hours: Sun 11-6. Mon & Tue, Thu & Fri 10-9. Sat 10-6. Wed 11-9.
Services: Accepts want lists.
Travel: From Raleigh: Duke St exit off Rte 147 (Durham Expwy). Continue on
                   Duke to Markham. Left onto Markham. Shop is after university cam-
                   pus, on left, and is set back from street about 50 feet.
Credit Cards: Yes
Owner: Richard Lee & Gordon Matthews
Year Estab: 1983
Comments: Unlike similar shops that sell comics, records and paperbacks, we
                   noted a better than average selection of hardcover volumes in this
                   shop. If you're into light fiction and are not searching for a rare or
                   esoteric item you might enjoy browsing here.

Books On Ninth   **Open Shop**
716A Ninth Street 27705   (919) 286-3170
                                          E-mail: jbrowner@mindspring.com

Collection: General stock of mostly paperback.
# of Vols: 25,000.
Hours: Daily 11-8.

Chelsea Antiques   **Open Shop**
2631 Chapel Hill Boulevard 27707   (919) 683-1865

Collection: General stock.
# of Vols: 1,000
Specialties: Fine bindings.
Hours: Tue-Sat 11-6.
Services: Accepts want lists.
Travel: Rte 15/501 exit off I-40. Continue on Rte 15/501 (Chapel Hill Blvd)
                   for about four miles. Shop is one right.
Credit Cards: Yes
Owner: Laura Kotchmar
Comments: Primarily an antique shop with perhaps 500-1,000 older books in inter-

esting bindings. Some of the titles may well be rare but this is not a place that you would spend much more than 5-10 minutes visiting, unless, that is, you also enjoyed browsing antiques.

McGowan Book Company   **By Appointment**
39 Kimberly Drive 27707   (919) 403-1503

Collection:	Specialty
# of Vols:	1,500
Specialties:	Civil War; American Revolution; black studies; southern history.
Services:	Catalog, accepts want lists.
Credit Cards:	Yes
Owner:	R. Douglas Sanders
Year Estab:	1987

Nice Price Books   **Open Shop**
3415 Hillsborough Road 27705   (919) 383-0119

Collection:	General stock of hardcover and paperback and records.
# of Vols:	50,000
Hours:	Mon-Sat 10-10. Sun 12-10.
Services:	Appraisals, accepts want lists.
Travel:	From I-85 southbound: Rte 15/501 exit. Make an immediate exit to the right, then at light turn left onto Hillsborough. Turn right after first light. Shop is just ahead in Festival Plaza shopping center. From I-85 northbound: Hillandale exit. Turn right on Hillandale. After crossing Club Blvd, turn right at next light onto Hillsborough.
Credit Cards:	Yes
Owner:	Cynthia Kamoroff
Comments:	Owner also operates similar shops in Carrboro and Raleigh.

The Readery   **Open Shop**
611 Broad Street 27705   (919) 286-6676
                                                        Fax: (919) 416-0716
                                                E-mail: readery@mindspring.com

Collection:	General stock of paperback and hardcover.
# of Vols:	10,000
Hours:	Mon-Fri 11-8. Sat 11-9. Sun 12-5.
Services:	Appraisals, search service, accepts want lists, mail order.
Travel:	Northbound on I-85: Exit 174B (Hillsborough Rd). Proceed east on Hillsborough (Rte 70) to Broad St, then right on Broad. Shop is at corner of Broad and W. Main, across from east campus of Duke University. Shop is in Bull City Market (a cluster of shops).
Credit Cards:	No
Owner:	Frank Parker
Year Estab:	1992
Comments:	This bi-level shop offers a little bit of everything; some interesting collectibles, a common variety of paperbacks and both recent and vintage hardcover items. While many subjects are covered, few are represented in depth.

Wentworth And Legett Rare Books   **Open Shop**
905 West Main Street 27701   Shop: (919) 688-5311
                                                   Home: (919) 479-1938

Collection:	General stock, post cards and prints.
# of Vols:	8,000
Specialties:	Medicine
Hours:	Mon-Sat 11-6.
Services:	Appraisals, accepts want lists.
Travel:	Duke St exit off Rte 147 (Durham Expwy). Proceed on Duke to Brightleaf Square parking lot. Shop is across the square in the courtyard.
Credit Cards:	Yes
Owner:	David & Barbara Wentworth
Year Estab:	1976
Comments:	An upscale book shop in an upscale mall with a stock devoted exclusively to hardcover books, many of which have unusual titles and a few of which may even be scarce or rare. The shop is relatively small but the books are of high quality.

Fayetteville

B.J. Exchange   **Open Shop**
4905 Murchison Road 28311   (910) 488-5920

Collection:	General stock of mostly paperback.
# of Vols:	50,000
Hours:	Mon-Sat 9-5.

The Bookworm   **Open Shop**
211 Hope Mills Road 28304   (910) 425-8415

Collection:	General stock of mostly paperback.
# of Vols:	60,000
Hours:	Mon-Sat 10-6.

Edward McKay Used Books   **Open Shop**
824 Santee Drive 28303   (910) 868-1001
Web page: www.jbcmedia.com

Collection:	General stock of mostly paperback.
# of Vols:	70,000
Hours:	Mon-Sat 9-9. Sun 12-6.

Warpath Military Collectibles, Books & Antiques   **Open Shop**
3805 Cumberland Road 28306   (910) 425-7000
                                                E-mail: warpathmil@aol.com

Collection:	Specialty books and ephemera.
# of Vols:	2,000+
Specialties:	Military; arms and armor; Japanese art; World War I & II; Vietnam War unit histories; Civil War; medieval history; American history; southern history; first editions.
Hours:	Mon-Thu 10-6. Fri & Sat 10-6. Call to confirm weekend hours.

Services:	Accepts want lists, mail order.
Travel:	Owens Dr exit off Bus I-95. Proceed on Owens to Cumberland, then left (at third light) onto Cumberland.
Credit Cards:	Yes
Owner:	Ed Hicks
Year Estab:	1988

Flat Rock

The Book Exchange   **Open Shop**
Route 25 28731   (704) 693-8311

Collection:	General stock of mostly paperback.
# of Vols:	4,500
Hours:	Mon-Sat 10-4,

Fletcher
(Map 11, page 212)

Book End   **Flea Market**
At Smiley's Flea Market   (704) 684-0482
Highway 25
Mailing address: PO Box 1356 Hendersonville 28739

Collection:	General stock of mostly used paperback and hardcover.
# of Vols:	10,000+
Hours:	Wed-Sat 10-5.
Travel:	About 10 miles north of Hendersonville.
Credit Cards:	No
Year Estab:	1990
Comments:	An indoor store that is part of an indoor/outdoor flea market. The stock is approximately 60% paperback.

Foscoe
(Map 11, page 212)

The Blue Ridge Book Gallery   **Open Shop**
9189 Highway 105 South   (704) 963-5001
Mailing address: Route 1, Box 975-23 Banner Elk 28604
Web page: www.mercury.net/~wgwinter   E-mail: wgwinter@mercury.net

Collection:	General stock of hardcover and paperback.
# of Vols:	20,000+ (hardcover)
Specialties:	Natural history; fishing; automobiles; hunting; Carolinas.
Hours:	Mon-Sat 10-5. Sun 1-5.
Travel:	On Rte 105, eight miles south of Boone. Traveling south from Boone, the shop is on the left. Look for a large "Books" sign.
Credit Cards:	Yes
Owner:	W. G. Winter
Year Estab:	1992

Comments: What one might call a "complete" book shop. There is very little that this
               shop does not offer, if only in modest numbers. The shop is well orga-
               nized, easy to browse and the books are reasonably priced. One room is
               devoted almost exclusively to paperbacks while the other rooms offer
               hardcover books and trade paperbacks in good to very good condition.

Franklin
(Map 11, page 212)

Smoky Mountain Books   **By Appointment**
407 West Main Street 28734   Tel & Fax: (704) 369-5342
                                                               (800) 883-8711

Collection: General stock, records and ephemera.
# of Vols: 6,000
Services: Appraisals
Owner: Jo & Wendell "Jeff" Davis
Year Estab: 1996 (See Comments)
Comments: A second location for the owner of the long established Raintree Books
                shop in Eustis, FL. The owners expect to be open for business in 1998.

Fuquay-Varina
(Map 11, page 212)

October Farm Books   **Open Shop**
At Bostic & Wilson Antiques 27526   (919) 552-3248
105 South Main Street

Collection: General stock, prints and ephemera.
# of Vols: 1,000
Hours: Tue-Sat 10-5. Sun 11-3.
Travel: Exit 298A off I-40. Proceed south on Rte 401 which becomes S. Main St.
Credit Cards: Yes
Owner: Barbara Cole
Year Estab: 1977
Comments: The owner's specialty collection of books and related items dealing
                 with horses is located in Raleigh, NC. See below.

Greensboro
(Map 11, page 212 & Map 12, page 233)

The Book Rack   **Open Shop**
5701 West Friendly Avenue 27410   (910) 854-4057

Collection: General stock of mostly used paperback and hardcover.
# of Vols: 10,000 (used)
Hours: Mon-Sat 9-9.
Travel: Eastbound on I-40. Exit 213 (Guilford College). Turn left at bottom of
                 exit ramp onto Guilford College Rd, then right onto Friendly. Shop is
                 just ahead on right, next to Quaker Village Shopping Center.
Credit Cards: Yes

Year Estab: 1980
Comments: Used stock is approximately 70% paperback.

The Book Trader   **Open Shop**
312 South Elm Street 27401   (910) 272-4091
                                                                            Fax: (910) 378-1183

Collection: General stock of hardcover, paperback and magazines.
# of Vols: 200,000
Hours: Tue-Fri 11:30-5:30. Sat 11-5.
Travel: Elm-Eugene exit off I-85. Proceed north on Elm-Eugene for about
                  three miles. Right onto Washington and proceed three blocks. Then
                  right onto Elm. Shop is in middle of block on right.
Credit Cards: Yes
Owner: Cordelia Faber
Year Estab: 1980
Comments: A good sized shop with a mix of approximately 50% paperback and 50%
                  hardcover. With few exceptions, most of the hardcover volumes we saw
                  were of a more recent vintage and not particularly unusual in terms of
                  either title or subject area. Most subjects are covered. Prices are moderate.
                  Lots of stools for the browser's comfort and convenience. As the shop is
                  just two blocks away from another used book store, we recommend that if
                  you're in the neighborhood, you drop by here.

The Browsery   **Open Shop**
504-506 South Elm Street 27406   (910) 370-4648

Collection: General stock of hardcover and paperback.
# of Vols: 100,000
Hours: Mon-Sat 12-6 but best to call ahead.
Services: Accepts want lists.
Travel: Lee St exit off I-40. Proceed west on Lee to Elm, then right on Elm.
                  Shop is two blocks ahead on left.
Credit Cards: No
Owner: Ben Mathews
Year Estab: 1976
Comments: Although our return visit to Greensboro for this new edition took place
                  early in the morning before this shop's scheduled opening time, we
                  went out of our way to drive by this shop, curious to see if there had
                  been any change in the store's overall ambience since our earlier visit.
                  From what we could see looking through the front window, there
                  appeared to be none.

                  The name of this shop is most apt. However, come early and plan to
                  stay for a while if you really want to see what is on the shelves as the
                  shop is extremely crowded and you'll need to be careful maneuvering
                  around the books (not always piled neatly) in the aisles. Also many of
                  the shelves are high and we didn't spot too many stools or ladders.
                  Having provided these caveats, we can also say that while the books
                  are of mixed condition (with some having seen far better days), there

are also many quite interesting and unusual titles here and the shop's second floor (in the same condition as the first) also offers shelf after shelf after shelf for your browsing enjoyment and/or challenge. To sum up, despite any drawback we may have cited, a true book lover with patience may find some real winners here.

Dramore Antiques   **Antique Mall**
526 South Elm Street 27406   (910) 275-7563
Hours: Mon-Sat 10-5.
Travel: See The Browsery above.

Edward McKay Used Books   **Open Shop**
2118 Lawndale Drive 27408-7102   (910) 274-4448
Web page: www.jbcmedia.com
Collection: General stock of mostly paperback.
# of Vols: 80,000
Hours: Mon-Sat 9-9. Sun 12-6.

The Exchange   **Open Shop**
338 South Tate Street 27403   (910) 273-2243
Collection: General stock of paperback and hardcover.
# of Vols: 2,000
Hours: Mon-Fri 11:30-9:30. Sat 10-10. Sun 10-2:30.
Comments: Stock is approximately 60% paperback. The shop also features a full
                   service restaurant.

Family Books & Gifts   **Open Shop**
2912 Randleman Road 27406   (910) 378-1999
Collection: General stock of mostly used paperback and hardcover.
# of Vols: 10,000+ (used)
Specialties: Religion; history.
Hours: Mon-Fri 10-6. Sat 10-5.
Travel: Randleman Rd exit off I-40. Proceed south on Randleman.
Credit Cards: Yes
Owner: Ronnie Crotts
Year Estab: 1993
Comments: Used stock is approximately 60% paperback.

John Neal, Bookseller   **By Appointment**
PO Box 9986 27429   (800) 369-9598   (910) 272-6139
Web page: www.johnnealbooks.com   Fax: (910) 272-9015
                                                    E-mail: jnealbooks@aol.com

Collection: Specialty new and used.
# of Vols: Small (used)
Specialties: Calligraphy; illumination; book arts.
Services: Catalog
Credit Cards: Yes
Year Estab: 1981

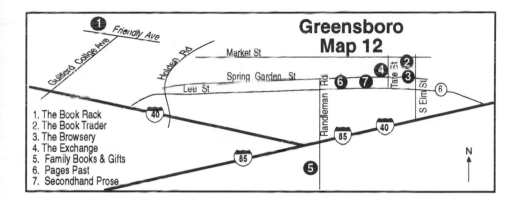

Greensboro
Map 12

Friendly Ave
Guilford College Ave
Holden Rd
Market St
Spring Garden St
Lee St
Randleman Rd
Tate St
S Elm St

1. The Book Rack
2. The Book Trader
3. The Browsery
4. The Exchange
5. Family Books & Gifts
6. Pages Past
7. Secondhand Prose

N

Pages Past   **Open Shop**
1837 Spring Garden Street 27403   (910) 574-1877

Collection:	General stock.
# of Vols:	8,000+
Specialties:	Americana; regional; religion.
Hours:	Tue-Sat 10-6, Sun 1-5.
Services:	Appraisals, accepts want lists, catalog.
Travel:	Highpoint Rd exit off I-40. Proceed north on Highpoint Rd to South Chapman, then left onto South Chapman and right onto Spring Garden. Shop is second building on right. Parking in rear.
Credit Cards:	Yes
Owner:	Roger W. March
Year Estab:	1996
Comments:	A shop that certainly meets the "antiquarian" definition with interesting titles, several multi volume sets and a respectable number of rare volumes in addition to a general stock of fiction and non fiction. For the serious book aficionado, definitely worth a visit.

Alice Robbins, Bookseller   **By Appointment**
3002 Round Hill Road 27408   (910) 282-1964

Collection:	Specialty
# of Vols:	3,000+
Specialties:	Modern first editions; women writers; southern writers.
Services:	Catalog, accepts want lists.
Credit Cards:	No
Year Estab:	1986

Secondhand Prose   **Open Shop**
1713 Spring Garden Street 27403   (910) 279-8433

Collection:	General stock of hardcover and paperback.
# of Vols:	22,000
Specialties:	Religion (Christianity); science fiction; fantasy.

Hours:	Mon-Sat 10-7.
Services:	Accepts want lists.
Travel:	Eastbound on I-85/I-40: Exit 128. Proceed west on Lee (Rte 6) to Aycock, then right on Aycock and left on Spring Garden. Westbound on I-85/I-40: Exit 121. Proceed north on Holden, then right on Spring Garden.
Credit Cards:	No
Owner:	Deborah Hill
Year Estab:	1996
Comments:	Almost an even mix between paperbacks and hardcover volumes, most of which were of fairly recent vintage. The books were nicely displayed and the shop is easy to browse. Reasonably priced. And for the comfort of its customers, there's a lounge area with coffee and cookies.

Greenville

Bookworm of Greenville   **Open Shop**
109B Arlington Boulevard 27858   (919) 321-6016

Collection:	General stock of mostly paperback and records.
# of Vols:	25,000
Hours:	Mon-Sat 10-8. Sun 12-5.
Travel:	Rte 264 into Greenville where it becomes Greenville Blvd. Turn right on Arlington.
Comments:	Primarily a paperback shop with less than 1,000 hardcover items, mostly on the top shelves. No doubt a shop that serves local interests and needs.

Hendersonville
(Map 11, page 212)

The Book Loft   **Antique Mall**
At Village Green Antique Mall   Mall: (704) 692-9057
424 North Main Street   28739   Home: (704) 693-0320

Collection:	General stock.
# of Vols:	2,000+
Hours:	Mon-Sat 10-5. Sun 1-5. Jan-Mar: closed Wed.
Travel:	See Southeastern Antiques & Collectibles below.
Owner:	Paula Dillman
Comments:	A nice surprise. Located on the mezzanine level of an antique mall, with exceptions, most of the books we saw were older, many were collectible, and a few very possibly one of a kind.

The Book Store   **Open Shop**
238 North Main Street 28792   (704) 696-9949

Collection:	General stock of hardcover and paperback.
# of Vols:	10,000
Hours:	Mon-Sat 10:30-5:30. Sun 1-4:30.
Services:	Search service.
Travel:	See Southeastern Antiques & Collectibles below.

Credit Cards:	No
Year Estab:	1994
Comments:	A crowded shop with an almost even mix of hardcover and paperback items of mostly recent vintage. Some book club editions and lots of "practical" books. At the time of our visit there were plenty of customers, suggesting that this was a popular community outlet.

Ben M. Jones III   **By Appointment**
115 Country Ridge Road 28739   (704) 697-8805

Collection:	Specialty
# of Vols:	3,000
Specialties:	Civil War; fine press; Western Americana.
Credit Cards:	No
Year Estab:	1977
Comments:	Sells primarily to dealers.

Southeastern Antiques & Collectibles   **Open Shop**
305 North Main Street 28792   (704) 697-6064

Collection:	Specialty
# of Vols:	1,500
Specialties:	Children's; boy scouts; Civil War.
Hours:	Mon-Sat 10-5.
Services:	Appraisals, search service, accepts want lists, mail order.
Travel:	Exit 18 off I-26. Proceed on Rte 64 to downtown Hendersonville. (Rte 64 becomes Main St.)
Credit Cards:	Yes
Owner:	James Sayers
Year Estab:	1962

Vintage Books   **Open Shop**
240 North Church Street   (704) 696-8387
Mailing address: PO Box 771 Hendersonville 28793

Collection:	General stock of hardcover and paperback.
# of Vols:	12,000 (see Comments)
Hours:	Tue-Sat. 11-5:30.
Travel:	Exit 18 off I-26. Proceed west on Rte 64 to Hendersonville. Left on Rte 25 South (Church St). Shop is at corner of 3rd Ave. The entrance is one flight down.
Credit Cards:	No
Owner:	John Gesser
Year Estab:	1996
Comments:	A mixture of paperbacks and hardcover volumes of mixed vintage and in mixed condition. Some collectibles. The shop is nicely organized, easy to browse and with at least two other book dealers just around the corner, certainly worth a visit. If you don't see what you're looking for, ask, as the dealer has an additional 24,000 books in storage, some of which are cataloged.

Hertford
(Map 11, page 212)

Bibliopath Bookshop & Bindery   **Open Shop**
103-105 North Church Street   (919) 426-8186
Mailing address: PO Box 154 South Kortright NY 13042

Collection:	General stock of hardcover and paperback.
# of Vols:	30,000
Hours:	Mon-Sat 10-5.
Travel:	Located just off Rte 17 in the business district.
Credit Cards:	No
Owner:	H.L. & Linda Wilson
Year Estab:	1984
Comments:	Considering the fact that there are few other used book dealers within miles, this shop is like an oasis for its region. The stock, a combination of paperback and hardcover, is in generally mixed condition and runs the gamut from older volumes to more recent popular fiction. The shop is easy to browse and reasonably priced. Visitors are advised that a call ahead is recommended as, at the time our visit, the shop was for sale.

Hickory
(Map 11, page 212)

Book Exchange   **Open Shop**
345 1st Avenue NW 28601   (704) 328-8407

Collection:	General stock of paperback and hardcover.
# of Vols:	100,000
Hours:	Tue-Sat 10-5.
Travel:	Exit 123 off I-40. Proceed north to Rte 70, then east on Rte 70 for two lights. Left on 4th St, then right at fourth light (immediately after railroad tracks) onto 1st Ave NW. Shop is just ahead on right.
Credit Cards:	No
Owner:	Sydney A. Bradley
Year Estab:	1976
Comments:	There well may be 100,000 paperbacks on the first level of this shop; we didn't bother to count. The second floor houses still more paperbacks, in addition to hardcover volumes consisting of recent items, library discards, book club editions and even some rebound library copies, all in fair to good condition. Almost without exception, many of the same titles we saw here were available elsewhere less expensively. Perhaps the owner makes up for it by having a summer sale offering 25% off on the "upstairs" books.

Book Rack   **Open Shop**
2122 US Highway 70 SE 28602   (704) 324-4230

Collection:	General stock of mostly paperback.
# of Vols:	60,000
Hours:	Mon-Sat 10-6. Sun 1-5.

Wonderland Books   **Open Shop**
5008 Hickory Boulevard 28601   (704) 396-7323

Collection:	General stock of mostly hardcover.
# of Vols:	100,000+
Specialties:	Southern Americana.
Hours:	Mon-Sat 11:30-5:30.
Services:	Appraisals, search service, accepts want lists, mail order.
Travel:	Exit 123 off I-40. Proceed north on Rte 321 (Hickory Blvd) towards Lenoir. Shop is on right, about one mile after the bridge.
Credit Cards:	No
Owner:	Avis O. Gachet
Year Estab:	1990
Comments:	One of the premier book dealers in the state. Yes, there are paperbacks here, but the number of hardcover volumes in good condition, many with dust jackets, includes some common titles but enough unusual and indeed rare titles to make this visit very worthwhile. Each category (and subcategory) was very well represented. Moderately priced. We could have left the shop with half a trunkful.

Highlands

Cyrano's Bookshop   **Open Shop**
Main Street, Box 765 28741   (704) 526-5488

Collection:	General stock of mostly new books.
Hours:	Mon-Sat 10-5.
Services:	Search service, accepts want lists.
Credit Cards:	Yes
Owner:	Randolph Shaffner
Year Estab:	1978
Comments:	Primarily a new book store with a limited selection of used books.

Hillsborough

Cover to Cover   **Antique Mall**
At Daniel Boone Antique Village   (919) 732-8882
387 Ja-Max Drive
Mailing address: PO Box 687 Chapel Hill 27514

Collection:	Specialty
# of Vols:	1,000
Specialties:	Children's; illustrated; sports; Civil War; southern history; crafts (19th century); antiques.
Hours:	Mon-Sat 11-5. Sun 1-5.
Travel:	Hillsborough exit off I-85. Mall is one block from exit.
Credit Cards:	Yes
Owner:	Mark Shuman
Comments:	The owner also displays at an antique mall in Pittsboro. See below.

Huntersville
(Map 11, page 212)

Book Nook at Lake Norman　　　　　　　　　　　**Open Shop**
9121 Sam Furr Road, #102 28078　　　　　　　　　(704) 892-1030

Collection:	General stock of paperback and hardcover.
# of Vols:	12,000
Specialties:	Science fiction.
Hours:	Mon-Sat 10-8.
Services:	Search service.
Travel:	At exit 25 off I-77.
Credit Cards:	Yes
Owner:	Stuart Madow
Year Estab:	1991
Comments:	Stock is approximately 70% paperback

Jacksonville

Book End Bookstore　　　　　　　　　　　　　　**Open Shop**
119 North Marine Boulevard 28540　　　　　　　　(910) 347-7778

Collection:	General stock of mostly paperback.
# of Vols:	70,000
Hours:	Mon-Sat 10-8. Sun 12-5.

Kill Devil Hills
(Map 11, page 212)

North Carolina Books　　　　　　　　　　　　　**Open Shop**
1500 North Croatan Highway 27948　　　　　　　　(919) 441-2141

Collection:	General stock of mostly used paperback.
Hours:	Mon-Sat 10-5. Sun 2-5. Longer hours in summer.
Travel:	Located on Outer Banks. Rte 158 is Croatan Hwy.

Roanoke Press & Croatan Bookery　　　　　　　**Open Shop**
2006 South Croatan Highway　　　　　　　　　　　(919) 480-1890
Mailing address: PO Drawer 809 Kill Devil Hills 27948

Collection:	General stock of mostly used.
# of Vols:	20,000+
Hours:	Easter-Christmas: Mon-Sat 10-5. Sun 2-5. Longer hours during summer. Jan & Feb: weekends only but best to call ahead.
Services:	Accepts want lists.
Travel:	On Outer Banks. Rte 158 is Croatan Hwy.
Owner:	Francis Meekins
Comments:	Shop also houses a museum of antique printing equipment.

Lincolnton
(Map 11, page 212)

North State Books   **Open Shop**
109 SE Court Square 28092   (704) 732-8562
                                                      E-mail: norstatc@interloc.com

Collection:	General stock of hardcover and paperback.
# of Vols:	50,000
Specialties:	Modern first editions; North Carolina; southern writers; mystery.
Hours:	Mon-Sat 10-6.
Services:	Appraisals, search service, accepts want lists, mail order.
Travel:	I-85 to Gastonia. Proceed north on Rte 321 to Lincolnton then west on Rte 27 to downtown. Shop is on the town square.
Credit Cards:	Yes
Owner:	Richard & Lori Jones
Year Estab:	1989
Comments:	The first time we visited this shop (about three years prior to our most recent visit) the owner was in the process of expanding his shop and we could only report that the books we saw were of mixed vintage and in mixed condition. As luck would have it, on our return visit, the owner had recently removed the wall separately the two halves of his shop in order to provide for more display space. Unfortunately, this made it difficult for us to see more than a small portion of his stock as the vast majority of the books were in the process of being reshelved. The dealer also displays at the Cherry Street Antique Mall in Black Mountain and the Conover Antique Mall in Conover. See above.

Little Switzerland
(Map 11, page 212)

Grassy Mountain Shop   **Open Shop**
Route 226A   Tel & Fax: (704) 765-9070
Mailing address: PO Box 448 Little Switzerland 28749
                                                     E-mail: grassymt@interloc.com

Collection:	General stock.
# of Vols:	30,000
Specialties:	Regional; southern literature.
Hours:	Apr-Oct: Daily 10-5.
Services:	Search service.
Travel:	Just off the Blue Ridge Pkwy, opposite the post office. Rte 226 exit off I-40. Proceed on Rte 226 to Blue Ridge Pkwy. Take Pkwy south one exit (Little Switzerland exit). Turn right at tennis courts and right at second stop sign onto Rte 226A.
Credit Cards:	Yes
Owner:	Curtis & Kathryn Johnson
Year Estab:	1987
Comments:	If you enjoy pretty vistas and traveling up (and later down) curvy mountain roads, you may discover the charm of this out of the way

book shop that stocks reading copies of recent vintage books in generally good condition. The lack of antiquarian and/or truly rare books should not necessarily detract from the charm of this country store situated on the top of a mountain.

Lumberton
(Map 11, page 212)

Reflections   **Antique Mall**
At Somewhere In Time Antique Mall   Mall: (910) 671-8666
4429 Kahn Drive   Home: (910) 867-6071
Mailing address: PO Box 53216 Fayetteville 28305-3216

Collection: General stock.
# of Vols: 500
Specialties: North Carolina; children's; military.
Hours: Mon-Sat 9-5:30. Sun 1-5:30.
Travel: Lumberton exit off I-95. Mall is on I-95 service road.

Manteo
(Map 11, page 212)

Burnside Books   **Open Shop**
612 North Virginia Dare Road 27954   (919) 473-1112

Collection: General stock of new and used hardcover and paperback.
Hours: Mon-Fri 8-5:30. Sat 8-12.
Travel: Across from elementary school and next to library.
Owner: Francis Meekins
Comments: Used stock is evenly divided between paperback and hardcover.

Island Nautical   **Open Shop**
207 Queen Elizabeth Avenue   (919) 473-1411
Mailing address: PO Box 1399 Manteo 27954   Fax: (919) 261-6439
Web page: www.nauticalsource.com

Collection: Specialty books and related items.
# of Vols: 500
Specialties: Nautical
Hours: Mon-Sat 10-5:30.
Services: Mail order.
Travel: Located at the waterfront.
Credit Cards: Yes
Owner: Jack Hughes
Year Estab: 1989

Marion

Paperback Traders   **Open Shop**
121 South Main Street 28752   (704) 652-1606

Collection: General stock of mostly paperback.
Hours: Mon-Sat 9-5:30.

Mebane
(Map 11, page 212)

Paula Boyd, Bookseller   **Open Shop**
112 West Clay Street 27302   (919) 304-4343

Collection:	General stock of hardcover and paperback.
# of Vols:	12,000
Hours:	Tue-Fri 10-5. Sat 9-1.
Services:	Accepts want lists.
Travel:	Exit 153 off I-85. Proceed north on Rte 119 for about three miles. After crossing railroad tracks, turn left onto Clay.
Credit Cards:	Yes
Owner:	Paula Boyd
Year Estab:	1995
Comments:	A modest sized shop with a collection consisting primarily of reading copies (book club editions, library discards, etc.) in mixed condition. On the bright side, the books are priced to sell; we saw several hardcover items that were a step above average in both condition and quality selling for a fraction of what we've seen them selling for elsewhere. It is of course possible that by the time this book is in your hands scouts will have emptied the shelves of such bargains.

Monroe
(Map 11, page 212)

Sweet Union Flea Market   **Flea Market**
4420 West Highway 74 28110   (704) 283-7985

Hours:	Sat & Sun 7-5.
Travel:	Between Monroe and Indian Trail.

Morehead City

Bill Mason Books   **Open Shop**
104 North 7th Street 28557   Tel & Fax: (919) 247-6161

Collection:	Specialty used and new.
# of Vols:	10,000 (combined)
Specialties:	Military; Civil War.
Hours:	Fri 10-5. Sat 11-4. Other times by appointment.
Services:	Search service, accepts want lists, catalog.
Travel:	Proceeding east on Arendell St in downtown, make left onto 7th St.
Credit Cards:	Yes
Year Estab:	1978
Comments:	A very neat and well organized shop which, while specializing in military books, has a heavier emphasis on the Civil War than on other campaigns. The books were in fine to excellent condition and a military or Civil War buff looking for something special stands an excellent chance of locating it here. About three fourths of the stock consists of used titles.

Nashville
(Map 11, page 212)

Valentine-Fuller Antiques   **Open Shop**
225 West Washington Street 27856   (919) 459-7770

Collection:	General stock.
# of Vols:	2,500
Hours:	Mon-Sat 10-5.
Travel:	Nashville exit off I-95. Follow signs into Nashville. Shop is across from courthouse.
Credit Cards:	Yes
Owner:	David & Betsy Fuller
Year Estab:	1989
Comments:	This combination used book/collectibles shop is less likely to have a rare first edition than it is to have simply a general stock of older books that one could best categorize as reading copies. If you enjoy visiting antique malls that also carry used books, you may find this shop to your taste.

New Bern

Middle Street Book Store   **Open Shop**
215 Middle Street 28560   (919) 514-2622

Collection:	General stock of mostly paperback.
# of Vols:	8,000
Hours:	Mon-Sat 10-5:30. Sun during Christmas and some holidays.

Pineville
(Map 11, page 212)

Town & Country Antique Mall   **Antique Mall**
601 North Polk Street 28134   (704) 889-1616

Hours:	Mon-Sat 10-6. Sun 1-6.
Travel:	I-485 exit off I-77. Proceed east on I-485 to South Blvd exit, then south on South Blvd. Shop is about 1/2 mile ahead on right.

Pittsboro

Cover To Cover   **Antique Mall**
At 52 Hillsborough Street Antique Mall   (919) 542-0789
52 Hillsborough Street
Mailing address: PO Box 687 Chapel Hill 27514

Collection:	Specialty
# of Vols:	1,500
Specialties:	Children's; illustrated; Civil War; sports; southern history; crafts (19th century); antiques; aviation; modern literature.
Hours:	Wed-Sat 10-5. Sun 1-5.
Travel:	One block from intersection of Rtes 64 & 15/501.

Credit Cards: Yes
Owner: Mark Shuman
Comments: Owner also displays at an antique mall in Hillsborough.

Raleigh
(Map 11, page 212 & Map 13, page 244)

The Book Cellar, LLC   **Open Shop**
Raleigh/Durham International Airport   (919) 840-0402
Mailing address: AMF, PO Box 80033 Raleigh 27623-0033
                                          E-mail: wmhigh@bellsouth.net

Collection: General stock of paperback and hardcover.
# of Vols: 15,000
Hours: Daily 6am-9pm.
Travel: On second floor of terminal A.
Credit Cards: Yes
Owner: Judy Burnham & Walter High
Year Estab: 1984
Comments: One of the two used book shops located in airport terminals that we have come across in our research and travels. Most of the stock in this shop consists of paperbacks, clearly marked and in most cases one half the cover price, but there are also some hardcover fiction and non fiction titles. While you're only likely to visit this shop while flying in our out of the Triangle area (since this is not a shop one would normally visit on a biblio vacation), should the opportunity present itself, we suggest you drop in and give the place a once over, either before your flight or while waiting for your baggage or for a passenger.

The Bookroom   **By Appointment**
416 Chamberlain Street   (919) 821-5625
Mailing address: PO Box 5131 Raleigh 27650

Collection: Specialty
# of Vols: 3,000
Specialties: Americana; Civil War; first editions.
Services: Appraisals, catalog.
Credit Cards: No
Owner: Kenneth E. Parrish
Year Estab: 1984
Comments: Also displays a general collection at the Collectors Antique Mall in Asheboro. See above.

Books & Things   **Flea Market**
At Raleigh Flea Market   Store: (919) 664-8466
1924 Capitol Boulevard   Home: (919) 787-4567
Mailing address: 2119 Kipawa Street 27607

Collection: General stock of mostly paperback and some hardcover.
# of Vols: 10,000

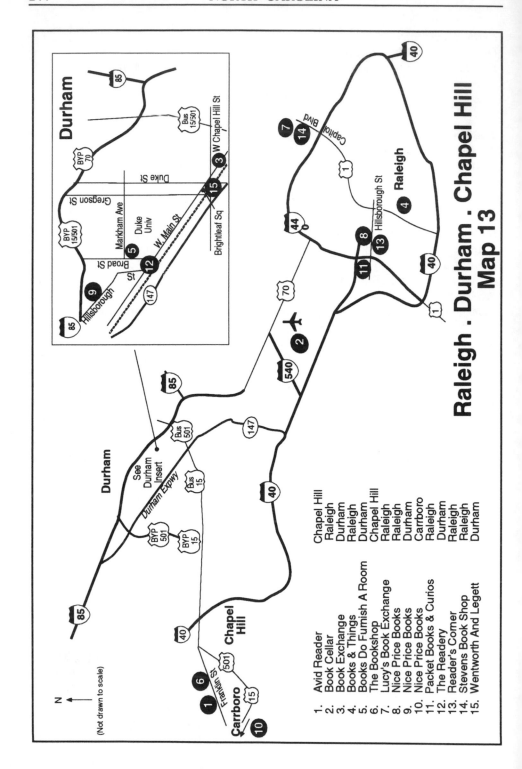

Raleigh . Durham . Chapel Hill
Map 13

1. Avid Reader   Chapel Hill
2. Book Cellar   Raleigh
3. Book Exchange   Durham
4. Books & Things   Raleigh
5. Books Do Furnish A Room Durham
6. The Bookshop   Chapel Hill
7. Lucy's Book Exchange   Raleigh
8. Nice Price Books   Raleigh
9. Nice Price Books   Durham
10. Nice Price Books   Carrboro
11. Packet Books & Curios   Raleigh
12. The Readery   Durham
13. Reader's Corner   Raleigh
14. Stevens Book Shop   Raleigh
15. Wentworth And Legett   Durham

Hours:	Sat & Sun 9-5.
Travel:	Capitol Blvd exit off I-440. Proceed south on Capitol (towards Raleigh).
Owner:	Jimmy Carter
Comments:	Stock is approximately 75% paperback.

Edward McKay Used Books   **Open Shop**

Web page: www.jbcmedia.com

Comments:	At press time, the location for this new shop had not been finalized. For current information, check the shop's web site or contact the owner's other shops in Greensboro or Fayetteville.

David Lenat, Bookseller   **By Appointment**

3607 Corbin Street 27612   (919) 787-8087

E-mail: lenatbks@aol.com

Collection:	Specialty
# of Vols:	3,000
Specialties:	Mystery (especially southern and bibliomysteries); southern literature; some natural history.
Services:	Catalog, accepts want lists.
Credit Cards:	No
Year Estab:	1995

Lucy's Book Exchange   **Open Shop**

6911 Capital Boulevard 27616   (919) 878-0625

Fax: (919) 790-9696

Collection:	General stock of mostly used paperback and hardcover.
# of Vols:	250,000
Hours:	Tue-Sat 10-5.
Travel:	Three blocks north of Plantation Inn on Rte 1 north.
Credit Cards:	Yes
Owner:	Lucy Morris
Year Estab:	1982
Comments:	We estimate that at least 80% of the books in this spacious, well organized shop, consist of paperbacks with the remaining 20% hardcover titles representing recent best sellers and older volumes without dust jackets. This is not a place to find rare or antiquarian books, but one which offers the general reader a good run for his or her money.

Nice Price Books   **Open Shop**

3106 Hillsborough Street 27607   (919) 829-0230

Collection:	General stock of hardcover and paperback and records.
# of Vols:	50,000
Hours:	Mon-Sat 10-10. Sun 12-10.
Services:	Appraisals, accepts want lists.
Travel:	Wade Ave exit off I-40. Proceed east on Wade to Faircloth, then right on Faircloth and left on Hillsborough. Shop is two blocks ahead on left. Parking is available in the rear.
Credit Cards:	Yes

(Raleigh)

Owner:	Cynthia Kamoroff
Comments:	The stock is about evenly divided between paperback and hardcover. The store is roomy, the shelves well marked and there are lots of chairs. Most of the hardcover volumes we saw were recent books and fairly common. Since the shop is just a block away from another used book dealer, you would not be going out of your way to visit it - and you might find something up your alley. The owner also has shops in Carrboro and Durham.

October Farm	**By Appointment**
2609 Branch Road 27610	(919) 772-0482
	Fax: (919) 779-6265

Collection:	Specialty books and ephemera.
# of Vols:	2,500
Specialties:	Horses (everything to do with them).
Services:	Search service, catalog, accepts want lists.
Credit Cards:	Yes
Owner:	Barbara Cole
Year Estab:	1977
Comments:	Owner also has a booth with a general stock at a multi dealer antique mall in Fuquay-Varina, NC. See above.

Packet Books & Curios	**Open Shop**
State Fairgrounds, Bldg #1, Hillsborough Street	(919) 828-7456
Mailing address: 659 Cary Towne Boulevard, #281 Cary 27511	
	E-mail: packetbook@aol.com

Collection:	General stock and ephemera.
# of Vols:	2,000
Specialties:	Guns; boats; planes; trains; sports; travel; fine and applied art; humanities; classic literature.
Hours:	Sat & Sun 9-5. Closed in October.
Services:	Search service, accepts want lists, mail order.
Travel:	Exit 290 off I-40. Proceed east on Rte 54 (Hillsborough St) to fairgrounds.
Credit Cards:	No
Owner:	John S. Atherton
Year Estab:	1994

Raleigh Creative Costumes	**Open Shop**
616 Saint Mary's Street 27609	(919) 834-4041
	Fax: (919) 834-0061

Collection:	Specialty
Specialties:	Theater, including play scripts and some makeup books.
Hours:	Mon-Sat 10-5.
Services:	Mail order.
Credit Cards:	Yes

Owner: Ms. Douglas T. Haas
Year Estab: 1977
Comments: Books are located in a costume shop.

The Reader's Corner   **Open Shop**
3201 Hillsborough Street 27607   (919) 828-7024
                                                                         Fax: (919) 664-8794
                                                                         E-mail: irvan@aol.com

Collection: General stock of hardcover and paperback and records.
# of Vols: 100,000
Specialties: Technology; art; mystery; science fiction.
Hours: Mon-Fri 10-8. Sat 10-6. Sun 12-6.
Travel: See Nice Price Books above.
Credit Cards: Yes
Owner: Irv Coats & Christine Baukus
Year Estab: 1975
Comments: We would definitely recommend a visit here and suggest that you not
be put off by the inexpensive paperbacks displayed outside the store.
(The books can be purchased even when the store is closed and the
proceeds from the sales, dropped through a slot in the front door, are
donated to the local National Public Radio station.) While the number
of paperbacks may at first seem overwhelming, a careful monitoring of
the shelves reveals a good sampling of hardcover titles and the persistent buyer who asks the right questions may be allowed to visit a
second site that houses real treasure trove of collectibles in many
fields. Bargains top be had.

Stevens Book Shop   **Open Shop**
7109 Old Wake Forest Road 27616   (919) 872-5995
                                                                         Fax: (919) 872-5881

Collection: General stock of mostly hardcover.
# of Vols: 500,000
Specialties: Religion
Hours: Mon-Sat 9-6.
Services: Catalog, accepts want lists.
Travel: Exit 11 off I-440. Proceed north (away from Raleigh) on Capitol Blvd
(Rte 1) for four miles. Shop is at intersection of Capitol and Old Wake
Forest Rd. Left on Old Wake Forest.
Credit Cards: Yes
Owner: Dick Stevens
Year Estab: 1954
Comments: If you're interested in any aspect of religion, chances are you'll find
enough material here to keep you browsing for hours on end. For those
with more lay tastes, there are books (both paperback and hardcover)
in most other subjects as well. In comparing volumes that we've seen
elsewhere, prices here tend to be a bit higher.

Tales Resold
3936 Atlantic Avenue 27604-1700

Open Shop
(919) 878-8551

Collection: General stock of mostly paperback and comics.
# of Vols: 30,000
Hours: Mon-Sat 10-6:30. Sun 1-5.

Rocky Mount
(Map 11, page 212)

J.J. Harper's Bookshop
142 SW Main Street 27804

Open Shop
(919) 442-7722

Collection: General stock of mostly hardcover.
# of Vols: 95,000
Specialties: First editions.
Hours: Wed-Sat 10-4.
Services: Appraisals, search service, accepts want lists, mail order.
Travel: Exit 138 off I-95. Proceed east on Rte 64 towards Rocky Mount, then Bus Rte 64 (Sunset Ave) to Main St. At the railroad, turn right. Shop is 1/2 block ahead on the right in a former bank building.
Credit Cards: No
Owner: Charles A. Cooley
Year Estab: 1985
Comments: A real find. The shop, which looks quite ordinary from its front windows, stocks a very large collection of books in every subject area and is particularly rich in its collection of older volumes. Divided into a series of rooms and alcoves, the shop offers book hunters an abundance of browsing opportunities. Whether you're looking for a familiar title or an unusual one you may not know about in a field that's of interest to you, there's a reasonable chance that you'll find it here. The books are priced most reasonably and we believe there are bargains to be had. The shop also stocks some paperbacks and remainders. If you don't see what you want, ask, as the owner has more than an equal number of volumes in storage.

Salisbury
(Map 11, page 212)

Lillian's Library
3024 South Main Street 28147

Open Shop
(704) 636-4671

Collection: General stock of hardcover and paperback.
# of Vols: 12,000
Specialties: North Carolina; Southern Americana.
Hours: Wed-Sat 12-5. Best to call ahead.
Travel: Jake Alexander exit off I-85. Proceed south on Main St to Red Acres Rd. Shop is a one story free standing building on the corner.
Credit Cards: No

Owner:	Lillian Gascoigne
Year Estab:	1988
Comments:	This combination collectibles/used book shop may very well be considered a sleeper in that it is not located on a major route. The used book portion of the shop was quite crowded during our visit and the casual browser might have some difficulty perusing the shelves carefully. Nonetheless, a patient browser should be able to find some older titles, not a few of which could be considered unusual and even rare. Prices were quite reasonable. The books were of mixed vintage and in mixed condition.

Salisbury Emporium   **Antique Mall**
230 East Kerr Street 28144   (704) 642-0039

Hours:	Tue-Sat 10-6. Sun 1-5.
Travel:	Exit 76B off I-85. Proceed west on Innes St then north on Depot to Kerr.

Shelby
(Map 11, page 212)

The Book Mill   **Open Shop**
213 South Lafayette Street 28150   (704) 481-9225

Collection:	General stock of hardcover and paperback and records.
# of Vols:	30,000
Specialties:	World War II, science fiction; children's.
Hours:	Mon-Fri 10-5:30. Sat 10-4.
Services:	Accepts want lists.
Travel:	Rte 18 exit off Rte 74. Proceed north on Rte 18 (S. Lafayette St) to uptown square. Shop is on right just before the square.
Credit Cards:	No
Owner:	Christine Berg & Reiner Van Rossum, Manager
Year Estab:	1986
Comments:	Located on the mezzanine level (an elevator is available) of another shop, this establishment offers a combination of records, paperbacks and hardcover fiction and non fiction in generally good condition and reasonably priced. Some nice titles, particularly among the mysteries which were separated by book club and original editions. Certainly possible to pick up a sleeper here.

Statesville
(Map 11, page 212)

DR. Books   **Antique Mall**
At Riverfront Antique Mall   Mall: (704) 873-9770
1440 Wilkesboro Road   Home: (803) 254-5444
Mailing address: 4015 Beverly Drive Columbia 29204

Collection:	General stock.
Hours:	Mon-Sat 9-8. Sun 9-6.

Travel:	Exit 150 off I-40. Proceed north on Rte 115 north for 1/4 mile.
Comments:	Also displays at Vista Books in Columbia, SC. See comments in South Carolina chapter.

Lester's Bookshop   **Open Shop**
118 West Broad Street 28677   (704) 871-2424

Collection:	General stock.
# of Vols:	10,000
Specialties:	Theology; music; philosophy.
Hours:	Mon-Sat 11-5:30.
Services:	Appraisals, accepts want lists, mail order.
Travel:	Exit 50 off I-77. Proceed west on East Broad St about one mile.
Credit Cards:	Yes
Owner:	Lester Chambers
Year Estab:	1991
Comments:	A modest sized shop whose decor and ambience brought to mind Christopher Morley. Whether or not you make a purchase here, you'll certainly admire the shop's decor of old fashioned wall lamps, busts and collection of Sherlock Holmes memorabilia. In addition to the specialties listed above, the shop offers a modest collection in other fields. Most of the books we saw in good condition and moderately priced.

Merri-Mac's Paperback Exchange   **Open Shop**
126 East Broad Street 28677   (704) 872-3805

Collection:	General stock of mostly paperback.
# of Vols:	10,000
Hours:	Mon-Sat 10-5.

Sylva

City Lights Bookstore   **Open Shop**
3 East Jackson Street 28779   (704) 586-9499

Collection:	General stock of new and mostly used paperback.
# of Vols:	3,000 (used)
Hours:	Summer: Mon-Thu 9-9. Fri & Sat 9am-10pm. Remainder of year: Mon-Thu 9-8. Fri & Sat 9am-10pm.

Troy
(Map 11, page 212)

Grandson's House   **Open Shop**
159 Saunders Road 27371   (910) 572-3484
                                                                   E-mail: gransons@ac.net

Collection:	General stock, ephemera and magazines.
# of Vols:	30,000
Hours:	Mon-Sat 10-4. Sun 1-4.
Services:	Accepts want lists, mail order.
Travel:	Proceed on Rte 24/27 west of Troy for about two miles. Left onto Saunders Rd. Shop is 1/2 block ahead on left.

Credit Cards:	Yes
Owner:	James M. Parks
Year Estab:	1970's
Comments:	Since our earlier visit three years ago when we saw a collection of mostly older, often obscure and difficult to find items in two dusty old buildings, the owner has reorganized his shop. For this new edition, we were advised that while the collection consists of approximately 30,000 volumes, only a small portion of the collection is available for browsing in the traditional "open shop" sense; the bulk of the collection is accessed by perusing lists. Based on that information, we decided to give this shop a "pass" on our most recent trip through North Carolina; while a visit would have enabled us to update our comments relating to the shop's ambience, we would have been at a loss to describe what really counts -- the books.

Tryon
(Map 11, page 212)

Village Book Shoppe **Open Shop**
102 Maple Street 28782 (704) 859-0273

Collection:	General stock of mostly hardcover.
# of Vols:	3,000-4,000
Hours:	Mon-Fri 10-5:30. Sat 10-5.
Travel:	Columbus exit off I-26. Proceed on Rte 108 for about five miles into Tryon where Rte 108 becomes Trade St. Left on Maple.
Credit Cards:	No
Owner:	Gina & Chris Amato
Year Estab:	1997

Wallace

Chapter Two **Open Shop**
110 West Main Street 28466 (910) 285-4595

Collection:	General stock of mostly paperback.
# of Vols:	50,000
Hours:	Mon-Sat 8:30-6.

Waxhaw

Theoria Scholarly Books **Open Shop**
30 Church Road 28173 (704) 843-4033
Web page: www.theoria.org E-mail: mlipper@theoria.org
Mailing address: PO Box 328, New York, NY 10159

Collection:	Specialty
# of Vols:	100,000
Specialties:	Religion; philosophy; linguistics; social sciences.
Hours:	Call for hours.

Travel:	Located near Charlotte. Call for details.
Services:	Appraisals, search service, catalog, accepts want lists.
Credit Cards:	No
Owner:	Marvin Lipper
Year Estab:	1976
Comments:	A warehouse location for a New York City based mail order dealer. The warehouse will open to the public in Spring '98.

Waynesville
(Map 11, page 212)

Saints & Scholars   **Open Shop**
36 North Main Street 28786-3809   (704) 452-3932

Collection:	General stock of new and used paperback and hardcover.
# of Vols:	3,000 (used)
Specialties:	Religion; fiction.
Hours:	Mon-Sat 10-5:30.
Travel:	From I-40, take Rte 19/23 to Waynesville, then Rte 276 south which becomes Main St.
Credit Cards:	Yes
Owner:	Jeff Minick
Year Estab:	1983
Comments:	Used stock is approximately 70% paperback.

Wall Street Book Exchange   **Open Shop**
181 North Wall Street 28786   (704) 456-5000

Collection:	General stock of mostly paperback.
# of Vols:	30,000
Hours:	Tue-Sat 10-7. Sun 1-6.

Wendell

Broadfoot Publishing Company   **Open Shop**
6624 Robertson Pond Road   (919) 365-6963
Mailing address: 1907 Buena Vista Circle Wilmington 28405   Fax: (919) 365-6008

Collection:	Specialty new and used.
# of Vols:	Limited (used)
Specialties:	Civil War.
Hours:	Mon-Fri 8:30-5.
Services:	Catalog. Also publishes new books dealing with the Civil War and North Carolina.
Travel:	Rolesville exit off I-64.
Credit Cards:	Yes
Owner:	Tom & Jan Broadfoot
Year Estab:	1973
Comments:	For catalog and mail order sales, contact the Wilmington location. (800) 537-5243, Fax (910) 686-4379. Retail sales are in Wendell.

Whispering Pines
(Map 11, page 212)

Edward J. Kearin-Books   **By Appointment**
135 Pine Ridge Drive 28327   (910) 949-3978

Collection: General stock.
# of Vols: 3,000
Specialties: Americana; southern history and fiction.
Credit Cards: No
Owner: Edward J. & Jeanne Kearin
Year Estab: 1976

Wilmington
(Map 11, page 212)

Daughtry's Books   **Open Shop**
22 North Front Street 28401   (910) 763-4754

Collection: General stock.
# of Vols: 28,000
Hours: Mon-Sat 9:30-5.
Travel: Downtown Wilmington.
Credit Cards: No
Year Estab: 1982
Comments: A rather good sized tightly packed shop with mostly older volumes.
                   Organization was spotty and the condition of many of the books was
                   questionable, with many volumes suffering from water damage. If
                   you're into older books, have patience and don't mind occasionally
                   stumbling over piles of books in the aisles, you may find some items of
                   interest here (although we had the sense that the shop's better books
                   had already been spoken for).

Dog Eared Book Exchange   **Open Shop**
6766 Wrightsville Avenue 28480   (910) 256-0079

Collection: General stock of paperback and hardcover.
# of Vols: 30,000
Hours: Mon-Sat 10-5:30.
Travel: On Rte 74/76 in Galleria Shopping Mall.
Credit Cards: No
Year Estab: 1994
Comments: Stock is approximately 60% paperback.

McAllister & Solomon Books   **Open Shop**
4402-1 Wrightsville Avenue 28403   (910) 350-0189
                                          E-mail: mcsolbooks@worldnet.att.net

Collection: General stock.
# of Vols: 20,000
Specialties: North Carolina; military; mystery; natural history.
Hours: Mon-Fri 10-7. Sat 10-6.

Services: Appraisals, catalog, search service, accepts want lists.
Travel: Rte 132 exit off I-40. Proceed south on College to Wrightsville, then
                 right onto Wrightsville. Shop is 1½ blocks ahead on the left.
Credit Cards: Yes
Owner: Steve McAllister & Linda Solomon
Year Estab: 1987
Comments: Sometimes travelers have to make difficult choices about which shops
                 to visit and which have to be passed up, at least for the trip in question.
                 Regrettably, this shop fell into that category. Just getting started when
                 the first edition of this book was published, the collection has almost
                 tripled in size in the intervening years, and based on what we saw the
                 first time, we very much wanted to pay a return visit. We just couldn't
                 work it into our itinerary. For our readers who do not have the first
                 edition of this book, we noted the following after our earlier visit:

                 A nice, just opened "open shop" that is, we believe, on its way to be
                 being nicer. The books we saw during our visit were in good condition
                 and represented most subject areas although limited in terms of num-
                 bers. Clearly, the owners take care in the selection of items they dis-
                 play suggesting that a discriminating buyer who stops to visit may,
                 unless another buyer has beaten him to the punch, find some items of
                 real interest. Prior to 1993, the owner operated a mail order business.

Winston-Salem
(Map 11, page 212)

Again & Again   **Open Shop**
708 Brookstown Avenue 27101   (910) 724-0599
Collection: General stock of mostly used hardcover and paperback.
# of Vols: 15,000
Hours: Tue-Sat 11-6. Sun 1-5. Longer hours in summer.
Travel: Broad St exit off Bus Rte 40. Proceed north on Broad, then right onto
                 Brookstown.
Credit Cards: Yes
Owner: Janet Wells
Year Estab: 1990
Comments: Used stock is approximately 60% hardcover.

Brookstown Antiques   **Open Shop**
1004 Brookstown Avenue 27101   (910) 723-5956
Collection: General stock.
# of Vols: 2,000+
Hours: Mon-Sat 10-5.
Travel: Broad St exit off Bus Rte I-40. Right onto Broad, then left onto
                 Brookstown. Shop is three blocks ahead on left.
Credit Cards: No
Owner: James E. Tatum
Year Estab: 1989

The Corner Antiques   **Open Shop**
749 Summit Street 27101   (910) 723-1825

Collection:	General stock.
# of Vols:	2,000
Hours:	Tue-Sat 10:30-6. Sun 1-5.
Travel:	Broad St exit off Bus Rte I-40. Proceed north on Broad to 4th St, then left onto 4th St and right onto Summit.
Credit Cards:	Yes
Owner:	Betsy Allen
Year Estab:	1981

Larry D. Laster   **By Appointment**
2416 Maplewood Avenue 27103   (910) 724-7544
                                                                   Fax: (910) 724-9055

Collection:	Specialty books, prints and maps.
# of Vols:	8,000-10,000
Specialties:	Fine bindings.
Services:	Appraisals
Credit Cards:	No
Year Estab:	1981

Triad Book Trader   **Open Shop**
3834 Reynolda Road 27106   (910) 922-2737

Collection:	General stock of mostly paperback.
# of Vols:	25,000
Hours:	Mon 1-7. Tue-Sat 10-7.

On the road again.

Michael E. Bernholz, Antiques & Books   (919) 929-3533
1 Sycamore Drive Chapel Hill 27514

Collection:	General stock.
# of Vols:	10,000
Specialties:	Military; nautical; North Carolina; medicine; science.
Services:	Appraisals, accepts want lists, catalog.
Credit Cards:	Yes
Year Estab:	1967

BookSearch   (704) 643-5800
4026 Bramwyck Drive Charlotte 28210   Fax: (704) 643-5802
Web page: www.bookgroup.com   E-mail: booksearch@vnet.net

Collection:	General stock.
# of Vols:	3,000+
Specialties:	Southern literature; children's series.
Services:	Search service.
Credit Cards:	Yes
Owner:	Barbara Svenson
Year Estab:	1969

Cape Lookout Antiquarian Books   (919) 728-5700
PO Box 910 Beaufort 28516-0910

Collection:	General stock.
# of Vols:	7,000+
Specialties:	Natural history; sporting; nautical.
Services:	Occasional catalog, accepts want lists.
Credit Cards:	Yes
Owner:	Barbara Z. Phillips
Year Estab:	1982
Comments:	Note: best times to call are 6-8am or 6-8 pm.

The Carolina Trader   (704) 282-1339
PO Box 769 Monroe 28111-0769   E-mail: carotrader@trellis.net
Web page: www.trellis.net/carotrader

Collection:	Specialty
# of Vols:	200+
Specialties:	Boy scouts.
Services:	Catalog, accepts want lists, appraisals, search service.
Credit Cards:	Yes
Owner:	Richard Shields
Year Estab:	1980

Charlie's Books   (910) 313-0649
PO Box 4625 Wilmington 28406

Collection:	General stock.
# of Vols:	3,000
Specialties:	North Carolina; modern first editions.
Services:	Accepts want lists.
Owner:	Charles B. Andrews
Year Estab:	1990

Collectors Exchange-National Geographics　　　　(919) 870-8407
10600 Lowery Drive Raleigh 27615　　　　　　Fax: (919) 870-8416
　　　　　　　　　　　　　　E-mail: KoopmanN@ix.netcom.com

Collection:	Specialty books, magazines and ephemera.
# of Vols:	15,000
Specialties:	National Geographic Society publications.
Services:	Appraisals, search service, catalog, accepts want lists.
Credit Cards:	Yes
Owner:	Nick Koopman
Year Estab:	1988
Comments:	Collection may also be viewed by appointment.

Chris Hartmann, Bookseller　　　　　　　　(704) 433-5478
219 W.A. Harris Road Morganton 28655　　　　Fax: (704) 433-1914

Collection:	General stock.
# of Vols:	18,000
Specialties:	Southern Americana; Civil War; military; natural history.
Services:	Catalog, accepts want lists.
Credit Cards:	No
Owner:	Chris & Lucille Hartmann
Year Estab:	1979

Daniel Hirsch - Fine & Rare Books　　　　　(919) 542-1816
PO Box 5096 Chapel Hill 27514　　　　　　Fax: (919) 542-1817

Collection:	Specialty
# of Vols:	1,100
Specialties:	Children's
Services:	Appraisals, accepts want lists, catalog.
Credit Cards:	No
Year Estab:	1972

JPH Books　　　　　　　　　　Tel & Fax: (919) 376-9778
PO Box 3741 Chapel Hill 27515　　　E-mail: jphbooks@interloc.com

Collection:	General stock and ephemera.
# of Vols:	500
Specialties:	Religion; modern first editions; science fiction.
Services:	Search service, catalog, accepts want lists.
Credit Cards:	Yes
Owner:	Perry Hardison
Year Estab:	1996

Paul Keene, Books　　　　　　　　　　　(919) 493-9539
119 Forestwood Drive Durham 27707　　E-mail: pkbooks@mindspring.com

Collection:	Specialty
# of Vols:	700
Specialties:	Nautical; naval and related fiction.
Services:	Occasional catalog, accepts want lists.
Year Estab:	1995

Lorien House   (704) 669-6211
PO Box 1112 Black Mountain 28711
Collection: General stock.
# of Vols: 1,500
Specialties: North Carolina; New York; technical.
Services: Appraisals, search service, accepts want lists.
Credit Cards: No
Owner: David A. Wilson
Year Estab: 1989

Murder For Fun Books   (919) 469-9473
2115 Marilyn Circle Cary 27513   E-mail: wembley@ibm.net
Collection: Specialty
# of Vols: 2,000 (used)
Specialties: Mystery; detective.
Services: Search service, accepts want lists.
Credit Cards: No
Owner: Pat O'Keefe
Year Estab: 1990

Not Forgotten Books   (910) 855-1929
1009 Condor Drive Greensboro 27410
Collection: Specialty
Specialties: Civil War (primarily first edition and out-of-print).
Services: Occasional catalog, accepts want lists, appraisals, search service.
Credit Cards: Yes
Owner: Russ Cummings
Year Estab: 1990

Tamarind Books   (910) 852-1905
PO Box 49217 Greensboro 27419   Fax: (910) 852-0750
                                                    E-mail: tamarind@interloc.com
Collection: Specialty
# of Vols: 2,000
Specialties: Southeast Asia.
Services: Catalog, accepts want lists.
Credit Cards: No
Owner: Frederic C. Benson
Year Estab: 1990

Triduum Books   Tel & Fax: (919) 929-7753
PO Box 1145 Chapel Hill 27514   E-mail: lynn@email.unc.edu
Web page: www.intrex.net/triduum
Collection: Specialty
# of Vols: 5,000
Specialties: Southern history; southern writers; Louisiana and New Orleans; modern
                   first editions; Huey P. Long; religion (Catholicism); fine arts; Orient.
Services: Appraisals, search service, catalog, accepts want lists.
Owner: Mr. Lynn Roundtree
Year Estab: 1988

South Carolina

Alphabetical Listing By Dealer

A touch of class

Alphabetical Listing By Location

Area Code Changes

Beginning March 22, 1998, the 803 area code in eastern South Carolina will be split into two codes. All 803 numbers listed below that are preceded by an * will become 843.

Aiken
(Map 14, page 273)

Janet Cornwell, Bookseller
At Aiken Antique Mall
112 Laurens Street SW 29801

Antique Mall
Mall: (803) 648-6700

Collection:	General stock.
# of Vols:	3,000+
Specialties:	Cookbooks; Civil War; Southern America.
Hours:	Mon-Sat 10-6. Sun 1-6.
Travel:	Rte 19 exit off I-20. Proceed south on Rte 19 which runs into Laurens St.

Twice-Sold Tales
At Aiken Antique Mall
112 Laurens Street SW 29801
Mailing address: 309 Ascauga Lake Road Graniteville 29829

Antique Mall
Mall: (803) 648-6700
Home: (803) 663-3498

Collection:	General stock and ephemera.
Specialties:	Children's; Christmas; magazines; South Carolina.
Hours:	Mon-Sat 10-6. Sun 1-6.
Services:	Search service, accepts want lists, mail order.
Travel:	See above.
Owner:	Jeanette Kirkland
Year Estab:	1990

Anderson
(Map 14, page 273)

Christian Book Store
1012 Whitehall Road, #A 29625-2122

Open Shop
(864) 225-6193

Collection:	Specialty used and new paperback and hardcover.
# of Vols:	3,000+
Specialties:	Religion
Hours:	Mon-Sat 9-8, except Wed closed at 6:30.
Travel:	Exit 19 of I-85. Proceed east on Whitehall.

Cottage Bookstore & Coffeehouse
2202 North Main Street 29621

Open Shop
(864) 261-3280

Collection:	General stock of mostly used paperback.
# of Vols:	8,000
Hours:	Mon-Fri 9:30-6. Sat 10-4.

McDowell's Emporium   **Open Shop**
104 Oak Drive 29625   (864) 231-8896
                                              E-mail: Neatstuffs@aol.com

Collection:	General stock.
# of Vols:	5,000+
Hours:	Tue-Fri 11-5. Sat by chance.
Services:	Search service, mail order, accepts want lists.
Travel:	Exit 19 off I-85. Proceed toward Anderson on Clemson Blvd which becomes N. Main St. Turn right on Oak Drive.
Credit Cards:	Yes
Owner:	Judith McDowell
Year Estab:	1988

Beaufort
(Map 14, page 273)

McIntosh Book Shop   **Open Shop**
917 Bay Street 29902   * (803) 525-1066

Collection:	General stock of used and new.
# of Vols:	4,000
Specialties:	South Carolina; World War II, Civil War.
Hours:	Mon-Sat 10-5.
Travel:	Located in Old Bay Market Place.
Owner:	G. Wilson McIntosh
Year Estab:	1995
Comments:	Stock is approximately 60% used. A smaller selection of used books is also available at the owner's second shop, The Beaufort Bookstore, 2127 Boundary St, which is primarily a new book shop.

Charleston
(Map 14, page 273)

Atlantic Books   **Open Shop**
310 King Street 29401   * (803) 723-4751
                                                E-mail: awoolf@awod.com

Collection:	General stock mostly used hardcover and paperback.
# of Vols:	15,000
Specialties:	South Carolina; southern authors, Civil War; Americana; Native Americans; children's; military; modern first editions.
Hours:	Mon-Sat 10-6. Sun 1-6.
Services:	Appraisals, accepts want lists, mail order.
Travel:	King St exit off I-26. Proceed south on King. Shop is between George and Society in downtown historic district.
Credit Cards:	Yes
Owner:	Amelia Woolf
Year Estab:	1986
Comments:	Want to buy a 24 volume collection of the works of Leo Tolstoy for only $300? Or a 38 volume collection of British essayists for $250?

They're available here (or were at the time of our visit) along with a collection of paperback and hardcover books, some new, some vintage and many interesting, in a shop that displays its books in an attractive and inviting manner

Atlantic Books   **Open Shop**
191 East Bay Street 29401   * (803) 723-7654
                                     E-mail: awoolf@awod.com

Collection:	General stock of mostly used hardcover and paperback.
# of Vols:	10,000-15,000
Specialties:	South Carolina, southern authors, Civil War; military; Americana; modern first editions; children's; Native Americans.
Hours:	Mon-Sat 10-6. Sun 1-6.
Services:	Appraisals, accepts want lists, mail order.
Travel:	King Street exit off I-26. Proceed south in King to Broad St, then left onto Broad and right onto East Bay. Shop is on the left.
Credit Cards:	Yes
Owner:	Gene Woolf
Year Estab:	1986
Comments:	The second of two shops with the same name owned and managed by a husband and wife team. The stock and ambience here is similar to its sister shop on King St.

Boomer's Books & Collectibles   **Open Shop**
420 King Street 29403   * (803) 722-2666
Web page: www.charleston.net/com/boomers   Fax: * (803) 722-1168
                              E-mail: boomers@charleston.net

Collection:	General stock of mostly hardcover.
# of Vols:	30,000
Hours:	Mon-Sat 10-6. Sun 2-6.
Services:	Search service, accepts want lists, mail order.
Travel:	See Atlantic Books above. Shop is between John and Hutson Streets.
Credit Cards:	Yes
Owner:	Jim & Lee Breeden
Year Estab:	1995
Comments:	A long narrow shop with a series of small rooms along the right hand wall. Most of the hardcover volumes we saw were in generally good condition, well organized and were of more recent vintage although there were also some collectibles and rare items. If you've travelled a distance and can identify yourself as a serious book person, the owner will gladly let you visit a room in the rear of the shop where additional books are stored.

Cavendish Rare Books   **By Appointment**
PO Box 1036 29402   * (803) 883-3994
                                 Fax: * (803) 883-5008

Collection:	Specialty
# of Vols:	2,000

(Charleston)

Specialties:	Voyages and travel; polar exploration; mountaineering; Asia; Pacific; maritime history; yachting.
Services:	Appraisals, search service, catalog, accepts want lists.
Credit Cards:	Yes
Owner:	Barbara Grigor-Taylor
Year Estab:	1960

The Charleston Rare Book Company   **Open Shop**
66 Church Street 29401   * (803) 723-3330
Mailing address: PO Box 774 Charleston 29402   Fax: * (803) 723-3233
                                       E-mail: chasrarebk@chrleston.net.com

\Collection:*	Specialty
# of Vols:	2,000
Specialties:	Charleston; low country and regional; antebellum Americana; Civil War; Victorian literature with emphasis on Anthony Trollope; naval and maritime history of US and Britain; British history; European history; Winston Churchill; children's.
Hours:	Mon-Sat 10-6. Other times by appointment.
Services:	Appraisals, search service, accepts want lists.
Travel:	Meeting St exit off I-26. Proceed south on Meeting to Broad St, left on Broad then right on Church. Shop is just past Tradd St on left across from church.
Credit Cards:	No
Owner:	Bob Schindler
Year Estab:	1994
Comments:	It's not often we get to visit a specialty shop carrying the kind of quality material we were able to view here. What the shop lacks in numbers it more than makes up for in the quality and condition of the volumes on hand. Of the specialties listed above, we noted a particularly strong emphasis on early American history. We also spotted several different editions of *Porgy*. Visiting here was like visiting a rare book room elsewhere.

D & D Books & Antiques   **Open Shop**
190 King Street 29401   * (803) 853-5266

Collection:	Specialty
# of Vols:	500
Specialties:	Charleston; Southern Americana; Civil War; nautical; fishing; hunting; travel; adventure.
Hours:	Mon-Sat, except closed Tue, 10-5.
Travel:	Two doors from Horlbeck Alley.
Credit Cards:	Yes
Owner:	Tony DiRest
Year Estab:	1993

Noble Dragon Book Shop
106 Church Street 29401

Tel & Fax: * (803) 577-9334
E-mail: noblebks@charleston.net

Collection:	General stock of mostly hardcover.
# of Vols:	3,500
Hours:	Mon-Sat 11-5:30. Summer: Tue-Sat 11-5:30. Other times by appointment.
Services:	Appraisals, search service, accepts want lists, mail order.
Travel:	See Charleston Rare Book Company above.
Credit Cards:	Yes
Owner:	Judith Swartzel
Year Estab:	1995
Comments:	We had better luck visiting this shop for this revised edition than we had three years earlier. What we found was a rather small shop with books in many subject areas, most of them reading copies. Some interesting. A few collectible. If you're looking for a place to have a cup of coffee and perhaps a snack, you might even find something you wish to purchase here.

Northbridge Books
1688 Old Town Road 29407

Open Shop
* (803) 556-5383

Collection:	General stock of mostly paperback.
# of Vols:	45,000
Hours:	Mon-Sat 10-6.

Palmetto Books
PO Box 12753 29422

By Appointment
* (803) 795-1996
Fax: * (803) 795-8591
E-mail: dkcupka@worldnet.att.net

Collection:	Specialty
# of Vols:	1,000
Specialties:	South Carolina; hunting; fishing.
Services:	Appraisals, search service, catalog.
Credit Cards:	No
Owner:	David Cupka
Year Estab:	1952

Parnassus Books
PO Box 1883 29402

By Appointment
* (803) 588-9008

Collection:	Specialty
# of Vols:	1,000
Specialties:	South Carolina; Charleston.
Services:	Mail order.
Owner:	Stephen Nolan
Year Estab:	1988

Terrace Oaks Antique Mall   **Antique Mall**
2037 Maybank Highway   * (803) 795-9689

Hours: Mon-Sat 9:30-5:30. Sun 1-5.
Travel: Rte 17 south to Rte 171 (towards Folly Beach), then right on Rte 700
                (Maybank Hwy). Shop is about 1½ miles ahead on left.

Columbia
(Map 14, page 273)

Bluestocking Books   **Antique Mall**
At City Market Antique Mall   (803) 799-7722
701 Gervais Street 29201

Collection: General stock of hardcover and paperback.
Hours: Mon-Sat 10-5:30. Sun 1:30-5:30.
Travel: See Books Finders below.

The Book Dispensary #1   **Open Shop**
1600 Broad River Road 29210   (803) 798-4739   (800) 798-6908
                                                        Fax: (803) 750-0286
                                                E-mail: tbd@cdickens.com

Collection: General stock of hardcover and paperback.
# of Vols: 20,000
Specialties: Children's; Civil War; Southern Americana; alcoholism; religion.
Hours: Mon-Sat 10-9. Sun 12-6.
Services: Appraisals, search service, mail order, accepts want lists, book restora-
                tion, repair and binding.
Travel: In Boozer Shopping Center at intersection of Bush River and Broad
                River Rds, just off I-20. From I-26, proceed west on Bush River Rd.
Credit Cards: Yes
Owner: Tom Hamm
Year Estab: 1975
Comments: The larger of two stores in Columbia owned by the same dealer. The
                hardcover items we saw were selected with care and, whether newer or
                older, were generally in very good condition. A section labeled "col-
                lectibles" had some interesting titles. Prices here, as well as in the
                chain's other shop, were for the most part, a tad higher than similar
                books found elsewhere. If you're time is limited and you can only visit
                one of the two stores, this is the one we would recommend.

The Book Dispensary #4   **Open Shop**
7384 Two Notch Road 29223   (803) 736-4033
                                                E-mail: tbd@dickens.com

Collection: General stock of hardcover and paperback.
# of Vols: 5,000
Specialties: Children's; science fiction; mystery; military.
Hours: Mon-Sat 10-6:30. Sun 12-6.
Services: Appraisals, search service, mail order.

Travel: Two Notch Rd exit off I-20. Proceed on Two Notch Rd for a short
                   distance (towards Columbia). Shop is located in Garden Place Plaza.
Credit Cards: Yes
Owner: Tom Hamm
Year Estab: 1975
Comments: Considerably smaller than it's sister store with the hardcover books up
                   front and along the side walls and paperbacks taking up the center of
                   the shop. Better books, and perhaps rarer items, are displayed closer to
                   the front counter.

Book Finders International/Eccentricities   **Open Shop**
701 Gervais Street 29201   Store: (803) 254-5444
                                                               Home: (803) 788-1368
                                                                Fax: (803) 736-0028

Collection: General stock.
# of Vols: 6,000
Specialties: English modern first editions; children's; pop-ups (20th century).
Hours: Mon-Sat 10-5:30. Sun 1:30-5:30.
Services: Appraisals, search service, accepts want lists.
Travel: Huger exit off I-126. Left onto Gervais. Shop is two blocks ahead on
                   left in the City Market Antique Mall.
Credit Cards: Yes
Owner: Elizabeth Wessels
Year Estab: 1985
Comments: A delightful little shop set off by itself in an antique mall. Lots of
                   "good stuff" in good to fine condition. In addition to the specialties
                   listed above, we noted a particularly nice mystery section. The owner
                   is chatty, gracious and a fountain of knowledge. Worth a visit.

The Book Place   **Open Shop**
3129 Millwood Avenue 29205   (803) 799-6561

Collection: General stock.
# of Vols: 20,000
Specialties: Civil War; South Carolina; modern first editions; hunting; fishing;
                   genealogy; military.
Hours: Mon-Sat 10-5.
Services: Appraisals, accepts want lists.
Travel: Proceeding east on Gervais St, Millwood is about two miles east of the
                   State House. Right onto Millwood and proceed for about one mile.
Credit Cards: Yes
Owner: Hampton Alvey
Year Estab: 1978
Comments: What we would classify as a "typical used book shop" with lots of
                   stock, nicely marked, easy to browse shelves and an establishment that
                   very well may have an item or two of interest for you. The books were
                   of mixed vintage and almost every subject category was covered in
                   some depth. Books were quite reasonably priced.

(Columbia)

Columbia Athenaeum   **By Appointment**
PO Box 7875 29202   Tel & Fax: (803) 779-4048

Collection:	Specialty
# of Vols:	2,500
Specialties:	South Carolina; genealogy; Civil War; Americana.
Services:	Appraisals, search service, catalog, accepts want lists.
Credit Cards:	Yes
Owner:	Carol Fairman & Ron Bridwell
Year Estab:	1987
Comments:	The owners also display at Vista Books in Columbia (see below) and at the Terrace Oaks Antique Mall in Charleston (see above).

DR. Books   **Antique Mall**
At The Antique Mall (Vista Books)   Mall: (803) 256-1420
1215 Pulaski Street   Home: (803) 787-5732
Mailing address: 4015 Beverly Dr Columbia 29204

E-mail: drbooks@cyberstate.infi.net

Collection:	General stock and ephemera.
# of Vols:	5,000
Specialties:	American archaeology; language.
Hours:	Mon-Sat 10-6. Sun 1:30-6.
Services:	Search service, accepts want lists, mail order.
Travel:	See Vista Books below.
Owner:	Don Rosick
Year Estab:	1990
Comments:	See Vista Books below.

First Corps Books   **By Appointment**
42 Eastgrove Court 29212   (803) 781-2709

E-mail: firstcorps@msn.com

Collection:	Specialty new and used.
# of Vols:	1,200
Specialties:	Civil War.
Services:	Appraisals, search service, catalog, accepts want lists.
Credit Cards:	Yes
Owner:	Mike Wadsworth
Year Estab:	1992
Comments:	Stock is approximately 70% new.

Gumshoe Books   **Antique Mall**
At The Antique Mall (Vista Books)   Mall: (803) 256-1420
1215 Pulaski Street   Home: (803) 799-5740
Mailing address: 1300 Pickens St, Ste 120 Columbia 29201   Fax: (803) 799-6504

Collection:	Specialty books and ephemera.
# of Vols:	6,500

Specialties:	Modern first editions; mystery; black studies; jazz; South Carolina; law; medicine; fine bindings.
Services:	Appraisals, catalog, accepts want lists.
Travel:	See Vista Books below.
Owner:	Skipp Webb
Year Estab:	1990
Comments:	One of the four dealers that make up Vista Books (see below). We were most pleasantly surprised to find such an outstanding collection of vintage mysteries (many of them dust jacketed and/or first editions) in an antique mall setting, along with pulp magazines and big little books. Many of the items seen here should be of great interest to those specializing in this genre.

Vista Books   **Antique Mall**
At The Antique Mall   (803) 256-1420
1215 Pulaski Street 29201

Collection:	General stock.
# of Vols:	5,000-8,000
Hours:	Mon-Sat 10-6. Sun 1:30-6.
Travel:	I- 126 exit off I-26. Right on Huger St, left on Gervais and left on Pulaski. From I-20: Rte 1 exit. Proceed north on Rte 1 to Pulaski, then left on Pulaski.
Comments:	This is a group shop (with, at the time of our visit, four dealers) in a multi dealer antique mall. It was clear to us that the dealers displayed some of their finer wares, including the works of several well known writers, some in signed first editions, e.g., *To Kill a Mockingbird*, as well as other high end fiction and non fiction volumes. When four separate first class dealers come together in one place, it's a combination that's hard to beat.

Conway
(Map 14, page 273)

Hidden Attic Antiques   **Antique Mall**
1014 Fourth Avenue 29526   * (803) 248-6262

Hours:	Mon-Sat 10-5.
Travel:	From Myrtle Beach: Rte 501 to Conway. Follow Bus Rte 501 to Main Street in town, then left onto Fourth Ave.

Florence
(Map 14, page 273)

Books+   **Open Shop**
2015J West Evans Street 29501   Tel & Fax: * (803) 665-0054
                                        E-mail: jroberts@interloc.com

Collection:	General stock of paperback and hardcover.
# of Vols:	7,000 (hardcover)

Specialties:	Francis Marion; modern first editions; biography; cookbooks; history; Archibald Rutledge; children's.
Hours:	Tue-Sat 12-6.
Services:	Search service, accepts want lists, mail order.
Travel:	At intersection of I-95 & I-20, take McLeod Blvd into Florence. Turn left at fifth light onto Evans. After one light, shop is in Park Place Mall on left.
Credit Cards:	Yes
Owner:	Patricia & Brandi Roberts
Year Estab:	1995

Florence Book Exchange   **Open Shop**
617 West Palmetto Street 29501   * (803) 665-6784

Collection:	General stock of mostly paperback.
# of Vols:	85,000
Hours:	Mon-Sat 10-5:30.
Travel:	Palmetto St is Rte 76.

Fountain Inn
(Map 14, page 273)

Bygone Books   **Open Shop**
201D-1 North Main Street 29644   (864) 862-2213

Collection:	General stock.
# of Vols:	2,700
Specialties:	Military
Hours:	Mon, Tue, Thu, Fri 9-5:30. Wed 9-12. Sat 9-5.
Travel:	Exit 24 off I-385. Proceed east on Fairview St. Shop is at the intersection of Fairview and Main, on the right, in a shopping center.
Credit Cards:	No
Owner:	Dennis Hutchinson
Year Estab:	1997

Goose Creek
(Map 14, page 273)

Book Exchange   **Open Shop**
104 Berkeley Square Lane, #25 29445   * (803) 797-5500

Collection:	General stock of paperback and hardcover.
# of Vols:	20,000
Hours:	Mon-Sat 10-8. Sun 12:30-6.
Travel:	On Rte 52 in Berkeley Square Shopping Center.
Credit Cards:	Yes
Owner:	Theresa Herian
Year Estab:	1972
Comments:	Stock is evenly mixed between paperback and hardcover.

South Carolina
Map 14

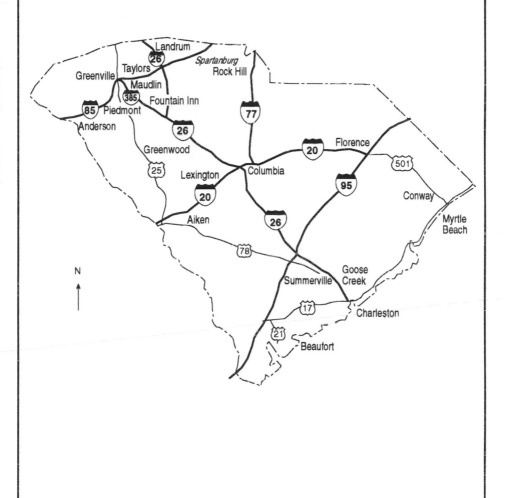

Greenville
(Map 14, page 273)

Bentley's Bookshop   **Open Shop**
3010 East North Street 29615   (864) 268-7802
E-mail: bentleysbooks@mindspring.com

Collection:	General stock of hardcover and paperback.
# of Vols:	20,000
Hours:	Mon-Sat 10-6.
Services:	Search service, accepts want lists, mail order.
Travel:	I-385 north exit off I-85. Proceed north on I-385 to Rte 291 north (Pleasantburg Dr) exit, then north on Rte 291 to East North St. Right on East North. Shop is about one mile ahead on right.
Credit Cards:	Yes
Owner:	Kerry Hughes & James Trusko
Year Estab:	1994
Comments:	Aesthetically, we would have to classify this as a warm and inviting place to browse. The books "ain't bad" either. Most of the books are in very good to excellent condition, are nicely arranged and, at the time of our visit, included several items worth going out of one's way for. Quite reasonably priced. Don't overlook the separate children's room.

Booklovers   **Open Shop**
1112 Rutherford Road 29609   (864) 232-0909

Collection:	General stock of mostly used hardcover.
# of Vols:	4,000
Specialties:	Non fiction; religion.
Hours:	Tue-Fri 10-5. Sat 10-2.
Services:	Mail order.
Travel:	From Rte 291 bypass, turn west onto Rutherford Rd. Shop is 1/4 mile ahead, on left, in Stone Plaza Shopping Center.
Credit Cards:	No
Owner:	Billy Stevens
Year Estab:	1995

Bookquest   **By Appointment**
19 Otis Street 29605   (864) 233-1063
Fax: (864) 233-3168
E-mail: baileybq@juno.com

Collection:	General stock.
# of Vols:	2,000
Specialties:	South Carolina; local history; modern first editions.
Services:	Search service, catalog, accept want lists.
Credit Cards:	No
Owner:	Michael & Dianne Bailey
Year Estab:	1986
Comments:	Also displays at antique malls in Taylors and Greenville. See below.

Robbins' Rarities   **Open Shop**
2038-C Laurens Road 29607   (864) 297-7948

Collection:	General stock, documents and prints.
# of Vols:	7,000+
Specialties:	Civil War; military; first editions; autographs.
Hours:	Mon-Sat, except closed Wed, 11-5.
Services:	Search service.
Travel:	Exit 48B off I-85. Proceed west on Rte 276 for about 1½ miles toward Greenville. Shop is on Rte 276, on the left.
Credit Cards:	Yes
Owner:	LeRoy A. Robbins
Year Estab:	1985
Comments:	Quite a nice shop where you can find a mix of first editions, reading copies and some rare items of yesteryear within several feet of one another. As with most stores with limited display space, the books you see when you visit here may be quite different from those we viewed when we visited, particularly since the owner indicates that he is constantly purchasing new stock. In addition to books, the shop also carries prints, confederate money and other miscellaneous collectibles.

St. Anthony's Catholic Bookstore   **Open Shop**
480 North Academy Street 29601   Tel & Fax: (864) 370-2086

Collection:	Specialty
# of Vols:	3,000
Specialties:	Religion (Catholic).
Hours:	Mon-Sat 9:30-5:30.
Services:	Search service.
Travel:	Academy exit off I-385. Turn right and proceed through two lights. Shop is on left.
Credit Cards:	Yes
Year Estab:	1990

Southern Estates Antique Mall   **Antique Mall**
415 Maudlin Road 29605   (864) 299-8981

Hours:	Mon-St 10-6. Sun 1-6.
Travel:	Exit 46 off I-85.

Greenwood
(Map 14, page 273)

The Attic   **Open Shop**
1500 Highway 246 North 29649   (864) 229-1022

Collection:	General stock.
# of Vols:	100,000+
Specialties:	South Carolina.
Hours:	Sat 9-5. Other times by appointment.
Services:	Appraisals, catalog.

Travel:	Six miles east of Rte 25 north.
Credit Cards:	No
Owner:	Donald Hawthorne
Year Estab:	1958
Comments:	A real find for any true book lover. Plan to spend several hours or more here but do call ahead for an appointment as the shop is only open one day a week. The shop has a warehouse appearance with tall shelves and fairly narrow aisles and there are no labels on the shelves indicating categories. However, once you've walked down each aisle looking carefully at the books, you can get a sense of the owner's organizational patterns. Don't come here looking for current best sellers. What you'll find are thousands of titles representing every possible subject area and some extraordinarily unique books in every field from the 18th century to the middle and late 20th century. The shop is chock full of wonderful books, some unfortunately that are worn, but most in good to better condition.

Noah's Ark Book Attic   **Open Shop**
1500 Highway 246 North 29649   (864) 229-1022

Collection:	Specialty
# of Vols:	30,000
Specialties:	Religion
Hours:	Sat 9-5. Other times by appointment.
Services:	Appraisals, catalog.
Travel:	Six miles east of Rte 25.
Credit Cards:	No
Owner:	Donald Hawthorne
Year Estab:	1954
Comments:	See above comments.

Greer

Book Exchange   **Open Shop**
109 Trade Street 29651   (864) 877-1548

Collection:	General stock of mostly paperback.
Hours:	Mon-Sat 10-5, except Fri till 6.

Hilton Head

The Antiquarian's Attic   **By Appointment**
35 Tucker Ridge Court 29926   * (803) 342-2050
                                                    E-mail: snyderr@fcae.nova.edu

Collection:	Specialty
# of Vols:	2,000+
Specialties:	Children's; Oz; pop-ups; children's series; first editions.
Services:	Search service, accepts want lists.

Credit Cards:	No
Owner:	Richard & Debbie Snyder
Year Estab:	1992

Landrum
(Map 14, page 273 & Map 11, page 212)

Blue Moon Books   **Open Shop**
118 East Rutherford Street 29356   (864) 457-2001
E-mail: blumnbks@interloc.com

Collection:	General stock.
# of Vols:	12,000
Specialties:	Carolinas; horses; fox hunting; history.
Hours:	Thu-Sat 10-5:30. Call for additional hours.
Services:	Appraisals, search service.
Travel:	Exit 1 off I-26. Proceed west on Rte 14 for two miles.
Credit Cards:	No
Owner:	Jerry & Mary Hardvall
Year Estab:	1991
Comments:	Modest in size but not in quality. This shop is nicely organized. The books we saw were in good to excellent condition with an emphasis on regional issues and uncommon titles. Quite reasonably priced.

Lexington
(Map 14, page 273)

Rainy Day Pal Used Books   **Flea Market**
Barnyard Flea Market, Bldg H 6 & 7   Bus: (803) 951-2780
4414 August Road 29073   Home: (803) 955-9078

Collection:	General stock of hardcover and paperback and ephemera.
# of Vols:	28,000+
Specialties:	Civil War.
Hours:	Fri-Sun 9-6.
Travel:	On Rte 1, between Lexington and Columbia.
Credit Cards:	Yes
Owner:	Calvin Lyles
Year Estab:	1989
Comments:	Stock is approximately 60% hardcover.

Maudlin
(Map 14, page 273)

George D. Hedgepath Old & Rare Books   **Antique Mall**
At L & L Market Place   Mall: (864) 862-6170
206 South Main Street   Home: (864) 244-3239
Mailing address: 316 Richbourg Road Greenville 29615

Collection:	General stock.
# of Vols:	3,000

Hours:	Tue, Thu, Fri, Sat 9-6.
Travel:	On Rte 276.
Year Estab:	1982

Myrtle Beach
(Map 14, page 273)

Bookstall   **Open Shop**
10497 Highway 17N 29572   * (803) 272-2607
                                                  E-mail: cdeese@aol.com

Collection:	General stock of hardcover and paperback.
# of Vols:	50,000
Specialties:	History; fiction.
Hours:	Mon-Sat 10-6.
Services:	Appraisals, search service, accepts want lists, mail order.
Travel:	On Rte 17, between Briarcliffe Mall and Barefoot Landing. Proceeding north, the shop is on the left in a former private residence set back from road.
Credit Cards:	Yes
Owner:	Cliff Deese, Manager
Year Estab:	1979
Comments:	A mix of newer vintage hardcover books, several shelves of older books labeled "do not touch" as they appeared too fragile to handle, and paperbacks. Once entering the shop, the size of the establishment turns out to be a bit larger than it appears from the outside. The manager advises us that he has close to 150,000 additional books in storage. The prices we saw on the books were as varied as the books themselves. While you may not want to travel out of your way to visit here, the attractions of Myrtle Beach may be such that you find yourself in the area; under these circumstances, we definitely recommend a visit.

Myrtle Beach Flea Market   **Flea Market**
3820 South Kings Highway 29577   * (803) 477-1550

| *Hours:* | Jul & Aug: Daily 9-6. Sep-Jun: Thu-Sun 9-6. |
| *Travel:* | Located on Bus Rte 17. |

Letty Wilder-Books   **By Appointment**
212 South Highland Way 29572   * (803) 449-3466

Collection:	General stock.
# of Vols:	1,000 (See Comments)
Specialties:	South Carolina; Southern Americana; Civil War; modern first editions.
Services:	Accepts want lists, search service.
Credit Cards:	No
Year Estab:	1973
Comments:	Also displays an additional 3,500 books at Hidden Attic Antiques in Conway. See above.

Newberry

Opera House Mysteries   **Antique Mall**
At Antiques Etc.   Mall: (803) 276-1073
1213 Main Street   Home & Fax: (803) 276-1575
Mailing address: PO Box 1064 Newberry 29108

Collection:	Specialty. Mostly hardcover.
# of Vols:	8,000
Hours:	Mon-Sat 10-5.
Specialties:	Mystery; modern first editions.
Services:	Mail order, accepts want lists.
Travel:	Rte 216 exit off I-26. Proceed south on Rte 219 to Newberry where Rte 219 becomes Main St.
Credit Cards:	No
Owner:	Jane C. Britt
Year Estab:	1996

North Charleston

Green Dragon   **Open Shop**
7671 Northwood Boulevard, Ste. 5T 29406   * (803) 797-2052
Web page: www.starlightgraphics.com/grdragon

Collection:	Specialty. Mostly new.
# of Vols:	250-500 (used)
Specialties:	Science fiction; horror; fantasy.
Hours:	Mon-Fri 11-9. Sat 10-9. Sun 12-6.
Travel:	From Charleston: Ashley-Phosphate Rd exit off I-26. Cross Ashley-Phosphate and continue straight through light. Shop is on left just before Northwoods Mall.

Piedmont
(Map 14, page 273)

Papa's Book Haven Antiques & Collectibles   **Open Shop**
2510 River Road 29673   (864) 269-5700

Collection:	General stock.
# of Vols:	20,000
Specialties:	Religion; history; literature; children's; poetry; art; self help; Civil War; South Carolina; fiction; westerns.
Hours:	Tue & Wed 10-5. Thu & Fri 10-6. Sat 10-5.
Services:	Accepts want lists.
Travel:	Exit 39 off I-85. At exit, look for a grey pre fab building.
Credit Cards:	Yes
Owner:	David & Eyonne Sherwood
Year Estab:	1993

Comments: With the exception of some older books focusing on southern history
                 and the Civil War, most of the books we saw in this pleasant shop (that
                 also sells antiques and collectibles) were an assortment of titles in most
                 subject areas but without much depth. Most of the books were reading
                 copies of mixed vintage with a majority being of more recent vintage.
                 The books were priced to sell.

Rock Hill
(Map 14, page 273)

The Book Shelf   **Open Shop**
119 North Spruce Street 29730   (803) 328-9062

Collection: General stock of paperback and hardcover.
# of Vols: 55,000
Specialties: Science fiction; mystery; occult; new age.
Hours: Mon-Sat 11-6.
Services: Appraisals, search service, accepts want lists.
Travel: 1/2 block off Main St.
Credit Cards: No
Owner: Andy & Shelby Hawkins
Year Estab: 1979
Comments: Stock is approximately 70% paperback.

Spartanburg
(Map 14, page 273)

Books 'n Stuff   **Open Shop**
8027 Greenville Hwy 29301   (864) 587-0887

Collection: General stock of mostly paperback.
Hours: Mon-Sat 10-6.

Your Town   **By Appointment**
516 Maverick Circle 29307-3707   Tel & Fax: (864) 579-2112

Collection: General stock and ephemera.
Specialties: Southern writers and subjects.
Services: Appraisals; markets entire libraries.
Credit Cards: No
Owner: Henry Barnet
Year Estab: 1990

Summerville
(Map 14, page 273)

Book Outlet   **Open Shop**
10030 Dorchester Road 29485   * (803) 873-4655

Collection: General stock of mostly paperback and hardcover and ephemera.
# of Vols: 25,000

Hours:	Tue 1-6. Wed-Sat 10-6.
Travel:	Exit 205 off I-26. Proceed west on Rte 78 towards. Left at light onto Ladson and proceed 4½ miles to Oakbrook Shopping Center.
Credit Cards:	Yes
Owner:	Robert Morris
Year Estab:	1991
Comments:	Stock is approximately 75%-80% paperback.

Taylors
(Map 14, page 273)

Buncombe Antique Mall   **Antique Mall**
5000 Wade Hampton Boulevard 29687   (864) 268-4498

Hours: Mon-Sat 10-5:30. Sun 1:15-5.
Travel: Exit 56 off I-85. Proceed north on Rte 14 for about five miles, then make left onto S. Buncombe Rd. Proceed for about three miles, then make left onto Rte 29 (Wade Hampton Blvd). Shop is about three to four miles ahead.

West Union

Deeliteful Designs   **Open Shop**
961 West Union Road 29696   (864) 638-5057

Collection: General stock of mostly paperback.
# of Vols: 3,000
Hours: Tue-Fri 9-5.

Mail Order Dealers

Kitemaug Books   (864) 576-3338
229 Mohawk Drive Spartanburg 29301

Collection:	Specialty
Specialties:	Naval and maritime books published under the Kitemaug Press imprint.
Services:	Appraisals
Owner:	Frank J. Anderson

Southern First Editions   (803) 799-8001
PO Box 50192 Columbia 29250

Collection:	Specialty
# of Vols:	4,000
Specialties:	Southern literature and history; modern first editions.
Services:	Appraisals, search service, catalog, accepts want lists.
Credit Cards:	No
Owner:	William Starr & Carol Reis-Starr
Year Estab:	1995

St. Andrews Books   (803) 425-4080
PO Box 210756 Columbia 29221

Collection:	Specialty
# of Vols:	2,000
Specialties:	D.H. Lawrence; Virginia Woolf; ship design and models.
Services:	Search service, catalog, accepts want lists.
Credit Cards:	No
Owner:	Tom Bettendorf
Year Estab:	1984

Virginia

Alphabetical Listing By Dealer

Some are like jewels and should be treated accordingly.

Alphabetical Listing By Location

Abingdon
(Map 15, page 294)

Hill's Books	**Antique Mall**

At Abingdon Mercantile   (540) 628-2788
130 Wall Street   E-mail: maynard@tricon.net
Mailing address: PO Box 1037 Kingsport TN 37662

Collection:	General stock.
# of Vols:	4,000
Specialties:	Appalachia; Tennessee; Civil War; regional.
Hours:	Mon-Thu 10-5:30. Fri & Sat 10-7. Sun 1-5.
Services:	Accepts want lists.
Travel:	Abingdon exit off I-81. Proceed into Abingdon on Rte 75 north (Cummings St). Make left at second light onto Main St, then left at next light. Shop is ahead in a three story brick building in heart of downtown. The books are located on the second floor.
Owner:	F.M. & Ann Hill
Comments:	Considerably more than a typical (if there is such a thing) "booth" in a multi dealer antique mall setting, the books we saw in this dealer's room, and a similar display in the next room belonging to Tauscher Books (see below), were sufficient in number, vintage, condition, and general content to make a visit worthwhile for the serious book person.

Tauscher Bookstore	**Antique Mall**

At Abingdon Mercantile   Mall: (540) 628-2788
130 Wall Street   Home: (540) 669-2994
Mailing address: PO Box 1311 Bristol 24201   E-mail: tausch@preferred.com

Collection:	General stock.
# of Vols:	25,000
Specialties:	Civil War; Southern Americana.
Hours:	Mon-Thu 10-5:30. Fri & Sat 10-7. Sun 1-5.
Services:	Appraisals, search service, catalog, accepts want lists.
Travel:	See above.
Credit Cards:	Yes
Owner:	Bill & Judy Tauscher
Year Estab:	1977
Comments:	See above.

Alexandria
(Map 15A, page 294 & Map 2, page 154)

Aeronautical Classics & Fine Arts	**Open Shop**

1305 King Street 22314   (703) 548-7122

Collection:	Specialty books and memorabilia.
Specialties:	Aviation
Hours:	Mon-Sat 11-6. Sun 1-5.
Travel:	In Old Town Alexandria between West and Payne Streets.

(Alexandria)

Air, Land & Sea   **Open Shop**
1215 King Street 22314   (703) 684-5118

Collection:	Specialty used and some new.
# of Vols:	4,000
Specialties:	Aviation; military; naval.
Hours:	Daily 11:30-6.
Services:	Search service, accepts want lists.
Travel:	Between Payne & Fayette Streets.
Credit Cards:	Yes
Owner:	Buzz Polistock
Year Estab:	1983

Bird-in-the-Cage Antiques   **Open Shop**
110 King Street 22314   (703) 549-5114

Collection:	General stock of hardcover and paperback, ephemera and records.
# of Vols:	2,000
Hours:	Daily 10:30am-10pm, except Fri till 11pm. Jan & Feb earlier closings.
Travel:	Near Union St. Shop is on second floor.
Owner:	Vivian Temes
Year Estab:	1972

The Bookshelf   **Open Shop**
8742 Cooper Road 22309   Tel & Fax: (703) 360-3202
                                                E-mail: redobooks@erols.com

Collection:	General stock of mostly paperback.
# of Vols:	150,000
Hours:	Tue-Fri 10-6, except Wed till 8. Sat 9-3.
Travel:	From Rte 1, turn west on Cooper. Shop is located in Burke & Herbert Shopping Center.

Collectorama & Book Niche   **Open Shop**
2008 Mount Vernon Avenue 22301   (703) 548-3466

Collection:	Specialty used and new paperback and hardcover and comics.
# of Vols:	2,000
Specialties:	Science fiction; fantasy; mystery; movie memorabilia.
Hours:	Mon-Fri 11-7. Sat 10:30-6:30.
Owner:	D.E. Webb
Comments:	Stock is approximately 60% used, 60% of which is paperback.

Comic & Card Collectorama   **Open Shop**
2008 Mount Vernon Avenue 22301   (703) 548-3466

Collection:	General stock of paperback and hardcover, comics and cards.
# of Vols:	1,000+
Hours:	Mon-Fri 11-7. Sat 10:30-6:30.
Comments:	Used book stock is approximately 60% paperback.

Donna Lee's Collectibles & Rare Books   **Open Shop**
419 South Washington Street 22314   (703) 548-5830

Collection:	General stock, maps and autographs.
# of Vols:	15,000
Specialties:	Americana
Hours:	Daily 11-5.
Services:	Appraisals, search service, accepts want lists, mail order.
Travel:	Alexandria exit off I-495. Proceed south on Alt Rte 1 (South Washington St). Shop is in Old Town Alexandria.
Credit Cards:	Yes
Owner:	Donna Lee Wilson
Year Estab:	1982

Annandale
(Map 2, page 154)

Edward N. Bomsey Autographs   **By Appointment**
7317 Farr Street 22003   Tel & Fax: (703) 642-2040
Web page: www.abaa-booknet.com/usa/bomscy   E-mail: enbainc@compuserve.com

Collection:	Specialty
Specialties:	Autographs; signed books.
Services:	Appraisals, occasional catalog, accepts want lists.
Credit Cards:	Yes
Year Estab:	1975

Kruger's Antique Plus   **Open Shop**
7129 Little River Turnpike 22003   (703) 941-3644

Collection:	General stock.
# of Vols:	4,000-5,000
Specialties:	Vintage paperbacks; first editions.
Hours:	Tue-Sat 10:30-6:30. Sun 12-6.
Services:	Appraisals
Travel:	Exit 6 off I-495. Proceed east on Rte 236 (Little River Tpk). Shop is in the Annandale Antique Center.
Credit Cards:	Yes
Owner:	Kurt Kruger
Year Estab:	1981

The Manuscript Company of Springfield   **By Appointment**
3902 Cherrywood Lane 22003-1901   (703) 256-6748

Collection:	Specialty
Specialties:	Handwritten items (letters, diaries, collections of correspondence, ledgers, etc.) of national and local historical interest.
Services:	Appraisals, mail order.
Credit Cards:	No
Owner:	Terry Alford
Year Estab:	1974

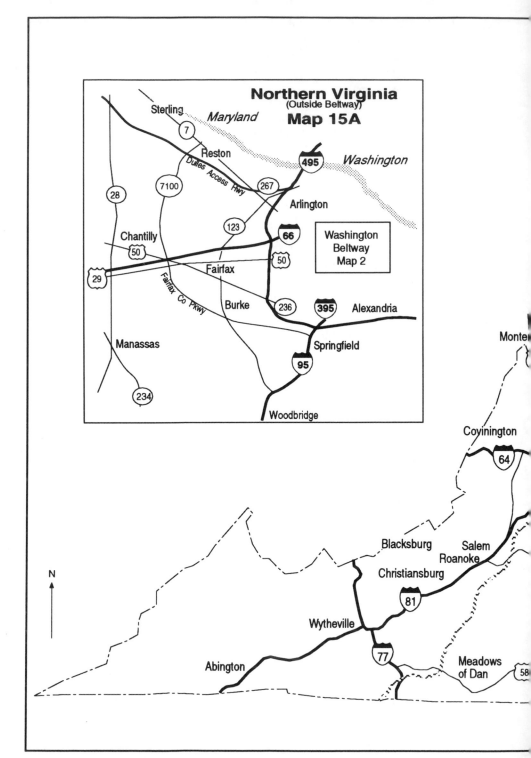

Northern Virginia
(Outside Beltway)
Map 15A

Sterling

Maryland

7

Reston

Dulles Access Hwy

7100

267

Washington

495

28

123

Arlington

Chantilly

50

66

Fairfax

50

Washington
Beltway
Map 2

29

Fairfax Co Pkwy

Burke

236

395

Alexandria

Manassas

Springfield

95

Monte

234

Woodbridge

Covinington

64

N

Blacksburg

Salem
Roanoke

Christiansburg

81

Wytheville

77

Abington

Meadows
of Dan

58

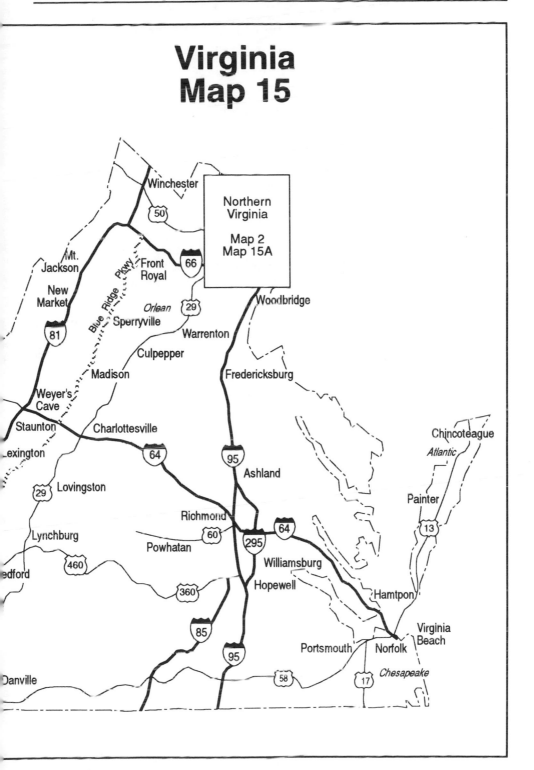

Virginia
Map 15

Winchester

Northern
Virginia

Map 2
Map 15A

50

Mt.
Jackson

Front
Royal

66

New
Market

Orlean

29

Woodbridge

81

Sperryville

Warrenton

Culpepper

Madison

Fredericksburg

Weyer's
Cave

Staunton

Charlottesville

Lexington

64

95

Chincoteague

Atlantic

Ashland

Lovingston

29

Painter

Richmond

13

Lynchburg

60

64

Powhatan

295

Bedford

460

Williamsburg

360

Hopewell

Hamtpon

85

Virginia
Beach

Portsmouth

Norfolk

95

Danville

58

17

Chesapeake

Arlington
(Map 15A, page 294 & Map 2, page 154)

Book Ends   **Open Shop**
2710 Washington Boulevard 22201   (703) 524-4976

Collection:	General stock of mostly hardcover.
# of Vols:	30,000
Specialties:	American history; military; cookbooks.
Hours:	Fri-Mon 12-6.
Travel:	Washington Blvd exit off I-395. Proceed north on Washington for about three miles to Clarendon. The shop is in a two story frame house.
Credit Cards:	No
Owner:	Janet & Mike Deatherage
Year Estab:	1979
Comments:	This bi-level shop offers book lovers a healthy mix of hardcover and paperback volumes selected primarily for the off the street reader more so than the book connoisseur. Prices generally are most reasonable and the stock is well organized.

Bookdogs   **By Appointment**
1600 South Eads Street, #1035 S 22202   (703)685-3812
                                                   E-mail: bookdog@erols.com

Collection:	General stock.
# of Vols:	5,000
Specialties:	First editions (fiction).
Services:	Search service, catalog in planning stage.
Credit Cards:	No
Owner:	John Draper
Year Estab:	1995

Bookhouse   **Open Shop**
805 North Emerson Street 22205   (703) 527-7797
Web page: www.bookhouse.com   E-mail: nhughes@idsonline.com

Collection:	Specialty
# of Vols:	30,000-50,000
Specialties:	Americana: all aspects including WPA guides; Civil War; American Revolution; art; literature, biography, regional histories; natural history.
Hours:	Daily, except closed Mon, 12-6, but open holiday Mondays.
Services:	Appraisals, accepts want lists.
Travel:	Glebe Rd exit off I-66. Proceed south to Wilson Blvd, then west on Wilson for about 1/2 mile to Emerson. Left on Emerson. Shop is just ahead on left in a white frame house. Parking and entrance is at the rear.
Credit Cards:	Yes
Owner:	Natalie & Edward Hughes
Year Estab:	1972

Comments:	The many rooms in this bi-level shop contain fabulous titles in almost every area of interest that in one way or another touches on Americana. In addition to being scholarly, the titles are most unusual. Considering the amount of traveling and visiting we have done, we found the titles here most unique. The owner emphasizes that she has no paperbacks, no magazines and no contemporary titles.

Evangelical Used Books   **By Appointment**
1815 North Nelson Street 22207-3628   (703) 522-0596
Web page: www.evangelicalbooks.com   E-mail: jinewman@evangelicalbooks.com

Collection:	Specialty
# of Vols:	10,000
Specialties:	Religion (Evangelical Protestant).
Hours:	Open Sat 1-5. Other times by appointment.
Services:	Accepts want lists.
Credit Cards:	No
Owner:	James I. Newman
Year Estab:	1978

Squire Books   **By Appointment**
5101 North 10th Street 22205   (703) 243-7288
Web page: www.abebooks.com   Fax: (703) 516-0013
                                                      E-mail: myslynch@erols.com

Collection:	Specialty
# of Vols:	5,000
Specialties:	Economics; economic history; history of science; mathematics; statistics.
Services:	Search service, accepts want lists, mail order.
Credit Cards:	No
Owner:	Michael P. Lynch
Year Estab:	1994

Ashland
(Map 15, page 294)

Bell Book & Candle   **Open Shop**
106 Robinson Street 23005   (804) 798-9047

Collection:	General stock.
# of Vols:	5,000-10,000
Hours:	Mon-Fri 10-5, except Tue 10-2. Sat 10-2.
Services:	Search service, accepts want lists, occasional catalog, mail order.
Travel:	Ashland exit off I-95. Proceed west on Rte 54. Left onto Virginia St, then right onto Robinson. Proceed to parking lot at end of street.
Credit Cards:	Yes
Owner:	Patricia Ewald
Year Estab:	1983

Comments:	Not among the most organized shops we have visited. The shop displays perhaps 5,000 or so mixed vintage hardcover books in mixed condition. We did spot a few collectible items and it may be that someone with a well trained eye will see much more here than we did.

Atlantic
(Map 15, page 294)

Irene Rouse - Bookseller   **By Appointment**
PO Box 310 23303   (757) 824-4090
                                          E-mail: irbooks@dmv.com

Collection:	General stock.
# of Vols:	30,000
Specialties:	Folklore; folklife; cookbooks; hymnology.
Services:	Accepts want lists, occasional catalog (primarily folklore and Americana and hymnology).
Credit Cards:	No
Year Estab:	1972

Bedford
(Map 15, page 294)

Hamilton's   **Open Shop**
155 West Main Street   (540) 586-5592
Mailing address: PO Box 932 Bedford 24523   Fax: (540) 586-6235
Web page: www.peterV.com   E-mail: otterV@aol.com

Collection:	General stock.
# of Vols:	2,000
Hours:	Mon-Sat 10-3.
Services:	Accepts want lists, mail order. Also publishes books dealing with regional history and aviation.
Travel:	Bedford exit off Rte 460. Follow signs into Bedford.
Credit Cards:	Yes
Owner:	Peter Hamilton
Year Estab:	1980

Blacksburg
(Map 15, page 294)

Past Pages Bookshop   **Open Shop**
103 NE Jackson Street, #2 24060   (540) 552-2665
Web page: www.ptiweb.com/~books   E-mail: books@ptiweb.com

Collection:	General stock of hardcover and paperback and ephemera.
# of Vols:	25,000
Specialties:	Science fiction; history; periodicals; Virginia; Southern Americana.
Hours:	Mon-Thu 10-8. Fri 10am-11pm. Sat 10-8.
Services:	Search service, accepts want lists, mail order.

Travel:	Exit 118 off I-81. Take Rte 460 bypass to Blacksburg, then Bus Rte 460 into downtown Blacksburg. Follow Main St through six lights, then first right onto Jackson St. Shop is located behind post office.
Credit Cards:	No
Owner:	Georgette Yakman
Year Estab:	1996
Comments:	A nice shop that had just acquired some additional space for expansion at the time of our visit. What we saw (before the reorganization) were several small rooms featuring a mix of paperback and hardcover volumes in generally good condition. Some reading copies. Some collectibles. Some unusual titles. Some more recent items.

Bristol

Christian Book Exchange   **Open Shop**
2042 Euclid Avenue 24201   (540) 466-5867

Collection:	Specialty. Mostly used paperback and hardcover.
# of Vols:	20,000
Specialties:	Religion
Hours:	Mon-Fri 10-6.
Travel:	Northbound Rte 11W exit off I-81. Proceed east on Rte 11. When road forks, bear left onto Euclid. Shop about two blocks ahead on the right, across from a school. Southbound on I-81. I-381 exit. Proceed south on I-381 to Euclid, then right on Euclid. Shop is about 10-12 blocks ahead on left.
Credit Cards:	No
Owner:	Dave Ashford
Year Estab:	1987
Comments:	Stock is approximately 60% paperback.

Burke
(Map 15A, page 294)

Burke Centre Books & Comics   **Open Shop**
5741 Burke Centre Parkway 22015 (see Comments)   (703) 250-5114
E-mail: joe-mike-gum-bookmen@worldnet.att.net

Collection:	General stock of paperback, hardcover and comics.
# of Vols:	12,000+ (used hardcover)
Specialties:	Science fiction.
Hours:	Daily 10-8, except Christmas day.
Services:	Search service, accepts want lists, mail order.
Travel:	Exit 55A off I-66. Proceed south on Rte 7100 to Burke Centre Pkwy, then left on Burke Centre Pkwy. At second light turn left into Burke Centre Plaza.
Credit Cards:	Yes
Owner:	Joe Gumbinger
Year Estab:	1984

Comments: Two shops in one with comic book related materials taking up what
                 could well be a separate shop in one half of the establishment and
                 many many alcoves containing paperback and hardcover volumes in
                 the other half. The books were well organized and the shelves fully
                 stacked. While most of the hardcover items were of fairly recent vin-
                 tage, there were a fair share of vintage items on hand as well. Note: the
                 store may relocate within the same shopping center.

Centreville

Richard McKay Used Books   **Open Shop**
14245B Lee Highway (Rte 29) 22020   (703) 830-4048

Collection: General stock of mostly paperback.
# of Vols: 100,000
Hours: Mon-Sat 9-9. Sun 11-7.
Travel: Exit 52 off I-66. Shop is on Rte 29, 1/4 mile from intersection of Rtes
                 28/29 in Centreville Square Shopping Center.

Chantilly
(Map 15A, page 294)

C & W Used Books   **Open Shop**
13816 Metro Tech Drive 20151   (703) 968-7323

Collection: General stock of hardcover and paperback.
# of Vols: 150,000
Hours: Mon-Sat 10-9. Sun 11-7.
Travel: Rte 50 exit off I-66. Proceed west on Rte 50 for five miles, then turn
                 right on Metro Tech. Located in Sully Place Shopping Center.
Credit Cards: Yes
Owner: Gail Charlesworth
Year Estab: 1994
Comments: See comments for Woodbridge store.

Charlottesville
(Map 15, page 294 & Map 16, page 301)

Antiquer's Mall   **Antique Mall**
2335 Seminole Trail 22901   (804) 973-3478

Hours: Mon-Sat 10-5. Sun 12:30-5.
Travel: On Rte 29. Proceeding north from Charlottesville, mall is on right just
                 north of the river.

The Avocado Pit   **Open Shop**
310 East Market Street (Terrace Level)   (804) 295-1314
Mailing address: PO Box 2187 Charlottesville 22902-2187
                                            E-mail: avocado@ubix.com

Collection: General stock.

# of Vols:	3,000
Specialties:	Children's; children's series.
Hours:	Tue-Sat 10-5.
Services:	Search service, mail order.
Travel:	Rte 29 to Bus Rte 250 (follow signs to historic district). Right on McIntire Rd, then left on Market St (Bus 250 East). Shop is between 3rd & 4th Streets, on right, at the end of a small courtyard.
Credit Cards:	Yes
Owner:	Andrew & Robin Gutterman
Year Estab:	1991
Comments:	At the time of our visit the owners had just moved in and their shelves were in the process of being stacked. Based on both our conversation with them and what we saw, the shop will continue to be modest in size, housing approximately 3,000-5,000 hardcover books with an emphasis in the specialties listed above and some more general titles. Note: the owners were previously located in Staunton and did business under the name Staunton Book Review.

Blue Whale Books   **Open Shop**
115 West Main Street 22902   (804) 296-4646

Collection:	General stock.
# of Vols:	25,000
Specialties:	Books about books; mystery.
Hours:	Mon-Sat 10-10. Sun 12-5.
Services:	Accepts want lists, search service, catalog.
Travel:	See Avocado Pit above. From Market St, turn right on 4th St and park. Shop is on downtown pedestrian mall between 1st & 2nd Streets.
Credit Cards:	Yes
Owner:	Scott Fennessey
Year Estab:	1995
Comments:	Plush carpeting and spacious browsing space mark this most attractive shop. The books "ain't bad" either. Most of the books we saw were in very good to excellent condition with a few vintage items lacking dust jackets but not character. Prices were moderate; whoever is pricing the books knows their value. If you're in town, this is one of the "must visit" shops.

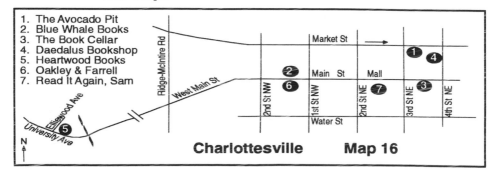

1. The Avocado Pit
2. Blue Whale Books
3. The Book Cellar
4. Daedalus Bookshop
5. Heartwood Books
6. Oakley & Farrell
7. Read It Again, Sam

Charlottesville   Map 16

(Charlottesville)

The Book Broker   ** Open Shop/By Appointment
310 East Market Street   (804) 296-2194
Mailing address: PO Box 1283 Charlottesville 22902

Collection:	General stock. **
# of Vols:	5,000
Specialties:	Fine bindings; children's; Virginia; Southern Americana; first editions.
Hours:	Tue-Sat 11:30-5.
Services:	Appraisals, search service, catalog.
Travel:	See the Avocado Pit above.
Owner:	Vesta Lee Gordon
Year Estab:	1985
**	The owner will be switching to a "by appointment" mode in 1998, with a smaller specialized collection of Southern Americana, Virginia and cookbooks.

The Book Cellar   Open Shop
316 East Main Street 22902   (804) 979-7787

Collection:	General stock of mostly used hardcover and paperback.
# of Vols:	30,000
Specialties:	Art; literary criticism; philosophy; history; children's.
Hours:	Mon-Thu 10-9. Fri & Sat 10-10.
Services:	Accepts want lists.
Travel:	On downtown pedestrian mall between 3rd and 4th Streets. Entrance to the shop is downstairs through The Hardware Store Restaurant.
Credit Cards:	Yes
Owner:	Tom Tiede
Year Estab:	1988
Comments:	You have to look twice to identify the used books from the remainders or the limited selection of new books (dealing mostly with regional interests) as the store's policy is to purchase very recently published used books in good condition and with dust jackets. While you're not likely to find any antiquarian items or any truly rare books here, you will find less expensive copies of recent fiction and non fiction titles with a strong emphasis on the specialties listed above.

Carousel Books   Open Shop
1924 Arlington Blvd, # 101   (804) 984-5555
Mailing address: PO Box 4444 Charlottesville 22905   Fax: (804) 984-1984

Collection:	Specialty
# of Vols:	10,000
Specialties:	Children's, from pre-school to middle school.
Hours:	Tue-Fri 11-5:30. Sat 11-3:30.
Services:	Accepts want lists.

Travel:	Proceeding south on Rte 29 into Charlottesville, turn right onto Arlington Blvd (after Barracks Rd Shopping Center).
Credit Cards:	Yes
Owner:	Joan & Claude Ripley
Year Estab:	1995

Daedalus Bookshop   **Open Shop**
121 4th Street, NE 22902   (804) 293-7595

Collection:	General stock of hardcover and paperback.
# of Vols:	90,000
Specialties:	Fiction; Modern Library; literary magazines.
Hours:	Mon-Sat 10-6. Sun 10-5.
Services:	Search service, mail order.
Travel:	See Avocado Pit above. Shop is between Market and Main Streets.
Credit Cards:	Yes
Owner:	Sandy McAdams
Year Estab:	1968
Comments:	This tri-level shop is packed to the brim with titles in almost every subject imaginable. The books are in mixed condition and of mixed vintage, some hot off the press, most a bit older (which for some people can be a boon, particularly if they're looking for an elusive item long out of print.)

Franklin Gilliam Rare Books   **By Appointment**
218 South Street 22901   Tel & Fax: (804) 979-2512
                                                 E-mail: fgrare@comclin.net

Collection:	General stock and ephemera.
# of Vols:	5,000-10,000
Specialties:	American literature (especially southern); English literature; bibliography; Americana.
Services:	Appraisals, accepts want lists, mail order.
Credit Cards:	Yes
Owner:	Mary Cooper Gilliam
Year Estab:	1950's
Comments:	At the time of our visit to this shop the owner had not yet gone to a "by appointment" mode and so we were privileged to view a portion of a most impressive collection, strong in the specialties listed above but also offering other, more general subjects. Clearly a shop for the serious collector and, in our opinion, worth making the appointment to visit. Our experiences are not always typical but we do believe that our readers can benefit from them. We spotted a book we wanted to purchase in an "off limits" section of the shop but were told that it had not yet been reevaluated for a price. As the owner did not wish to "price" the book during our visit, she indicated that she would contact us. Some weeks later when we inquired about the book we were advised that it had already been sold to a friend of the owner's. And so it goes.

(Charlottesville)

Heartwood Books   **Open Shop**
5 & 9 Elliewood Avenue 22903   (804) 295-7083

Collection:	General stock of hardcover and paperback.
# of Vols:	50,000 (see Comments)
Specialties:	Scholarly; Thomas Jefferson; Virginia; Civil War.
Hours:	Mon-Fri 10-7:30. Sat 10-6. (See Comments)
Services:	Appraisals, search service, catalog, accepts want lists, mail order.
Travel:	From Bypass Rte 29, take Bus Rte 250 east exit and proceed straight for approximately 1½ miles. Turn left onto Elliewood.
Credit Cards:	Yes
Owner:	Paul Collinge & Sherry Joseph
Year Estab:	1975
Comments:	Heartwood Books is really two separate shops a few doors away from one another. The shop at 5 Elliewood carries a strong general collection of hardcover and paperback books, which, as might be expected from its location near the University of Virginia campus, has an academic bent. The books were in generally good condition and most reasonably priced. Unlike other used bookshops near university campuses that carry primarily more serious subjects, this one also had an ample supply of popular fiction, mysteries, entertainment related titles, etc. The second shop, located at 9 Elliewood, is a smaller, more crowded shop that carries rare and antiquarian items of a mostly scholarly nature. This shop is usually open by appointment or chance 10-5.

Alfred Hirshoren Fine Art Prints & Books   **By Appointment**
2307 Greenbrier Drive 22901   (804) 975-1521
                                          E-mail: ahirshoren@aol.com

Collection:	Specialty
Specialties:	Fine art prints (original); books with original prints or books relating to prints.
Services:	Appraisals, accepts want lists.
Credit Cards:	No
Year Estab:	1982

Oakley & Farrell Books   **Open Shop**
At York Place   (804) 977-3313
112 West Main Street 22902   E-mail: farrells@comet.net

Collection:	General stock of hardcover and paperback.
# of Vols:	6,000+
Specialties:	Irish; children's; science fiction.
Hours:	Mon-Thu 11-6. Fri & Sat 10-6. Sun 12-5.
Services:	Accepts want lists, mail order.
Travel:	On downtown pedestrian mall between 1st and 2nd Streets.
Credit Cards:	Yes
Owner:	Chris Oakley & Krista & Pat Farrell

Year Estab: 1995
Comments: A mix of hardcover and paperback books, most of which appear to be
                of fairly recent vintage. What makes this shop special is its collection
                of Irish and Celtic related items. If that's your "thing," you may want
                to call ahead to see if the title you're looking for is on hand.

Oliver & Co. Books   **By Appointment**
1417 Ricky Road 22901   (804) 296-4041
                                                    E-mail: charlestoo@aol.com

Collection: Specialty
# of Vols: 2,000
Specialties: Modern first editions; literary biography.
Services: Catalog, accepts want lists.
Credit Cards: No
Owner: Tod & Helen Oliver
Year Estab: 1987

Read It Again, Sam   **Open Shop**
214 East Main Street 22902   (804) 977-9844
                                                            Fax: (804) 977-9845
                                                    E-mail: readit2sam@aol.com
Collection: General stock of hardcover and paperbacks.
# of Vols: 80,000
Specialties: Mystery; vintage paperbacks.
Hours: Mon-Wed 10-7. Thu-Sat 10-10. Sun 12-5.
Services: Accepts want lists.
Travel: On the downtown pedestrian mall, between 2nd & 3rd Streets.
Credit Cards: No
Owner: David Taylor & Gene Ford
Year Estab: 1991
Comments: At the time of our visit to Charlottesville, the owner was in the process
                 of packing up his books at his previous location in Lovingston in
                 preparation for his move to this new home close to several other qual-
                 ity dealers. We're sorry we missed him as we enjoyed our visit to his
                 shop three years ago. If you stop by for a visit, we'd welcome your
                 impressions.

L & T Respess Books   **By Appointment**
PO Box 1604 22902   (804) 293-3553
Collection: General stock.
# of Vols: 4,000
Specialties: Americana; Southern Americana; English and American literature;
                 fishing; hunting.
Services: Catalog, accepts want lists.
Credit Cards: Yes
Owner: Lin & Tucker Respess
Year Estab: 1980

20th Art & Antiques   **Open Shop**
201D East Main Street 22902   (804) 296-6818

Collection:	Specialty
# of Vols:	1,000
Specialties:	Philosophy; mathematics; literature; politics; science; foreign language books.
Hours:	Tue-Sat 10-5:30. Sun 12-5.
Travel:	On the downtown pedestrian mall between 2nd & 3rd Streets.
Credit Cards:	Yes
Owner:	Jonathan McVity
Year Estab:	1992

Chesapeake
(Map 15, page 294)

Great Bridge Books Ltd.   **By Appointment**
PO Box 15512 23328   (757) 548-3858
                                          E-mail: gbbkerr@gr8brdg.net

Collection:	General stock.
# of Vols:	8,000
Specialties:	Virginia; military.
Services:	Appraisals, search service, accepts want lists.
Credit Cards:	No
Owner:	Judith H. Kerr
Year Estab:	1975

Chincoteague
(Map 15, page 294)

Daedalus East Used Books   **Open Shop**
700 North Main Street 23336   (804) 336-3564

Collection:	General stock of hardcover and paperback.
# of Vols:	5,000
Hours:	May-Oct only: Fri-Sun 3-8.
Travel:	Left turn off Main St and proceed seven blocks.
Owner:	Sandy McAdams

Christiansburg
(Map 15, page 294)

Dalley Book Service   **By Appointment**
90 Kimball Lane 24073   (540) 382-8949
                                               Fax: (540) 382-1728
                                          E-mail: dalleybk@swva.net

Collection:	General stock of mostly hardcover.
# of Vols:	4,500
Specialties:	Vietnam War; religion; Virginia; Southeast Asia.
Services:	Search service, catalog, accepts want lists.

Credit Cards: Yes
Owner: George W. Dalley
Year Estab: 1973

Stagecoach Antiques Mall   **Antique Mall**
3980 Mudpike Road 24073   (540) 639-0397
Hours: Mon-Sat 9-5. Sun 1-5.
Travel: Exit 109 off I-81. Proceed west on Rte 177 for 2/10 mile.

Covington
(Map 15, page 294)

Mountain Book Company   **Open Shop**
310 West Main Street 24426   (540) 962-9196
                                                               Fax: (540) 965-4294
Collection: General stock of used and new hardcover and paperback.
# of Vols: 20,000
Hours: Mon-Fri 10-6. Sat 10-5.
Services: Search service, accepts want lists.
Travel: In downtown.
Owner: Melinda Snedd-Johnson
Year Estab: 1989
Comments: Stock is approximately 60% used, 60% of which is hardcover.

Culpepper
(Map 15, page 294)

Ace Books and Antiques   **Open Shop**
120 West Culpepper Street 22701   (540) 825-8973
Collection: General stock of hardcover and paperback.
# of Vols: 250,000+
Hours: Mon-Sat 9:30-6. Sun 12-5.
Services: Accepts want lists, mail order.
Travel: Located in center of town, just off Main St near post office. The entrance
                  to the second floor book shop is through the street level pet store
Credit Cards: Yes
Owner: James & Mary Lou Leftwich
Year Estab: 1984
Comments: Although located in the heart of downtown, this shop has the general
                  ambience of an old book barn with aisles and aisles of books contain-
                  ing mostly older volumes. And, when you think you've explored the
                  entire shop, there's more. Once you pass through an unassuming rear
                  door (we didn't see any signs so ask for directions at the front counter)
                  you'll be able to explore two additional rooms carrying still more
                  books (mostly hardcover) and magazines. Prices were inexpensive.
                  While we don't think you're likely to find a long lost treasure here,
                  because of the size of the collection, it's certainly possible that could
                  find some items that may prove worth buying. We regretted the fact
                  that our tight schedule did not leave us with more browsing time.

Danville
(Map 15, page 294)

Ye Olde Bookstore   **Open Shop**
512 Westover Drive 24541   (804) 792-5522

Collection:	General stock of paperback and hardcover.
Hours:	Mon-Sat 8-7. (Subject to change)
Travel:	Westover Dr exit off Rte 58. Proceed west on Westover. Shop is on the right, just after Piedmont Dr intersection, in a free standing Goodwill superstore.
Credit Cards:	Yes
Owner:	Dick Pretty, PR Director
Year Estab:	1992
Comments:	Operated by Goodwill Industries. All books are donated. Shop also sells bookcases (manufacturer's seconds) and antiques and collectibles.

Fairfax
(Map 15A, page 294)

Greentree Books   **Open Shop**
10409 Main Street 22030   (703) 691-9095
                                               E-mail: grntrbks@interloc.com

Collection:	General stock of hardcover and paperback.
# of Vols:	10,000
Specialties:	Military
Hours:	Mon, Tue, Sat 10-6. Thu & Fri 10-8. Sun 1-5.
Services:	Search service, accepts want lists.
Travel:	Fairfax exit off I-66. Proceed south on Rte 123 or about two miles to Fairfax. Left on Main St. Shop is on right at end of a row of shops.
Credit Cards:	Yes
Owner:	Marie Claveloux
Year Estab:	1996
Comments:	Stock is approximately 65% hardcover.

Mike's Books & Records   **Open Shop**
5618 Columbia Pike 22041   (703) 820-5051

Collection:	General stock of mostly hardcover and ephemera.
# of Vols:	4,500
Specialties:	Civil War; history; military; philosophy; literature.
Hours:	Mon-Fri 10-6. Sat 10-2.
Services:	Accepts want lists, search service.
Travel:	On Columbia Pike, three blocks east of Rte 7. From Washington, DC, proceed west on Rte 50 to Carlin Springs Rd. Left on Carlin Springs, then right on Columbia Pike. Shop is just ahead on right.
Credit Cards:	Yes
Owner:	Mike Hardesty
Year Estab:	1970

Comments: We have visited a number of book stores that had secondary businesses attached to them but this is the first time in our many travels that we've come across a legitimate book dealer whose store also houses a TV repair shop, also operated by the book dealer. The collection, while not great in number, offers an interesting mix of paperbacks and hardcover titles. Some of the hardcover volumes we saw would definitely fit into the collectible category. While your trip here may be brief, it could also prove satisfying.

Fairfax Station
(Map 15A, page 294)

Squirrel's Nest Books   **By Appointment**
PO Box 7214 22039   (703) 352-3454
                                          E-mail: squirrelnest@worldnet.att.net
Web page: www.bibliofind.com/squirrelnest.html

Collection: General stock.
# of Vols: 15,000+
Specialties: Cookbooks; mystery; modern first editions.
Services: Accepts want lists, search service, occasional catalog, mail order.
Credit Cards: No
Owner: Babette V. Polzer
Year Estab: 1993

Falls Church
(Map 2, page 154))

The ASSOCIATES, Rare Books   **By Appointment**
PO Box 4747 22044-0747   (703) 578-3810
Web page: www.abaa-booknet.com/usa/associates   E-mail: assoc@clark.net

Collection: Specialty
# of Vols: 5,000
Specialties: First editions of: books into film; literature; Vietnam War, pop culture.
Services: Catalog
Credit Cards: Yes
Owner: William Selander & Nanci Langley
Year Estab: 1979

Hole in the Wall Books   **Open Shop**
905 West Broad Street 22046   (703) 536-2511
                                          E-mail: cosmicat@erols.com
Collection: General stock of paperback and hardcover.
# of Vols: 10,000+
Specialties: Science fiction; mystery.
Hours: Mon-Fri 10-8. Sat & Sun 10-6.
Services: Appraisals, occasional catalog, mail order.
Travel: On Rte 7 across from church.
Credit Cards: Yes

Owner:	James Nally
Year Estab:	1979
Comments:	Stock is approximately 75% paperback. The owner operates a second store in Manassas. See Cosmic Books below.

Fredericksburg
(Map 15, page 294)

The American History Co.   **Open Shop**
701 Caroline Street 22401   (540) 371-6822
Web page: www.american-history.com   E-mail: ahc@american-history.com

Collection:	Specialty. Mostly new.
Specialties:	American history.
Hours:	Mon-Sat 10-5. Sun 12-4.
Services:	Search service.
Credit Cards:	Yes
Owner:	Chris Landon & Pat Conway
Year Estab:	1994

Beck's Antiques and Books   **Open Shop**
708 Caroline Street 22401   (540) 371-1766

Collection:	General stock.
# of Vols:	5,000
Specialties:	Virginia; Civil War; art; architecture; antiques; American history.
Hours:	Mon-Sat 10:30-5. Sun 12:30-5.
Travel:	See Riverby Books below.
Credit Cards:	Yes
Owner:	Bill Beck
Year Estab:	1973
Comments:	An attractive shop with antiques in the front and a very strong collection of non fiction titles in the back room. If you're looking for an unusual Civil War or Virginia volume, there's an excellent chance you'll find it here.

Riverby Books   **Open Shop**
805 Caroline Street 22401   (540) 373-6148
                                                      Fax: (202) 544-7995
                                               E-mail: cymrot@paltech.com

Collection:	General stock.
# of Vols:	6,000
Hours:	Daily 11-5.
Services:	Accepts want lists, mail order.
Travel:	Exit 130A (Rte 3) off I-95. Proceed east on Rte 3 to downtown. Right on Princess Anne, left on Hanover and right on Caroline.
Credit Cards:	Yes
Owner:	Steven L. Cymrot
Year Estab:	1995

Comments:	Located on the second floor of a gift shop, the books displayed here are, for the most part, in quite good condition and are well organized. Although modest in number, lots of subjects are represented in an easy to browse fashion. One can find antiquarian items as well as collectibles, scholarly tomes and items of recent vintage. The owner also displays at the nearby Fredericksburg Antique Mall, 211 William Street.

Sergeant Kirkland's Museum & Historical Society   **Open Shop**
912 Lafayette Boulevard 22401   Tel & Fax: (540) 899-5565
E-mail: civil-war@msn.com

Collection:	Specialty
Specialties:	American Revolution; Civil War; autographs; manuscripts.
Hours:	Daily 10-5.
Services:	Appraisals, search service, catalog, accepts want lists, mail order.
Travel:	Exit 130E off I-95. Museum is located near Fredericksburg National Battlefield.
Credit Cards:	Yes

Front Royal
(Map 15, page 294)

Royal Oak Bookshop   **Open Shop**
207 South Royal Avenue 22630   (540) 365-7070
Fax: (540) 636-2599

Collection:	General stock of mostly used hardcover and paperback.
# of Vols:	30,000
Specialties:	Civil War; Virginia.
Hours:	Mon-Sat 10-6. Sun 12-5.
Services:	Informal search service, accepts want lists, mail order.
Travel:	From I-66 in Front Royal, turn south on Rte 340 (South Royal Ave). Shop is in heart of downtown.
Credit Cards:	Yes
Year Estab:	1975
Comments:	This seemingly small shop on the outside turns out to be much larger once you get inside and start exploring its many nooks and crannies. Most of the hardcover titles are of a much more recent vintage although some older titles are shelved behind glass.

Hamilton

Hamilton, Virginia Books   **By Appointment**
38983 East Colonial Highway 20158   (540) 338-2220

Collection:	General stock.
# of Vols:	1,000
Services:	Appraisals
Credit Cards:	No
Owner:	Robert Daniels
Year Estab:	1985

Hampton
(Map 15, page 294)

Odyssey Books   **Art Gallery**
At Blue Skies Gallery   (757) 727-0028
26 South King Street   E-mail: BAConway96@aol.com
Mailing address: 1620 Willow Cove Newport News 23602

Collection: General stock.
Specialties: Children's; classics; prayer books; Virginia; English history and coun-
                   tryside.
Hours: Mon-Sat 10-6. Sun 12-6.
Services: Search service, accepts want lists, mail order.
Travel: Exit 267 off I-64. Follow signs to Virginia Space Museum. Just after
                   crossing King St, turn right into parking lot across from the Space
                   Museum.
Credit Cards: Yes
Owner: Carol Conway
Year Estab: 1990
Comments: We have to admit that the number of books on display at this gallery are
                   limited in number. They are, however, of generally good quality, and,
                   considering the setting in which they are displayed, they are quite reason-
                   ably priced, with special bargains, we think, among the children's books.

Old Village Books   **Art Gallery**
At Blue Skies Gallery   (757) 727-0028
26 South King Street 23669

Collection: General stock.
# of Vols: 1,500 rotating stock.
Specialties: 19th century illustrated; fine bindings; children's; Virginia.
Hours: Mon-Sat 10-6. Sun 12-6.
Travel: See Odyssey Books above.
Credit Cards: Yes
Owner: Tonya Thompson Yonkos
Year Estab: 1976
Comments: See comments for Odyssey Books above.

The Way We Were   **Open Shop**
32 East Mellen Street 23663   (757) 726-2300

Collection: General stock.
# of Vols: 3,000
Hours: Wed-Fri 10:30-4:30. Sat 10:30-5. Sun 12:30-4:30.
Services: Accepts want lists, mail order.
Travel: Exit 268 (Phoebus) off I-64. Proceed north on Mallory St then right on
                   Mellen.
Credit Cards: No
Owner: Charles Felts
Year Estab: 1996

Comments: At the time of our visit there were almost as many books on the floor in waist high piles with signs requesting the browser "Not To Disturb" as there were books on the shelves, not necessarily a bad sign since clearly the owner was acquiring more books than he could display. And if you really wanted, you could purchase one of the items from the pile. Along with a mixed variety of hardcover books representing many periods, we saw more than a few books of both historical and collectible interest, speaking of which, the shop also sells memorabilia, collectibles and antiques.

Harrisonburg

Downtown Books **Open Shop**
49 West Water Street 22801 (540) 433-1155

Collection: General stock of new and mostly paperback used.
# of Vols: 1,200 (used)
Hours: Mon-Sat 9-6.

Hopewell
(Map 15, page 294)

Selected Used Books **Open Shop**
331 Cavalier Square 23875 (804) 452-0755

Collection: General stock of paperback and hardcover.
# of Vols: 40,000
Hours: Mon-Sat 11-7. Sun 12-5.
Travel: Hopewell exit off I-295. Proceed east on Rte 36 to Cavalier Sq, then left on Cavalier. Shop is in the Cavalier Shopping Center.
Credit Cards: No
Year Estab: 1992
Comments: Stock is approximately 70% paperback.

Leesburg

Clio's History Bookshop **Open Shop**
103 Loudoun Street, SW (703) 777-1815
Mailing address: PO Box 168 Leesburg 20178 E-mail: cliobooks@aol.com

Collection: Specialty. Mostly used and some new.
# of Vols: 6,000
Specialties: Military; extraordinary social and political movements; J.H.L. Mencken.
Hours: Mon-Sat, except closed Tue, 11-6. Sun 12-5.
Services: Catalog, accepts want lists.
Travel: From Washington, DC, take Rte 7 (Leesburg Pike) west, then Bus Rte 7 into town. When road splits, bear left on Loudoun.
Credit Cards: Yes
Owner: Jason Duberman
Year Estab: 1994

Lexington
(Map 15, page 294)

Beech & Crow Rare Books   **By Appointment**
334 Enfield Road 24450   Tel & Fax: (540) 464-1023
                                              E-mail: beecrow@cfw.com

Collection: Specialty books and ephemera.
Specialties: Emphasis on 19th century (any subject), plus manuscripts; maps; phographica; primitive folk art.
Services: Catalog, accepts want lists.
Credit Cards: No
Owner: Michael Hopkins
Year Estab: 1986
Comments: Also displays at Lexington Antique Mall in Lexington. See below.

The Bookery, Ltd.   **Open Shop**
107 West Nelson Street 24450   (540) 464-3377

Collection: General stock of new and used hardcover and paperback.
# of Vols: 29,000 (combined)
Specialties: Civil War; Virginia; local writers.
Hours: Mon-Sat 10-5:30.
Services: Search service, accepts want lists, mail order.
Travel: Rte 60 exit off I-81. Proceed west on Rte 60 which becomes Nelson St in Lexington. Shop is second block west of Main St.
Credit Cards: Yes
Owner: Gary Baggs
Year Estab: 1989
Comments: An attractive combination new/used book shop with an ample supply of used books about evenly divided between hardcover and paperback. Most of the hardcover books were in good condition with dust jackets. Prices were reasonable. Some first editions and collectibles.

Christiansen's Books   **Antique Mall**
At Lexington Antique Mall   (540) 463-9511
Route 11   E-mail: christiansen@hotmail.com
Mailing address: Route 1, Box 248 Natural Bridge 24578

Collection: General stock.
# of Vols: 4,000
Hours: Mon-Sat 10-6. Sun 12:30-5.
Services: Search service, accepts want lists, mail order.
Travel: See Lexington Historical Shop below.
Credit Cards: No
Owner: Arvid Christiansen
Year Estab: 1988

Comments: Generally we don't become too enthusiastic when describing used book booths in multi dealer antique malls. In the case of this site, however, we're pleased to report that the four dealers who displayed here at the time of our visit offered books of far better quality than we have usually found at such establishments. A further bonus is the fact that the mall is located in the same shopping center as two other dealers (see below), offering the travelling book person more books per gallon mile travelled.

Lexington Historical Shop   Open Shop
Route 11   (540) 463-2615
Mailing address: PO Box 1428 Lexington 24450   Fax: (540) 463-1182
E-mail: books@rockbridge.net

Collection: Specialty books and ephemera.
# of Vols: 10,000
Specialties: Civil War (first edition Confederate); World War II; Virginia.
Hours: Mon-Sat 10-6. Other times by appointment.
Services: Appraisals, search service, accepts want lists, mail order.
Travel: Exit 191 (I-64 West) off I-81, then first exit off I-64. Proceed south on Rte 11. Shop is at the second light in College Square Shopping Center.
Credit Cards: Yes
Owner: Bob Lurate
Year Estab: 1981
Comments: One of the largest, if not the largest, collections of confederate history that we have seen in an open shop in our travels. In addition to these volumes, the shop also offers a healthy selection of other books and ephemera of historical and military significance. If this is your area of interest, you'll feel like a small child in a candy store when visiting.

Second Story Bookshop   Open Shop
Route 11   (540) 463-6264
Mailing address: PO Box 1384 Lexington 24450   E-mail: books@rockbridge.net

Collection: General stock of hardcover and paperback.
# of Vols: 10,000
Specialties: Horses; children's.
Hours: Mon-Sat 10-6. Sun by appointment.
Services: Appraisals, search service, catalog, accepts want lists.
Travel: Shares space with the Lexington Historical Shop. See above.
Credit Cards: Yes
Owner: Nancy Coplai
Year Estab: 1992
Comments: The books on display here are modest in number and are in generally good condition.

Lynchburg
(Map 15, page 294)

Bookshop on the Avenue   **Open Shop**
3407 Memorial Avenue 24501   Tel & Fax: (804) 845-1336
                                                   E-mail: wc@earthlink.net
Web page: http://members.tripod.com/~ghostbook/index.html

Collection: General stock of hardcover and paperback.
# of Vols: 80,000+
Specialties: Religion; children's; science fiction; mystery.
Hours: Mon-Sat 10-7.
Services: Search service, mail order.
Travel: Southbound on Rte 29: Exit 4 (Stadium Rd). Turn right on Wythe Rd,
                     then left at second light onto Memorial Ave. Shop is three blocks
                     ahead. Northbound on Rte 29: Exit 5 (James St). Turn left on James, go
                     under overpass, then left on Stadium, right on Wythe and left at second
                     light onto Memorial.
Credit Cards: Yes
Owner: Walt & Maggie Carey
Year Estab: 1990
Comments: Three levels of books in a patriotically painted former residence that
                     should not be difficult to miss as long as you recognize the stars and
                     stripes. The shop is nicely organized with a healthy collection of both
                     hardcover and paperback books that are intershelved. The majority of
                     the hardcover items are reading copies but we also noted some col-
                     lectibles. While there were few rarities to be seen here, there were
                     enough collectibles and other good reading matter in most categories
                     to satisfy the average buyer.

Givens Books   **Open Shop**
2345 Lakeside Drive 24501   (804) 385-5027

Collection: General stock of new and used.
# of Vols: 100,000
Hours: Mon 9-6. Tue -Fri 9-7. Sat 9-5.
Services: Appraisals, mail order.
Travel: From Rte 29 southbound, take Rte 501 north, then turn right (north)
                     onto Rte 221. Shop is 1/4 mile east of intersection of Rtes 501 and 221,
                     on the right, in a stand alone building.
Credit Cards: Yes
Owner: George & Sylvia Givens
Year Estab: 1976
Comments: We revisited this shop three years after our first visit and found an
                     extremely attractive shop on the first level offering a fine selection of
                     new books as well as used paperbacks. Unfortunately, the used books
                     we saw in the basement level were even less attractive in terms of both
                     condition and variety of titles than we recalled seeing on our earlier
                     visit when we commented:

A bi-level shop with new books and a small selection of rare and more expensive used titles on the first floor and the remaining used books on the basement level. Most of the used books we saw were older (circa 1920's-1950's). Most were in mixed condition and few, if any, had dust jackets. One had the impression that the better books had been picked over and that what was left were the less desirable titles.

Inklings Bookshop   **Open Shop**
1206 Main Street 24504   (804) 845-2665
Web page: www.inklingsbooks.com   E-mail: ehop@inklingsbooks.com

Collection:	General stock of used and used hardcover and paperback.
# of Vols:	6,000
Specialties:	Civil War; Southern Americana; religion; C.S. Lewis.
Hours:	Mon-Sat 10-6 (but often closed on Thu). Best to call ahead.
Services:	Search service, accepts want lists, mail order.
Travel:	Main St exit off Rte 29 bypass. Follow Main St to downtown.
Credit Cards:	Yes
Owner:	Ed Hopkins
Year Estab:	1995
Comments:	A small shop located in the heart of the city directly across from a farmer's market. In addition to the specialties listed above, the shop offers a modest collection of general titles, mostly of a scholarly nature. Some new books.

Madison
(Map 15, page 294)

Second Chance Books & Search Service   **Antique Mall**
At Roaring Twenty Antiques   Mall: (540) 948-3744
Route 29 North   Home: (540) 672-2343
Mailing address: HCR 03, Box 224 Rochelle 22738
                                        E-mail: vwalrond@ns.gemlick.com

Collection:	General stock.
Hours:	Mon, Thu, Fri, Sat 10-5. Sun 12-5.
Services:	Search service
Travel:	Two miles south of Madison.
Owner:	Veronica Walrond

Manassas
(Map 15A, page 294)

Cosmic Bookstore   **Open Shop**
10953 Lute Court 20109   (703) 330-8573
                                        E-mail: cosmicat@erols.com

Collection:	General stock of hardcover and paperback.
# of Vols:	30,000
Specialties:	Science fiction; mystery.

(Manassas)

Hours:	Wed-Mon 10-6.
Travel:	I-66 west to Rte 234 south. At first light, turn right onto Balls Ford Rd, then right at next light onto New Market Ct. Follow New Market to the end (look for a fence) then walk around the court to the left. Shop is second door on the left.
Credit Cards:	Yes
Owner:	Edith Nally
Year Estab:	1991
Comments:	It always gives us pleasure to discover what we consider a sleeper, realizing, of course, that by the time this book is in print, others may make that same discovery and some of the wonderful volumes we saw during our visit may no longer be available. One's initial impression upon entering the shop is: paperbacks and comics. Toward the rear of the shop, however, there is a solid collection of hardcover volumes of every caliber. Perhaps only as a result of a recent buy, there were several fine mystery items on hand that we thought were underpriced in addition to a large number of dust jacketed "out of the ordinary" science fiction titles, some classics and books in several other collectible categories. If the scouts don't get here before you, and if you're a discerning collector, you should find a visit here satisfying. We did.

Manassas Treasures   **Open Shop**
9023 Centreville Road 20110   (703) 368-8222

Collection:	General stock.
# of Vols:	5,000
Hours:	Mon-Sat 10-6. Sun 12-4.
Travel:	I-66 exit off I-495. Proceed west on I-66 to Rte 28 (Centreville Rd) then south on Rte 28. Shop is on left.
Credit Cards:	Yes
Owner:	Sharon Wolfword
Year Estab:	1988
Comments:	Judging from the outside (the store was not open at 10am on the day of our visit), this shop sells antiques and collectibles in addition to books. Looking through a window we were able to see at least one section of the store where books appeared to be somewhat haphazardly placed on shelves. We're sorry we can't say more.

Richard McKay Used Books   **Open Shop**
8079 Sudley Road 22110   (703) 361-9042

Collection:	General stock of mostly paperback.
# of Vols:	100,000
Hours:	Mon-Sat 9-9. Sun 11-7.
Travel:	Manassas exit (Rte 234) off I-66. Proceed south on Rte 234 for five lights. Shop is in Westgate Shopping Center on left.

RW Books   **Open Shop**
9129 Center Street 20110   (703) 257-7895
                                            E-mail: rwbooks@tidalwave.net

Collection: General stock of hardcover and paperback and ephemera.
# of Vols: 75,000
Specialties: Military; modern first editions; history.
Hours: Mon-Thu 10-8, except Fri & Sat till 9. Sat 10-7. Sun 12-5.
Services: Appraisals, search service, accepts want lists, mail order.
Travel: Exit 47A off I-66. Proceed south on Rte 234 (Sudley Rd) which be-
                    comes Grant Ave. Left onto Center St. Shop is one block ahead on
                    right in Old Town Manassas.
Credit Cards: Yes
Owner: Raymond R. Willis
Year Estab: 1993
Comments: We've seen well organized book stores in the past and this shop cer-
                    tainly makes the Best 10 list in that category. In addition to well
                    labeled sections, several major categories were meticulously subdi-
                    vided (and labeled); the literature section was divided into popular
                    fiction, fiction between 1930's-1950's and pre-1930's fiction and al-
                    phabetical tabs made it easy to find specific authors. The vast majority
                    of the books we saw were in good to excellent condition. Books in the
                    owner's specialty areas were particularly interesting as were several
                    shelves of "collectible" items. If you're into historical maps, you'll
                    find an ample supply here as well.

McLean
(Map 2, page 154)

The Old Book Company of McLean   **Open Shop**
6829 Redmond Drive 22101   (703) 734-0858
                                                    Fax: (703) 734-0885

Collection: General stock.
# of Vols: 12,000
Specialties: Military; espionage (non fiction); Americana; fine bindings.
Hours: Mon-Sat 11-8. Sun 1-6.
Services: Appraisals; search service; accepts want lists.
Travel: Exit 11 off I-495. Proceed north on Rte 123 (Dolley Madison) for
                    about one mile, then right onto Old Dominion and proceed two blocks.
                    Right at light onto Beverly, then left into shopping center parking lot.
Credit Cards: Yes
Owner: Chet Hanson
Year Estab: 1993
Comments: A cozy shop with a modest sized collection of mostly more recent titles
                    with a fair representation of some older volumes interspersed. Quite
                    reasonably priced. The books are attractively displayed, the coffee is
                    always hot, and the comfortable sitting area is an invitation to leisurely
                    browse the shop.

Mike Tecton Books
1469 Spring Vale Avenue 22101

By Appointment
(703) 893-7945
E-mail: mtecton@erols.com

Collection: Specialty new and used.
Specialties: Architecture, with emphasis on traditional architectural plans and detail books.
Services: Catalog
Credit Cards: No
Year Estab: 1973

Meadows of Dan
(Map 15, page 294)

Remember These
Route 58
Mailing address: PO Box 736 Meadows of Dan 24120

Open Shop
(540) 952-1211

Collection: General stock of mostly hardcover and ephemera.
# of Vols: Several hundred.
Hours: Daily 9-5.
Travel: Located at intersection of Rte 58 and Blue Ridge Parkway.
Owner: William Mankins

Mechanicsville

Book Place
8151 Atlee Road 23111

Open Shop
(804) 746-7410

Collection: General stock of mostly paperback.
# of Vols: 45,000
Hours: Wed, Fri, Sat 12-6.

Midlothian

Book Exchange
13198 Midlothian Turnpike 23113

Open Shop
(804) 379-2642
Fax: (804) 378-6072

Collection: General stock of mostly paperback.
# of Vols: 85,000
Hours: Mon-Fri 10-6. Sat 10-5. Sun 12-5.

Monterey
(Map 15, page 294)

Field Books
Spruce Street (Route 636)
Mailing address: PO Box 249 24465

Open Shop
Tel & Fax: (540) 468-3339
E-mail: fieldbks@cfw.com

Collection: General stock of hardcover and paperback ephemera.
# of Vols: 3,000+ (see Comments).

Hours:	Mar-Oct: Fri & Sat 10-6, plus extended hours in summer. Best to call ahead. Nov-Apr: by appointment only.
Services:	Accepts want lists, mail order, book and paper restoration, makes blank books.
Travel:	Exit 225 off I-81. Proceed west on Rte 250. Upon entering Monterey, turn left after the courthouse. Shop is third building on the right.
Credit Cards:	No
Owner:	John & Suse Field
Year Estab:	1996
Comments:	The owners describe their relatively new shop as a "work in progress" that has evolved from their hand bookbinding business and 30 years of collecting books.

Mount Jackson
(Map 15, page 294)

Nostalgia Mart   **Open Shop**
5946 Main Street   (540) 477-2182
Mailing address: PO Box 745 Mt. Jackson 22842

Collection:	General stock and ephemera.
# of Vols:	10,000
Specialties:	Black Americana; children's.
Hours:	Fri-Mon 10-5. Closed Mid-Jan to Apr.
Services:	Accepts want lists.
Travel:	Exit 273 off I-81. Proceed on Rte 11 into Mt. Jackson where Rte 11 becomes Main St.
Credit Cards:	Yes
Owner:	Sheila Padoll
Year Estab:	1989
Comments:	For the second time, our schedule took us to this part of northern Virginia on the "wrong" day of the week.

New Castle

O'Nale-20th Century First Editions   **By Appointment**
Route 2, Box 1293 24127   (540) 864-6288
    Fax: (540) 864-6088

Collection:	Specialty
Specialties:	First editions of fantasy and science fiction (emphasis on 1940's thru 1979); mystery (especially 1920-1960), books to film; modern literature.
Services:	Catalog, accepts want lists.
Credit Cards:	Yes
Owner:	Jan L. O'Nale
Year Estab:	1976

New Market
(Map 15, page 294)

New Market Battlefield Military Museum   **Open Shop**
9500 George R. Collins Drive 22844   (540) 740-8065

Collection: Specialty new and used.
Specialties: Civil War; American history.
Hours: Mar 15-Dec 1: Daily 9-5.
Travel: From I-81 southbound: Exit #264. Right at bottom of hill and proceed
                 west on Rte 211. Right onto George R. Collins Dr.

Paper Treasures   **Open Shop**
9595 Congress Street   (540) 740-3135
Mailing address: PO Box 1160 New Market 22844

Collection: General stock and ephemera.
# of Vols: 50,000
Specialties: Magazines; Civil War; children's; local history; vintage paperbacks.
Hours: Mon-Sat 10-6. Sun 12-6. (Winter: open till 5).
Services: Appraisals, search service, accepts want lists, mail order.
Travel: Exit 264 (New Market) off I-81. Proceed east on Rte 211 for two
                 blocks then right onto Rte 11 south. Shop is about five blocks ahead on
                 right.
Credit Cards: Yes
Owner: Mike Lewis
Year Estab: 1985
Comments: This unexpectedly, and most welcome, large and spacious shop (a
                 former car dealership) carries a mix of well displayed ephemera and
                 generally older books, many of which fall into the collectible category.
                 Prices were most reasonable.

Norfolk
(Map 15, page 294)

Bargain Books   **Open Shop**
7524 Granby Street 23505   (757) 587-3303

Collection: General stock of mostly used paperback.
# of Vols: 50,000 (used).
Hours: Mon-Fri 9-9. Sat 9-7. Sun 12-6.
Travel: From I-64 eastbound: Granby St exit. Proceed on Granby to second
                 light. Left at light onto Little Creek Rd, then right into Ward's Corner
                 Shopping Center. From I-64 westbound: Little Creek Rd exit. Make
                 left at exit onto Little Creek then left turn into shopping center just
                 before Granby intersection.
Credit Cards: Yes
Owner: Harvey Eluto
Year Estab: 1966
Comments: Stock is approximately 80% paperback.

Beacon Books of Ghent   **Open Shop**
821 West 21st Street 23517   (757) 623-5641

Collection:	General stock.
# of Vols:	40,000
Specialties:	Military
Hours:	Summer: Mon-Sat 12-7:30. Winter: Mon-Sat 12-7.
Travel:	In Ghent section, near intersection of Colley Ave and 21st St.
Credit Cards:	No
Owner:	Tommy Warren
Year Estab:	1991
Comments:	This is a shop one must see to believe. As you approach it, you may think you're visiting a combination antique/collectible and book shop because of the "interesting" novelty items the owner has chosen to decorate his shop with. The shop itself does specialize in books though, and there are at least as many volumes as noted above. On the day of our visit, the owner indicated that he had just acquired a large holding which might account for some of the books we saw in the aisles. Tempted as I was, however, to explore the nooks and crannies of this unique establishment, I would have had to loose 50 or 60 more pounds and take lessons from a contortionist in order to do the shelves true justice. The little I could see does suggest that along with the shop's more common stock, there may well be some hidden gems that a far more patient browser could discover. At any rate, a visit here will certainly give you a fresh perspective on the world of used books.

Bibliophile Bookshop   **Open Shop**
251 West Bute Street 23510   (757) 622-2665

Collection:	General stock of mostly hardcover.
# of Vols:	20,000
Specialties:	Civil War; military; history; mystery; fiction; modern first editions.
Hours:	Mon-Sat 10-7. Sun 1-6.
Travel:	Waterside exit off I-264. Continue on Waterside, then left on Bute.
Credit Cards:	Yes
Owner:	Uwe Wilken & Susan Lendvay
Year Estab:	1996
Comments:	A store we had visited three years ago now under new ownership but still, because it has a fine selection of books in generally quite good condition, is easy to browse and offers reasonable prices for its stock, is, in our judgment, well worth visiting.

John Lynch Bookstore   **Open Shop**
116 East Little Creek Road 23505   (757) 531-9441

Collection:	General stock of new, remainders and mostly paperback used.
Hours:	Mon-Sat 9-9. Sun 11-8.

Oakton

E. Wharton & Co.
3232 History Drive 22124

By Appointment
(703) 264-0129
Fax: (703) 860-4923
E-mail: ewhartonco@aol.com

Collection:	Specialty
# of Vols:	1,000
Specialties:	Women writers.
Services:	Accepts want lists, catalog.
Credit Cards:	Yes
Owner:	Sarah Baldwin
Year Estab:	1979

Orlean

Blue Ridge Books
PO Box 36 20128

By Appointment
(540) 364-4595
Fax: (540) 364-9770
E-mail: brbooks@erols.com

Collection:	General stock.
# of Vols:	10,000
Services:	Appraisals, search service, accepts want lists, occasional catalog.
Credit Cards:	Yes
Owner:	Robert Jordan
Year Estab:	1994
Comments:	Also displays at Sperryville Antique Market in Sperryville. See below.

Painter
(Map 15, page 294)

Kit & Caboodle
At Pinchpenny Antiques, Books & Collectibles
Railroad Street
Mailing address: 11502 Swan Drive Machipongo 23405

Antique Mall
(757) 442-6018

Collection:	General stock.
# of Vols:	8,000
Specialties:	Modern first editions.
Hours:	Wed-Sat 10-5.
Travel:	From Rte 13, turn at light. Shop is in Old Bundick Variety Store.
Services:	Search service
Credit Cards:	No
Owner:	Judith Hale
Year Estab:	1988

Petersburg

Cartographic Arts
239 South Adams
Mailing address: PO Box 2202 Petersburg 23804
Web page: www.dogstar.com/carto

By Appointment
(804) 861-6770
Fax: (804) 861-3021
E-mail: carto@dogstar.com

Collection:	Specialty
Specialties:	Antique maps (with emphasis on America from 1600-1800); books containing maps, about maps and map makers.
Services:	Appraisals, accepts want lists, mail order.
Credit Cards:	Yes
Owner:	Luke & Patricia Vavra
Year Estab:	1975

Louis Ginsberg Books & Prints
1642 Avon Way 23805

By Appointment
(804) 732-8188

Collection:	General stock.
# of Vols:	10,000
Specialties:	Books on books; Judaica; manuscripts.
Owner:	Shirley Ginsberg

Second Corps Civil War Books
209 High Street 23803

By Appointment
(804) 861-1863
E-mail: usger@mnsinc.com

Collection:	Specialty
Specialties:	Civil War; Ulysses Grant.
Services:	Appraisals, search service, catalog, accepts want lists, Civil War area tours.
Credit Cards:	No
Owner:	Merlin E. Sumner
Year Estab:	1987

Portsmouth
(Map 15, page 294)

Smithfield Rare Books
429 High Street 23704

Open Shop
(757) 393-1941
Fax: (757) 357-9149

Collection:	General stock, prints and maps.
# of Vols:	5,000-6,000
Specialties:	Southern Americana; travel; natural history; fishing; fine bindings.
Hours:	Tue-Sat 9-5.
Services:	Appraisals, accepts want lists, catalog, search service.
Travel:	Located in downtown, four blocks from Elizabeth River ferry.
Credit Cards:	Yes
Owner:	Elizabeth Goldman
Year Estab:	1981

Comments: Modest in size and eclectic in its collection. During our visit, we saw some good first editions with dust jackets of Hemingway, Faulkner and other noted American writers, a nice selection of travel books, some scholarly volumes and several more pedestrian titles.

Powhatan
(Map 15, page 294)

Book Treasures   **Open Shop**
3810 Courthouse Tavern Road 23139   (804) 598-1260
Collection: General stock of paperback and hardcover.
# of Vols: 5,000
Hours: Tue-Fri 10:30-5:30. Sat 10-3.
Travel: Proceeding west on Rte 60 from Richmond, turn left at Powhatan Historic District sign. Shop is in historic district.
Credit Cards: No
Year Estab: 1993
Comments: Stock is approximately 70% paperback.

Reston
(Map 15A, page 294)

Antiquarian Tobacciana   **By Appointment**
11505 Turnbridge Lane 20194-1220   (703) 435-8133
Collection: Specialty
# of Vols: 500
Specialties: Tobacco, including technology, smoking, pipes and other smoking utensils.
Services: Appraisals, search service, catalog, accepts want lists.
Credit Cards: No
Owner: Ben Rapaport
Year Estab: 1979

W.B. O'Neill - Old & Rare Books   **By Appointment**
11609 Hunters Green Court 20191   (703) 860-0782
                                                                 Fax: (703) 620-0153

Collection: Specialty
# of Vols: 2,000
Specialties: Eastern Mediterranean countries (all subjects).
Services: Catalog, appraisals.
Credit Cards: No
Owner: William B. O'Neill
Year Estab: 1950

Reston's Used Book Shop   **Open Shop**
1623 Washington Plaza 22090   (703) 435-9772
Collection: General stock of hardcover and paperback.
# of Vols: 26,000

Hours:	Mon-Fri 11-7. Sat 10-6. Sun 12-5.
Travel:	Rte 267 (Dulles Access Rd) exit off I-495. Proceed on Rte 267 to Reston Pkwy. Right turn onto Baron Cameron, then right onto Village Rd to Lake Anne Village Center.
Credit Cards:	Yes
Owner:	Sue Schram & Sue Wensell
Year Estab:	1978
Comments:	A small, tightly packed shop with paperbacks and hardcover titles of a fairly recent origin. Most of the books are in quite good condition and represent most areas of general interest although we saw little that was out of the ordinary. Reasonably priced.

Richmond
(Map 15, page 294 & Map 17, page 330)

Ardent Reader   **Open Shop**
11 East Grace Street 23219   (804) 225-0281
                                                               (800) 773-5079

Collection:	General stock.
# of Vols:	10,000
Hours:	Tue-Sat 10-5. Open till 6 in summer.
Services:	Search service, mail order.
Travel:	Southbound on I-95: Broad St West exit. Proceed west on Broad St to 1st St, then left on 1st, and right on Grace. Shop is 1/2 block ahead. Northbound on I-95. Broad St exit. Proceed west on Broad St and follow directions above.
Credit Cards:	Yes
Owner:	Al House
Year Estab:	1991
Comments:	This shop has relocated to a new and most attractive location (and changed its name) since our last visit to Richmond. The new shop is roomy and books are displayed with taste; one can browse comfortably in well lit surroundings. The vast majority of the books we saw (some of the stock was still being unpacked and shelved at the time of our visit) were in very good to excellent condition and most were of fairly recent vintage and reasonably priced.

Autumn's Books & Printing   **Open Shop**
5013 Forest Hill Avenue 23225   Tel & Fax: (804) 231-0883

Collection:	General stock of hardcover and paperback.
# of Vols:	30,000
Hours:	Mon-Fri 10-9. Sat 10-5. Sun 12-5.
Services:	Search service, mail order.
Travel:	See Stories below.
Credit Cards:	Yes
Owner:	Richard & Courtney Haynes
Year Estab:	1996

(Richmond)

Comments: The shop is large and could, quite comfortably, hold many more vol-
                 umes then were on display. (At the time of our visit, there were far
                 fewer than the 30,000 volumes noted above.) The shop offers a mix of
                 paperbacks and hardcover books with the hardcover volumes repre-
                 senting both the older variety as well as those of more recent vintage.
                 A few collectibles and some sleepers but by and large mostly reading
                 copies. Reasonably priced.

Black Swan Books   **Open Shop**
511 North Meadow Street 23220   (804) 353-9476
                                                              Fax: (804) 353-3198
                                                      E-mail: blckswn@interloc.com

Collection: General stock.
# of Vols: 8,000-10,000
Specialties: 20th century first editions.
Services: Search service, accepts want lists, mail order.
Travel: From downtown, continue west on Grace to Meadow, then left on
                 Meadow. Shop is just after crossing Monument Ave, on the left.
Credit Cards: Yes
Owner: Nicholas Cooke
Year Estab: 1997
Comments: A new shop that opened shortly after our visit to Richmond.

Book Rack   **Open Shop**
8801G Three Chopt Road 23229   (804) 288-3418
Collection: General stock of mostly paperback.
# of Vols: 20,000
Hours: Mon-Fri 10-7. Sat 10-5. Sun 1-5.

Book People   **Open Shop**
536 Granite Avenue 23226   (804) 288-4346
                                                              Fax: (804) 282-7327
Collection: General stock of mostly new books and ephemera.
# of Vols: 20,000
Hours: Mon-Fri 9-9. Sat 9-7. Sun 9-6.
Services: Search service, accepts want lists, mail order.
Travel: From I-95 or I-64, follow signs for University of Richmond. At Patterson
                 Ave, turn left (east), then right on Granite.
Credit Cards: Yes
Owner: Ruth Erb

Books Plus   **Open Shop**
7151 Staples Mill Road 23228   (804) 262-7558
Collection: General stock of paperback and hardcover.
# of Vols: 30,000
Hours: Mon 1:30-5:30. Tue & Thu 10-6. Wed & Fri 10-5. Sat 12-5. Sun 1-5.

Travel:	Rte 33 exit off I-64. Proceed west on Staples Mill Rd for 1½ miles (five lights) past corner of Hilliard and Staples Mill. Shop is on right in Dumbarton Square Shopping Center.
Credit Cards:	No
Owner:	Susanne Lyman
Year Estab:	1992
Comments:	Stock is approximately 70% paperback.

Chapter Two Books   **Open Shop**
422 East Main Street 23219   (804) 643-7568

Collection:	General stock.
# of Vols:	20,000
Specialties:	History; art; mystery; science fiction; theology.
Hours:	Tue-Sat 10-5. Other times by appointment.
Services:	Appraisals, accepts want lists, mail order.
Travel:	I-95 southbound: 3rd St exit. Proceed to Franklin St, then left on Franklin and right on 5th and continue to Main. I-95 northbound: Broad St exit. Proceed west on Broad, left on 1st St, right on Franklin and right on Fifth. Shop is located at corner of 5th & Main in the English basement of the Hancock-Writ Caskie House built in 1808.
Credit Cards:	Yes
Owner:	Betty Hubbard and William Blair
Year Estab:	1995
Comments:	This is a shop we really don't want to tell you about as, given the opportunity, we would like to return and purchase more books than the dozen or so we did buy during our initial visit. Need we say more? If any of the specialties listed above are of interest to you, try to get to this shop before your nearest competitor. The selections were broad, the books were in good condition and the prices were fantastic.

Collectors' Old Book Shop   **Open Shop**
15 South Fifth Street 23219   (804) 644-2097

Collection:	General stock.
# of Vols:	15,000
Specialties:	Virginia; Civil War; literature.
Hours:	Mon-Fri 11-5. Sat 11-3.
Services:	Appraisals, search service
Travel:	See Chapter Two Books above. Shop is at intersection of 5th & Carey.
Credit Cards:	No
Owner:	Mary Clark Roane
Year Estab:	1945
Comments:	A three room, thickly carpeted shop located on the lower level of an historic house dating back to 1844. A piano in the center of one room adds a touch of refinement to the surroundings that blends well with the shop's concentration on southern authors and history. If you're searching for books dealing with the deep south, you're certainly likely to find items of interest here.

Ex Libris Bookshop   **Open Shop**
6921 Lakeside Avenue 23228   (804) 262-9217

Collection:	General stock of used and new hardcover and paperback.
# of Vols:	5,000-6,000 (used)
Hours:	Mon-Fri 10-7. Sat 10-5.
Services:	Search service, accepts want lists, mail order.
Travel:	Lakeside Ave exit off I-95. Proceed north on Lakeside for about two miles. Shop is at the intersection of Hilliard and Lakeside in The Hub.
Credit Cards:	Yes
Owner:	Jim Martinelli
Year Estab:	1989
Comments:	Used stock is evenly divided between hardcover and paperback.

Fountain Bookstore   **Open Shop**
1312 East Cary Street 23219   (804) 788-1594

Collection:	Specialty (See Comments)
# of Vols:	250+
Specialties:	Literary first editions.
Hours:	Mon-Fri 10-8, except Fri till 9. Sat 11-9. Sun 12-5.
Travel:	Shockoe Slip exit off I-95. Turn right onto 10th St, then right onto Cary St. Shop is three blocks ahead on left in historic Shockoe Slip district.
Comments:	A "new" book store with a limited number of specialty used books on consignment.

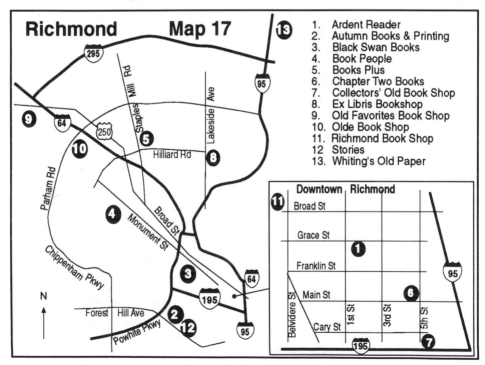

Richmond   Map 17

1. Ardent Reader
2. Autumn Books & Printing
3. Black Swan Books
4. Book People
5. Books Plus
6. Chapter Two Books
7. Collectors' Old Book Shop
8. Ex Libris Bookshop
9. Old Favorites Book Shop
10. Olde Book Shop
11. Richmond Book Shop
12 Stories
13. Whiting's Old Paper

Old Favorites Book Shop   **Open Shop**
3055 Lauderdale Drive 23233   (804) 364-2055

Collection: General stock.
# of Vols: 12,000
Specialties: Military; science fiction; fantasy; Civil War; genealogy.
Hours: Mon-Fri 11-6. Sat 11-4.
Services: Appraisals, search service, catalog, accepts want lists.
Travel: Exit 178A (Short Pump) off I-64. Proceed west on Broad St (Rte 250)
                   for about one mile, then left on Lauderdale Rd. Shop is about one mile
                   ahead on left in Lauderdale Square Shopping Center.
Credit Cards: Yes
Owner: Gary O'Neal
Year Estab: 1982
Comments: When we visited this shop at its previous location we indicated that the
                   dealer's specialties were well represented in a small, neat and well
                   organized shop. The books were in generally fine condition, most with
                   dust jackets. Prices represented the scarcity of some of the titles and
                   the shop was definitely worth a visit if the shop's specialties were of
                   interest to you. Visiting the shop three years later in its new location
                   reaffirms our earlier observations to the point where we left the shop
                   filling the last few inches of truck space in our car. The shop also
                   carries some antiquarian items.

Olde Book Shop   **Open Shop**
1551 Parham Road 23229-4604   (804) 282-6990

Collection: General stock of mostly hardcover.
# of Vols: 5,000-10,000
Specialties: Virginia; Civil War; history.
Hours: Tue-Sat 10-6, except Fri till 8.
Services: Accepts want lists, mail order.
Travel: Parham Rd exit off I-64. Proceed west on Parham for about three
                   miles. Shop is located in the Ridge Shopping Center on the left.
Credit Cards: Yes
Owner: Barbara H. Clower
Year Estab.   1990
Comments: A pleasing, relatively small shop with a modest but good selection of
                   mixed vintage books in rather good condition. Reasonable prices.

Owens & Ramsey Historical Booksellers   **Open Shop**
2728 Tinsley Drive 23235-2448   (804) 272-8888
                               E-mail: mramsey@rmond.mindspring.com

Collection: Specialty used and new.
# of Vols: 5,000
Specialties: Civil War; Americana; Virginia; Richmond; World War I & II; West-
                   ern Americana; military.
Hours: Mon-Sat 10-5.
Services: Appraisals, accepts want lists, catalog.

(Richmond)

Travel:	I-195 exit off I-95. Proceed south on I-195. Take first exit (Forest Hill Ave) after crossing river. Proceed west on Forest Hill for about three miles, then right onto Tinsley. Shop is just ahead in shopping center.
Credit Cards:	Yes
Owner:	Marc & Jill Ramsey
Year Estab:	1984
Comments:	Stock is approximately 75% used.

Scott Partridge, Bookseller   **By Appointment**
121 Wyck Street, Ste 104 23225   (804) 674-4971
                                         E-mail: delscott@worldnet.att.net

Collection:	General stock.
# of Vols:	15,000
Specialties:	Modern first editions; science fiction; mystery.
Services:	Search service, accepts want lists, mail order.
Credit Cards:	Yes
Year Estab:	1992

Religious Goods Shop   **Open Shop**
20 North Belmont Avenue 23221   (804) 355-6634

Collection:	Specialty used and new and limited general stock.
# of Vols:	12,000 (used)
Specialties:	Religion (Catholicism).
Hours:	Mon-Fri 9-5:30. Sat 9-5.
Services:	Accepts want lists.
Travel:	Boulevard exit off I-95. Proceed south on Boulevard to Grove Ave. Right onto Grove and proceed three blocks to first light. Left onto Belmont. Shop is 1½ blocks ahead.
Credit Cards:	Yes
Owner:	Taylor Campbell
Year Estab:	1945

Richmond Book Shop   **Open Shop**
808 West Broad Street 23220   (804) 644-9970

Collection:	General stock of hardcover and paperback.
# of Vols:	30,000
Specialties:	Original cartoon art; art; history; architecture.
Hours:	Mon-Fri 2-5. Sat 11-5.
Travel:	Eastbound from I-95 or I-64: Belvidere exit. Proceed straight to Broad St, then one block right. Westbound from I-95/64: 5th St/Coliseum exit. Right turn onto Broad St. Proceed for 12 blocks.
Credit Cards:	Yes
Owner:	Robert Lewis
Year Estab:	1995

Comments: Unfortunately this shop was not open at the time of our visit to Richmond. We did, however have an opportunity to stop and look through the front window — not a very accurate way, we confess, to evaluate any business. There seemed to be a sufficient number of hardcover volumes to suggest a legitimate reason for traveling book hunters to stop by. Should you have an opportunity to visit here, we would be happy to have you share your impressions with us. Be advised that a sign in the window notes that the shop is "open by appointment, chance or scheduled sales," suggesting that despite the hours listed above, you may want to call ahead if you plan to visit. Another sign notes that the owner also displays at the Antique Gallery at 3140 West Cary Street and the West End Antique Mall at 6504 Horsepen Road, both in Richmond.

Stories   **Open Shop**
5065-7 Forest Hill Avenue 23225   (804) 231-4213

Collection: General stock of paperback and hardcover and comics.
# of Vols: 200,000+
Hours: Mon, Tue, Thu & Sat 10-6. Wed 10-8. Fri 10-7. Sun 12-6
Travel: Forest Hill Rd exit off Chippenham Pkwy. Proceed east on Forest Hill. Shop is between Jahnke Rd & Belt Blvd.
Credit Cards: No
Owner: Barry Pryor
Year Estab: 1985
Comments: A large shop with an extremely large collection of comic related materials and paperbacks. It also has a few thousand hardcover items (some up front and many in the rear of the store), both fiction and non fiction.

Whiting's Old Paper   **Antique Mall**
At Antique Village   (804) 746-4710
Route 301
Mailing address: PO Box 25058 Richmond 23260

Collection: General stock and ephemera.
# of Vols: 1,000
Specialties: Magazines
Hours: Mon-Sat, except closed Wed, 10-5. Sun 12-6.
Travel: On Rte 301, four miles north of I-295.
Credit Cards: No
Owner: John Whiting
Year Estab: 1975

Roanoke
(Map 15, page 294)

Carriage House Antiques   **Antique Mall**
5999 Franklin Road 24014   (540) 776-0499

Hours: Daily 10-6.
Travel: On Rte 220, south of Roanoke.

(Roanoke)

The Dusty Corner Bookstore   **Open Shop**
3639 Brambleton Avenue 24018   (540) 774-3249

Collection:	General stock of used and new hardcover and paperback.
# of Vols:	15,000 (used)
Hours:	Mon-Sat 10-6. Sun 12-5.
Travel:	Rte 221 exit off Rte 419. Proceed north on Rte 221 (Brambleton Ave).
Credit Cards:	Yes
Owner:	Sharon & Brady Perdue
Year Estab:	1987
Comments:	This store sells a little bit of everything. In addition to a modest number of hardcover used books, (our guess would be fewer than 3,000-4,000 volumes), most of which were reading copies of fairly new titles, there's an entire room devoted to romance paperbacks and hardcovers, another area overflowing with comic books, an ample supply of new titles, and, at the time of our visit, even a supply of beads and jewelry. The owners operate a second shop in Salem.

Foundation Books   **By Appointment**
PO Box 7086 24019   (540) 366-9075
                                                       Fax: (540) 362-1302

Collection:	Specialty
# of Vols:	10,000
Specialties:	Religion
Services:	Catalog
Credit Cards:	No
Owner:	Rick Harvey
Year Estab:	1989

Roanoke Antique Mall   **Antique Mall**
2302 Orange Avenue, NE 24012   (540) 344-0264

Hours:	Mon-Sat 10-6, except till 8 during summer. Sun 12-6.
Travel:	Orange Ave East exit off I-581. Proceed east on Orange for about 1¾ miles. At fifth light, turn left into Orange Plaza Shopping Center.

Too Many Books   **Open Shop**
2311B Colonial Avenue 24015   (540) 982-8172

Collection:	General stock of paperback and hardcover.
# of Vols:	30,000
Hours:	Mon-Sat 10-5:30.
Services:	Search service, accepts want lists.
Travel:	I-581 (Roanoke) exit off I-81. Turn left off exit onto Colonial Ave then an almost immediate left at light and left into parking lot. The entrance to the shop is from the rear parking lot, not Colonial Ave.
Credit Cards:	Yes
Owner:	Linda Steadman & Ellen Troland
Year Estab:	1993

Comments: A tri-level shop with a nice collection of attractively displayed paperbacks and mixed vintage hardcover books, mostly reading copies, but some collectibles. Hardcover and paperback books are shelved together. Note: The owners are looking for larger quarters in Roanoke.

Rural Retreat

Bookworm And Silverfish   **Open Shop**
Church Street   (540) 686-5813
Mailing address: PO Box 639 Wytheville 24382   E-mail: bookworm@cnaxs.com

Collection: Specialty
# of Vols: 8,000-10,000
Specialties: Genealogy; Virginia; local history; Civil War; trade catalogs; technology; Americana.
Hours: Mon-Fri 8-4.
Services: Appraisals, search service, catalog, accepts want lists, collection development.
Travel: Exit 60 off I-81. Proceed east on Rte 90 for about two miles, then right onto Buck Street. Proceed for one block and make left onto Church Street. Shop is about 75 feet ahead at Gammon Avenue in a two story brick house.
Credit Cards: Yes
Owner: Jim Presgraves
Year Estab: 1973
Comments: If you're looking for books in specific subject areas, you'll have to browse all the shelves in this modest sized shop since, at least at the time of our visit, there appeared to us to be no rhyme or reason as to how the books were shelved. The inventory is computerized, however, and if you know what you're looking for, the management will be more than happy to direct you to the right book case. During our visit, we saw some very unusual titles that without question would classify this shop as one specializing in truly rare and antiquarian books. Prices reflect the nature of the stock.

Salem
(Map 15, page 294)

The Dusty Corner Bookstore   **Open Shop**
27 & 29 East Main Street 24153   (540) 387-4192

Collection: General stock of new and used hardcover and paperback.
# of Vols: 20,000 (used)
Hours: Mon-Fri 12-6. Sat 10-6. Sun 12-5.
Travel: See Wright Place Antique Mall above. Shop is across from library.
Credit Cards: Yes
Owner: Sharon & Brady Perdue
Comments: See comments for Roanoke store.

(Salem)

Givens Books   **Open Shop**
1641 East Main Street 24153   (540) 986-1103

Collection:	General stock of hardcover and paperback.
# of Vols:	50,000
Specialties:	Western Americana; Civil War; American history.
Hours:	Mon-Sat 10-6.
Services:	Appraisals, mail order.
Travel:	Exit 141 off I-81. Proceed south on Rte 419 for about two miles to Main St. Left on Main. Shop is on the left.
Credit Cards:	Yes
Owner:	Chip & Susan Givens
Year Estab:	1983
Comments:	A healthy number of hardcover volumes, most of which were reading copies in mixed condition. A knowledgeable scout might find some items here.

Christopher Gladden Bookseller   **Open Shop**
211 South College Avenue 24153   (540) 389-4892

Collection:	General stock, ephemera, prints and maps.
# of Vols:	1,000+
Hours:	Tue-Fri 10:30-3. Other times by chance of appointment. (See Comments)
Travel:	See Wright Antique Mall below. Right on Main, then left on College.
Credit Cards:	No
Year Estab:	1993
Comments:	An elusive bookseller whose telephone answering machine announces the above hours. Intrepid as we are, we nonetheless took the chance of stopping by the shop at 2pm on a Friday afternoon. Sure enough, the shop was closed but there were signs of book life within. (A sign on the door confirmed the above hours.) In addition to a number of volumes spread out on the floor (no doubt new acquisitions about the be sorted and shelved) we were able to see, but not appreciate, a dozen or so bookcases filled with hardcover volumes, a sign suggesting that there may indeed be quality books within. At least one of our reader friends was lucky enough to visit the shop and spoke well of it. Regrettably, we were unable to share that experience.

Green Market Antique Mall   **Antique Mall**
8 East Main Street 24153   (540) 387-3879

Hours:	Mon-Sat 10-6. Sun 12-6.
Travel:	See Wright Place Antique Mall below. Turn right onto Main.

Wright Place Antique Mall   **Antique Mall**
27 West Main Street 24153   (540) 389-8507

Hours:	Mon-Sat 10-6. Sun 12:30-6.
Travel:	Exit 140 off I-81. Proceed south on Rte 311 into Salem. Right at Main St.

Shipman

Buteo Books
3130 Laurel Road 22971
Web page: www.buteobooks.com

Open Shop
(804) 263-8671
Fax: (804) 263-4842
E-mail: allen@buteobooks.com

Collection:	Specialty
# of Vols:	2,000
Specialties:	Ornithology
Hours:	Mon-Fri 9-5.
Services:	Appraisals, search service, catalog, accepts want lists
Travel:	From Rte 29, turn east on Rte 6, then right on Rte 639 (Laurel Rd). Shop is about four miles ahead.
Credit Cards:	Yes
Owner:	Allen M. Hale
Year Estab:	1971

Sperryville
(Map 15, page 294)

Sperryville Antique Market
2 River Road

Antique Mall
(540) 987-8080

Hours:	Daily, except closed Wed, 10-5.
Travel:	Rte 211 exit off Sklyline Dr. Proceed east on Rte 211 for six miles to River Rd (Rte 1003). Right on River Rd. Mall is just ahead on left.

Springfield
(Map 15A, page 294 & Map 2, page 154)

Bob's Books
6230-D Rolling Road 22152

Open Shop
(703) 644-7330

Collection:	General stock of paperback and hardcover.
# of Vols:	15,000
Hours:	Mon-Fri 10-8. Sat 10-6. Sun 12-5.
Travel:	Exit 169B off I-95. Proceed west on Old Keene Mill Rd for three miles, then right on Rolling Rd and left at light into West Springfield Center.
Credit Cards:	No
Owner:	Bob Seltzer
Year Estab:	1996
Comments:	The shop has far more paperbacks than hardcover books although the hardcover collection, mostly reading copies, did have some interesting titles and more than a few vintage items. Quite reasonably priced.

Felicia's Used Books
7627 Fullerton Road 22153

Open Shop
(703) 866-3966

Collection:	General stock of paperback and hardcover.
# of Vols:	15,000

Hours:	Mon-Fri 10-6. Sat 10-4.
Travel:	Backlick/Fullerton exit off I-95. Proceed south on Fullerton for about one mile. Shop is on left.
Credit Cards:	Yes
Owner:	Felicia Rotter
Year Estab:	1992
Comments:	This bi-level shop carries a respectable number of both paperbacks and hardcover volumes. Some of the hardcover books were nicely dust jacketed items of recent vintage but the shop also has a variety of older books in mixed condition. We did, however, note that several volumes we have seen frequently in other area shops were offered here at higher prices.

Jeff's Baseball Corner   **Open Shop**
5536A Port Royal Road 22151   (703) 321-9209
Web page: members.aol.com/jbcorner   (888) 867-6056
                                                          E-mail: jbcorner@aol.com

Collection:	Specialty books and memorabilia.
# of Vols:	15,000
Specialties:	All sports, except hunting and fishing.
Hours:	Open daily. Call for hours.
Services:	Accepts want lists, mail order.
Travel:	Exit 5W off I-495. Proceed one block west on Braddock, then left at first light onto Port Royal.
Credit Cards:	Yes
Owner:	Jeff Doranz
Year Estab:	1983

Staunton
(Map 15, page 294)

Blue Moon Books   **Open Shop**
9 East Beverly 24401   (540) 886-6913

Collection:	General stock of hardcover and paperback.
# of Vols:	40,000
Hours:	Mon-Sat 11-6. (Hours may change so a call ahead is advised.)
Travel:	Exit 225 off I-81. Proceed west on Rte 275 to first light (Rte 11), then left on Rte 11 and proceed to downtown (keep right on Rte 11). Turn right onto East Beverly.
Credit Cards:	No
Owner:	Agnes Sobszak
Year Estab:	1996
Comments:	A fledgling shop just getting underway at the time of our visit. Based on the little we were able to see, we believe that the store holds promise. Most of the books on hand were reading copies and inexpensively priced. The owners plan a separate rear room for paperbacks.

Sterling
(Map 15A, page 294)

Crest Books   **Open Shop**
1113 West Church Road 20164   (703) 450-4200

Collection:	General stock of paperback and hardcover.
# of Vols:	40,000
Hours:	Mon-Wed 10-6. Thu-Sat 10-5.
Travel:	Rte 28 exit off Rte 50. Proceed north on Rte 28, then right on Church.
Credit Cards:	Yes
Owner:	Patricia Jacobs
Year Estab:	1989
Comments:	Stock is approximately 75% paperback.

Tappahannock

Book'N   **Open Shop**
154 Prince Street   (804) 443-2262
Mailing address: PO Box 1757 Tappahannock 22560

Collection:	General stock of mostly paperback.
# of Vols:	1,000 (hardcover)
Hours:	Mon-Thu 10-5. Fri 10-7. Sat 10-5. Sun 11-3:30.

Vienna

Audubon Prints and Books   **By Appointment**
9720 Spring Ridge Lane 22182   (703) 759-5567

Collection:	Specialty
Specialties:	Audubon books.
Services:	Catalog, accepts want lists, search service.
Credit Cards:	No
Owner:	Ed Kenney, Manager
Year Estab:	1978

Jo Ann Reisler   **By Appointment**
360 Glyndon Street, NE 22180   (703) 938-2967
Web page: www.clark.net/pub/reisler   Fax: (703) 938-9057
E-mail: reisler@clark.net

Collection:	Specialty
# of Vols:	5,000
Specialties:	Children's; illustrated; original illustrative art; early paper dolls and toys.
Services:	Catalog
Credit Cards:	Yes
Owner:	Jo Ann & Don Reisler
Year Estab:	1970

Virginia Beach
(Map 15, page 294)

Brimmers' Books   **Open Shop**
236 London Bridge Shopping Center 23454   (757) 631-6357

Collection:	General stock of hardcover and paperback.
# of Vols:	15,000
Specialties:	Black studies; history.
Hours:	Mon, Wed, Fri 12-6. Tue, Thu Sat 10-6. Sun 2-6.
Services:	Search service, mail order.
Travel:	Lynnhaven Pkwy north exit off Virginia Beach Expy. Proceed on Lynnhaven Pkwy to Virginia Beach Blvd, then right on Virginia Beach Blvd, left on Great Neck Rd and immediate left into shopping center.
Credit Cards:	Yes
Owner:	Louise Brimmer
Year Estab:	1995
Comments:	In addition to the more typical books seen in generally smaller shops (paperbacks and recent vintage hardcover reading copies) this shop carries a modest number of truly antiquarian items as well as some outstanding books in the shop's specialty areas. If you're not charmed by the shop's owner, we'll be surprised.

Classic Books of Virginia   **Open Shop**
3029 Shore Drive 23451-1242   (757) 496-8110
                                                    E-mail: bjvolker@interloc.com

Collection:	General stock of mostly used hardcover and paperback.
# of Vols:	10,000
Hours:	Tue-Sat 10-7. Sun (summer only) 12-5. Other times by appointment.
Services:	Appraisals, search service, accepts want lists.
Travel:	From I-64: Northampton Blvd exit. Continue north on Northampton, then right onto Shore Dr. From Rte 13 (the Maryland eastern shore), exit at Bay Bridge Tunnel and proceed east on Rte 60 (Shore Dr). Shop is at corner of Starfish and Shore Dr.
Credit Cards:	Yes
Owner:	Bonita Volker
Year Estab:	1996
Comments:	A few new items and a fair selection of paperbacks and hardcover books that were a combination of mostly mixed vintage reading copies with and without dust jackets. Reasonably priced. The shop also sells gift items, greeting cards and books on tape.

Encore Consignment Department Store   **Open Shop**
3636 Virginia Beach Boulevard 23452   (757) 431-6941

Collection:	General stock new and mostly hardcover used.
# of Vols:	10,000
Hours:	Mon-Thu 10-7. Fri & Sat 10-6. Sun 12-5.
Travel:	At corner of Rosement and Virginia Beach Blvd.

Credit Cards:	No
Year Estab:	1988
Comments:	All books are on consignment from dealers and collectors.

First Landing Books & Fine Art   **Open Shop**
2708 Pacific Avenue 23451   (757) 422-4072
E-mail: tdebear@aol.com

Collection:	General stock of hardcover and paperback.
# of Vols:	7,500
Specialties:	Fine bindings; science; World War I & II; art; religion; philosophy; literature; poetry; Civil War.
Hours:	May-Sep: Mon-Fri 9-9. Sat & Sun 9am-11pm. Oct-Apr: Daily, except closed Wed, 10-6. Best to call ahead in winter.
Services:	Appraisals, search service, accepts want lists, mail order.
Travel:	I-64 to Rte 44 East. Continue on Rte 44 to oceanfront. Left on Pacific. Shop is on left just after 27th St.
Credit Cards:	Yes
Owner:	Ted Logue
Year Estab:	1997
Comments:	Just a block from the beach, one would expect to find a shop offering lots of "beach reading" and in that respect this shop has its fair share of paperbacks and hardcover novels. What is both surprising and gratifying though, is that the shop ALSO carries a goodly number of historically significant items, including many related to the Civil War, several bound long runs of *Scribner's* (1871-1877) and *Atlantic Monthly* (1858-1871) and other similar items. We also saw a number of single author sets with fine bindings. All in all, a shop we believe that should satisfy the esoteric taste of any antiquarian collector.

Warrenton
(Map 15, page 294)

BJ's Books   **Open Shop**
381 West Shirley Avenue 20186   (540) 347-4111

Collection:	General stock of mostly paperback.
# of Vols:	100,000
Hours:	Mon-Sat 10-8. Sun 12-5.
Travel:	On Rte 29 in Waterloo Station Shopping Center.
Comments:	Stock is approximately 80% paperback.

Waynesboro

Karl Altau   **By Appointment**
800 Warwick Circle 22980   (540) 949-8867

Collection:	Specialty
# of Vols:	15,000
Specialties:	Americana

Services: Appraisals, mail order.
Year Estab: 1968

Weyer's Cave
(Map 15, page 294)

Ann's Pens & Buttons   **Antique Mall**
In Rocky Simonetti's Antique Mall   (540) 234-8935
Route 11   24486

Collection: General stock.
# of Vols: 4,000
Specialties: Antique reference.
Hours: Thu-Mon 9-5.
Travel: Exit 235 off I-81. Proceed south on Rte 11 for about one block.

Williamsburg
(Map 15, page 294)

Aeroplane Books   **Open Shop**
114 Deer Path Road 23188   (757) 565-4814
                                                            Fax: (757) 253-1089
                                                    E-mail: aerobook@hroads.net

Collection: Specialty used and new.
# of Vols: 7,000+
Specialties: Aviation; aviation magazines.
Hours: Mon-Sat 9-6.
Services: Appraisals, search service, catalog, accepts want lists.
Travel: Exit 234 off I-64. Turn northeast and proceed for .9 mile to Barlow.
               Right on Barlow, left on Skimino, right on Deer Path.
Credit Cards: Yes
Owner: Bill & Barbara Byrd
Year Estab: 1970

The Book House   **Open Shop**
421-A Prince George Street 23185   (757) 229-3603
                                                            (757) 229-2901

Collection: General stock of mostly used hardcover and paperback and ephemera.
# of Vols: 5,000
Specialties: Virginia
Hours: Mon-Sat 10-5. Sun (seasonal) 1:30-5.
Travel: In heart of historic Williamsburg, just off Merchant Square and 1½
               blocks from the Wren Building at the College of William & Mary.
Credit Cards: Yes
Owner: Mary Lewis & Andrew Chapman
Year Estab: 1977
Comments: Down a flight of stairs, this well organized shop caters to a variety of
               tastes with mostly used hardcover books of mixed vintage, some new
               and used paperbacks and a few new miscellaneous items.

The Bookpress Ltd.   **Open Shop**
1304 Jamestown Road   (757) 229-1260
Mailing address: Box KP Williamsburg 23187   Fax: (757) 229-0498
Web page: www.bookpress.com   E-mail: bookpress@widowmaker.com

Collection:	General stock.
Specialties:	Art reference; architecture; books about books; fine printing; Americana (colonial).
Hours:	Mon-Sat 10-5.
Services:	Appraisals, search service, catalog.
Travel:	Rte 199 exit off I-64. Proceed towards Jamestown. Left on Jamestown Rd. Shop is in fifth building on left.
Credit Cards:	Yes
Owner:	John Robert Curtis Jr. & John Ballinger
Year Estab:	1972
Comments:	We returned to this shop three years after our first visit as the owners had moved to a new location. The books, located on two levels, are attractively displayed with rarer items behind glass. The shop offers something for everyone's taste. While the prices of difficult to find books (which can be found here) may reflect their rarity, prices of other books were most reasonable. This is a place that true book aficionados, and especially scholars and antiquarians, will enjoy browsing.

Hamilton's Book Store   **Open Shop**
1784 Jamestown Road 23185   (757) 220-3000
Web page: www.goodbooks.com   Fax: (757) 220-1820
      E-mail: goodbook@goodbooks.com

Collection:	General stock and ephemera.
# of Vols:	35,000
Specialties:	Virginia; illustrated; history; book arts; children's; historical documents and autographs.
Hours:	Mon-Sat 10-5.
Services:	Appraisals, mail order.
Travel:	See Bookpress above. Continue on Jamestown Rd.
Credit Cards:	Yes
Owner:	Jack D. Hamilton
Year Estab:	1978
Comments:	We liked this shop three years earlier when we first visited it and found it equally attractive on our return visit. It is large and has excellent books fitting the true antiquarian definition as well as vintage items, collectibles, new material and scholarly volumes. You name it, you can find a reasonable number of volumes to whet your appetite at this location. We did and left the shop somewhat lighter in our wallet.

Henry Stevens, Son & Stiles   **By Appointment**
PO Box 1299 23187   (757) 229-1809

Collection:	Specialty
Specialties:	Early Americana, including maps, engravings and manuscripts.

Services: Appraisals, catalog, accepts want lists.
Credit Cards: No
Owner: Thomas MacDonnell
Year Estab: 1843

Winchester
(Map 15, page 294)

The Book Shelf   **Open Shop**
106 Featherbed Lane 22601   (540) 665-0866
Collection: General stock of mostly paperback used and new books, gifts and
                  candles.
# of Vols: 5,000 (used)
Hours: Mon-Thu 10-6. Fri 10-7. Sat 10-5. Sun 12-4.

Rainbow's End Used Books   **Open Shop**
9 West Boscawen Street 22601   (540) 665-0334

Collection: General stock of hardcover and paperback.
# of Vols: 10,000
Hours: Mon-Sat 11-5. Sun 11-5.
Travel: Rte 7 exit off I-81. Proceed west on Berryville, then left on Piccadilly,
                  left on Braddock and left on Boscawen.
Credit Cards: No
Owner: Gary Braithwaite
Year Estab: 1982
Comments: A small shop with mostly older books in mixed condition. Nothing
                  outstanding in terms of quality.

Woodbridge
(Map 15A, page 294 & Map 15, page 294)

C & W Used Books   **Open Shop**
14583 Potomac Mills Road 22192   (703) 491-7323
Collection: General stock of paperback and hardcover.
# of Vols: 75,000-100,000
Hours: Mon-Sat 10-9. Sun 11-7.
Travel: Exit 156 (Potomac Mills Rd) off I-95. Follow signs to Potomac Mills.
                  Shop is in the Potomac Festival Shopping Center.
Credit Cards: Yes
Owner: Gail Charlesworth
Year Estab: 1974
Comments: A shop that is most friendly to consumers but not dealers (The sign
                  above the front counter that reads "No Sales To Dealers" is strictly
                  enforced.) While the shop is heavily paperback, it does have a good
                  selection of hardcover books. Prices for most of what we saw were
                  quite competitive. The owner operates a second shop in Chantilly.

Parker's Book Stop   **Open Shop**
14439 Jeff Davis Highway 22191   (703) 494-2683
                                   E-mail: parkerbk@tidalwave.net

Collection:	General stock of paperback and hardcover.
# of Vols:	55,000
Specialties:	Religion; history; military; Civil War; cookbooks; mystery; science fiction; modern first editions.
Hours:	Mon-Sat 10-7. Sun 12-5.
Services:	Search service, accepts want lists, mail order, book repairs.
Travel:	Exit 156 (Potomac Mills) off I-95. Turn right on Smoketown/Opitz Blvd and proceed to Rte 1. Left on Rte 1 (Jeff Davis Hwy) and proceed for 3½ blocks. Shop is on right in Lynwood Shopping Center.
Credit Cards:	Yes
Owner:	Michael Parker
Year Estab:	1995
Comments:	A good sized shop that carries both paperback (the majority of the stock) and hardcover items (a respectable number) in mixed condition. One can find older items here, some collectibles and several shelves of first editions along with more common materials. Paperbacks and hardcovers are intershelved by subject. The shop is both customer and dealer friendly.

Wytheville
(Map 15, page 294)

Blue Ridge Books   **Open Shop**
148 West Main Street 24382   (540) 228-8303
                                        E-mail: cwing@vt.edu

Collection:	General stock of new and used hardcover.
# of Vols:	15,000+ (combined)
Specialties:	Southwest Virginia; Appalachian history and authors.
Hours:	Mon-Fri 9:30-6. Sat. 9:30-3. Sun by appointment.
Services:	Search service, accepts want lists, mail order.
Travel:	From I-81 take one of Wytheville exits to Main St in town.
Credit Cards:	Yes (Discover only)
Year Estab:	1983
Comments:	This combination new/used book store offers nothing out of the ordinary in terms of its mixed vintage used book collection. With the exception of the specialty used books located in the front of the shop, most of the used books (which we estimate numbered between 2,000-3,000) were shelved in the rear of the store.

Astor House Books (757) 220-0116
PO Box 1701 Williamsburg 23187   E-mail: cookbooks@widomaker.com

Collection:	Specialty
Specialties:	Cookbooks; food history; beverages.
Services:	Search service, catalog, accepts want lists.
Credit Cards:	No
Owner:	Mary B. Haskell
Year Estab:	1986

Best Beloved Books (703) 532-1928
6301 North 19th Street Arlington 22205   E-mail: seoneepack@aol.com

Collection:	Specialty books and ephemera.
# of Vols:	5,000+
Specialties:	Dogs; horses.
Services:	Search service, accepts want lists.
Credit Cards:	No
Owner:	Heather Hanna
Year Estab:	1991

Bubbe's Bookshelf Tel & Fax: (703) 255-7028
PO Box 1455 Vienna 22183   E-mail: bbooks@worldnet.att.net

Collection:	Specialty
# of Vols:	1,500
Specialties:	Judaica
Services:	Search service.
Credit Cards:	No
Owner:	Susan & S.J. Dilles
Year Estab:	1994

Clover Hill Books (804) 973-1506
PO Box 6278 Charlottesville 22906   Fax: (804) 974-9749
Web page: www.cloverhillbooks.com   E-mail: cloverh@cfw.com

Collection:	Specialty
# of Vols:	6,000
Specialties:	Modern first editions (British and American); poetry; literary ephemera; little magazines. Small selection of older gardening books.
Services:	Catalog, accepts want lists (for literary wants only).
Credit Cards:	No
Owner:	Candace Carter Crosby
Year Estab:	1982

Thomas L. Coffman, TLC Books (540) 389-3555
9 North College Avenue Salem 24153

Collection:	Specialty
# of Vols:	5,000-10,000
Specialties:	Mystery

Services: Appraisals, accepts want lists, search service, catalog.
Credit Cards: No
Year Estab: 1990
Comments: Also displays general collection at Wright Place Antique Mall and Green Market Antique Mall in Salem.

Collector's Companion (804) 321-9212
PO Box 935 Mechanicsville 23111-0935 E-mail: bookscc@aol.com

Collection: Specialty new and used hardcover and paperback.
# of Vols: 5,000+
Specialties: Antiques and collectibles.
Services: Search service, accepts want lists.
Credit Cards: Yes
Owner: Perry Franks
Year Estab: 1982
Comments: Stock is approximately 25% used, half of which is hardcover.

Dr. Nostalgia (804) 384-8303
3237 Downing Drive Lynchburg 24503

Collection: Specialty
# of Vols: 3,500
Specialties: Children's series.
Services: Catalog
Credit Cards: No
Owner: Dr. & Mrs. Bob Gardner
Year Estab: 1973

Eastern Front/Warfield Books (540) 338-1972
36734 Pelham Court Philomont 20131 Fax: (540)338-1910
E-mail: rwarfiel@erols.com

Collection: Specialty new and used.
# of Vols: 2,000 (used)
Specialties: Military.
Services: Search service, accepts want lists, catalog.
Credit Cards: Yes
Owner: Richard Warfield & Lawrence Wilson
Year Estab: 1987

From Out Of The Past (703) 768-7827
2821 Franklin Street Alexandria 22306

Collection: General stock.
# of Vols: 40,000
Specialties: Magazines
Services: Catalog, accepts want lists.
Credit Cards: Yes
Owner: Mike Keck
Year Estab: 1974

German Historica   (540) 659-9349
2020 Admiral Drive Stafford 22554

Collection: Specialty
# of Vols: 1,000
Specialties: German books, magazines and newspapers from 1933–1945 (plus some
                  World War I material), with emphasis on military and political subjects.
Services: Accepts want lists.
Credit Cards: No
Owner: Clemens Lemke
Year Estab: 1994

Ron Griswold, Bookseller   (703) 525-9794
1811 North Highland Street Arlington 22201

Collection: Specialty
Specialties: Modern British and American first editions.
Services: Catalog
Credit Cards: No
Year Estab: 1995

HPFRI   (540) 635-7107
PO Box 1434 Front Royal 22630   Fax: (540) 635-1818
                                              E-mail: hpfrigko@interloc.com

Collection: Specialty books and ephemera.
# of Vols: 5,000
Specialties: Russia; Alaska; American history; Genealogy; petroleum.
Services: Appraisals, search service, accepts want lists.
Credit Cards: No
Owner: Gary Olsen
Year Estab: 1997

Jonathan Byrd's Rare Books & Bibles   (703) 323-8787
9521 Draycott Court Burke 22015   E-mail: Director@greatsite.com
Web page: www.greatsite.com

Collection: Specialty
Specialties: Religion; bibles; biblical manuscripts and leaves.
Owner: John Lawton Jeffcoat, Director of Marketing
Comments: Books sell for generally not less than $500.

Magnum Opus Rare Books   (804) 978-3700
PO Box 1301 Charlottesville 22902

Collection: General stock.
# of Vols: 5,000
Specialties: England and American literature since 1800; Americana; sports; mys-
                  tery; books about books.
Services: Catalog
Owner: John Guillot
Year Estab: 1984
Comments: Approximately 60% of collection is devoted to literature. Collection
                  can also be viewed by appointment.

MCL Associates (703) 356-5979
PO Box 26 McLean 22101-0026

Collection:	Specialty
# of Vols:	10,000
Specialties:	Cookbooks
Services:	Catalog, accepts want list, search service.
Credit Cards:	No
Owner:	Phyllis H. King
Year Estab:	1978

Mark E. Mitchell Inc. (703) 591-3150
3002 Winter Pine Court Fairfax 22031   E-mail: meminc@ix.netcom.com

Collection:	Specialty
Specialties:	Historic newspapers.
Services:	Appraisals, catalogs, search service.
Credit Cards:	Yes
Year Estab:	1976
Comments:	Collection can also be viewed by appointment.

Night Owl Books (703) 590-2966
Box 2187 Woodbridge 22193   E-mail: bangzoom@ix.netcom.com

Collection:	Specialty books and ephemera.
# of Vols:	50,000 (excluding comics).
Specialties:	Pulps; vintage paperbacks; circus; popular culture; back issue comics.
Services:	Subject catalogs, search service, accepts want lists.
Credit Cards:	No
Owner:	Glenn C. Goggin
Year Estab:	1973

J.G. Norman, Bookseller (804) 633-4015
PO Box 378 Milford 22514   E-mail: jgorman@crosslink.net

Collection:	Specialty
# of Vols:	3,000
Specialties:	Southern literature; Virginia; history.
Services:	Catalog, accepts want lists, search service.
Credit Cards:	No
Owner:	Gary Norman
Year Estab:	1995

George Bernard Norris, Bookseller (540) 886-5742
8 Alleghany Avenue Staunton 24401

Collection:	Specialty
# of Vols:	500-1,000
Specialties:	Irish literature (late 19th & 20th C.); Irish history; German history (20th C).
Services:	Appraisals, catalog, accepts want lists.
Credit Cards:	No
Year Estab:	1989

Old Dominion Books   (804) 749-4536
PO Box 370 Rockville 23146   E-mail: haypellow@aol.com

Collection:	Specialty
# of Vols:	2,000
Specialties:	Modern first editions; sets; illustrated; book art; press books.
Credit Cards:	No
Owner:	Dan Pellow
Year Estab:	1990

Oracle Books   Tel & Fax: (703) 620-9619
10905 Howland Drive Reston 20191   E-mail: oraclebk@interloc.com

Collection:	Specialty
# of Vols:	3,000
Specialties:	Modern fiction; mystery; galleys & proofs; signed first editions.
Services:	Catalog, accepts want lists.
Credit Cards:	No
Owner:	Geoffrey & Bonnie Hughes
Year Estab:	1995

Ed Schaefer Associates   (703) 920-1457
1600 South Eads St, 924N Arlington 22202   Fax: (202) 662-7569

Collection:	Specialty
Specialties:	World War I & II (political and military aspects).
Services:	Accepts want lists.
Credit Cards:	No
Year Estab:	1980

Secondhand Prose   (703) 860-4303
2103 Lirio Court Reston 20191   Tel & Fax: (703) 860-1705
Web page: www.bksearch.com   E-mail: sndprose@erols.com

Collection:	General stock.
# of Vols:	3,000
Specialties:	American historical novels; American history (colonial to Civil War); Americana; mystery; cookbooks.
Services:	Catalog, accepts want lists.
Credit Cards:	Yes
Owner:	Ken Baumgartner
Year Estab:	1995

Southside Virginia Historical Press   (804) 392-8300
PO Box 865 Farmville 23901

Collection:	General stock of used and new hardcover and paperback and ephemera.
Specialties:	Virginia (Southside).
Services:	Catalog, accepts want lists.
Credit Cards:	No
Owner:	Robert G. Flippen
Year Estab:	1996
Comments:	Stock is approximately 50% used.

13th Hour Books   (703) 960-3461
5714 Fenwick Drive Alexandria 22303

Collection: Specialty hardcover and paperback.
Specialties: Horror; science fiction; fantasy.
Services: Catalog, accepts want lists.
Credit Cards: No
Owner: Les Thomas
Year Estab: 1989
Comments: Stock is approximately 80% hardcover.

P.F. Thomas Vintage Books   (703) 912-9806
PO Box 4051 Merrifield 22116   E-mail: pfthomas@tidalwave.net

Collection: General stock of hardcover and paperback.
# of Vols: 5,000
Specialties: Vintage paperbacks.
Services: Catalog
Credit Cards: Yes
Owner: Philip Thomas
Year Estab: 1995

Walker Creek Press Used Books   Tel & Fax: (540) 688-3832
PO Box 709 Bland 24315   E-mail: walkrbks@interloc.com

Collection: General stock of hardcover and paperback and some ephemera.
# of Vols: 1,200
Specialties: Mountains of Virginia and Appalachia; Virginia publishers.
Services: Search service, accepts want lists.
Credit Cards: No
Owner: Richard & Courtney Haynes
Year Estab: 1994

"I found Paradise."

Specialty Index

The Used Book Lover's Guide Series
Your guide to over 6,000 used book dealers.

New England Guide (Rev Ed)
750 dealers • 383 pp • $16.95
ISBN 0-9634112-4-1

Mid-Atlantic Guide (Rev Ed)
1,100 dealers • 439 pp • $18.95
ISBN 0-9634112-7-6

South Atlantic Guide (Rev Ed)
950 dealers • 375 pages • $17.95
ISBN 0-9634112-8-4

Midwest Guide (Rev Ed)
1,000 dealers • Due Sum. '98 • $18.95
ISBN 0-9634112-9-2

Pacific Coast Guide
1,350 dealers • 474 pp • $18.95
ISBN 0-9634112-5-X

Central States Guide
1,250 dealers • 465 pp • $18.95
ISBN 0-9634112-6-8

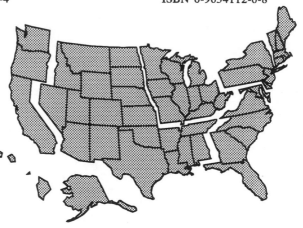

Keeping Current

As a service to our readers, we're happy to make available, at cost, Supplements for each of our guides.

The Supplements, published annually, provide our readers with additional listings as well as information concerning dealers who have either moved or gone out of business.

Much of the information in the Supplements comes to us from loyal readers who, in using our guides, have been kind enough to provide us with this valuable data based on their own book hunting experiences.

Should you wish to receive the next Supplement for the book(s) you currently own, complete the Order Form on the next page and enclose $2.50 for each Supplement, plus postage. Please note the date of any earlier Supplement/s you may have. **The new Supplements will be mailed as they become available.**

ORDER FORM

Book Hunter Press
PO Box 193 • Yorktown Heights, NY 10598
(914) 245-6608 • Fax: (914) 245-2630
E-mail: bookhuntpr@aol.com

GUIDES	Price	# of Copies	Disc.	Unit Cost	Total
New England (Rev)	16.95				
Mid-Atlantic (Rev)	18.95				
South Atlantic (Rev)	17.95				
Midwest (Rev) *	18.95				
Pacific Coast	18.95				
Central States	18.95				

ANNUAL SUPPLEMENTS   (See Keeping Current on previous page)

	Price	# of Copies	Disc.	Unit Cost	Total
New England (Rev)	2.50				
Mid-Atlantic (Rev)	2.50				
South Atlantic (Rev)	2.50				
Midwest	2.50				
Pacific Coast	2.50				
Central States	2.50				

Available Summer, 1998

SPECIAL DISCOUNTS
Any combination of books
2-5 copies: 20%
6 or more copies: 40%

Subtotal	
Shipping	
(NYS residents only) Sales Tax	
TOTAL	

SHIPPING   Guides: $3.00 for single copies. Add $1.00 for each add'l. copy.
Supplements: 50¢ each.

Name_____

Company_____

Address_____

City_____ State_____ Zip_____

Phone_____

MC Card _____ Visa _____ Exp Date _____

Card # _____

Signature_____